# BILLY WILDER

# BILLY WILDER
# IN HOLLYWOOD

MAURICE ZOLOTOW

G. P. PUTNAM'S SONS, NEW YORK

SBN: 399-11789-X
Library of Congress Catalog Card Number 77-75684

PRINTED IN THE UNITED STATES OF AMERICA

This Book Is Dedicated to Charlotte Zolotow

*If you came this way,*
*Taking any route, starting from anywhere,*
*At any time or at any season,*
*It would always be the same . . .*

# CONTENTS

# FOREWORD

# HOW I MET BILLY WILDER

I didn't plan it. It happened in this way. I was in Hollywood in 1953. My home was in New York. I used to go to Los Angeles twice a year and interview glamorous personalities for magazines. I would gad all around Beverly Hills and the studios and interview the stars and make notes and then I would go back to my home and write these fascinating magazine articles. So I was out there, on this occasion, to do Marlon Brando, or George Jessel and Martin and Lewis. It was invariably a hectic experience—rush, rush, rush, from early morning until late evening. I was going to funerals and banquets with Jessel, who is the town's leading toastmaster and eulogist. I was in hot pursuit of Brando, who was eluding me: He has always spurned the members of the press. I was also attempting to get coherent statements from Jerry Lewis and Dean Martin, separately and together. One morning, I went out on the golf course with Martin. I do not play golf. I followed him around while he played eighteen holes with three friends at the Lakeside Country Club. It took hours. It was boring. I learned that some persons are very happy when they drop a little white ball into a little hole. Then good old Dino and I went to the clubhouse and we drank Scotch whisky. Martin really likes to drink. I found that out. It was the real thing with him. He reminisced about his days as a professional gambler and card shark in Steubenville, Ohio. I could not decipher my interesting notes the following morning. My writing was illegible. There had been a day, at a rehearsal, when I had made some great notes, very legible notes, and Jerry said he wanted to see how I made notes. I handed him my folded up copy paper. He struck a match and set the notes on fire. He thought that was hilarious. He also cut my tie. He gave me two beautiful Countess Mara ties in exchange. I remember one terrible day when I was tracking down Marlon Brando on the Metro-Goldwyn-Mayer lot: I went here and I went there, and every place I went they said Brando had been there and gone. In despair, I went to see my friend, Ernest Lehman, a screenwriter who was working on his first major screenplay, *Executive Suite.* Lehman said he had seen Brando in the commissary a few moments before. I dashed from the Thalberg Building to the commissary and ran into a secretary I knew who said she heard that he was in the makeup department. He was doing makeup tests for his role of Sakini in *Teahouse of the August Moon.* I tracked him down. He was sitting in a barber chair and getting Oriental makeup slapped on him. He knew who I was. He had promised to give me an interview. He had been stalling for days. Every day I went and waited for him and now I had him. He spoke for almost an hour. He gave me the Stanley Kowalski treatment. He told me what liars and ingrates we writers were. He said I was no different than anybody else. He didn't want to tell me about his personal life. He didn't mention the Napoleonic Code. I took very legible notes. I hated to read them but I had them. I had to see dozens of Brando's colleagues, friends, enemies, technicians who had worked on his films. That's how it was on this trip in 1953. People, appointments, broken promises, golf courses, burned-up notes, funerals, on the phone from my Beverly Hills Hotel bungalow, in and out of the rented car, talking, listening. I am by nature shy and introverted. I am uneasy with strangers. I came back to the hotel after another terrible session on the golf course with Dean Martin. That was, he insisted, the only place where he felt relaxed and able to speak to reporters. It is tiring to walk for miles and miles up and down a golf course, especially when you are bored by this stupid game. I came back to my room and was grateful that I had an evening to myself. I didn't want to talk to a soul. I took a hot bath. I changed into slacks and a sport shirt. I put on a jacket. My plan was to have a drink, alone. To have dinner, alone. To sit quietly in my room and perhaps read a novel by Jane Austen—to get as far away

as I could from the mad world of these egomaniacs and temperamental stars, these deranged geniuses. I wanted to be, at least, mentally, out of it. I went down to the famous Polo Lounge. I sat at the
small bar. I had a dry martini. I had a second martini. Then I was
paged. I picked up the phone. If I had not answered that call, I
would never have met Billy Wilder and you would not be reading
this book. The caller was Herb Stein, who wrote a column for the
*Hollywood Reporter.* He invited me to attend a banquet that evening
in honor of Walter Winchell. He said I could do myself good and
meet some real important people because Twentieth Century-Fox
was laying on the banquet and I would get to meet Darryl Zanuck.
The idea of going to another banquet was repulsive. It seemed as
though I had been to dozens of them with Jessel—and I enjoyed Jessel's company. I didn't want to go. I was in a state of total antipathy
to Hollywood people, to all people. I should have said no. I said yes,
why not. The Los Angeles Press Club was honoring Winchell. Winchell would like to see a New York writer like me at the banquet. I
would do myself a lot of good. Herb and I went to this private dining
room at the Ambassador Hotel. Winchell was sitting at the head table. There were about eighty persons present. On Winchell's left
was Zanuck and on his right was a gorgeous blonde woman in a very
low-cut sequin gown, skintight gown. She didn't say a word. She listened to Winchell, who was a nonstop talker and talked almost entirely about himself and his deeds. She seemed to be listening atten-
tively. She had a heavy layer of makeup and long fake eyelashes and
enormous vermilion-lipsticked lips. She looked like the quintessence of the studio-manufactured sex body. She looked empty inside. She was Marilyn Monore. I had never seen her before. She
was about to become famous. She was an obscure, though up-and-
coming, actress at that time. She had just finished *Niagara* with Joseph Cotten.

The dinner partner on my right was Charles Brackett, an eminent
screenwriter and producer. He had cowritten and produced *Niagara.* I was thrilled to be sitting beside Brackett. He was one of those
Algonquin Round Table sophisticates. He had been the first drama
critic of the *New Yorker.* Previously, he had been a Paris expatriate
during the 1920s. He knew F. Scott Fitzgerald and Hemingway and
Edmund "Bunny" Wilson and Gerald Murphy and Harry Crosby
and Gertrude Stein. He was a piece of American literature. I was
probably the only man in that banquet room, that big private dining

room of the Ambassador, who knew that Brackett, long before he became a screenwriter, had written these bright, sardonic novels: crisp, lean books, written in the manner of Aldous Huxley and Ronald Firbank, books about rich, decadent people. I pumped Brackett about Alexander Woollcott and the Lunts and Dorothy Parker and Gertrude Stein, all friends of his. I didn't talk about the movies. Later I realized that it must have been such a comfort to Charlie Brackett that this man from New York thought of him as a novelist, put him in the category of Evelyn Waugh. I had loved *Entirely Surrounded,* this *roman à clef* about Woollcott and his friends on Bomoseen Island in Vermont. I even knew *Week-End.* I even owned a copy. They served the banquet finally and while we were eating, Brackett asked me if I had ever met Marilyn Monroe. I said not yet. He said her life was a strange one. He said I should write one of those magazine articles I used to write, about Marilyn Monroe. I couldn't believe he was serious. She was just another dumb Hollywood starlet with a fat ass and big tits. She was certainly not worthy of my penetrating analysis.

Then, he said suavely, a twinkle in his grey eyes, "Why, you should write a *book* about Marilyn Monroe."

"Why should I do that?"

"Because she is going to be a great star," he said. "Because the story of her life is like a Dickens novel. Let me tell you about her." And, as we sipped the wine, he murmured the story of her days in the orphanage, of her struggle as an aspiring model and actress, of her insane mother, and her mysterious father. These events, which are now universal knowledge and a part of one of the great myths of our time, were then unknown. Brackett revealed them to me. After the coffee and the baked alaska, after the speeches and the handshakings, there were pictures to be taken and I stood close to Marilyn Monroe. I had my photograph taken with Winchell and the blonde. For one moment, our eyes made contact. I looked into her soul. I glimpsed a fear and a vulnerability. I shivered. What she was inside was not what she was outside. I suddenly said to myself I will write a book about her. It was in 1956 that I began to explore the shabby and forlorn episodes of her past and re-create her character. There were magazine articles at first and then I began, finally, to write the biography—the first time in my life I had tried to write an entire book about an actress. It was to be the first serious study of Marilyn Monroe and by the time it was published she was already married to Arthur Miller and had created an astounding series of classic roles in pictures. It was published in 1960. It became the source of the hundreds of magazine articles and books which have since been published about this legendary woman.

Had I not said yes when I was so weary that evening and got the phone call in the Polo Lounge, all this would never have happened, as I would not have been sitting beside Charlie Brackett. It was in the course of seeking answers to the mystery of Marilyn Monroe that I made the acquaintance of Billy Wilder. He had made two films with her—*Seven Year Itch* and *Some Like It Hot*.

I will never forget our first meeting. It was in the lobby of the St. Regis Hotel in New York. I was waiting for him by the elevator. When I first saw him, I couldn't believe it was he. His photographs led me to expect a cherubic-faced, plump, short gentleman. On the contrary, he was quite tall and he moved gracefully and he was not at all plump. He was elegantly dressed. He had a narrow-brimmed black English-type hat on his head. A maroon ascot was furled around his neck. He looked like a dandy. I could almost see him twirling a cane. Ultimately, I was to see him twirling canes and batons and riding crops until I was sick to death of Wilder and his twirlings. I didn't realize it then, of course, but it is an essential aspect of his defense against the emotional intrusions of others on his privacy for him to be aggressive, mean, nasty, sarcastic, and, in a word, abrasive. His films are abrasive and often nasty. And the man comes on like this. Politeness, gentleness, affable tenderness, *bonhomie*—this is definitely not the Wilder manner. He wants you to hate him. He seems to feel more vibrant and alive when you hate him. I'll try to explain this as we go along, though, frankly, it is very hard to understand and it has taken me almost three years to put it all together. When Erich von Stroheim was playing ruthless German officers in American propaganda films made during World War I, he was billed as "The Man You Love To Hate."

One might say that Wilder has made a career out of being "The Man You Hate To Love."

It has been one of the failures of his life that, in spite of all his attempts to be hated, many persons admire and like him very much and there are even a few, a very few, who love him. As a screenwriter he has been loved very much. He has scored twenty-three Academy Award nominations and twelve Writers Guild nominations for his screenplays. He has won two Oscars as a writer and eight Writers Guild awards. In 1957, he received the greatest honor his colleagues can bestow—the screenwriters Laurel Award for a lifetime of writing achievement. It is a sterling-silver wreath of laurel. All in all, he has six of those Oscar statuettes, those art moderne golden geezers, standing on a shelf in his office. In 1960, he hit a triple—he received three Oscars on one night for *The Apartment*—one as writer, one as director, and one as producer of what was named the Best Movie of the Year.

At our first encounter, we repaired to the King Cole Room and we had brandy stingers and I asked him about Marilyn. That's when he started in trying to make me hate him. He assumed I was emotionally ravished by her beauty and her talent.

"Marilyn Monroe is a monster," he said, sharply. He spoke with a slight German accent. He spoke in a manner that would brook no disagreement. "She is perhaps the most cruel person with whom I ever worked. What I went through with her—nobody will ever know. Certainly not you. I will not tell you. You would not believe it anyway."

"I am willing to give it a try, Mr. Wilder," I said.

"They all say that, but nobody believes it," he said. "Come on, let's get out of here; let's take a walk."

For hours and hours and more hours, I trudged about Manhattan with Billy Wilder. That is how he likes to give an interview or be with a friend. Walking and shopping. Shopping and walking. Well, I guess it is more interesting than following a baritone on a golf course. We went in and out of many stores in the East Fifties that afternoon—haberdashery shops and art galleries and jewelry shops and glassware shops. Mr. Wilder is a lecturer and teacher at heart. This is his real pleasure in life, as many of his friends will attest subsequently and as I can attest, having been a shopping companion of his on several occasions. Mr. Wilder is one of those unique parties who simply knows everything about everything, be it the erotic paintings of Schiele or the varieties of fine European crystal or the difficulty of finding narrow ties—these being some of the subjects upon which I was lectured on this occasion. He is one of those men with an insatiable curiosity; the memory of a computer bank; the reading ability of a manic speed-reader; and, those rarest of human attributes, eyes and ears which look and hear with freshness, looking upon all things as if he is seeing them for the first time—looking with the eyes of a child and hearing with the ears of a musician who

can hear melodies not heard by everyone. He has the sensitivities of
a musician and a painter; and both his musical and his pictorial talents are revealed in his films. Basically, however, he is a writer. He
is a screenwriter who became a director because his screenplays
were, he thought, being destroyed by incompetent directors and
egocentric actors. He conceives of existence in terms of scenes, of
stories, of acts, of events leading up to climaxes and resolutions, as
a writer conceives of the flow of events. And, since he is possessed
of so many rare and wonderful gifts, it was perhaps inevitable that
the gods would make him imperfect and give him a certain impa-
tience with humanity, a certain bitterness, a caustic tongue, which
would spoil everything—for him and for others. On the other hand,
it is his caustic tongue which has made him socially exuberant and
interesting and the subject of many anecdotes. He feels restless and
anxious when he senses that you are getting too close to him, too
much in love with him. He was constantly trying to get me to hate
him. Now and then he succeeded. I will give you a typical example
of his technique. I once showed him a few chapters of an early draft
of this book. He looked at it with an intense expression of nausea.
He made corrections on my mistakes in German and what he conceived to be equally erroneous English usage. He said I had absolutely no feeling for a gag. Every time I tried to report one of his
gags, I ruined the punch line. I had simply no ear for wit. He just
took me apart right there in his office. He took me apart culturally
and as a human being. I finally said, "Billy, when I leave here, the
way I feel, I think I'm going to drive my car over a cliff and kill myself."

"Aaagh," he said leering at me, "you make my mouth water."

Now and then, we would meet for an hour or two in his office at
Universal. We would talk. I would ask questions. He would lecture
me, usually on my incompetence. Frequently he would tell me I had
made a terrible mistake in commencing such a book, as nobody
would read a book about him, certainly not such a book as a loutish
person like me would write, and he had been out of his mind to let
me come here and ask him questions. Of course, I did not know
what I was getting into when I had started this. It became, as all such
journeys have to become, a journey to find out the secret springs of
this most devious and perverse of Hollywood personalities.

He was a man, for instance, who in one moment could express the
most delicate of sensibilities in commenting on the later paintings of

Ingres and Renoir—and in the next tell you the most crude and vile obscene story or joke, and sometimes it was not even funny. As an author, I have the last word and I have to say, in revenge, that Wilder's jokes were not always that funny, just as his funny pictures were not always that funny. You see he eventually got me so mad I would start to hate him now and then. I would hate him and love him at the same time. I developed a tremendous identification with his first and second wives. His lovely and bright and keen present wife, Audrey, once told me that Billy reminded her of that old popular song which went, "You always hurt the one you love."

She said I had to understand that if Billy did not love me he would not say all these cruel things to me.

I'll give you another example.

I had seen Billy on several occasions during the 1960s, when I was delving into his experiences with La Monroe. We would meet in Manhattan. We would interrupt our traveling to have a drink now and then. I was a constant drinker at that time. He had seen me belt stingers and martinis and highballs along with him. He had seen me enjoy alcohol. Now we dissolve to the spring of 1974. I am going to write a book about Wilder. I begin my exploration by going to the set at Universal where he is directing a remake of *The Front Page* with Jack Lemmon and Walter Matthau. I observe. I listen. I make notes. On the second day, after the noon break, he asks me over to his trailer to have a shot of *schnapps*. I say no.

The next day I passed again. I refused his offer of wine at the studio commissary on the fourth day and the fifth day. While strolling from the sound stage to the commissary on the sixth day, a Monday, he asked me what the hell was the matter. I said I was no longer able to drink. I had been living a sober life since 1971.

"How boring," he said. "Why?"

I said I was an alcoholic.

"Nonsense," he said. "One drink can't hurt you."

In front of us was Lemmon ambling to the restaurant. I pointed to him. "Remember Jack in *The Days of Wine and Roses*? That's me if I take a drink."

"Aaagh, you're stupid."

He got my goat. "Billy," I said sharply, "how can you of all people say that? You made *The Lost Weekend*. Remember?"

He stopped walking. He looked up. "You mean, one drink is too many and a thousand isn't enough?"

"Yeah—me and Ray Milland."

From then on, however, almost every time we came together, he would go throught the same challenge. We would have suffered through a long and sometimes tiresome recollection of his ancient history. He would complain of my banality or ignorance. Then it would be noon. He would summon his secretary, Kay Taylor, and ask her to bring out a bottle of something. Always he would wave a glass at me. Sometimes he would pass it under my nostrils. He would ask me if I weren't tempted, if I didn't crave just one *little* shot of whiskey. Sometimes he would have hot saké. Wouldn't I like just a little touch of hot saké? But the same sadist, when I was in the hospital for two weeks following a serious operation, not only sent me a lovely plant and three new books but telephoned many times with genuine concern in his voice. I think if I were in real trouble and needed help, he would help me as fast as any man in the world.

But he wouldn't want anybody to know he had helped me.

Since *Irma La Douce* in 1963, Wilder has not had a single critical or commercial success. He has made interesting films and, in several cases, films I think were elegant and at the top of his form. But he has been a failure for more than ten years. *Kiss Me Stupid, The Fortune Cookie, The Private Life of Sherlock Holmes, Avanti, The Front Page*—all failures. It has been an ordeal for him. He has suffered. He has persisted but he has suffered. *Sherlock Holmes,* a beautiful film, was cut before release and withdrawn after a few weeks. *Kiss Me Stupid* not only was a failure—but was violently denounced as immoral and degrading. It was one of his most brilliant films and it went down the drain.

Wilder's reaction to disaster was not to moan. It was not to allow himself a moment of self-pity. He went on the attack. He gloried in his disasters. He has granted innumerable interviews to journalistic vultures who have come to gnaw on his flesh. He has almost seemed to take pleasure in the delicious irony of it all. He has pointed out that in Hollywood when you have two commercial failures in a row you are no longer asked to be a pallbearer at funerals. Formerly he had been invited to bear palls all the time. Now he was getting only one or two a year—and then only after the demise of old crocks, very close personal friends, like Jack Benny. In the days when he was making *Double Indemnity, Sunset Boulevard, Some Like It Hot, Witness for the Prosecution,* why, he had two funerals a month—many for corpses of persons whom he had hardly known when they were thriving as producers and directors. So, you see, the cloud had a silver lining. He didn't have to worry about hernias any more. Another advantage of Hollywood failure was you can't get your agent on the phone, which spares you many tedious conversations. And then all those friends who were having script problems and casting problems, who used to badger him on the phone and drop into the office for advice—for Wilder, in another one of his contradictory moves, is the most generous of men with suggestions and criticism—well, now they leave him in peace. Actors down on their luck don't borrow money from him any more. That hurts. He makes believe he is gloating over his own misfortunes, but you know it pains him deeply. He has to win. He has a competitor's need to win. He makes films anyway. He has to make films.

"I'll never retire," he once told me. "They'll have to take my camera away before I'll stop making pictures. I'll die making pictures. Renoir painted even when they had to tie a brush to his arthritic fingers. Renoir didn't paint with his fingers anyway. He painted with his prick, as he once said. That's how you make movies—with a prick—unless you're Lina Wertmuller, and I wouldn't be surprised if she has one."

He used to say that his career had become like the Ford Motor Company after the Edsel catastrophe. Every year he would say that he was retooling, and this time "we shall come out with the Mustang and sweep the market." Each season it has been another Edsel. I think that the verdict of film historians will be that his films from 1964 to 1974 were, on the whole, splendid and interesting ones. But Billy Wilder lives in the present. The present has been a harsh and frustrating time for him. But you would never know this. He sails through life with all his flags flying and his cannons firing. He is as insulting as he is when his pictures are grossing big numbers and he is winning awards at home and abroad. He was, I have been told, the same kind of nasty man when he was a down-and-out screenwriter in Hollywood during the 1930s.

He was always, as someone once put it, Billy Wilder—even before he became Billy Wilder.

He always had to be The Man You Hated To Love.

# I

# A FIRST-CLASS REPORTER
# IS AVAILABLE

It is reasonable to assume that persons like Billy Wilder, in whom all traits are extreme and clash one with the other, must be men who have grown up amidst great tension—social tension, historical tension, family tension, and, ultimately, artistic tension. It is also evident that any man who comes out with his fists clenched and ready to fight even when nobody is threatening him, is a man who has experienced his environment as a hostile territory. He has learned to protect himself against all dangers, real and imaginary. One seeks for explanations for such a phenomenon. What was there in his genetic pool, his acculturation in the family setting, in the political and social turmoil of the period, which went into the making of his personality? You find one clue. You find a second here, a third there. But when you put all the parts together, the whole is greater than the sum of its parts. Because he is a writer of films and a maker of films, you search his work for repetitions of themes and moods and characters which will reveal his ultimate secret, the secret which is concealed from the world, that primal secret which is even concealed from himself. Do you find it?

He was born Samuel Wilder on June 22, 1906, in Sucha, a small town 100 miles east of Vienna, in the province of Galicia, then part of the Austro-Hungarian Empire and now part of Poland. He was born in the reign of the Emperor Franz Josef, ruler of a sprawling and polyglot kingdom. Franz Josef had been reigning since 1848. He died in 1916 at the age of eighty-six. Papa took Samuel to the second floor of the Café Edison on the Ringstrasse so he could watch the funeral cortège. Generals and ambassadors on horseback from the wartime allies of Austria-Hungary—leaders from Bulgaria, from Kaiser Wilhelm's Germany, from Turkey—all in somber black uniforms, with black helmets and black horses, then the long black coffin, followed first by the new emperor Karl, and then by a small boy who wore a white uniform and rode a white horse. Papa put his hand on Billy's shoulder and said, pointing to the coffin, "There is the last of your old emperor, and that is your new emperor, Karl Josef; and behold, that little boy is your future emperor."

And then, many years and two world wars later, Wilder, now a famous director at Paramount Pictures, received a call from Luigi Luraschi, who was in charge of foreign publicity. Luraschi said a countryman of Wilder's was visiting the studio. Perhaps Mr. Wilder would be gracious enough to take him on a guided tour? In Luraschi's office, he saw a haggard little man, bald and nervous, in a rumpled business suit and a tie askew. "May I introduce Otto von Hapsburg?" Luraschi said. So that was what had become of the little boy in the white uniform with the white shako on the white horse. So that was the future emperor, was it? He was in exile. He was the pretender to the throne. There was not very much of an empire remaining any more. It had been cut up in many pieces after the war. Only a sliver of old Austria remained. And Otto von Hapsburg was an old man who eked out a living lecturing on international relations at American colleges. He had come to lecture at UCLA.

Wilder remembers the past as an ironic juxtaposition of incidents. He began cultivating in himself this armor of sardonic detachment, for it became evident to him at an early age that life was an illusion, that visions of success and love were bubbles, that men and women were actors in a play who did not know their parts. The producer and director of the play, who knew the truth, seemed to keep it from the performers, who therefore made fools of themselves. To paraphrase Lear, like Method actors to wanton directors are we to the Gods; they let us improvise for their sport . . .

Once, while Wilder was filming *Sabrina,* the king and queen of Greece visited his set. They were treated most deferentially. Wilder borrowed two thrones from the prop department so they could sit in grandeur. A red carpet was rolled from the stage door to the thrones. Wilder, a royalist at heart, presented the monarchs to Audrey Hepburn, Bill Holden, and Bogart. Suddenly, an electrician shouted, "Hey, queen, where were you last night when I needed you to fill a straight?"

Wilder loves this story, for it sustains his conviction that kings and queens are playing-cards, like the characters in *Alice in Wonderland.*

Billy's mother and father lived on illusions, of course, and he believed in their dreams until he became cynical, which happened when he was about twelve years old. His mother, Eugenia Baldinger, had a dream. Her dream was America. She was a dark-haired, vivacious, stylish and amusingly articulate lady. She came from Zakopane and her family owned a resort hotel in the Carpathian Mountains. His father was Max Wilder. Max Wilder's dream was to become a rich businessman. He was a headwaiter in a Krakow restaurant when he met Eugenia, or Genia. Krakow was the capital city of Galicia. She fell in love with Max at first sight. He was tall and handsome and his eyes were brown and sharp. He had a sophisticated Kaiser Wilhelm moustache. They were married in 1903. They lived at Fleischmarkt 7 in the fashionable first district in Vienna. They had two sons. Wilhelm, nicknamed Willie, was born in 1905; and Samuel, nicknamed Billy, came along two years later. Mrs. Wilder loved the name Bill. Once, Wilder confided to Ray Milland that his mother had had a crush on Buffalo Bill and named her sons after the famous cowboy. She had once seen his Wild West show in Madison Square Garden. She had become infatuated with America. She had lived in New York for several years when she was a young girl. She lived with an uncle and his family on Madison Avenue. He owned a jewelry shop on Madison. Her dream was to emigrate to America. Her children were brought up on stories of the excitement and wonders of America—the freedom, the elevated trains, the wealth, the democratic atmosphere, the Atlantic Ocean. She loved the ocean. She had often gone to Coney Island and regaled her sons with vivid descriptions of the rides and sideshows at this resort. She would tell over and over again about the Indians and the cowboys in the Buffalo Bill Wild West show and it played on little Billy's imagination. She had a favorite story: It was about a wooden Indian at a cigar store. She said the cigar shops in New York had wooden Indians standing outside—large wooden Indians with wooden feathers and wooden tomahawks. She had once lost her way coming home and found her place only because of the familiar wooden Indian on the corner. The wooden Indian was to surface thirty years later in *The Lost Weekend*.

Max Wilder went into the railway-café business. He owned a chain of small cafés at railroad stations throughout Galicia. Most of the year before Billy was born the family traveled on trains, as papa stopped at one, then another, of his branches, each for a few days. Billy likes to think of his papa as being the Fred Harvey of Austria; Harvey used to operate similar cafés on the main line of the Atchison, Topeka, and Santa Fe Railroad.

There must be something to prenatal influence. Billy Wilder is obsessed with trains and speed. He is a restless man. He cannot remain still for more than a few moments. Racketing around Austria in his mother's belly, Billy then and there began to plot his future movies; and it is surely more than a coincidence that his first film as a director (*The Major and the Minor*) centered its action in a railroad train, and that the wildest scenes of *Some Like It Hot* occurred in and out of the berths of a sleeping car on a train.

Later, papa opened a four-story hotel and restaurant in Krakow. Its name, in English, was Hotel City: Max thought it gave the joint a little class. He had rooms, a restaurant, an outdoor terrace, and a billiard room and card tables. It is in the gaming room that we first see a clear sign that the child is becoming father to the man. By watching the pool sharks, Billy became adept in handling a cue at the age of three or four. He became a prodigy at three-cushion billiards. Since he was so diminutive, he was placed on a chair as he made his shots. He was soon beating the regulars. He became a kind of juvenile Minnesota Fats. When the regulars saw a stranger walk in, they would bet him that this little kid could beat the lederhosen off him. Little Billy always came through. The winners paid him off in sweets. He loved sweets. He also learned how to play cards, chess, and checkers and has been a lifelong devotee of parlor games. In fact, games in general. Athletic games. Sports contests. Love games. In a game—well, this is the only human situation in which one can win. All else is vanity and vexation of spirit. And winning, he quickly learned, is the only thing. Winning not only gets you a pat on the rump and a stroke on the head, it gets you money. He saw how greedy the bettors were. He didn't get money at first. He got candy. But he liked the idea of money. He saw customers leaving *kronen* on the table. He knew these were tips for the waiters. Sometimes the waiters were not fast enough. Little Billy would sweep the coins from the table surreptitiously. He liked the jingle of money in his pants. He didn't know what to do with it but he knew that money was good. The waiters caught him stealing tips. "They beat the shit out of me," recalls Wilder. His father was angry and wanted to know why the waiters were thrashing his young son. They told him. Then papa beat him up. He also lectured him on honesty. Billy realized that money was not everything, though most people seemed to think it was. A large hotel for transients and a gaming room, Billy believes, is a good school for a growing boy. "I learned many things about human nature—none of them favorable," he says.

On a hot afternoon, one Sunday in June 1914, as the string trio was playing von Suppé waltzes on the terrace and the customers were sipping their coffee and eating pastry, at the hour of *Jause,* similar to the English teatime, papa, attired in his striped trousers and cutaway, came to the bandstand. He raised his hand. He said,

"*Meine Damen und Herren,* there will be no more music today. We have received the sad news that our Crown Prince has been assassinated at . . . Sarajevo."

Galicia, which bordered on Russia, was invaded when the war started. The Wilders were evacuated. They fled to their Vienna domicile. Here they lived the next eleven years, years of increasing hardship and hunger. The British blockade was starving out Germany and Austria. There was no coal or wood. No warm clothes. Little food. By 1917, Billy, like other children, was being commandeered as a street cleaner. He shoveled snow. He collected garbage. Papa was on guard duty with the reserve. Mama was with the Austrian Red Cross. Billy remembered being on the ration line to get the family's food. He once stood in line for twenty hours, on a very cold day, without a coat or hat, and all he got were three small potatoes. He was taught to blame the English for the trouble. He wore a button: GOTT STRAFE ENGLAND. He was in school when the war ended on November 11, 1918. He saw the mobs in the street as he trudged home. They ran amok—looting shops, tearing down royal statues, beating up every army officer in sight, ripping away the "*K und K*" insignia: *Kaiser und König.* He saw them make bonfires and kill soldiers. He never forgot these sights. And how could one have any illusions after this, and after the events of 1919 and 1920? Because it got worse. There was the partition of the old Empire. Formerly there had been fifty-six million souls subject to Emperor Franz Josef. Now there was only one small country of seven million, and three million of these had crowded into Vienna to starve collectively.

Only one dream remained. America. America came to the rescue. Billy learned to admire another American the way he already admired Buffalo Bill. This man was Herbert Hoover, a Quaker, who had organized the American War Relief. Wilder never forgot the first morning he received a bowl of a strange hot gruel, something he had never tasted; they called it Cream of Wheat. They gave him cream and sugar for it—these beautiful Americans. They had white bread and canned beef and chocolate and coffee cake. They introduced him to chewing gum. Yes, mama was right, Americans were magicians. Americans were kind and generous. Americans could perform miracles. He dreamed of America. Now he had an American illusion of his very own. He dreamed of America when school became boring. He hated the iron discipline of the Vienna public school and then the high school. He was a natural-born fast reader and had a fast mind. He was terrible in math and science but did well in history and foreign languages. He got carried away by German literature and knew the lyrics of Heine and the contemporary von Hoffmannsthal by heart. But he had an American passion for sports—which was, in those days, unusual in a young Austrian. By fifteen, he was five feet ten inches tall, a wiry, tough, muscular lad. He played soccer football. He rode a bicycle. He skated. He skied. He became a lover of automobiles and motorcycles. Once, recalls his older brother Willie (who had to change his name to W. Lee Wilder, when he became a Hollywood producer-director himself during the 1940s) Billy stole a Zündapp motorcycle. He drove it around and around the block in an ecstasy, until it ran out of petrol. He was a constant truant from school. He ran away. He stole cars as well as motorcycles. He was almost what you might call a juvenile delinquent, a rebel against authority, a kid who had been made into a premature adult by the disasters of the war. He was tough and hard.

And he loved the movies. He had discovered the movies. He had discovered the Rotenturm Kino and the Urania Kino. He had found a place in which one could lose one's self in the darkness and live a thousand lives through the images on the screen. It was a life that was more beautiful than real life. Willie recalls that many times he was sent out into the streets to locate his kid brother, who was missing. Like as not he would be watching the picture show. Hollywood films were now exhibited in Austria and he made the acquaintance of famous cowboys like William S. Hart, Tom Mix, Hoot Gibson, and Dustin Farnum.

"The guy I really went for," Wilder says, "was Douglas Fairbanks. He conquered a screen. And he had such panache in his whole life-style. I remember hearing that during the inflation, he offered to buy Austria! He made a firm price of ten million dollars for the whole country—lock, stock, and waltzes. We were by now a little country, but still . . . I liked this. Another millionaire would buy a French chateau, a Greek island. Not Fairbanks. He wanted a whole country. That is what I call class. He was my kind of a hero."

The inflation convinced Billy that money was another illusion. The Hotel City vanished like a lady in a conjuror's cabinet. The emotions which we feel in relation to money, and what it symbolizes for us, are usually signals of our deepest attitudes. Billy's feeling about money—about currency, about the numbers in the bank account—is that it is unreal. Objects—now these are real. He had seen the prices of objects, be they loaves of bread or antiques or houses, rise insanely during the inflation, and he had seen paper money burst like bubbles. He had seen his father lose the hotel and, from then on, papa lived only on dreams and went from one business failure to another: he had a trout hatching business and a watch business and a leather goods business, and he was not a good businessman in any of them.

Billy was not interested in business and he was not interested in studies. His mother was determined that he should go to college and become a lawyer and he went along with the scheme more out of Oedipal resignation than anything else. By now his pulses were beating to American dance music. He had discovered American jazz on records and American dances. He was a fantastic dancer. He memorized the American lyrics of all the new hits. He was collecting Paul Whiteman records. He was one of the first in Vienna to own Whiteman's big hit—*Japanese Sandman,* with *Whispering* on the flip side. He was crazy about American automobiles. He knew about American cars. He learned the fox-trot. He spurned the Viennese waltz. He wanted to own an American car. He wated to go to America. He wanted to be an American. He fell madly in love, for the first time in his life, just like in an American movie, like Gloria Swanson and

Thomas Meighan. There was a girl named Ilse, who was a clerk in a phonograph and record shop on the Ringstrasse. She was mad about *Tiger Rag, St. Louis Blues, Yes, We Have No Bananas, The Sheik of Araby, Dardanella,* just as he was, and they danced the nights away in the new casino dance-halls along the Kaertnerstrasse. Billy could even do a tango, imitating Valentino in *Four Horsemen of the Apocalypse.* Ilse was a beautiful dancing partner. They made beautiful music together in the casinos and the parks. She was truly a modern girl who smoked cigarettes and wore short skirts and short hair. He wrote poems to her. He dreamed of marrying her and going to America with her.

Meanwhile he registered at the University of Vienna in September 1924. He would be a lawyer—maybe. And now a strange and mysterious event took place. He went to college for three months. Then suddenly, in December, he quit cold.

He ceased going to classes. He stopped seeing Ilse. He got a job and moved out of the house. Billy has never discussed this turn of events; and brother Willie, who was living in London at the time, does not know why he changed course so abruptly. There have been two books written about Wilder. There have been many newspaper articles and magazine essays about him—including long and searching pieces by Lincoln Barnett, Richard Lemon, and Jon Bradshaw. This abrupt withdrawal from college has been noted by these and other writers without any further investigation. It intrigued me and puzzled me.

It took me a long time to formulate an explanation for what went on in Vienna in 1924. And it explained, to a great extent, the cynical attitude which became the fixed way of his mind, and which he was able to impose on his Hollywood movies, though Hollywood pictures were supposed to be fraudulent, happy-ending stories . . .

The idea that Billy might be a writer was suggested to him by a high school teacher, Alfred Spitzer, who admired his compositions and helped to fashion his tastes in literature. Spitzer said he could be a writer, and should be a writer. Being without a profession, Billy became a writer. He started as a reporter. Spitzer gave him a letter of recommendation to Hans Liebstöckl, drama critic and Redakteur of *Die Stunde* ("The Hour"), a new paper started in 1922 by the Hungarian, Imre Bekessy, who also put out a show-business weekly, *Die Bühne* ("The Stage.") One day, Billy went to Canisiusgasse 9 to see Herr Liebstöckl. There was nobody in the reception room.

He heard strange sounds from the Redakteur's office. He slowly opened the door. He saw a scene that made his blood run hot. The Redakteur was making violent love to his secretary who was sprawled, limbs akimbo on a sofa.

"Good afternoon, sir," Billy said, coughing.

Liebstöckl buttoned his fly. It was like a scene out of Arthur Schnitzler. The Viennese know how to carry these things off gracefully.

"Do you have an appointment?" the secretary inquired.

"I have a letter from Professor Spitzer. If *Die Stunde* is looking for a first-class reporter, I'm available."

"What experience have you?"

"None, but I'm a keen observer." He coughed.

"You're hired."

Wilder proved to be a fast writer. He wrote short features and news breaks. He became the regular man covering the Vienna Archdiocese and met Cardinal Pacelli, later Pope Pius XIII. Pacelli was the papal nuncio to Vienna. Billy loved covering crime stories. He hung out at a little café across from the Polizei Praesidium; when a red light came on in the café it was a signal a story was breaking and the boys ran over and covered it. They drank coffee and *schnapps* and shot the breeze. The suicide and murder of Marie Vetsera and Crown Prince Rudolf at Mayerling in the 1890s was always being hashed over. The Sunday supplements were always publishing new versions of the great murder story. Billy's already cynical philosophy became harder as he saw the worst side of humanity in trouble and heard the stories of greed, lust, hypocrisy, and political corruption from his fellow reporters. Billy worked a long night. He picked up his stories at night and came into the office at two A.M. He was at his desk until ten A.M., when the paper went to press. *Die Stunde* was a gossipy scandal-mongering sheet which came out precisely at noon. It was what they called a "boulevard paper" in Vienna.

He now lived in a small furnished room. Landladies became a serious problem. They haunted him for several years. In Vienna and later in Berlin, it was *verboten* to bring a girl home. Wilder played a cat-and-mouse game to outwit landladies. He wished he could go to the whores, many of whom were fantastic, but he could not afford the money. It was better to pick up a girl at a casino, and he always could because he was a superb dancer and knew how to sweet-talk his way into a bed. It was fine when *they* had the beds. When it was *his* bed, there were problems. Often, he had to satisfy his libidinous urges while standing up in hallways. He sometimes says bitterly—I don't think he is serious about this theory, but who knows?—that when he was about thirty-five years old he began to suffer from terrible backaches which no doctor could cure. They could not even diagnose the condition. "I finally came up with my own diagnosis," he says, "and I think it is all the result of those hot nights in Vienna when I was screwing girls standing up in doorways—and sometimes, alas, no girls—*just doorways.* That would ruin any person's back, yes?"

Where reporter Wilder broke fresh ground in Viennese journalism was that he took sportswriting seriously at a time when European papers, on the whole, ignored the field. He started writing tough, realistic personality pieces about star players in soccer, tennis, and six-day bicycle riding. He was always looking for visiting American celebrities to interview and was making Americans one of his specialties. Once he interviewed Molnar, the great Hungarian playwright, whose latest hit had just opened. Molnar was at a hotel on a mountaintop near Vienna. Billy had the interview in the garden of the hotel. Molnar started talking. He was a fine raconteur and wit. He hated being interrupted. A large red chicken kept coming around and clucking. Molnar kicked it away. It kept returning. He finally looked at the hen severely and said, "Go away—or I'll order you for dinner!"

Wilder's greatest Vienna coup was the day he interviewed—in one day—Richard Strauss, Arthur Schnitzler, Alfred Adler, and Sigmund Freud. *Die Stunde* was preparing its annual Christmas issue. The theme was Mussolini and Italian Fascism. Fascism was a new political development. What did it mean? What did our leading Austrian personalities think of it? Each of the reporters got some subjects to query. Billy first went to see the great composer. Strauss was—as Wilder recalls it—rather impressed by Benito Mussolini, who seemed to be a man of heroic stature and whose life was truly *Ein Heldenleben.* Austria needed a man like Mussolini. Next he took a long trolley ride out to Schnitzler's elegant villa in the suburbs. The playwright was a dapper and elegantly dressed gentleman who smoked a cigar and sipped sherry. He was not apprehensive about Italian Fascism. He thought Italians were like Viennese—love, food, and music were their elements. Mussolini would not last very long. Billy went back to the city and located Dr. Adler in his sumptuous flat on Nussdorferstrasse. Dr. Adler was a great fat man with pince-nez glasses who talked and talked and talked. He was a compulsive lecturer. He lectured Wilder about the nature of Mussolini's inferiority complex and his compensations. Billy was happy to get out of there. Then, finally, he went to the Bergasse, where Freud lived in an apartment. Previous biographers of Wilder have stated that he pretended to be suffering from a severe neurosis to worm his way in but this is not so. He presented his card to the maid. Freud was having lunch. Billy could see, through an open door, Freud's consulting room and *the* couch. It was a disappointingly small couch with a throw rug over it. Dr. Freud came out with a napkin tucked under his chin. He asked if Wilder were a reporter from *Die Stunde*. Yes. He said he did not give interviews. Freud pointed to the door. *"Raus,"* he said.

Wilder departed. Later, as he says, it proved to be more interesting that he had been rejected by Freud than any other journalistic experience he ever had. For years, he was able to dine out on his Freud story, which he embellished with dramatic details.

In May, Paul Whiteman and his twenty-six piece orchestra came to play concerts in England and the continent. It was 1926. The General Strike hit England. The concerts were canceled. There were three weeks to kill until the next engagement. Whiteman decided to see Vienna. Looking through registrations of new guests at the Hotel Bristol, Billy saw the name of Whiteman. He rushed back to the office and cried to Bekessy that Paul Whiteman was actually in Vienna and no paper had reported it. Bekessy had never heard of Whiteman and he thought Wilder was crazy anyway, with his mania for soccer players and movie stars. Wilder said he had a good angle for a story. He said Whiteman was known as the King of Jazz. He said he would bring the King several recent songs written by Viennese composers and get the King's opinion of them. Bekessy said he would use 300 words but no more. He sent a photographer with him. Wilder brought the fat maestro two pieces: "Wenn der Weisse Flieder Wieder Blühn," ("When the White Lilacs Bloom Again") and "Madonna, Du Bist Schöner als der Sonnenschein" ("Madonna, You Are Lovelier than the Sunlight"). Wilder knew a dozen words of English—mostly broken, but he charmed Whiteman. When he ran out of English phrases, he would resort to a line from an American song and Whiteman would just flip out. Billy showed him the songs. Then he and Whiteman made a tour of the Vienna night spots.

Three weeks later the band was reunited at Scheveningen, Holland. Matty Malneck, who was playing hot fiddle with the band, will never forgot a moment when Whiteman gave out sheet music of "Madonna," just the melody line, and he ad-libbed an oral arrangement, saying the strings take this passage, brass here, saxes here. Ray Turner, one of the two pianists with the band, remembers Henry Busse, the trumpet man who loved using a mute, taking his first chorus on it that night and just improvising the damndest second chorus. The audience went wild. "Madonna" was played as an instrumental the rest of the tour. Later Buddy de Sylva put words to it. He changed the sunlight to twilight. We all know it now as "When Day Is Done."

Wrede, publisher of "Madonna," told Wilder the good news. He also said that Whiteman was going to Berlin from Paris for concerts and he wished Wilder to be his companion and guide in Berlin. Wrede said he would pay the expenses and a small salary. Billy got three days' leave from the paper. He had never been to Berlin. For a young Viennese writer, to go to Berlin was to go to the promised land. He never returned to Vienna, except to visit.

He became a Berliner for many years.

# 2

# WAITER, BRING ME A DANCER

Berlin in the 1920s was a seething cauldron of energy in every art. There were 120 newspapers and 45 weekly and monthly magazines, there were 40 legitimate theatres, and 360 large and small movie studios, including the world-famous UFA. Berlin was the magnet which drew every ambitious young man and woman. It was the big league for all of central and northern Europe. It was filled with aspiring Hungarians, Austrians, Czechs, Danes, Swedes, Poles, Germans from the other cities like Hamburg and Dresden, an intensely boiling center for experimental poets, novelists, painters, architects, musicans, dancers. It attracted Frenchmen and Englishmen also. It was where new ground was being broken. There were great symphony orchestras and ballet companies and brilliant political reporters and cultural anthropologists. It was the most exciting city in Europe. It was also the most decadent and vice-ridden city in the world and the most sophisticated. It was a city of great wealth and corruption—and also a city of poverty and exploitation. Political passions ran high. Street riots were a popular sport.

You had to be fast and smart and sharp to push your way into this world. Billy became a hardworking free-lance writer. His friendship with Whiteman and knowledge of American jazz and American culture was the wedge he used. He sold a personality piece on Whiteman to the *Berliner Zeitung am Mittag,* known affectionately as the *"B.Z."* It was a chic afternoon paper. (The narrator in Isherwood's *Berlin Stories* chose the *B.Z.* as the paper to advertise his English lessons.) For several years Billy lived a hand-to-mouth existence in Berlin. He never had a staff job. Sometimes he got an offer but he made a reckless comment or a wisecrack and lost the chance. He liked his freedom anyway. He would bring ideas in to the *B.Z.* or the *Nachtausgabe* or *Tempo* or *Boersenkurier.* He was always reliable when it came to an American story. He wrote articles on such now forgotten American recording stars of the 1920s as Whispering Jack Smith and Gene Austin. These men were to Europeans of that period like Louis Armstrong and Ellington were to Europeans of a later generation. Whispering Jack Smith's concerts were sellouts in Europe. Austin's disc of "My Blue Heaven" was number *eins* on the Berlin Hit Parade. Through a rave he wrote about Whispering Jack, Wilder got to know another one of Jack's Berlin admirers, a young stage and movie actress appearing in the intimate revue, *Zwei Kravatten.* They went around now and then to the decadent late night spots like the Eldorado and the Trocadero. There were interesting rumors that the lady, who was Marlene Dietrich, was having a tumultuous affair with young Wilder. He was a dashing figure and he was always having affairs with one lady or another. Who knows? Besides, Marlene had so many lovers that Wilder did not particularly stand out in the crowd. Wilder recalls that they talked more about American singers than about sexual positions. They have remained good friends all of their lives and she starred in two of his films.

Wilder recalls interviewing Cornelius Vanderbilt, Jr., in Berlin. He asked the millionaire how much money he had on him at this moment. Vanderbilt looked in his wallet and his pockets. All he had were a few coins. Three marks, eight pfennigs. "You get the angle, baby? A free-lancer's life is not an easy one. You either invent an interesting slant on the same old story or you dig up a personality or a story which nobody on the staff is writing or you don't pay the rent. This week you eat one meal a day."

Another American he interviewed was Jackie Coogan, making personal appearances in Europe. Coogan was a fine little boy with a Prince Valiant haircut. Wilder was intrigued by the parents who kept eyeing The Kid like two birds of prey. In his mind he saw an angle for the story. The exploitation of a child star. He asked a few questions about how the money was being handled. He was told to get out and stay out. He wrote the story, slanting it with innuendos. Coogan, as he suspected, was picked clean, and all the money he made as a child star went up in smoke.

Lindbergh flew nonstop across the Atlantic in 1927. New York to Paris. Chamberlain and Levine announced they would make a longer flight—New York to Vienna. *Die Nachtausgabe* sent Billy to Vienna to await the arrival of the fliers. Already a Chamberlain-Levine Welcoming Committee was formed. Thousands of schoolchildren would be given flags and go to the airport. Choral societies would sing. Bands would play. Banquets had been arranged. Wilder was filing exciting advance stories.

Unfortunately, the fliers never got to Vienna. They crashed in Germany—in a place called Kottbus.

After the war, Wilder, now a colonel with the American army of occupation, was in Vienna. He was staying at the Bristol. While having a hot roll and coffee for breakfast, he read a morning paper and he saw a feature on page one which made him so hysterical that he sprayed coffee from his mouth. He couldn't stop laughing. There was a story telling of the nineteenth annual reunion of the Chamberlain-Levine Welcoming Committee! Evidently, the members had become so fond of each other, that they had maintained their little society—even though it it was based on an international aviation fiasco!

Another one of Billy's coups was sitting behind Prince Youssopoff, the man who had led the gang which assassinated Rasputin, at the Piscator Theater during the opening night of a documentary play called *Rasputin*. After the performance, Billy questioned Youssopoff as to his opinion of the play.

"Rubbish," he replied, "cheap and vulgar and historically untrue."

"Are you going to sue for libel?"

"Suing is for the bourgeoisie. Besides the author has missed the real tragedy."

"And what is the real tragedy, Your Highness?"

"We killed the wrong man. We should have killed Lenin. And Trotsky too while we were about it."

Life was not easy on Grub Strasse. Sometimes there were weeks without an assignment. Sometimes he would put in a week writing a story and it was rejected. Everything he did was on speculation. He wrote everything—from reflective essays to pornographic revelations. He was trying to write movie scenarios, for every reporter in Berlin was writing movies on the side and trying to get into the picture business.

To survive, he had to sometimes take curious nonliterary jobs. Once, Joe Pasternak hired him to be a personal guide to famed Hollywood director, Allan Dwan. Dwan, who had recently done *Robin Hood* with Fairbanks, had taken his fourth wife, a gorgeous Ziegfeld showgirl. They were touring Germany on their honeymoon. Pasternak, who later became a brilliant Hollywood producer of such confetti as the Deanna Durbin musicals, was then Berlin manager for Universal Pictures, along with Paul Kohner, who is now the leading independent agent in Hollywood. Dwan paid Billy $50 a week and expenses. Wilder knew nothing of Germany outside of Berlin. But he had a Baedecker guidebook which he secretly studied the night before and he was able to keep one step ahead of his clients. Anyway, he soon realized that, like many thirsty Americans coming to Europe from Prohibition-dry America, Dwan wanted to drink, more than to see the sights. He loved martinis. He introduced Wilder to the martini. The first bar they hit, Dwan ordered a dry martini and got a glass of Martini and Rossi vermouth, which he spat out. Eventually he and Wilder worked out a German formula to tell bartenders: *"Fünfzehn Teile Gin zu einem Teil Wermut, und zwei Oliven."* When Dwan got enough martinis under his belt, he and Mrs. Dwan were ready to go to museums and cathedrals. Billy bluffed his way through Berlin, Hamburg, and Cologne, and they got to Heidelberg and went to see some old *schloss,* and Billy made up some random date for it and a ridiculous story about a mad baron and his mistress. Unfortunately, a real guide was taking a party of English tourists and telling them the dull truth about this castle. Dwan overheard the truth.

"He found out I was faking and fired me," Billy says. "After all, since he already knew how to order a martini in German, what did he need me for now?"

Pasternak has another version. He remembers Dwan phoning him from Heidelberg and screaming that Pasternak had given him a terrible guide. He had gone on the make for his new wife and she was falling for him. He was a fine dancer and Mrs. Dwan loved to dance and when he got back to Hollywood, he was going to get Pasternak's ass for this mistake . . . .

Frequently, Wilder got so desperate that he became a gigolo, or, in German, an *Eintänzer.* The Eden Hotel and the Adlon Hotel employed male ballroom dancers to dance with the single women who came to the afternoon *thes dansants.* Billy worked at the Eden. There were eight *Eintänzers.* They sat at a table. They looked over the ladies—who ranged in age from forty to seventy-five. The protocol was that the gigolo went through a ritual of asking a lady to dance with him. They worked on a small salary and tips. The fatter and older ladies gave the best tips. It was hard work. It paid well. He could make as much as 100 marks a day, which was about $25 and paid the rent. He worked evenings also. He had to wear white tie and tails. At night, couples came, elderly husbands and lovers who wanted to keep their ladies happy. At night, the protocol was for the man to summon a waiter and ask that a dancer be sent over to the table. *"Waiter, I'd like to order one extra-dry dancing partner."* He also gave Charleston lessons on the side. Billy believes he was the first Berliner to master the Charleston, which did for him what the Twist did for Chubby Checker. He had the best American discs for Charlestoning. He charged 25 marks for a Charleston lesson. He threw the Black Bottom in free.

I don't have to tell you how beautifully Wilder has employed popular music and dancing in his films—"Tangerine" heard off-camera from a distant radio as Barbara Stanwyck and Fred MacMurray are shooting each other in *Double Indemnity,* Marilyn singing "I Wanna Be Loved by You" in *Some Like It Hot* and Joe E. Brown tangoing to "La Comparsita," with Jack Lemmon in drag, in the same film; or Swanson and Holden also tangoing, alone in her enormous mansion on New Year's Eve in *Sunset Boulevard?* Wilder has known how to evoke deep emotions and human conflicts in moments of dancing and singing as no other American or European screenwriter or director has done—there are superb dancing sequences in *Ninotchka; Arise, My Love; Avanti!; Sabrina; Love in the Afternoon.* Matty Malneck, who worked with Billy as musical adviser on *Love in the Afternoon,* told me that his knowledge of hit songs of the 1920s and 1930s was virtually encyclopedic. He seemed to remember every good tune of that period and, as a writer or director or both, he would know how to integrate a song into the action so it enhanced a character's trait or feeling or heightened a moment. To be a dancer as Billy was a dancer, with the feeling for rhythmic flow and body language, was one of the finest elements he was to bring to his directorial craft.

Wilder blew his cover as a gigolo when he wrote a series of three articles for *B.Z. am Mittag* exposing the behind-the-scenes intrigues and amorous scandals of the gigolo business. It ran under the title: WAITER, BRING ME A DANCER! It was the talk of Berlin. It made Billy's reputation. It also ended his career as an *Eintänzer*. He didn't dare show his face in the Eden for a long time.

Billy was now assigned by the *B.Z.* to give them an exposé of system gamblers at Monte Carlo. He was given his expenses and 5,000 marks. He blew the bankroll in two days at chemin de fer. He had no story. He tried to salvage the piece when he espied Sir Basil Zaharoff, the munitions king of Europe and owner of the casino, taking the sun one morning. Perhaps he could wangle an interview with Sir Basil. But, though some of his biographers have stated that Billy was the only journalist who ever got an interview with this mysterious figure, he never got to first base. Like Dr. Freud, Zaharoff wanted no publicity. Billy returned to Berlin—poor once more. He never felt discouraged. He never felt downhearted. He knew he was a hack today but tomorrow he would write a good novel. His writing was getting better. Someday he would write a novel and get rich. Or perhaps someday he would land an important high-paying position as an editor, like this friend of his, who ran *Die Dame*, a glossy, high-priced, women's magazine. He told his travails to this man at lunch. The man told him he was leaving his post at *Die Dame*. He was going to write a novel about the war from the viewpoint of the German soldiers in the trenches. As he described it, it sounded like a grim piece of antiwar realism, which, felt Billy, readers would shun. He warned his friend not to leave the highest paying position in Berlin journalism to write such a dreary noncommercial book.

The book turned out to be *All Quiet on the Western Front*. The author was Erich Maria Remarque. Not only did Billy give him terrible literary advice, but he also was rumored to have been caught by Remarque in flagrant delectation with the first Mrs. Remarque. At least so the scandal went as the gossipmongers passed on this story. Perhaps she and Billy had been discussing the contemporary novel or new dance steps. Anyway, the rumors went that Remarque, like a nineteenth-century Prussian nobleman, had horsewhipped Wilder. Another version was that the confrontation had taken place on a street and that both men had fought with fists until they were bloody and quite bowed.

It was Billy's custom to have breakfast at seven-thirty at the Café Kranzler near the Zoo station. He got the Vienna papers hot off the train. At nine, another Austrian writer, from Graz, usually joined him. Carl Mayer was a gloomy and cadaverous-looking fellow and the first great screenwriter. He had cowritten *The Cabinet of Dr. Caligari.* He wrote all the scenarios for E. A. Dupont and Murnau. Mayer wrote *Sunrise,* which Murnau made in Hollywood. He wrote *The Last Laugh,* a silent movie classic with Emil Jannings, in which there was not a single title. Mayer was truly a man of great visual imagination. He was the first screenwriter who took a pride in his profession. He did not permit directors to distort his scripts. He wrote meticulously detailed scenarios with camera directions. He was on the set every day. He considered himself the true creator of the film, and the director and actors merely the executors of his conceptions, as conductor and musicians interpreted a Beethoven score. He had invented camera angles and shots in which he asked that the camera swing to indicate a dizziness in a character. He was a brilliant innovator. He represented an ideal to Billy Wilder. It is strange that for all the cynicism Billy put on as a defense, he was still a romantic in some ways. He idolized Carl Mayer, as he later was to idolize Ernst Lubitsch. He admired men who were honest and dedicated and talented. He wanted to be like them—but on his own terms. He was a very unhappy man, this Mayer; and Wilder was the only person who could make him laugh, with his little stories, quips, and jokes. At least so says Walter Reisch, who is also from Vienna and was a newspaperman in Berlin in that period, and, like Wilder, became a successful screenwriter and won an Oscar for writing *Titanic.*

Wilder was now traveling in fast circles, theatrical and movie and literary. One of his best friends was Egon Erwin Kisch, one of Germany's best foreign correspondents and an avowed Communist. He came from Prague. He was a private in the Austrian Imperial Army. His brother was a general and in the war ministry. In 1918, Egon was the leader of a Bolshevik cell in Vienna. He led his comrades to take over the war ministry. He went to his brother and said, "General Kisch, in the name of the Third International—I order you to surrender."

General Kisch replied: "I surrender—but I'm going to tell mother."

Billy was now driving around Berlin in his first car—a beat-up old

Chrysler. He lived in a furnished room on the sixth floor of an apartment house on Victoria Luise Platz. He lived with a family. He had a nice room at a reasonable price. He still had not made enough money to get his own apartment and furniture. He remembers how he would come home late and exhausted after a night on the town, and lie down and close his eyes, and how his sleep was ruined by the fact that he was next door to the toilet. It was a broken toilet. The water went drip-drip-drip. He would lie there unable to sleep. Then he started imagining that the dripping noises were the splashings of a waterfall, "just to get my mind off that goddam broken toilet. Well, many years later, I was in Bad Gastein, an Austrian spa, where there is a splendid waterfall. I was lying in my king-size bed with a canopy over my head. It was very quiet and peaceful and all I could hear was the waterfall. Suddenly—after all I've been through, the money I've made, the awards I've won—I can't fall asleep because that goddam waterfall reminds me of a broken toilet!"

# 3

# NEXT TIME, ERICH POMMER

One night, Billy was awakened by a pounding on the front door. He heard screaming. He recognized the screamer. It was Heinz. Heinz was the boyfriend of Lulu, daughter of the landlady. Lulu was a lady of loose morals. Sometimes she entertained gentleman callers, who paid well for the entertainment. Not that Heinz was a clean-living man. He was a strong-arm guy, six foot five, and he owned a lesbian night club. Lulu rapped on Billy's door. She moaned, "Please help me. It is Heinz trying to break in. He is going to kill us!" Billy opened the door and she pushed her customer inside and shut the door. He locked it. Then Lulu let Heinz into the apartment and proclaimed her innocence.

Wilder switched the light on. He looked over Lulu's trick. To his delight, it was Galitzenstein, the president of Maxim Films, stark naked, his clothes bundled in his arms. He trembled as he dressed himself. "Please do you have a shoehorn?"

"Not only do I have a shoehorn, Galitzenstein, I also have a script."

"A . . . a . . . movie script?"

"I have many of them which are available to you."

"Come see me tomorrow in my office."

"Here, read one of them—now."

They could hear Heinz screaming that he would cut the throat of any bastard who fooled with his Lulu.

Galitzenstein weighed the script in his hand. "I'll buy it. It feels like a good story. Is five hundred marks suitable?"

He paid cash at once, and it was in this way that Wilder, as a result of lust and jealousy, made his entry into the film business. The next day he encountered a disheveled Lulu outside the toilet. He whispered,

"Thank you for sending me Galitzenstein. But he is a small-time producer. *Next time, please . . . Erich Pommer!*"

His second film sale came about when Carl Laemmle, head of Universal, sent over a nephew, Ernest, to learn how to be a director. He also sent over a washed-up Western star, Eddie Polo. Kohner and Pasternak were ordered to produce a movie starring Polo to be directed by Ernest Laemmle. Kohner said that hiring Wilder to write a scenario was his idea, as he had spoken with this young man in the Berlin cafés and liked his sense of humor and breezy writing style. Pasternak says it was his idea. He says Wilder had "borrowed a thousand marks from me and in order to get my money back I put him on the Eddie Polo picture. Wilder had lost all his money in a poker game with me and some others. He was a terrible poker player in those days." The script was *The Devil's Reporter.*

Apparently, Galitzenstein never produced Billy's first script, for the archives of the Deutsches Institut für Filmkunde in Wiesbaden, Germany, list *Der Teufelsreporter* as his first one. The credit reads: "*Drehbuch: Billie Wilder.*" The name was spelled "Billie" in Germany and it wasn't until he came to Hollywood, that Wilder learned that "Billie" was feminine, as in Billie Burke. Wilder's first produced scenario, or *Drehbuch*, was a story about a reporter who sells his soul to the devil. ("Ah-*hah*," as psychoanalysts like to say.) Polo, incidentally, became a big German star. The picture was released in 1929.

One night, Billy was sitting with his friend, Curt Siodmak, at the Romanisches Café, which was a gathering place of writers and other emotionally disturbed persons. Wilder was waxing wroth, in a loud voice, at a certain Robert Leibman, who was Pommer's right hand man, ran his story department, and was a prosperous scenario writer. Wilder accused Leibman of being afraid of young writers. He

said he couldn't stand the competition. He wanted to create a mono-
poly at UFA.

Wilder had never met the powerful Leibman. Suddenly, a chunky
man came over and said, "I'm Leibman. If you're only one percent
as talented in writing as you are in shooting off your mouth, I might
give you some work. Come see me."

Wilder did. He became a ghostwriter. He was a ghostwriter for
Leibman and for Franz Schulz and for many other leading movie
scenarists of the period. Then, as now, ghostwriting was a common
practice in the picture business. It was the way new writers learned
the tricks. They still do. Robert Towne, who wrote *Chinatown,* had
been a Hollywood ghostwriter without screen credit for years. Billy
remembers that in his ectoplasmic days he was paid under the table,
like blacklisted writers during the 1950s in Hollywood. Leibman was
under contract to write 10 pictures a month for UFA. He could not
do it alone. He set up a sort of factory system in which he processed
scripts. During this spectral period, Billy wrote about 200 scripts,
for which he never received screen credit. In the German film archives, he is listed as possessing 12 credits. It was during these
years—in 1928 and 1929—that Wilder learned visualization and construction and plotting. These 200 were all silent pictures. He did not
write titles. He only wrote "scenarios" which were, as the name
suggests, a scene by scene, action by action, narration of what was
to be photographed. It was here that one learned how to invent visual gags and visual drama. To tell a story with a minimum of words,
and with a maximum of poignant and significant actions—this was
the art of the silent-movie scenarist. For most of these two or three
years, Wilder lived a hazardous life. As a ghostwriter, he rarely got
more than $25 or $50 a script. Many weeks he sold nothing.

In 1927, papa came to see him in Berlin. Papa was making plans to
go to America. He was on his way to get mama in Vienna and then
they would leave for New York. At last, Eugenia Wilder's dream
would come true. He had come to Berlin to say good-bye to Billy.
During the visit, papa was stricken with an abdominal illness. He
died in the hospital within a few days. Wilder had no money to give
his father a decent burial. He went to several of the men for whom
he was ghostwriting and none of them would lend him money. He
did not even have enough to phone his brother in New York to break
the sad news. He was unable to talk to his mother and grandmother

in Vienna. He was alone—completely alone. The friends he knew, like Reisch, were out of the city, and the others—they were companions of the night, companions of the tables at the Romanisches and the El Dorado. They were not true friends.

He was the only person at his father's funeral.

In 1929, Robert Siodmak, a film cutter, directed *Menschen am Sonntag* ("People on Sunday"), from a story by his brother, Curt, and a scenario by Billy Wilder. He shot the film on the streets and in a park in Berlin with no professional actors. He used ordinary people. It was a story of two men and two girls and what they did on a typical Sunday. He shot it with a hand-held camera on a budget of less than one thousand dollars. Robert Siodmak went on to become an important Hollywood director and Curt Siodmak became a leading science-fiction writer, whose most famous work, *Donovan's Brain*, is a classic. *People on Sunday* was a springboard for many careers. The cameraman was an unknown genius, Eugene Shuftan, who was to become a great camera innovator (his Shuftan process is famous), and who won an Oscar for *The Hustler*. The assistant cameraman was Fred Zinnemann, who won Oscars for *From Here to Eternity* and *A Man For All Seasons*. The codirector was Edgar Ulmer, who became a darling of the *Cahiers du Cinema* critics for his crime and action films. As for Wilder, it made him famous overnight in Germany. Contrary to its reputation, *People on Sunday* is not a documentary. It is a fictional adventure, a romantic story, and in texture it resembles the Italian neorealist films of Rossellini and De Sica. Wilder kept the use of title cards to a minimum. He wrote one sequence in which a street photographer snaps pictures of people in the park. Shuftan got the idea of splicing "stills" into the action of the film. It was probably the first time that the "freeze frame" was employed in cinema.

Another sequence, as we can see in retrospect, embodies what came to be known as the Wilder touch—a grossness, a cynicism, a bawdiness. A boy, crazed with lust, chases a girl through the park. She falls. He mounts her. The camera now wanders poetically through leaves and branches and cloud patterns and then slowly pans back to the earth, and we see the lovers buttoning their clothes and then, the girl carefully reaches out and removes a rusty can of sardines under her buttocks. The can has been there, apparently unnoticed, all the time.

The film opened at the U.T. Kurfürstendamm Theater on April 2, 1930. It was hailed in the press. It ran for six months. In his treatise, on German movies of this period: *From Caligari to Hitler* (1947) the *behrümte* professor Siegfried Kracauer analyzes this happy-go-lucky film from the Marxist viewpoint. He saw it as revealing the "spiritual vacuum" of the German petty bourgeoisie and the "plight of the little man." *People on Sunday* raised the question of whether people like those in the picture would make a united front with the proletariat, or whether they would "cling to their middle-class prejudices." God held the pedant who class-angles a film about persons making love on a sunny Sunday afternoon . . .

Siodmak's next picture was *Der Kampf mit Dem Drachen*—how a tortured tenant murdered his "dragon," that is, his landlady. Billy, who had long enjoyed the fantasy of landlady-murder, suggested the idea. It was a brilliant twelve-minute surrealistic fantasy. The tenant was played by Felix Bressart. He is one of the three commissars in *Ninotchka.*

Siodmak was now given his own UFA unit under Pommer. He took Wilder with him. So at last, without the help of Lulu, Wilder was working for this greatest of all movie producers. Pommer had that same obsession with films, and making them with taste and quality, as Irving Thalberg or Sam Goldwyn. He toiled eighteen hours a day. He had four or five films in work at the same time. He was skinny, sensitive, and nervous; chain-smoked cigarettes; drove everybody relentlessly. Billy never met the directors of his UFA films. He wrote the scripts and deposited them in the Berlin office. The UFA production facilities were in the suburb of Neubabelsberg. There was no Writers' Building there. The writers wrote at home. They had meetings with Pommer.

Wilder says that an amusing thing happened when *Klangfilms* (i.e., talking pictures) started in 1929. UFA had a terrible problem insulating the sound-stage walls against outside noises. They heard that in Hollywood the problem had been licked. So they sent two UFA technicians out there to spy around and find out the secret materials used by MGM and Paramount and Warners'. After much espionage, the secret agents finally stole a sample of a certain type of heavy corrugated cardboard which was the mysterious insulator. UFA now began seeking a firm which could duplicate this American insulator.

After much searching, they found a factory about a mile away from UFA in Babelsberg. It was the same factory from which Hollywood had been importing all its insulating materials for two years!

During the next four years, Wilder wrote, alone or in collaboration, many interesting films. He wrote love stories, musicals, murder and crime stories, romantic fantasy stories.

Curt Siodmak, who collaborated with Billy on a fascinating film, *The Man Looking for his Own Killer,* recalls hectic story conferences with the Irving Thalberg of Germany: "I remember how Billy could never sit still in one place. We'd meet Pommer in his kingly office. There was me, Ludwig Hirschfeld, and Billy. Pommer had a trick to get his writers thinking up angles or new lines. He put out a stack of silver coins on his desk. Now you have to picture Billy: he's walking up and down, snapping his fingers, and Pommer would say like, maybe, we are stuck for a shot here. He sticks his finger on the script. Now who thinks of a good shot or an idea, he wins a silver coin. Well, you know that Billy is a very quick thinker and he has the will to win; he was always the first one to shoot out an idea, never stopping his marching up and down; and there's this world-famous man, Pommer, throwing him another coin; and Billy, he don't even break step, he just keeps up his marching and catches the coin so we don't stand a chance; and that pile of coins, it finished in Billy's pants."

So you thought only Hollywood moguls were weird, did you? You expect such childish behavior from a Zanuck, a Jack Warner, *nicht wahr?* But this dignified, cultured Pommer, who produced *Cabinet of Dr. Caligari* and *The Blue Angel?* Throwing coins to his writers like peanuts to an elephant?

Pommer's number one girl friend and favorite actress was the gorgeous British blonde, Lillian Harvey. She was in the 1932 *Blonde Dream,* written by Wilder with Walter Reisch. She was the Ginger Rogers of Germany. She sang in French, English, and German. The plot was about two window-washers who are in love with Lillian— Willi Forst and Willi Fritsch, two topline German *farceurs.* The film was written as a depression musical: the trio live in an abandoned railroad car. Lillian cannot choose between the two aspirants for her heart and so, in disgust, they leave her and go off together, womanless, as raindrops keep falling on their bicycles—just like Newman and Redford. Yes, they traveled around Berlin on bicycles, looking for dirty windows . . .

Miss Harvey was furious. How dare they—these two ignorant writers! These two faggots! How could there be a Lillian Harvey movie in which she is abandoned by *two* men? Even for *one* man to abandon her was unthinkable! And Pommer, who knew on which side his broad was buttered, agreed with her. "Fix it," he ordered. Reisch remembers that Wilder practically walked him off his feet trying to figure out how to placate the star, and also write an original movie. Finally he said, "I got it, I got it. We have a little dog. There ain't a dog alive that can't act the pants off Lillian Harvey anyway. One will get Lillian, and the other Willi, he'll get the dog; and I think who gets the dog is the winner."

And that's how it was: Willi Forst got the dog; Willi Fritsch got the girl; and one of the Willis, I forget which, went to America, which was what the other Willi, or Billy, also had in mind one of these days.

One of Billy's 1931 screenplays, *Ihre Hoheit Befiehlt* ("Her Majesty Requests") was bought by Fox and remade with Janet Gaynor as *Adorable*. This, like several other Wilder epics of this, his Pink Period, or Sigmund Romberg-type musical phase, was, in Wilder's words, "one of those pictures that you sum up so: little does the handsome soldier know that the little peasant girl at the fair is really a countess, and little does she know that the handsome soldier is really the crown prince." Another Wilder story, *Was Frauen Träumen* ("What Women Dream") was remade by Universal as *One Exciting Adventure*, with Neil Hamilton and Binnie Barnes. Miss Barnes was to have more exciting adventures when she married Mike Frankovitch, later head of Columbia Pictures.

Billy's best film for UFA was *Emil und die Detektive*, based on a best-selling novel by Erich Kastner. It is a fast and furious comedy about a thief who steals money from a boy, and is pursued by this boy and a gang of street rascals who imitate all the devices of detectives they've read about. I saw it in 1932 without subtitles at a student screening at the University of Wisconsin. (Little did the freshman know that decades later he would be writing a biography of the screenwriter.) I loved it then. I saw it again in 1975. It was just as good.

Billy's last screenplay for Pommer was *Der Frack mit der Chrysantheme* ("Tailcoat with the Flower") written with Reisch. It was an episodic movie, in which a full-dress suit goes through vicissitudes from one owner to another and finally is a scarecrow in a field of corn.

Erich Pommer never got around to producing it. He had left Berlin. By then, Wilder was also in another country.

# 4

# HELLO TO HOLLYWOOD

$B$y the time Billy Wilder fell madly in love for the second time, he was living the high life of a decadent Berliner. He was making more money than he could spend. He was driving a brand-new, rakish Graham-Paige convertible. He was driving it fast and recklessly. He lived in an *art moderne* flat in a contemporary building on fashionable Fasenenstrasse. His place was furnished with avant-garde Mies van der Rohe furniture. He was starting to collect prints and posters. He did not look like a screenwriter. German screenwriters, just like Hollywood ones, tended to be nervous, drunken, badly dressed, out-of-condition characters. Billy was tall and trim and athletic. He walked miles every day. He was attired in the best silk shirts, ties, custom-made suits, hats—everything was either British or American. He sported a cane. He was sophisticated. He loved being rich. He loved spending his money on *real* things that he could touch and see. He was a hedonist. He knew the best restaurants in town and had tasted of all their specialties. He was only twenty-five, and, at first glance he seemed like a rosy-cheeked cherub in a rococo painting. He had been cursed with an ungainly mane of curly red hair which made him look—well, *wrong*, for his boulevardier disguise. That's when he started wearing hats indoors and out-of-doors. If you looked at him more closely and saw the world-weariness in his eyes, you knew that this lad had lived—yes, he had been around the *strasse* a couple of times. As Kohner remarks, "Already in Berlin he was a man who has suffered and knows everything. Yes, he seemed to know everything. Yes, he seemed to know everything about everything. And only twenty-five—it was not to be believed. As we say, he was *mit allen Wassern gewaschen, und mit allen Hunden gehetzt.*" ("He had been washed in all the waters, and pursued by all the dogs.")

But who minds being pursued by yet another dog, especially if it is a comely bitch? Her name was Hella Hartwig. She had shining black hair, cut very short, and enormous black eyes, fringed with long black eyelashes, and long fingernails, and she was voluptuous. She had a nonchalant air. She was like Hedy Lamarr in appearance. She was rather dumb in matters of art and literature. She could not engage in high-flown conversation. She liked racing cars and skiing and jazz and dancing. She liked Billy Wilder. She was head over heels in love with him and her heels were, *Gott sei Dank*, round. She was a rich girl, an heiress. She drove a sleek blue Lancia. Wouldn't it have been nice, I once wondered, if they had met in what Hollywood calls a "meet-cute," maybe his blue Graham-Paige crashed into her blue Lancia? The way Gary Cooper meets Claudette Colbert in *Bluebeard's Eighth Wife*, when he wants to buy pajama tops and she wants to buy pajama bottoms? Or like when Jane Wyman and Ray Milland get his raincoat and her leopard coat mixed up at the opera in *Lost Weekend*? Billy is famous in Hollywood for his "meet-cutes." Billy shook his head despairingly when I told him of my yearning to know how he met Hella.

"You want my life to be a Billy Wilder picture," he shouted. "You are impossible. You are hopeless. I am only glad we are not collaborating on a movie together. Hella and I did not meet cute. We met the way lovers usually meet. We met at a party in somebody's apartment. I liked her. She liked me. We went out together. We made love. No, she did not talk like Claudette Colbert. In real life, no woman is talking like Claudette Colbert, including Claudette Colbert. In real life, most women are stupid, and so are persons who are writing biographies of Hollywood celebrities. Most people do not say clever or interesting things. That is why they have to pay clever screenwriters so much money to make up these clever things."

"That's only your opinion, Billy."

"My opinion is the true opinion."

"What was Hella's profession?"

"Her profession was to be a rich woman, and she did her work admirably. Her father owned a large pharmaceutical business in Frankfort an der Oder. Her family did not admire me. I did not make a good impression on them when she took me to meet them." (Wilder usually did not make a good first, or even second, impression on most people, since his unconscious desire was to irritate others so they would hate him.) "They did not want her to marry a screenwriter. A banker for a son-in-law was more what they had in mind. This was fine with me as I did not contemplate matrimony, then or ever. I did not like the idea of marriage. It was enslavement and the end of liberty."

One of the pastimes of Hella and Billy was to play dominoes. I'm afraid this is going to be terribly disillusioning, I mean when you think of everything you've heard about antebellum Berlin: the cocaine sniffing, the lesbians, the gay communities, the absolute and beautiful degredation of all humanity, those George Grosz cartoons, those Bertolt Brecht characters, that despair of the blues—decadent Berlin. Every Sunday, Hella and Billy went to Reisch's house and played dominoes until midnight, when Reisch's mistress made liverwurst and salami sandwiches and they drank beer and played more dominoes. There were a dozen or so regulars at the domino games.

Meanwhile, democratic Germany was being torn apart by the political extremists of the right and the left and the president of the country was a reactionary old man, the World War I general, von Hindenberg, after whom they named that ill-fated dirigible. The Nazis and their Storm Troopers were fighting in the streets and Hitler's party was getting more votes and more Reishstag members. In the 1930 elections they had won 107 seats.

In January 1933, Billy and Hella went to Davos for the skiing. They were skiing down the Parsenn one morning. Along the way, they paused at one of those huts. They had sausages, hot potato salad, and mulled wine. There was a radio in the chalet. There was an announcement that President von Hindenberg had appointed Adolf Hitler to be chancellor.

Wilder said to his girl, "I think it is time to leave." She said she would like to have some pastry and coffee first and he said he meant to leave Germany. It was the end. They must return at once and be prepared to flee. It was all over. He felt this in his bones. Many others waited until 1934 and even 1935 before they fled. Some waited until it was too late . . . .

Billy sold every possession he owned at distress prices. He converted his marks into American money. He had a thousand dollars in hundred-dollar bills. He did not, as has been erroneously reported in many stories, flee with valuable rolled-up paintings by Matisse and Cezanne. The reason was that he did not, at that time, possess any valuable works of art. On February 27, the night of the Reichstag fire, Billy and Hella were dining at the Kempinski and they saw the parliament building blazing and the streets were filled with the ominous whining of fire engines and police cars. The commissioner of police in Berlin was Hermann Goering. The fire, which the Nazis said had been done by Communists, became the excuse to put an end to political freedom.

Wilder decided to get out the next day. Hella's father drove them to the Zoo station. They took the night train to Paris. Hella had been given a large hoard of gold coins. She had many diamonds and fur coats. Billy had one suitcase with some clothes, and the thousand dollars—which was secreted in his hatband.

Hella still not did believe that Germany was lost. Many people—even persons with real political savvy like Billy's friend, Egon Kisch—thought Hitler and his hoodlums would soon be vanquished. Most of his friends remained. That was one way. Another was to go to another country where German was spoken—Austria or Switzerland. You could, thirdly, kill yourself; and many would soon be doing it. Or, finally, you could make a clean break and forget Germany and German and start all over—and that was what Billy proposed to himself in his mind. Hella thought in terms of what one lost. It was true he had lost his UFA prestige and apartment and Mies van der Rohe furniture and friends and a whole exciting way of life. He had also lost the city he loved so much, his Berlin, and the spirit of exuberance which animated Berlin.

But the most important thing he had lost was his country, and the real homeland of a writer—his native language.

They arrived in the Gare St. Lazare at six in the morning. They were refugees. You had to be careful. There were rumors that refugees were being returned to Nazi Germany. Wilder was on an Austrian passport. He was still an Austrian national. But he would have to register. He had come without a visa. He was worried about Hel-

la. He had a list of rather *louche* hotels which weren't too serious
about making you register. They carried their luggage to a fleabag on
the Boulevard Raspail. They had a little room upstairs. The shades
were drawn. They awoke at two. She pulled up the shade and
groaned. They had a fine view of the Montparnasse cemetery. Hella
said they had to get out of here fast. They did. They took a taxi to
the Hotel Ansonia, 8 Rue de Saigon, near Avenue Foch, which became a refuge for many refugees. Alice and Franz Waxmann (he later dropped one "n" and became a leading Hollywood composer),
and Friedrich Hollander, another composer, who had written "Falling in Love Again" for Marlene, and Peter Lorre, already famous
for *M*, and others lived at the Ansonia.

Wilder had a terrible time in Paris. He could not write under his
own name. He did not have a labor permit. He wrote under other
people's names. He first had to write in German and then translate it
into French. He spoke and wrote French fluently, though with less
control than his German. He was getting paid in unmarked en-
velopes by people who looked over their shoulders. He was working
illegally. Hella was wretched over their poverty. She didn't like
small rooms and cheap restaurants. She nagged at him. To her, the
luxuries were necessary. Necessities, she could do without. In April
1934, Reisch finally arrived in Paris and Billy met him at the station.
He at once took him, not to the Ansonia, but to the Roland Garros
Stadium, to see the Davis Cup matches—France against England.
Billy was excited. He was jumping up and down cheering the four
musketeers—Cochet, LaCoste, Brugnon, and Borotra. France won!
What a perfect day. The hell with Hitler and who cares about Hella.
France won. It reminds me of those two Englishmen in *The Lady
Vanishes* who are trapped on the continent, as Europe is about to go
to war, and their concern is who won some cricket matches . . . .

Among the many stories on which he worked was one with a couple of Berlin exiles, Max Kolpe and H.G. "Jon" Lustig, two former
UFA writers. It was a screenplay about a gang of young car thieves,
their tricks, their loves, their lives, and their deaths. Wilder found a
Hungarian-partner, Alex Esway, who found a colorful guy, General
Edouard Corniglion-Molinier, a hero of the first World War, an aviator, a man with some political influence. He backed the movie. He
was a movie producer. He owned a studio in Nice. With The General—as they called him—in their corner, Wilder could come out of
the closet. They couldn't afford a real director, so Wilder directed

his first movie—*Mauvaise Graine* ("Bad Seed"). The star was a seventeen-year-old actress playing her second movie role—Danielle Darrieux. She looked very plump and spoke her lines mechanically. She didn't even look beautiful. Wilder filmed the movie, in documentary style, out in the streets and in a garage. It is a dazzling picture. It is unbelievably good—unbelievably, because it was made in 1934 and it has a syncopated jazz score by Waxmann and fast cutting from scene to scene and car chases and gangsters and police and—hell, it still is a damn entertaining film, though only two prints of it are said to exist, one of them at the Cinemathèque Française and the other owned by a Los Angeles film collector who charged me forty dollars to see it last year.

Wilder did not like directing movies. It was hard on his nerves. He couldn't stand arguing with actors. He couldn't stand worrying about problems of lighting and placement and getting the cars to go the way they should go. He was praying to get back to the real business of his life, which was writing. He would, of course, never direct another movie—never.

Wilder wrote another story—*Pam-Pam*, a musical *strudel* about a girl runaway who takes refuge in an abandoned theatre on Broadway and gets mixed up with counterfeiters who help her put on an amateur musical show. They had not yet made those Judy Garland-Mickey Rooney type musicals, but one can see that this is the general line along which Wilder is working. He had to get to America. He was trying to invent a Hollywood-type musical movie. No more peasant girls and handsome soldiers, no more lieutenants and countesses, he was getting into that good old Warner Bros. musical, Busby Berkeley groove. *It don't mean a thing if it ain't got that swing . . .*

Billy sent the script to his friend Joe May. May was now a producer at Columbia Pictures. He had been the Cecil B. De Mille of German pictures. He made nine-hour spectacles starring his beautiful wife, Mia May. They were shown in separate installments.

In December 1933, May cabled. Eureka! Columbia liked the idea. They would pay his passage—one way—to Hollywood. He would get $150 a week to write the screenplay. He went alone, without his Hella.

He traveled on the *Aquitania* on January 22, 1934. He chose a British liner so he could practice his English. He was determined to learn English. He was studying phrase books and some new American novels he had picked up at Brentano's on the Place de l'Opéra: Hemingway's *A Farewell to Arms, Babbitt* by Sinclair Lewis, Wolfe's *Look Homeward, Angel.* When he danced with lady passengers on the ship, he tried out various English phrases, culling many from American song lyrics. If a woman asked him, in the ship's lounge, when she would see him again, he might reply, "When day is done, and shadows fall."

Asked once whether he longed for Berlin, he replied, "Gee, but I'd give the world to see that old gang of mine."

Soon the women passengers darted out of sight when they saw this lunatic . . . .

They landed in New York in a snowstorm. Finally he was reunited with brother Willie, whom he had not seen for twelve years; he met Willie's wife, and their little boy, who has since grown up to become Miles Wilder, a successful television writer.

After a few days, he boarded the Twentieth Century for Chicago and then the Chief for Los Angeles. He felt intoxicated by America. He had at last come to the place about which he had dreamed for so long. The Wild West. The place his mother had made up stories about. The place of the movies. As the train went through the cities which were so legendary—Kansas City, Santa Fe, Albuquerque, Yuma—he was uplifted. He was dizzied. He loved the spaces and the emptiness and the desert of the west.

Joe May was there at the old Second Street Station in downtown Los Angeles to meet him. They drove west on Second Street. It was a golden morning. Wilder was looking around for famous stars. He most wanted to see Clark Gable and Mae West—I know not why. That's what he told me. He thought the streets were paved with stars. He didn't see any stars. Along Melrose Avenue, May pointed out the Paramount studio, where Lubitsch was head of production now—our Ernst Lubitsch. He explained that in another place, west and south, was the mammoth studio of MGM in Culver City, and now, here, on your left, right down there on Gower Street, that was Columba Pictures, where he would be working. May turned right on Gower and then left onto a wide street, a very wide thoroughfare with stucco buildings, one or two stories high, and many empty spaces between them, and those weird palm trees like giraffe necks, and those houses in between stores, flamingo pink and pistachio green and cerulean blue and Mediterranean white—but they weren't villas; they were fruit markets, banks, bars, hamburger stands, tailor shops.

Billy was trying to figure out the words on billboards.

"What do they call this street, Joe?" he asked.

"Sunset Boulevard," was the reply.

# 5

# BOY MEETS BOY

On his first morning as a Columbia writer, Wilder was led into Sam Briskin's office. Briskin was first lieutenant to Harry Cohn, the roughneck president of Columbia. Unlike other studios, Columbia was not hospitable to European writers. What had appealed to Briskin and Cohn in Wilder's fable of the counterfeiters was that it had a Damon Runyonesque quality. Columbia had just had a success with *Lady for a Day*, based on a Runyon story.

Briskin was under the impression that Wilder was an American writer, a real New Yorker.

Hearing his first fumbling words, Briskin knew that *this* Wilder was definitely not a Broadway denizen.

"You French or something?" he muttered.

Wilder's vocabulary deserted him. "I—I—been—Austrian," he ventured.

"Billy—what kinda name is that for an Austrian?"

Billy wished he could think of the appropriate line from a song that fitted the situation. All he could remember was a line from Oscar Hammerstein's *Show Boat:* "He's just my Bill, an ordinary guy . . ."

Billy's office was in the writers' compound, a group of bungalows around a fountain courtyard. Wilder sat at the desk. He stared at the

American keyboard of his typewriter. His dictionary was on the desk. A ream of typewriting paper was on the table. He put a sheet of paper in the machine and he typed.

EXT. NEW YORK THEATRE. AFTERNOON.

His mind went blank.

An hour passed. Fearful that his silence would be interpreted as sloth, he started furiously typing a letter to Hella in German.

Subsequently he met other Columbia writers, mostly neophytes like himself. There was James M. Cain, with *The Postman Always Rings Twice* to his credit. Norman Krasna, younger than Billy, a former press agent who had written a Broadway hit at twenty-one— *Louder Please*—was another. There were Jo Swerling, Dorothy Parker, Sidney Kingsley, Sidney Buchman, young Dore Schary.

The senior member of the writers was thirty-seven-year-old Robert Riskin. Riskin liked composing outside in the sun. He wrote on a long legal pad in longhand. He liked being interrupted. Wilder timidly asked him questions. Riskin was helpful. So was Cain, a stocky gentleman, with horn-rimmed glasses, who talked out of the side of his mouth like a stevedore and knew more about grand opera than any Viennese.

Cain heard Wilder's typewriter crack in the mornings. He told him to take it easy until 11:45, as Harry Cohn never got to his office until noon.

Once, Harry Cohn arrived at ten. He strode through the courtyard of the writers' bungalows. Not a single typewriter was clacking.

He started screaming. "What the hell is going on around here? I pay you fuckin' writers a fortune to write and nobody is writing."

In a moment, from every office came the sounds of typewriters clicking, bells ringing, carriages returning.

This infuriated Cohn even more. He brandished his fist at the noisy typewriters and shouted,

"Liars! *Liars!* LIARS!"

Billy wrote the screenplay of *Pam-Pam*. Nothing happened.

He was boarding with Mia and Joe May. He paid them $75 a week for a room and his meals. They lived in a Spanish-style mansion on Courtney Avenue in the Hollywood hills.

Miss May, still vigorous at ninety-three, remembers Billy.

"Oh such a sweet boy he was," she murmured, pouring me Viennese coffee and pastry she had baked, "a sweet gentle person. A very nice boarder. He never gave trouble. Did I permitting him to bring ladies to his room? No. No. Never.''

In August, his six-month deal with Columbia would be up. So would his visitor's visa. He had to get an immigration visa. He loved America. He planned to make his life in Hollywood. He was going to become a citizen. He went to Calexico, California, and crossed over the border to Mexicali. He presented his affidavits and forms from the department of immigration. Five years later he went to federal courthouse in Los Angeles, accompanied by screenwriter Don Hartman. He satisfactorily answered the questions about our form of government and then, joining several hundred men and women in a courtroom, he took the pledge of allegiance. That day, in 1939, he considers one of the shining days of his life.

Joe May went over to Fox. He directed Gloria Swanson and John Boles in a musical film based on Jerome Kern's *Music in the Air.* Wilder received his first American screen credit when it was released in 1934. He shared it with Howard I. Young. It was a wretched picture. La Swanson's previous film had been *Queen Kelly*, directed by von Stroheim, financed by her lover, Joseph P. Kennedy. *Queen Kelly* was never released. The coming of talkies had seemingly wrecked her career. She made several other films after *Queen Kelly.* They failed. She hoped *Music in the Air* would rehabilitate her. He saw Gloria Swanson on the lot, her pride and desperation wrapped around her like a tattered ermine robe.

Billy, too, knew the desperation and bitterness of failure. He wrote and he wrote and all that he wrote was rejected. His agent was never in when he phoned. He was behind in his payments on a 1928 De Soto coupe that was a wreck when he bought it. He wore old clothes. He was behind in the rent. He lived in a small cell with a Murphy bed and a hot plate in the Chateau Marmont above Sunset Boulevard near Laurel Canyon. His room overlooked the back alley. Often he was lonely. Sometimes he was hungry. He sought to improve his English by listening to the radio, reading all the Los Angeles papers, and following the new books. Sometimes he would use food money to go dancing at the Pacific Ocean Pier in Venice. He had no phonograph and no records. Sometimes he just lay in the sun for a whole day on the beach at Santa Monica.

He had valuable contacts in Kohner, Pasternak, and Ernest Laemmle, but they could not find him work. Pasternak had become an important man on the Universal lot. He was able to get many talented German filmmakers on the payroll, including Herman Kosterlitz (who as Henry Koster directed many successful musical films), and Felix Jackson (who cowrote *Destry Rides Again* and other films and also wrote novels).

"I think," Pasternak told me, "that Carl Laemmle didn't want to hire Billy because he was too tall. Laemmle was a little shrimp. Billy was damn near six feet big. Laemmle didn't like big guys around him."

In all of 1935, he had only one screen credit, a collaboration with Franz Schulz, a romantic melodrama, a B picture for Fox, *Lottery Lover,* starring Lew Ayres. It was a five-week assignment at $200 a week. He got it through William Thiele, the director, also an ex-Berliner.

Wilder also remembers engaging in clandestine, ghostly rewrites as he had done at UFA. He shudders at the memory of one of his spectral assignments.

"It was an idiotic mishmash about two gentlemen known as sandhogs," Wilder says. "They are making a tunnel under some river by New York. They are friends. They like to get drunk and hit each other. They fight over broads. It was for Victor McLaglen and Edmund Lowe. My name did not appear on the credits, thank God."

He did not want to go on collaborating with Schulz. He had to have American collaborators. He tried to shun the German colony so he could master English but he was drawn into it out of loneliness.

Salka Viertel's salon at 165 Mabery Road in Santa Monica was a center for the exiles. An intense, slender lady with dark eyes and black hair, she was a vivacious talker and a lover of people. Her husband, Berthold, was a director. They had come to Hollywood in 1926. Frau Viertel played in films for a few years and later became a writer herself. She was a close friend of Greta Garbo. Frau Viertel was the queen of the emigrés.

Also present at the Viertel Sunday afternoons were Louise and Oliver H.P. Garrett, who were neighbors. Garrett was a rich screen writer. Scion of an old New England family, he wrote action films. He drove a rakish convertible. He sported a beret and attired himself in loud sport coats. He was the epitome of the respectable New York writer who "goes Hollywood." He was amused at Billy's wit. They became friends. Billy went out to Garrett's to play tennis. Peter Viertel, then fifteen, also played tennis with Billy.

Erich Pommer was under contract to RKO. He lived in a Beverly Hills mansion. He knew how insulted Billy would be if he loaned him money. Instead, during a lavish poolside party, he offered to bet Billy $50 that he would jump into the pool with his clothes on. Fully dressed and in his right mind, Billy danced along the board and then jackknifed into the pool.

It was the only splash he made in Hollywood that year.

Wilder denies any rumors that he became a professional pool jumper. Nor was he ever an Arthur Murray dancing teacher, as another rumor had it. All he did was write movies and starve.

Garrett began taking an interest in him. He advised him on American slang and revealed the secrets of screenwriting.

He stressed the importance of the opening boy-meets-girl scene or the "meet-cute."

There was a widespread conviction, not entirely baseless, that romantic love was the royal road to Hollywood success. This attitude was summed up in *Boy Meets Girl,* a Broadway hit of 1936 by Bella and Sam Spewack, made into a Warner Bros. comedy. This is the only film, as far as I know, in which a team of screenwriters are the heroes. They were played by Jimmy Cagney and Pat O'Brien. There is a scene, early on, in which the "boys" are trying to come up with something.

O'Brien asks, "What's our story?"

Cagney replies: "Boy meets girl, boy loses girl, boy gets girl, or love will find a way. Love never loses. Put your money on love."

Garrett and Wilder put their money on love and collaborated on *Encore,* a musical romance, and *Gibraltar,* a fable of spies, gamblers and boys meeting girls. Garrett had a notion that a new company, Pioneer Films, might be receptive to these charades. Pioneer Films started in 1934 and was owned by producer director Merian C. Cooper (involved in such exotic films as *Change, Grass* and *King Kong*), in partnership with two millionaires John Hay (Jock) Whitney and Cornelius Vanderbilt ("Sonny") Whitney. Pioneer was the first studio to make only Technicolor films. Technicolor, invented by Herbert Kalmus in 1918, was shunned by the major studios, still coping with sound. They announced an ambitious program of color films. They hired Robert Edmond Jones, a great theatrical designer, as their art director. Charles Vidor was to direct films.

Once, Billy ran into Jock Whitney at the Pioneer offices. "Mr. Whitney," Wilder said, "you got the right second name of everybody—but the wrong first names. You need Thornton Wilder. You got Billy Wilder. You need King Vidor; you got Charles Vidor. You need Gary Cooper; you got Merian Cooper. Every first name is wrong!''

Later, as Wilder says, ''Jock Whitney finally found a partner with the right first name and the right last name. He went in with David O. Selznick and not Myron Selznick. He had a piece of a movie. The movie had the right four names. *Gone With the Wind.*''

Billy got $5,000 for his share of the two originals and signed a long-term contract at Pioneer. He celebrated by going to Europe for six weeks. In Paris, he saw Hella. The old thrill was gone. She was just another stunning and illiterate female. He saw his mama and grandmama in Vienna. Mama had remarried. No, she did not want to come to America. Her husband, Herr Siedlisker, had a business here. No, Hitler would never bother the Austrians.

Back in Los Angeles, he now had a better room at the Chateau Marmont but it wasn't ready yet. It was the Christmas holidays. The hotel was booked solid. They suggested that he temporarily hole up in an anteroom in the basement. It was the anteroom leading to six women's toilets.

''This Christmas in 1935,'' he says, ''when I could not sleep, when women were coming in and peeing and looking at me funny, when I was worried about the knowledge that my mother was in danger, and knew that the war was on the way for Europe, suddenly I wasn't sure if I fitted in around here in Hollywood. I had the feeling I was not in the right country and I didn't know if there was a right country for me. Right here was the low point of my life.''

Around this time, Pioneer Films dissolved. *Encore* and *Gibraltar*, like *Pam-Pam,* were never filmed.

In collaboration with H.S. ''Hy'' Kraft, one of those new young writers imported from Broadway, Billy next wrote *Champagne Waltz,* a story about an American swing musician who brings his band to Vienna and conquers the waltz city. Lester Cowan, an independent producer working in the Fanchon and Marco unit at Paramount, paid $10,000 for the screenplay. Kraft and Wilder each received a $1,000 advance. Cowan could not get *Champagne Waltz* into production. Would Billy take a $250-a-week contract writing post at Paramount in lieu of the $4,000 he was still owed? Yes.

He was interviewed by Manny Wolfe, head of the writers department. He was put on salary—on a week-to-week basis—as a favor to Cowan.

Manny Wolfe—one of the few front-office men in Hollywood really called "Manny," a name traditional in Hollywood producer and agent jokes—was a shrewd judge of writing talent. He was a short, wiry fellow with a bald head and thick glasses. He dressed formally, by Hollywood standards—that is, his coat and trousers matched, he wore white shirts, and he wore ties.

There were 104 writers under contract to Paramount when Wilder signed. *One hundred and four.* Wilder started in a little room on the second floor of the Writers' Building. He was assigned to see what he could do in the way of adapting *Champagne Waltz* to fit Fred MacMurray, a former band singer and sax player who hailed from Kankakee, Illinois, and who was imported from Broadway shows to Hollywood in 1934. He had an infectious grin and a genial wise-cracking ring in his voice.

Suddenly Wolfe handed the story to Don Hartman and Frank Butler. They wrote a new script. It was filmed later with Gladys Swarthout playing the granddaughter of Johann Strauss, and MacMurray playing Buzzy Ballew, a swing musician.

"Yeah, I sure remember *Champagne Waltz*," MacMurray reminisced recently, grinning his eternally loveable MacMurray grin. "Yeah, it was where I chew gum all the time. I was a nice guy but fresh. That was how Paramount always cast me. Nice guy. But fresh. Hey—you know I didn't realize Billy wrote the story. I guess it hadn't been for Billy, I'd still be playing nice fresh guys. He made me a villain. Still, you think about it, the first fifteen minutes of *Double Indemnity,* I'm still doing the wisecracking smart aleck, getting fresh with Barbara Stanwyck, going on the make for her."

Another musical blintz which Wilder rolled during his early, or solfeggio, period at Paramount was *Rhythm on the River,* intended for Bing Crosby. He worked on this vehicle for The Groaner with his old friend, Jacques Théry. This was also taken away from Wilder's hot hands and given to Dwight Taylor.

Wilder thought he was doomed. Little did he know that Manny Wolfe had an idea. For his next project Ernst Lubitsch wished to remake an Alfred Savoir play, *La Huitième Femme du Barbe-Bleu,* previously done by Gloria Swanson in 1923. One day there was a knock on Wilder's door.

"Come in," he said.

The door opened. There stood Manny Wolfe, fastidiously attired. There was a thoughtful frown on his face.

*My God,* Wilder thought, *he has come to fire me. He certainly cannot be here to take a script away from me, because I do not have a script for him to take away, so he is here to fire me.*

"Do you know Lubitsch?" Manny Wolfe asked.

"No."

"Do you know the eighth wife of Bluebeard?"

"By Savoir?"

"Yes."

"*Her* I am acquainted with, Manny."

"Do you know Charlie Brackett?" Wolfe continued.

"I know him but I don't think he knows me."

"He is about to know you, Billy," Wolfe said. "We are going to give Mr. Brackett a little surprise present."

They proceeded to Brackett's office. "Charlie," Wolfe said, "I think you know Billy Wilder here. We have decided to team you boys up for our next Lubitsch picture—that's the Savoir property, the one about the eighth wife."

Brackett examined Wilder carefully.

"Billy," Brackett said, "it will be a pleasure to work with you. However, there is one thing I must know."

"And what is that?"

"Do you play cribbage?"

The date was July 17, 1936.

# 6

# THE CLOCKWORK
# MECHANISM

Socially and temperamentally, Billy Wilder and Charlie Brackett were at opposite poles. Brackett was a calm, suave, genteel individual. He thought and moved languidly. He had an imperious dignity. He was fourteen years older than Billy when they started the partnership. He never treated Billy as the junior partner. Nobody could ever get away treating Billy as a junior anything. Charlie was well-mannered and polite. Billy was rough and indelicate. Brackett came from a rich old upper New York State family. His father was a corporation lawyer and a state senator. Charlie, like his forebears, was a rock-ribbed conservative Republican. Charlie went to Williams College. He was a graduate of the Harvard Law School. He fought in World War I. He began writing stories and novels while he was still a lawyer. His roots were in Saratoga Springs, New York. He was a Victorian at heart. Nobody could understand how he and Billy collaborated so well. They couldn't either. Bracket had been seduced by Hollywood in 1930. After the talking picture revolution, the studio heads began sending for Broadway actors who could speak lines and for New York playwrights, novelists, and newspapermen who could write words for actors to speak. They had discovered that, just as certain silent movie stars like John Gilbert failed in talking pictures, so many of their best scenario writers

*63*

could not write dialogue. There was an old saying that it was easy to write a talking picture. All you had to do was write a silent movie scenario, and then "just dialogue it in." This is nonsense, Wilder says. A talking picture has to be conceived and structured along radically different lines from the very beginning. When the actors opened their mouths, the nature of the movies was violently altered, and so was the writing of pictures. Brackett wrote repartee for RKO, Paramount, and MGM. He hated story conferences. He hated talking out imaginary scenes with directors and producers. Wilder loved these moments. The burden of story conference strategy fell upon his glib tongue.

From their first meeting, Billy was in awe of Ernst Lubitsch and was to remain so until Lubitsch died. To him, Lubitsch was the master of film composition, a magician. Lubitsch was a stout little man with a beaming smile and a thick German accent and twinkling eyes. He smoked cigars all the time. He was a perfectionist. He was a believer in a well-made screenplay and he didn't start shooting until the screenplay was perfect. Lubitsch never improvised on a set—nor allowed his actors to utter spontaneous lines. He choreographed each word and gag. He made sure that there was not a single superfluous detail in the script. Once, B.P. Schulberg, then Paramount's head of production, asked him why he was shooting a scene a certain way, and he replied he couldn't remember exactly why at just this moment, "but it is in the script, which is good enough for me. If I didn't have a good reason, it would not have been in there when Sam Raphaelson was writing it in the first place."

Lubitsch was relentless in making the new team revise and polish. Once, Brackett and Wilder had completed a scene in which Claudette Colbert is being pursued by American multimillionaire Gary Cooper (playing a Howard Hughes character), who has married and divorced seven wives already. She eludes her suitor by leaping off a float in the Mediterranean. It was a wild scene, with Cooper in a white suit pedal-boating out to her and getting wet. Now what Lubitsch wanted was one word to be shouted by Colbert just before she dived into the water. Just one word. Nobody could come up with the right word. They tried a thousand words—and never found *le mot juste*. Again and again, Lubitsch, pantomiming Colbert's dive, would look at the writers appealingly and beg them to please give him the word, the perfect word. Long after they were past this scene, he would come back to it and suddenly ask if anybody had thought of the word for the diving bit.

In story conferences, Lubitsch acted out every role in the film as he read the lines aloud. He played Cooper and Colbert and David Niven, young male secretary of Cooper. He even played Herman Bing, as a private detective. Bing would disguise himself while shadowing Claudette. And, Billy reports in veneration, Lubitsch would do Bing better than Bing could do Bing, and he would make himself into the disguises of Bing—a teenage schoolgirl, a nun . . .

He had Wilder rolling on the floor and screaming with laughter. He even broke up Brackett, which was hard to do.

*Bluebeard's Eighth Wife* belonged to a now outmoded genre of Hollywood picture known as the UFF., or Unfinished Fuck. In the traditional, or Doris Day, UFF. picture, the heroine is a compulsive virgin, who defends her maidenhead in a series of episodes in which copulation is postponed until marriage. In *Bluebeard's Eighth Wife,* the heroine sexually frustrates the hero *after* they are married. It is one of the most salacious films ever made—and yet there is not one obscene word or frame in the movie. This was the time of the strict code laid down by the Motion Pictures Producers Association.

Wilder says "we had to operate cunningly to outwit the censors and this made us write more subtly. It was not permitted to have a character speak even a puny little curse like 'you bastard' or 'you son of a bitch.' Once Charlie and I figured out this substitute: 'if you had a mother, she would bark.'

"You couldn't show on the screen a man fucking a woman to whom he was not married, or even fucking a woman to whom he was married. For that matter, you couldn't even show a couple occupying the same bed at the same time. As far as the Hays office was concerned, every bedroom in the whole goddam world had twin beds. So, the problem is, how do you show that man and woman making love?

"Someone figured out a *shtick* like the maid is making up a man's bed the next morning; on the pillow she finds a hairpin. Lubitsch was the genius of what I call the hairpin-on-the-pillow tricks. He wants to show you, let us say, a man and a woman in a passionate affair. First a scene in which they are kissing ardently the night before. Then . . . dissolve to the following morning . . . We see them at breakfast. Ah, but regard how they are sucking their coffee and how they are biting their toast: This leaves no doubt in anybody's mind that other appetites have been satisfied. In those days, the butter was on the toast and not the ass, but there was more eroticism in one such breakfast scene than in all of *Last Tango in Paris*."

In July the partners completed the screenplay of *Bluebeard's Eighth Wife*. Now, in accordance with the Writer-Producer Code of Practice of the Screen Writers Guild, Paramount, after filming was completed in November, prepared a "notice of tentative credits." For the first time, the marriage of the two men was validated in writing:

*Screenplay by Charles Brackett and Billy Wilder.*

The document was signed by Manny Wolfe and stamped at 6:00 p.m., November 3, 1937.

Claudette Colbert starred in the next B and W comedy—*Midnight*, in my opinion, one of the most polished and beautifully written high comedies of the 1930s. Wilder and Brackett wrote it in seven months. I once made detailed notes while screening this film to see how smoothly each piece fitted into each scene and into the whole. There was not a single unnecessary detail in the movie—from the gold lamé gown in which Claudette Colbert is discovered in a railroad train in scene one, to the kidney stew served at a Sunday brunch, towards the end. One may compare such intricately constructed screenplays to those arrangements of lifelike figures in medieval town halls which—operated by an ingenious clockwork mechanism and a system of counterweights, wheels, gears, and levers—spring into action every hour to tell the time. In the 1930s and 1940s, a group of writers invented a clockwork mechanism which was a machine for laughter and unique to American films. We sometimes loosely call it "screwball comedy" because the energy which powers the machinery is produced by a conjuction of insane coincidences. Among the masters of the genre were Hecht, MacArthur, Riskin, Krasna, Nunnally Johnson, Preston Sturges, Charlie Lederer, Ring Lardner, Jr., Garson Kanin, and —yes—Brackett and Wilder.

When Charlie and Billy gave their meticulous screenplay to producer Arthur Hornblow, Jr., he decided, after reading *Midnight*, that he needed to get another writer to fix it up. This was a common practice and was known as "writing behind the script." The original writers were kept in ignorance that other writers were working behind their backs. It is now outlawed by the Screen Writers Guild.

Now you must realize that Hornblow liked the script. It was just that he would feel anxious and unimportant unless he had another writer "writing behind" B and W.

He assigned Ken Englund to "write behind." Englund did his version of *Midnight*. Hornblow was disappointed when he studied it. It was good—but it just didn't have that Brackett and Wilder flavor. He wondered aloud, "Who have we got under contract who writes like Brackett and Wilder?"

"Charlie Brackett and Billy Wilder," said Englund. "Why don't you send them my script and they'll give it some Brackett and Wilder flavor?"

"That's a hell of an idea."

Back went the script to B and W. They didn't even read it. They retyped their original script—with a few minor changes—and Hornblow just loved it. It was, of course, a power play. It was how a producer demonstrated to himself and the studio that *he* was in control of these eccentric writers. A Hornblow could shuffle writers about from one project to another. At $2,000 a week—during the Depression—one did not argue with these men. Except Billy Wilder; he argued with them. He argued with stars and directors. B and W worked with Mitchell Leisen on *Midnight* and other films at Paramount. Wilder and Leisen came to hate each other with a passion that never died. Leisen was one of the top directors on the lot. Formerly a costume and set designer for De Mille, he had graduated into direction and made several good screwball comedies, including *Hands Across the Table* and *Easy Living*. He was a tall, strikingly attired man. He was an ugly man. He was pop-eyed and large-nosed and had a clubfoot. He flaunted his sexual proclivities at a time when gay men kept them in the closet. There were no gay bars in Hollywood and no male brothels. Leisen turned his home into a homosexual rendezvous. His parties were *le dernier cri* among the gay set. Leisen was as narcisstic as any actor or actress. He changed clothes—at the studio—three or four times a day. He preened himself. He was a compulsive tie-knot tightener and hair comber. He wore startling colored slacks and embroidered Ecuadorian blouses and lurid sandals. Or he might appear in an elegant pongee suit and a panama hat. He was unpredictable. He had a feeling for design and texture in clothes and furniture that gave all his films an intensification of the usual high-camp Art Deco look that was a characteristic of most Paramount films of the '30s and '40s, because of the influence of studio art director Hans Dreier, a Bauhaus-oriented refugee from Berlin.

But was Leisen really a director, in the sense that he creatively interpreted a screenplay? Given a well-made screenplay and a company of superb actors, he was able to be a competent traffic policeman. Most directors of the period were traffic cops, not real directors like Lubitsch or John Ford or Hitchcock. Leisen hated words and did not understand screenplays. He was impatient with writers. Preston Sturges had written several of the films for which Leisen got credit. (We had an "auteur" theory operating in Hollywood when Andrew Sarris was so little he couldn't get into a picture house without his mother.) Leisen got Sturges so mad that Sturges went into the directing business himself. He was the first major Hollywood writer who became a writer/director in self-defense. After Sturges deserted him, Leisen's pictures were sloppy until he latched on to B and W. And when they deserted him, he never made a good film again.

He did have a talent of sorts for the *look* of a film, for he loved to fuss over a woman's costume or the design of a carpet. To his dying day—literally—Leisen burned with anger at Billy. He was in the last year of his life; he was up there in the Motion Picture Country Home, up in the Santa Monica Mountains, near Calabasas, a beautiful place, where old and sick and alcoholic members of the movie industry can live out their final years in flamboyant luxury. It's as lovely a place, and as well equipped in the way of sports and grounds and wine with the sumptuous meals and attendants, as your best country club—Hillcrest or Lakeside or the Bel-Air. So there is Leisen dying in 1970, and a young film scholar, David Chierichetti, comes to record his memories. (He published Leisen's biography as *Hollywood Director* in 1973.) Leisen speaks serenely of many matters in his career—until he comes to *Midnight* and to Billy Wilder.

Then the old wrath boils and bubbles in the dying man. He tells his interviewer that it was he, Leisen, who guided Brackett and Wilder in writing the screenplays of the films they made with him. He sat right there in the room with the writers. He explained to this crazy Wilder the unconscious motives of characters. You see, he Leisen, had been psychoanalyzed for eight years and he knew personality structure; he knew subconscious drives. Wilder was an arrogant, loud mouth son of a bitch. Leisen said they argued over the scripts sequence by sequence and *line by line*. He said: "Billy would scream if you changed one line of his dialogue." Leisen screamed back that

Wilder wasn't Shakespeare. Brackett, thank God, was a "leveling influence." He calmed down the madman. He made peace. "He would referee my quarrels with Billy."

In rebuttal, Wilder says: "Leisen spent more time with Edith Head worrying about the pleats on a skirt than he did with us on the script. He didn't argue over scenes. He didn't know shit about construction. And he didn't care. All he did was he fucked up the script and our scripts were damn near perfection, let me tell you. Leisen was too goddam fey. I don't knock fairies. Let him be a fairy. Leisen's problem was that he was a stupid fairy. He didn't have the brains to see that if Charlie and me, if we put in a line, we had a goddam reason for putting in that line and not a different line, and you don't just go and cut a line or a piece of action to please some actress, at least without putting another line or action in its place. I ask you, is that so difficult to understand? And Charlie hated him as much as I did. Because if we gave in to him, there would be holes in the script which he shot. Charlie never was a peacemaker. That's bullshit. It was Arthur Hornblow who refereed our fights.

"What can you do with a director that he comes on the set at 7:00 A.M. and puts exact marks where everybody *must* stand and he'll stop a camera which is rolling to fix the hem of a dress? He didn't know what was a plot. Charlie and I could always give him twenty alternative lines, but to him—cut, cut, cut, it didn't matter. Leisen wasn't the only director who didn't know what a script was. He was more arrogant and more ignorant than the average. He thinks he's smart when he cuts this, cuts that, this isn't necessary, that's extraneous.

"I tell you, in a good script, *everything* is necessary or it ain't good. And if you take out one piece, you better replace it with a different piece, or you got trouble.

"And about this Shakespeare—well, I didn't think our lines were the Ten Commandments chiseled with a platinum hammer out of Carrara marble. It was just—oh, hell, there were these voids in most of his films where any screenwriter could see Leisen has been chopping. *Midnight* is perfect because I fought him every inch of the way."

John Barrymore was in *Midnight*. He played Mary Astor's jealous old husband. Barrymore was in the last years of his career. He was married to Elaine Barrie. She had a supporting role in the film. Barrymore was sent only the pages of his part—about twenty pages or so. He sent Mrs. Barrymore over to B's and W's office to get the entire screenplay. She said that he never before wanted to read a whole script. An actor only cared about his own lines—his "sides," as they call them. But Barrymore loved *Midnight*. He subsequently told Wilder that it was the most fascinating screenplay he'd ever read. He considered it an authentic piece of literary comedy. And it is.

Once while Billy was discussing a problem with Don Ameche in Hornblow's office, Barrymore sauntered in. Hornblow made the introductions. He said, "Do you know Mr. Ameche?"

"Do I know Mr. Ameche?" Barrymore said, smirking. "I go down on him three times a day."

Another time, while en route to the sound stage, he rushed by mistake into a woman's toilet. He was pissing away, when a lady opened the door.

"This is for women!" she cried in outrage.

"And so is this," Barrymore replied, shaking his tool at her.

Barrymore respected the craft of the writer. But Leisen's attitude of contempt was more typical of the Hollywood of that period. Writers were servants who should know their place. They occupied a place in the pecking order below studio heads, executive producers, producers, directors, and stars. Just as the work of the screenwriter was unknown to the public, it was equally invisible around the studios. As screenwriter Joe Gillis bitterly remarks in *Sunset Boulevard:* "Audiences don't know somebody sits down and writes a picture. They think the actors make it up as they go along."

By 1939, Wilder was making $2,000 a week. He had a large office on the fourth floor of the Writers' Building. He and Charlie shared the best secretary in the pool, Helen Hernandez. She worked solely for them. They were at the highest level of movie writing—but Billy Wilder was not permitted to drive his new De Soto convertible coupe on the lot. He had to park it in an underground garage at the Green Gables apartments, near the studio. Writers, even those who made $3,000 a week—the highest then—were not permitted the status privilege of parking on the lot. You had to be a director or a producer. When producer Walter Wanger shot Jennings Lang (then an agent) in the parking lot of a Hollywood night club, the joke was that they had argued, not over Joan Bennett's affair with Lang, but over a *parking space*. That could really threaten a man's belief in himself—losing a good parking space.

Well, Billy Wilder (like Sturges, who had broken the ground for him at Paramount) was determined to get his parking space, so to speak. He would take no humiliations from others and he would not be deferential toward persons who just happened to be directors or producers.

He defied the Paramount regulations and got away with it, because he and Charlie were good. It was the rule at Paramount that each writer must turn in eleven pages every Thursday. At Warner's it was worse: you had to punch a time clock in at nine and remain until five, and work on Saturdays. Brackett and Wilder wrote their scripts in their own time and fashion. They sometimes did not put a word on paper for months. They talked out all the aspects of the story first. Brackett, shoeless, stretched on a couch, and Wilder, restlessly pacing—they talked.

When they were ready to put the show on paper, Billy, who had incredible mnemonic powers and recalled every line and idea they had already discussed, would dictate it to Brackett, who filled long legal-type yellow pads with his very fine, almost seismographic, lettering, which only Miss Hernandez could decipher. They did a first draft, a second draft, sometimes as many as ten, twelve, fifteen drafts, before they were satisfied enough to show one to the director. Billy, who remembered Carl Myer's dignity and pride in screenwriting, took pride in being a screenwriter. He was not a novelist *manqué* or a failed playwright. He had wanted to be a screenwriter and nothing but a screenwriter since—well, let us say, at least since 1930 . . . a decade, it was.

Around four o'clock, Brackett and Wilder ceased working. Sometimes they went over to Oblath's, which was a few steps away from the Bronson gate at Paramount, for a drink, or across the way on Melrose to Lucey's, a more luxurious watering hole. Sometimes they just had coffee at the office and then played cribbage or gin rummy, or inveigled two other writers into a bridge game. Wilder was becoming a bridge fanatic. At the writers' table in the commissary, they played the Word Game. Wilder always won. *Always.* By the way, movie writers had their own sense of status. They would not let actors or directors or producers sit with *them*. They found most of the other Hollywood natives to be terribly boring.

Friday brought a welcome change in the routine. The arrival of Larry Edmunds. Edmunds was a sensitive, poetic homosexual. He loved books. He had a small bookshop on Hollywood Boulevard.

He survived during the Depression by loading two suitcases with the latest novels and nonfiction books and trundling them about to the writers at the studios. Don't believe the clichés that movie writers are a barbaric tribe of unlettered drunks, driving fast sports cars and screwing dizzy blonde starlets in between playing tennis and backgammon and jaunting to Palm Springs or Acapulco. There are, of course, some writers who do these things. But they also read. They are, take them for all in all, as literate and wellread a class as you will find in this country. Some of them may dote on sexual sports and athletic sports; but, on the whole, their favorite diversions are traveling and reading. I would say that the Los Angeles citizenry, writers and otherwise, comprise the heaviest concentration of book buyers in our country today. Billy Wilder happens to be a more intense reader than the average, partly because his backaches keep him awake in the night. He reads as many as ten or more books a week. He reads new novels and biographies not only in English, but in French and German. He keeps *au courant* with the newer works, and rereads his favorite classics . . .

F. Scott Fitzgerald, (unlike Hemingway or Dos Passos) was not one of the American writers of the 1920s who had been popular in Europe. So when Wilder met him at Paramount, where Fitzgerald put in a stint, he did not at first realize Fitzgerald's importance. Billy does not have any dramatic Fitzgerald stories. He remembers him sitting in Oblath's and drinking cup after cup of black coffee. He was a remote man, pale and gray, with that washed-out complexion of the aged alcoholic. He seemed lost and desperate. He struck up conversations with Wilder many times. To Billy, it seemed as if Fitzgerald thought that Wilder knew certain secrets, and if only he could learn them, he too could be a good screenwriter. "It seemed to me as though he could never get beyond page three of a script," Billy says. "He made me think of a great sculptor who is hired to do a plumbing job. He did not know how to connect the fucking pipes so the water would flow. Sam Behrman was another beautiful writer who could not do plumbing. Give them a structured scene and they would write good lines, but they could not construct a scene themselves."

Many of the leading American writers were sucked into the Hollywood maw for a time. A junior writer came out from New York after college in 1940 to take a $150-a-week contract job at Paramount. He once described to me the thrill of seeing—at Paramount—W.R.

Burnett, Albert Maltz, Fitzgerald. Later, at Warner's, he rubbed
shoulders with John Collier and Christopher Isherwood. The junior
writer did not own a car. Once, he hitched a ride from the studio
with Isherwood, Burnett, and Gordon Kahn. Outside the gate, a
man with curly gray hair was sitting on the curbstone. He was
thoughtfully sucking a pipe. Kahn said, "Want a ride, Bill?" Bill got
in the car. He was silent. They dropped him at the Hollywood
Knickerbocker Hotel. The junior writer asked who was this quiet
man.

They all said: "Didn't you know? That was Faulkner."

The lad said: "You don't mean—William Faulkner? Gosh . . ."
The junior writer was I.A.L. Diamond.

# 7

# THE SECRET HISTORY
# OF *NINOTCHKA*

This movie is the most sublime and passionate political picture ever made in Hollywood. There have always been men and women who felt intensely about social issues. Their political emotions are a part of the passion in love. But movies were not at that time an arena in which political conflicts were described. *Ninotchka* broke every taboo of its time. It presented a woman in the role of a serious, dedicated, and intelligent member of the Communist party. She was an attractive and sympathetic person. She was a good human being. She came from the Soviet Union. She was not a caricature of a woman. She was not a caricature of a Communist. And she was not vaporized into one of those genteel euphemisms. She was not a "leftist." She was not a "radical." She believed in the dictatorship of the proletariat. She believed in the class struggle. She argued her viewpoint with intelligence. She fell in love with a Parisian gentleman who was a parasite, a gigolo, a sort of *Eintänzer,* as Billy Wilder had been, a man who lived off rich women by using his charms and his seductive badinage, a clever and a witty man, and also a person of some intelligence and taste. And to play this stalwart Communist, there was the supreme movie actress of all time—Garbo. Well, this simply could not happen, could it? At a Hollywood studio which epitomized the dream factory? Metro-Goldwyn-Mayer? And such a serious film, such a satiric film, a film of such subtlety, teeming with references which to grasp required a good deal of political sophistication. A movie about Five-Year Plans and the Purge Trials, interspersed with amorous intrigue? Ridiculous. Maybe they could make it in Paris or London—but not in bourgeois Hollywood. Well, they made it in Hollywood. In 1939. It was directed by Ernst Lubitsch and it was written, in an uncompromising spirit of irony, by Brackett and Wilder and Walter Reisch. Satire? Why everybody knows what satire is. As George S. Kaufman once said, "Satire is what closes Saturday night." This has never closed. *Ninotchka* is a classic. The movement for woman's liberation has a special banner marked *Ninotchka*. When there are film retrospectives of the great feminist films, *Ninotchka* is included. Compare *Ninotchka* to Lina Wertmuller's *Swept Away*—also a film in which a man and a woman are fighting a political struggle while playing the sex game. Here the woman is the parasite—but she is a hysterical idiot, a fool, a superficial crazy lady. The man, who is the Marxist, the Communist, is a primitive, a noble savage. It is a film of shouts, screams, chases, and physical brutality; and with all its obscenity and naked copulation— with all that—it can't even hold a phallus or a vagina to *Ninotchka*, in which Melvyn Douglas and Garbo never remove their clothes and never hit each other. Taste, subtlety, romance—but above all a kind of a serious intelligence permeates the film. A respect for human beings and a belief in human values are in Lubitsch's film. They are absent in Wertmuller's—and I say this as a guy who loved *Swept Away*.

Probably the hardest hurdle *Ninotchka* had to overleap was that it was anti-Soviet and anti-Communist. Now at the time (in 1938) when this film was being prepared, it was considered in bad taste to criticize the Soviet Union—at least among the Hollywood intelligentsia. Sure, the forced collectivation of small farms in the Ukraine had resulted in twelve million deaths, but as Robespierre had said, "You can't make omelettes without breaking eggs." To some liberals there seemed to be a suspicious stink of the frame-up in those notorious Moscow trials, from 1934 on, which dragged down all the leaders of the 1917 revolution, including Trotsky. One also heard disturbing news from Spain—that the Communists had executed Socialists and Anarchists. In Hollywood, one did not speak openly of these matters. Liberal writers like Orwell, Koestler, and Hemingway, who had started writing anti-Soviet books, were dangerous. It was necessary to fight Hitler and Nazi Germany. The Soviet Union, led by the great Stalin, was the main antagonist of Hitler. One must defend the Soviet Union. The Communist party had set up what was called a "Popular Front" organization: the Anti-Nazi League in Hollywood. In its heyday, it had four thousand members, only a handful of whom were Communists. And the Communists, the writers and actors and directors who were proud to call themselves Communists, honestly believed that Russia had the answer to unemployment, war, and race prejudice. I know some will find it hard to believe this, but many wise persons, even some college professors and literary critics, opposed any criticism of Stalin or Russia. Hundreds of leading American intellectuals and artists signed two of these "open letters" which were fashionable in the 1930s, "letters" defending the guilty verdicts of the "Moscow trials of the Trotskyite-Bukharinite traitors," and denouncing a committee of investigation (headed by John Dewey, James T. Farrell, and Carlo Tresca) which was looking into the charges against Trotsky.

Among the Hollywood luminaries who signed were Alan Campbell, Vera Caspary, Guy Endore, John Garfield, Lillian Hellman, H.S. Kraft, Ring Lardner, Jr., Albert Maltz, George Marshall, Lewis Milestone, Dudley Nichols, Samuel Ornitz, Dorothy Parker, Irwin Shaw, Lionel Stander, Samson Raphaelson, Tess Slesinger, and Nathanael West.

Now what makes the succeeding events curious is that, first, one of the centers of radical political activity was the home of Salka Viertel on Maberry Road in Santa Monica. Mrs. Viertel was a militant anti-Nazi and a Communist fellow traveler. She was the closest friend of Garbo. She was Garbo's intellectual duenna.

And she should have, of course, never, never, allowed her friend to become a "social fascist" or a "Red baiter." Yes, that's what they called you, in those days, if you didn't admire Joseph Stalin or ridiculed the USSR. Especially in the Hollywood film colony. It was mainly the Socialist *New Leader* and the Trotskyist *Militant* that published serious anti-Stalin criticism and vented hostility on the Communists then. These journals had less publicity in Hollywood than *samizdat* writers have nowadays in the Moscow film colony.

It was a strange and, in retrospect, an unreal historical period in which to live.

To learn how *Ninotchka* got made we have to begin back in 1936, when Lubitsch, like many other European and American notables, was invited to visit the Soviet Union. It was part of the new Popular Front line. En route to Russia, Lubitsch stopped briefly in Vienna to talk to Reisch. Reisch had gone to Vienna after a year in Paris and was now writing films for the Sascha Studio in Austria. Lubitsch liked many of Reisch's films—like *Zwei Herzen im Drei Viertel Takt*—and discussed with him the possibility of his writing a treatment and script of Strauss's *Der Rosenkavalier*. Lubitsch wanted to film this opera with Jeannette MacDonald as the Marschalin. The two men had a stimulating conference. Lubitsch was going to Moscow and Leningrad for eight weeks. He would return to Vienna and resume their discussions and perhaps make a deal. . . .

In three weeks (less than three weeks, really—nineteen days) Lubitsch suddenly reappeared in Vienna! Why? What had happened in Moscow? He would not talk about it. Reisch asked him questions and Lubitsch evaded him, saying that he was "committed to silence." Reisch remembers that Lubitsch didn't "speak ten words about what he saw in Russia."

And Herman G. Weinberg, a Lubitsch scholar, tells us in his *Lubitsch Touch:* "I have been unable to find out any details of his Moscow trip."

Had he seen at first hand the fear and terror that stalked Moscow? Had he been unable to see Eisenstein because he was in disrepute? Did he learn that many of his friends in the Russian film industry had been purged, were in jail, had lost their jobs, were dead? Did he see letters being censored, freedom crushed, the once world-famous Russian filmmakers degraded into making propaganda trash? Did he visit apartments and see people living in corners, with strangers occupying pieces of their apartments? Did he see the hunger and the fear? The fear, always the fear?

We do know that not long after Lubitsch came back from Russia he told Salka Viertel, as she reports, that he was withdrawing from the Anti-Nazi League. He said it was a tool of the Communists. He told her to get out of it also. She begged him to think it over and remain. She said it was the only way to fight fascism. He said he was warning her. He was getting out. They remained friends, despite their political differences.

Billy's political feelings at this time were on the radical side. He thought of himself as a "social democrat" in the European sense. He had had vague sympathies for socialism and was almost a fellow traveler. Egon Erwin Kisch had made him see the promise of socialism and Kisch believed that, in the long run, the Soviet Union would become a free, democratic society. Billy was for the Spanish Loyalists and he was of course a passionate anti-Nazi. However, he did not like to join organizations. He did not like meetings. He was, however, on friendly terms with many Communist and left-leaning writers. He recalls now that several of them ceased talking politics to him after *Ninotchka*. He thinks that Communists, by and large, lack a sense of humor. It was sacrilege to poke fun at them. Wilder, during the witch hunts of the 1950s, was a proponent of freedom of expression and took a stand against the investigations and the blacklist. He was one of the few writers at Paramount who would not sign a loyalty oath. He supported the Committee for the First Amendment, which defended the Unfriendly Ten. But he just couldn't keep a civil, or civil rights, tongue in his head.

Asked what he thought of the Unfriendly Ten, he said, "Two of them have talent. The rest are just unfriendly."

Anyway, *Ninotchka* didn't start as a political satire.

It started one day when Melchior Lengyel was lunching in the Vine Street Brown Derby. Salka Viertel came over to his table. She said Bernie Hyman, an MGM executive producer, wanted to make a comedy with Garbo so they could advertise it with the slogan "Garbo Laughs," as they promoted *Anna Christie* with "Garbo Talks."

She asked him if he happened to have a story up his sleeve in which Garbo would laugh? He looked up his sleeves. There were no plots there. He phoned her the next day. He said he had an idea. She said come right over, as Garbo is swimming in the pool. He did. Garbo swam over and perched on her elbows. "Tell me your idea," she said. She was naked. She liked to swim in the nude. He said,

"Russian girl saturated with Bolshevist ideals goes to fearful, capitalistic, monopolistic Paris. She meets romance and has an uproarious good time. Capitalism not so bad, after all."

MGM paid him $15,000 for these three sentences.

Gottfried Reinhardt was assigned to direct. Viertel and Lengyel were to write it. They failed. They were followed by Jacques Deval, author of *Tovarich*, a comedy about Russian exiles in Paris. He failed to lick it. So did S.N. Behrman, one of the most exquisite turners of a phrase, who had written dialogue for several of Garbo's films, including *Anna Karenina*. Behrman did compose an amusing love story about a lady commissar and a French gigolo.

She had come to Paris to make a deal for the ore in a Siberian nickel mine.

Reinhardt resigned. Garbo, a longtime admirer of Lubitsch, asked

for him. Metro got Lubitsch on loan. He was happy to be directing
Garbo. He liked much of the dialogue in Behrman's script. But the
plotting was loose. The pieces of the plumbing did not fit neatly. It
did not flow. Reisch was now a contract writer at Metro. Lubitsch
had Reisch put on the project. They went to Bernie Hyman's house
for a conference. On the way, Lubitsch told Reisch that he couldn't
make a movie out of this script. He was thinking of giving up the
project. It was hopeless. Poor Sam Behrman, such a fine man, but
he had written a botched-up script. And that stupid business with
the Siberian nickel mine. He had to have something he could show
on a screen. What the hell did it mean if you showed an ingot of
nickel or a pile of nickel? There was no glamour about a nickel mine.

At Hyman's, Lubitsch read the entire script, playing all the parts.
"Sam," he said, "I just want to prove to you that this script will not
play." And he read it with such exaggeration that even Behrman had
to laugh.

He finished. "See what I mean, Sam?"

"Yes, Mr. Lubitsch, I see. But if the man who owned the Globe
Theatre heard you read *Hamlet* like you read my script *Hamlet*
would never have been produced . . . "

Behrman would not collaborate with Reisch. Lubitsch's parting
words were that if this movie ever was made, which he doubted, he
would change the Siberian nickel mine into diamonds. He would
have the lady come to Paris to sell some Czarist diamonds confiscat-
ed in the Revolution. Maybe owned by a duchess, whose lover is the
gigolo . . .

"You might think it's a clich, Sam," he said, "but I like diamonds. They got a sparkle to them. You can photograph them sparkling on the tits of a woman."

"Good-bye, Mr. Lubitsch," said Sam and departed for Broadway.

At this juncture, Brackett and Wilder joined the team. At first, the
three writers and Lubitsch intended to make a typical Lubitsch sophisticated comedy romance. It would take place in Paris. The logic
of the plot and the heroine's character compelled them all to blurt
out on film what was then, in the popular arts, unthinkable and un-
speakable, and what Lubitsch had been silent about for three years.

Politics was the core of *Ninotchka*. If you really portrayed a woman of flesh and blood and brains, you had to write about her convictions and this inevitably led you to the nature of life in Russia and
the trials, the confessions, the purges, the terror. Wilder and Brack-

ett, like all the good high comedy writers in Hollywood, either knew or intuitively sensed that the mind is the most powerful erogenous zone. That was why they wrote strong roles for interesting women with exciting minds—for Colbert, Hepburn, Roz Russell, Stanwyck, Crawford, Dietrich, Garbo. Of all the writers on *Ninotchka,* Wilder was the most aware of the nuances of radical politics. Almost all of the anti-Soviet jibes came from him. And he didn't want it to be like that. He rather liked the Soviet Union. In a 1944 essay in *Life*—the first extended study of Brackett and Wilder—Lincoln Barnett wrote *en passant:* "Wilder has mixed feelings about *Ninotchka* because as a Russophile he had offended the USSR. 'I've always wanted to see Odessa and now I never will,' he said recently." Why Odessa, of all places? Barnett didn't pursue the question. The reason why it was Odessa and not Moscow was that Odessa was the scene of Eisenstein's *Potemkin,* which Wilder thought was the best film ever made. He still does.

And if Wilder was a Russophile, what of Salka Viertel? Why didn't she kill the movie in the early stages? For the strangest of reasons: one of her three sons was a Trotskyist! Hans Viertel, she tells us in her memoirs published years later, had forced her to face the Moscow trials, "with their inexplicable confessions, horrifying executions, and the growing Stalin terror." Hans was one of a group of radicals who picketed Stalinist meetings in Los Angeles. They gave out leaflets against Stalin. Mrs. Viertel remembers Hans and his friends being "insulted and beaten up" by Stalinists.

The script expressed insights which were unfashionable at that time but now seem to have been written out of prophetic inspiration. They wrote a decade before Krushchev's revelations. In 1939, who could have possibly foreseen that Stalin's own daughter would fall in love and become a Ninotchka?

The political line of *Ninotchka* is established early in the film when the three trade delegates, sent to Paris to negotiate the sale of the Grand Duchess's jewels to a French firm, come to meet Garbo at the Gare de l'Est. They ask her,

"How are things in Moscow?"

"Very good," she replies. "The last mass trials were a great success. There are going to be fewer—but better—Russians."

In the lobby of the hotel she observes a chic woman's hat in a display window. How decadent! How wasteful! Communism will not be long in triumphing over such a corrupt society.

After her encounter with Douglas, the amorous repartee begins.

How ingeniously the writers laced the love play with political jibes! Learning that she is Russian, Douglas cracks, "I have been fascinated by your Five-Year Plan for the last fifteen years." Following a sequence at a Paris restaurant where Garbo has confronted her rival, the duchess, and she has gotten tipsy, we dissolve to Ninotchka's suite. Douglas has a bottle of champagne. They will form a new party led by Ninotchka and her lover, Leon. Their slogan will be "Lovers of the World, Unite." They will not salute with clenched fists upraised.

"Our salute will be a kiss," Garbo says, as they passionately salute. Ah, she is so happy, she declares, and she must be punished for this anti-Communist joy.

"I want to confess," she says.

"I know . . . it's the Russian soul," Leon murmurs.

(One of the explanations given by Western experts on the Moscow trials was that Russian mysticism explained the confessions.)

Ninotchka says, "Everyone wants to confess and if they don't confess they make them confess. I am a traitor. When I kissed you I betrayed the Russian ideal. Leon, I should be stood up against the wall."

Leon stands her up against the wall. He ties a napkin over her face. The script called for him to open the champagne and "shoot" her with the exploding cork. While filming, Lubitsch suggested Douglas raise a corner of the napkin and bestow a final kiss on her lips. Later, they get one of the jewelry pieces—a coronet—from the safe and he crowns her. And Garbo, in one of her most exalted moments on the screen, spoke to an imaginary audience on Red Square:

"Comrades. People of the world. The revolution is on the march. I know . . . Wars will wash over us. Bombs will fall. All civilization will crumble. But not yet please. Wait, wait . . . what's the hurry? Let us be happy. Give us our moment."

After their moment of love, she is awakened the following morning by the grand duchess. The duchess informs Ninotchka that a White Russian waiter has taken the jewels.

However, if Garbo will at once return to Russia and leave Melvyn Douglas in Paris, she will give the jewels back to her.

Torn between her political ideals, which are the core of her being, and her love for this man, Garbo, in terms of her character, cannot forsake her ideology, for that would be to forsake herself. On the other hand, if she deserted Douglas, then they had no Act III.

The writers were at an impasse. Lubitsch was bewildered. So far, Lubitsch could have deceived himself into believing that *Ninotchka* was only a sophisticated comedy in romantic Paris.

And then, one day, Wilder shattered the roadblock.

"We will have to go to Moscow," he said.

And so the film did. Garbo gives up her lover and returns to Moscow. We cut to Garbo's life in Moscow. And it was now that Lubitsch's recollections of his nineteen Moscow days began seeping out and lending a realistic coloration to the last part of the film. Letters being censored. Garbo sharing an apartment with a lady cellist and a streetcar conductor. The atmosphere of fear and the ominous sense of helplessness. The scarcity of food.

There was a famous scene in which the three emissaries, whom Garbo had gone to Paris to investigate, come to her Moscow room for a reunion. Each has brought an egg. Garbo will make a real French omelette for their dinner. She breaks the eggs. Those of us who saw this picture in 1939 had heard Duranty's oft-repeated apologetic, and we felt that this was a conscious kick at those who said you could not make omelettes without breaking eggs.

Garbo's metamorphosis from ascetic Marxist into amorous Marxist was dramatized in the nightclub sequence in which she gets very drunk on champagne. Garbo refused to play it. She said she would look like a slut. She never drank alcohol. She was then in love with Gayelord Hauser, the natural foods philosopher. Her favorite beverage was not Dom Perignon or Taittinger Blanc de Blancs. It was Mr. Hauser's invigorating Sunshine Cocktail—one part orange juice, one part celery juice, one part carrot juice.

Lubitsch rarely deviated from a script and he would not budge on the scene. He worked on Garbo's anxiety for a week, calming her, cajoling her, until she played the sequence. Not only was she reluctant to play a drunk, but the sequence demanded a score of dress extras playing the nightclub patrons. So Lubitsch cleared the set and shot just her and Douglas, later intercutting with the group scenes.

Only once does Wilder remember Lubitsch fixing a line on the set. It was for Garbo. She was orating against capitalistic railroads. The first-class section, she cries, has velvet chairs, the second-class has leather seats, and the third-class wooden benches.

"We communists, we will change this from the bottom up," was the line.

Garbo objected to the word *bottom*. It had coarse overtones. Lubitsch took out *bottom*—not so much to placate Garbo, as because he agreed that it was a vulgarism which was out of character.

Wilder wanted to be on the set every day as Lubitsch filmed, but Garbo would not have strangers present, including screenwriters. On a few occasions, Wilder sneaked on the set. He usually hid behind a scenery flat or a prop. He came to know Garbo. He came to know the mystery of her art. He would peer out from behind his hiding place and see her play the page or two of the script. He would always marvel at the miracle that took place between the time she was before the camera and what happened on the film when it was developed, printed, and projected in the screening room. Suddenly she became a luminous presence of ineffable beauty. It could not be explained.

WILDER: "The face, that face, what was it about that face? You could read into it all the secrets of a woman's soul. You could read Eve, Cleopatra, Mata Hari. She became all women on the screen. Not on the sound stage. *The miracle happened in that film emulsion.* Who knows why? Marilyn Monroe had this same gift. That strange trick of flesh impact—that is to say, their flesh registered for the camera and came across on the screen as real flesh that you could touch, an image beyond photography."

Wilder became friends, of a sort, with Garbo. They both liked to walk. They went on long walks in Beverly Hills. Billy says that she was a simple woman of simple ideas and simple tastes. She wanted a quiet and peaceful existence. She was essentially a shy and frightened person, who desired a private life. Her withdrawal from the social whirl of Hollywood was not an eccentricity. She feared strangers. In this too, she was similar to Marilyn Monroe, who dreaded people, who was a solitary seeker, who was only at ease with small animals and lonely beaches. Yet both of them sprang to life when a camera was turned on their faces.

*Ninotchka* completed shooting on July 27, 1939. And then, between the completion of the film and its world premiere at Grauman's Chinese on October 6, 1939, burst the shattering news that those sworn enemies, the USSR and Nazi Germany, had signed a treaty of friendship, nonaggression, and mutual trade. We saw photographs of Molotov and von Ribbentrop shaking hands. The Hollywood Anti-Nazi League was disbanded at once. The Communists became fanatical pacifists, anti-British and anti-French.

Suddenly there was a climate of goodwill toward the political satire of *Ninotchka.* The film was praised to the skies. It deserved the praise, but would not that praise have been tinctured with reservations if the film had appeared before the strange alliance and the invasion of Poland by the Red Army from the east and by the Nazis from the west on September 1?

Their work on *Ninotchka* had drawn Wilder and Lubitsch into a close friendship. Wilder worshipped Lubitsch and Lubitsch adored Wilder. After the war, Wilder, excited by rumors of the neorealist Italian films, secured a print of *Shoe Shine*. He screened it for Lubitsch in September of 1947.

That was the last film Lubitsch ever saw. On Sunday, November 30, 1947, while showering, Lubitsch had a heart attack and died before a doctor could reach him.

One of the legendary Billy Wilder stories is that he arrived at Lubitsch's house a few minutes after the director's demise. In a corner of the living room, Wilder observed a blonde crying. Wilder approached her.

"Listen, baby," he murmured, "we are all shocked but get control of yourself. Stop crying. Look at me. Mr. Lubitsch was like a father to me. But I am not crying."

"It's easy for you to talk," she moaned, tears running down her face. "He didn't fuck you—and then stiff you for the money." Just before his heart attack, Lubitsch banged this lady. He owed her $50.

Wilder paid her $50. The tears dried up at once.

"An interesting story but absolutely not true," Wilder says. "It was Otto, the chauffeur, who paid her off. However it was true he made love before dying. Ernst Lubitsch had a younger brother, a famous pediatrician in Cologne. He also died after having a fuck with a hooker in Cologne's biggest whorehouse. A strange coincidence. Dr. Lubitsch was a respectable family man, so his corpse had to be sneaked out of the brothel by the back door to avoid scandal."

Lubitsch was buried in Forest Lawn on December 5, 1947. His pallbearers were Otto, Mervyn LeRoy, Richard Sale, Walter Reisch, and Billy Wilder. Charles Brackett spoke the eulogy. Leaving the services, Wilder said to Willy Wyler, also a close friend of Lubitsch, "No more Lubitsch."

"Worse than that," Wyler sighed, "no more Lubitsch films."

Wilder says that he has sought in vain for the secret of the Lubitsch touch. "That most elegant of screen magicians took his secret with him," Wilder wrote in an essay for *Action*, the magazine of the Screen Directors Guild.

A year after Lubitsch died, his devoted amanuensis, Steffi Trondl,

passed away. She had saved her money and bought a plot in Forest
Lawn. She is now buried beside the man she served so devotedly
during his life.

Every year, on the anniversary of Lubitsch's death, Billy and
Walter Reisch go to his grave. And, just as it was when Billy was at
Paramount and he had to pass Steffi Trondl to get to Lubitsch, he
still has to pass Steffi Trondl's grave to stand at Lubitsch's.

Billy received his first Academy Award nomination, along with
Reisch and Brackett, for writing *Ninotchka*. That year Sidney Howard won it for *Gone With the Wind*. *Ninotchka* was nominated for
best picture. *GWTW* won. Garbo was nominated for best actress.
Vivian Leigh, the Scarlett O'Hara, won. The year 1939 was a vintage year for Hollywood pictures: *Goodbye Mr. Chips, Stagecoach,
Dark Victory, The Wizard of Oz, Wuthering Heights, Mr. Smith
Goes to Washington*—and *Gone With the Wind*, which took the evening like Sherman took Atlanta.

# 8

# A COCKROACH
# FOR CHARLES BOYER

With *Ninotchka*, Brackett and Wilder—like jugglers manipulating billiard balls while kissing women—had finally made politics a part of the flirtation and tenderness between a man and a woman. They had written satire and it had not closed on Saturday night. As the golden age of the 1930s ended, they wrote two of the finest love stories of the period. The war had started in 1939. The war was part of these love stories. The issues and struggles of the period were in them. Neutrality, the civil war in Spain, the impending crisis in Europe, the Fascist threat, nonintervention, the democratic society, freedom and the Nazis, freedom and the Communists, the ultimate meaning of existence—all these they interspersed with romantic ardor. They did it with such control and finesse that it seems almost natural that men and women were excited by their ideas—as well as their sexual emotions. In *Arise, My Love*, Ray Milland was a soldier of fortune flying for the Spanish Loyalists and Claudette Colbert was an American correspondent modeled after Martha Gellhorn, Hemingway's third wife, who had covered the Spanish civil war for *Time–Life*. Leisen and Wilder pursued their own little conflict at Paramount. Wilder could not stand the sight of Leisen. He felt that Leisen had spoiled another one of their perfect scripts. He fought him every day over every line and alteration. They yelled and they screamed and, many times, they resorted to punching and slapping. The film was released in 1940. *Hold Back the Dawn*, the next one, was an equally powerful expression of love and politics. It was one of the loveliest films of 1941 and revealed Olivia de Havilland, hitherto stereotyped as a vapid consort to Errol Flynn in various Warner Bros. historical fantasies, to be an actress of wit and mind. The romance between Olivia de Havilland (who played an American schoolteacher in Mexico) and Charles Boyer (who played a Rumanian adventurer who plots to marry an American innocent so he can legally enter the United States) was loosely based on a real-life romance. Katharine Hartley was a free-lance fan magazine writer. She wrote for *Photoplay* and *Screenland*. While visiting Paris in 1937, she met a German refugee, Kurt Frings, formerly lightweight boxing champion of Europe. He was a Catholic. His uncle was the famous Cardinal Frings, who had denounced Hitler from his pulpit and been persecuted for it. Miss Hartley fell in love with Kurt Frings, and he with her and they were married. He was an American citizen now, but he still could not enter the United States, as he had once falsified a date when applying for a visa. Ketti Frings—as she now called herself—and Kurt settled in Tijuana, Mexico, to wait until he was able to clear up the misunderstanding and get his visa. She commuted back and forth to her Hollywood apartment. She came to know other refugees in the bungalow court in Tijuana, all waiting, waiting, waiting for documents to be stamped and signed, papers to come, quotas to be open for them, lost and frightened souls. She wrote a forty-page screen treatment about these people, and about her love and marriage to Kurt Frings. She knew Arthur Hornblow, Jr. She wrote her story in the form of a letter to him. She called it "Memo to a Movie Producer." Paramount paid $4,000 for it. Prior to the filming, she wrote her first novel on the same theme. It was called *Hold Back the Dawn*. It was published by the new house of Duell, Sloan, and Pearce. Her novel was about a prizefighter named Klaus Eckert and an American writer named Jennifer. It was laid in Tijuana.

Brackett and Wilder completely transformed the story. The amiable and noble prizefighter became a cunning gigolo. The sophisticated American woman became a kindhearted and naive and trusting girl from a small California town. The gigolo was Boyer. His partner in crime was Paulette Goddard. She had been his dancing partner in Paris. She had married a dumb, rich American to get her citizenship.

While in Hornblow's office one day, Billy got a call from Kurt
Frings. Frings was enraged. He said he had secured a copy of the
script. He had read it. He said that he had been libeled. He said that
the portrait of the scheming Iscovescu was nasty. "You're a bastard, Billy. Everybody in town knows Ketti was writing about us
and they'll say I'm a goddam pimp and she's a dumb schoolteacher.
That's not the way she wrote her book. You made up these lies. I
know Charlie Brackett did not. Only you would write such things
about me. Now you better change that script or I am suing you and
the studio and—"

Wilder put Hornblow on the phone. Hornblow listened to the
complaint. He asked Frings whether he had the script before him.

"Will you read what it says on page two? . . . Property of Paramount Pictures Corporation. . . . Now, tell me, Kurt, how did you
get this script?"

"None of your business."

"It's like this, Kurt: if you sue us, we will charge you with theft of
our property—and we will have you deported."

Kurt Frings did not sue. He became a successful agent. Ketti became a successful screenwriter and playwright. She won the Pulitzer in 1957 for *Look Homeward, Angel.*

The Mexican government was also unhappy with the script. The
ambassador protested to the State Department. The State Department put pressure on Paramount. Our Latin-American brothers said
that this screenplay painted Mexico and Mexicans in an unflattering
light. They said it would damage the friendship between the two
countries. These two terrible gringo writers, why they had described
the plaza in this border town (Wilder had harked back to his recollections in Mexicali, but it applied as well to Tijuana or Enseneda at
that period) as a dirty old place. I swear—they actually put all this in
writing through their diplomats. They insisted that the plaza in *Hold
Back the Dawn* must be landscaped! The *New York Times* reported
that instead of the "bedraggled and dusty" plaza originally conceived by Brackett and Wilder, "a sylvan glade with shrubs and
grass was substituted." The Mexican government objected to the
fat Mexican maid who worked around the Hotel Esperanza. The
Hotel Esperanza was also too sloppy. There was this Mexican mechanic who was sloppy and he couldn't fix Olivia de Havilland's station wagon when it broke down. They demanded that the hotel maid
be a woman "with dignity" and the garage mechanic also a man "of

dignity." To avoid a breach of diplomatic relations, Paramount made Brackett and Wilder change the mechanic to a Russian, a crazy, wild Russian. The maid became a comely, well-groomed lady. Taking no chances, the studio employed Señora Eva Puig, widow of a Mexican diplomat, to portray the maid.

Much as Wilder resented the interference from Mexico and Frings—it was Leisen and Charles Boyer and a cockroach who drove him to declare his independence. The writers had carefully wrought a clever visual scene to dramatize Boyer's demoralization as he waits for his visa. We have seen him as he was when he first strode into the Esperanza—elegant, homburg on his head, swinging his cane, an elegant continental. Six weeks later: medium shot of Boyer hopeless and flat broke, lying on his bed, unshaven, sloppy, an unholy mess, and he is teasing . . . a . . . cockroach . . . with his cane. Closeup of cockroach crawling on the wall towards a mirror. Cockroach tries to crawl on mirror, and each time Boyer shoves him away with the cane. He talks to him the way the immigration officers talk: "Where you going?" "What is the purpose of your trip?" "Let's see your papers."

Wilder was proud of this scene. He went on the set the morning they were shooting it. The scene was cut. Why? Leisen told him that Boyer did not want to do it. Boyer was a very big star. He did not want to make Boyer feel bad. Out the window went a scene on which the writers had worked for several days. Why, stormed Billy to Leisen, did he not ask them to write another scene to put in its place? They did not need another scene. Wilder looked around for Boyer. Somebody said he was having an early *déjeuner* at Lucey's. Billy tore across Melrose Avenue. He went into the restaurant. In one of the back booths, dining alone, sat the glamorous and urbane lover who had invited Hedy LaMarr to come to the Casbah with him.

Wilder inquired about the missing cockroach.

Boyer shrugged. "I could not speak such lines—to this—this cockroach. One does not talk to cockroaches. One does not ask a cockroach for his passport. You wish to make me look *stupide*?"

Wilder attempted to explain the importance of this transitional scene. Boyer loftily waved him away. He said, "I do not wish to have these discussions while I am at the table. Go away, Mr. Wilder. You disturb me."

Billy was seething. He stormed into the office. Brackett had never seen him so violent. He was thwacking the desk and chairs with a cane. "I'll kill him, I'll kill him," he cried. "I'll beat out his brains. No, he has no brains. He is an actor. I've got a better idea, Charlie. If that bastard ain't talking to cockroaches, he ain't talking to nobody. Let us give the rest of the picture to Olivia de Havilland."

Brackett thought it was a capital idea.

As a result of Boyer's arrogance, his importance in the final third of the film dwindled while de Havilland's rose and made her a full-fledged actress. Miss De Havilland, by the way, never knew about the intrigue. She only knew she was getting more lines of dialogue. I wrote her recently at her Paris home seeking information about the film and she replied: "I had no idea that I owed that Academy nomination to a cockroach spurned by Boyer and championed by Wilder, but I'm grateful, very grateful. . . . Billy was quite intimidating, from my point of view. He seemed so sharply witty, intelligent, sophisticated, urbane that I avoided encountering him."

Billy was outraged at the mayhem performed on the screenplay. He told William Dozier, the new head of the writers' department, that he and Charlie wanted to change the usual writers' credits. The form, dated May 5, 1941, read that *Hold Back the Dawn* was based on "a novel by Ketti Frings. Screenplay by Charles Brackett and Billy Wilder."

Billy crossed out "screenplay" and substituted "written by," for in his opinion a screenplay was an entity with a beginning, middle, and end, and this one had been cut up and now was not worthy of the label "screenplay."

Billy made a firm resolution that from now on he would have to direct the films written by the partners. Brackett could produce them. He no longer wished to be at the mercy of the actor's ego and the director's insensitivity. Brackett did not like this plan. He wanted everything to remain the way it was. He did not care for the responsibilities of a producer. Brackett did not think Billy had the calmness and patience required of a director. He flew off the handle. He had a short fuse. He had a nasty temper. He said mean and irascible things. He made fun of people. He was always making fun of Charlie. He was always saying terrible things about Charlie. He would keep on goading Charlie until Charlie, in his turn, finally exploded and started hurling imprecations at his partner, and after Charlie had used up his curses he would throw objects—heavy objects—telephone books and inkstands and wastebaskets. Charlie would try to hit Billy in the head; and he was serious. Behind closed doors, Helen Hernandez would tremble, as she listened to them screaming and then the sounds of breaking ashtrays and falling lamps. Billy defended himself, like a fencer, by stabbing at the objects and dodging about. I don't believe that Brackett ever nailed him. But it was not for lack of trying. The publicity stories that they were the "happiest couple in Hollywood," which was used in feature stories about them and in the *Life* article, were grossly inaccurate. But, like so many unhappily married people, they looked good in public, and so everybody thought it was a euphoric relationship, when it was as rent by fits of temperament and jealousy and spleen as the collaboration of Gilbert and Sullivan. And like the two Englishmen, Brackett and Wilder would have long periods during which they ceased talking to each other and communicated through their secretary. It was rather complicated to proceed with a literary collaboration during these Trappist-like phrases, but somehow they managed.

For his part, Wilder was determined to go it alone or with another collaborator, if Brackett did not want to get into a writer/director/producer amalgamation with him. Normally a man of great inventive ferment, film ideas just naturally bubbled out of him. Once, returning from New York, he fell in with Leland Hayward. Hayward had become one of the best agents in Hollywood. He represented Sonja Henie, among many other stars. He said Twentieth Century-Fox needed a good Sonja Henie story. Production chief William Goetz was desperate. Couldn't Billy think of something? Well, between Kansas City and Albuquerque, he improvised the plot for a musical, another ice-skating extravaganza. He forgot all about it, until Hayward phoned him a month later and said Goetz liked the idea and would he send it over. Wilder had long ago forgotten what the story was. He called Miss Hernandez in. He started snapping his fingers—which is how he sometimes conjures up ideas and gags out of the air. He composed a new story. It took him about thirty minutes to do so. He told her to type it up and send it along. No, he did not want to go over it. Hayward got him $2,500 for this little *jeu d'esprit*. Billy gave Miss Hernandez a check for $350. When she was a student at secretarial school, even in her wildest dreams she could not have imagined earning such a sum for less than an hour's work. And remember, dear reader, we are talking about 1941 money—real money. Wilder was attracted by Hayward's style. He appointed him as his agent.

Another story which he sold was one to Sam Goldwyn, who was looking for a Gary Cooper vehicle. Billy unearthed an old story written in his last Berlin year. It was unfilmed. It was entitled *From A to Z* . He asked Thomas Monroe, a Paramount junior writer, to fix it up. He sent it over to Goldwyn. Hayward was not yet Billy's agent. He handled the deal himself.

Goldwyn called. He said, in his high-pitched voice, "Frances read the story. She likes it. [Frances was Mrs. Goldwyn.] How much?"

"Ten thousand, Sam."

"Ridiculous."

"Take it or leave it."

"I'll tell you what. I give you seventy-five hundred now. If we ever get it made, I give you another twenty-five hundred."

Wilder agreed.

One day, Bill Dozier received an unexpected call from Goldwyn. He congratulated Dozier on his new position. He said, in his *castrato* voice, "Y'know , Bill, I am thinking it is time you and I started doing each other favors."

"Sure. What?"

"Let's start by you doing me one. . . . I would like to borrow Brackett and Wilder."

(It was like the time Goldwyn had telephoned Zanuck and said, "Darryl, you and I have a problem." and when Darryl wanted to know what was this mutual problem, Goldwyn said, "You have Tyrone Power—and I want him.")

Dozier said Paramount would not loan out these writers. Goldwyn said they had loaned them to Metro for the Garbo picture. Dozier explained it was a favor to Lubitsch. What, and Paramount did not care to do favors to Goldwyn? Well, it wasn't that exactly, you see, but—Goldwyn interrupted. He wanted Charlie and Billy to write a movie for Barbara Stanwyck and Gary Cooper based on an original by Wilder and some feller named Monroe. . . . As soon as Goldwyn said "Cooper" wheels started turning. Paramount had been seeking Cooper to play Robert Jordan in *For Whom the Bell Tolls*. Finally, after some negotiations, Paramount traded Wilder and Brackett and threw in Hope and Crosby (whom Goldwyn wanted for a Mel Shavelson musical) in exchange for Cooper.

Billy agreed to work on *Ball of Fire* (the new title of *From A to Z*) provided he could be at director Howard Hawks's side during the filming. He was going to learn how a master directed films.

*Ball of Fire* was, among other things, a tale into which Billy poured his love of American slang—which went back to his adolescent discovery of American popular songs during the early 1920s. He had labored strenuously to get a feeling for the nuances of the American vernacular, and he had succeeded. Although he still spoke with an accent, he had a marvelous feeling for the shadings of colloquial speech. He always made it a point to memorize the latest slang expressions. He loved American slang. The "macguffin" or "weenie" of *Ball of Fire* is that a pedantic and quite unworldly gentleman, one of eight professors isolated in a mansion while working on an encyclopedia, begins researching the essay on slang, and in the course of his research among the common people, he falls in with a stripteaser who is on the lam from the district attorney and takes refuge with Cooper and the professors. (It was an ingenious switcheroo on Disney's *Snow White and the Seven Dwarfs*, of 1937.) While preparing the script, Wilder, like the professor, decided to check out current slang among the younger set. He went to a drugstore near Hollywood High on Sunset and hung around for several days and started treating his respondents, especially the ones who were nubile and tight-sweatered, to sundaes and banana splits. He almost got arrested on suspicion of molesting minors. But everything, even this abominable experience, was interesting; and he started germinating an idea about an older man and a young woman. . . .

*Ball of Fire* was a smash in 1942. Wilder phoned Goldwyn for the $2,500 balance owing him. Goldwyn had suffered a memory lapse. He said he didn't owe Billy a penny. He asked if they had a written agreement.

Billy shouted, "Forget it, Sam. And if the two of us ever meet again—let's pretend we don't know each other."

He slammed down the phone.

It rang in a few moments. Goldwyn said, "Now, Billy, I just talked to Frances. She don't remember it, either."

"Now we both know you said you would pay me a balance of twenty-five hundred. So if you don't remember it, and Frances doesn't either, the hell with both of you."

He slammed down the phone.

Goldwyn rang him up at once. "Please, Billy," he moaned, "listen to me— I don't want a person going around Hollywood talking angry against me. All right, come over and pick up the . . . fifteen hundred!"

Wilder says, "That bastard had to screw me out of a thousand." He took the fifteen hundred, but he never wrote another movie for Goldwyn. Billy enjoyed Goldwyn's rascality, as he did Sam Spiegel's. He had made the acquaintance of this fat little man in Berlin. Spiegel had been a publicity man for Universal. Later he had produced unsuccessful pictures in Paris and London. He was down and out in Hollywood. Billy was surprised to run into Spiegel at the Goldwyn studio. Goldwyn had given him a little office and a phone. He embraced Wilder. He explained his terrible situation. He said if only he had a property he could make a deal over at Twentieth with Goetz, who was running the studio while Colonel Darryl Zanuck was on leave with the army. Didn't he have a story he could buy? Spiegel did not have a nickel. He had a large supply of brass, however. His charm was inexhaustible. His plight stirred Billy's heart. He remembered that old script he and Reisch had done for UFA— the one about that tailcoat. Through a Hungarian contact, Spiegel smuggled a copy of the script out of Nazi Germany. Goetz liked it. Twentieth put it into production, directed by Jules Duvivier, with an all-star cast: Boyer, Ginger Rogers, Paul Robeson, Marlene Dietrich . . .

It was *Tales of Manhattan.*

Spiegel was ever so grateful. What could he give Billy? Billy said he didn't want anything. Spiegel insisted. Well, there were these two matching chairs he'd seen in a decorator's shop on Rodeo Drive. . . .

"Those chairs, my friend, they are as good as yours," said Spiegel.

To Reisch, he promised a new Capehart with speakers set in the wall. Reisch was building an alpine chalet on Amapola Drive in Bel Air. He had the architect make two holes in the wall for the speakers. Weeks passed. No chairs. No Capehart. Holes in the wall. Then came the opening of *Tales of Manhattan* for charity. The writers each received a pair of tickets, $100 a ticket. They sent $400 to the charity. They didn't attend the premiere. They sent Spiegel an ironic telegram congratulating him and saying that they were, right now, sitting in the chairs and listening to the Capehart:

WE CAN FEEL THE DRAFT COMING THROUGH THE HOLES IN THE WALL.

Finally, Reisch got the phonograph and Wilder got the chairs. *They also got the bills.* Wilder sent his bill to Spiegel. It was not paid. The decorator threatened to sue. Billy paid the money. He would never have any dealings with Spiegel thereafter. He found his company amusing and dined on his yacht in the Mediterranean. He went to his New Year's Eve parties. For some years, Spiegel's year-end gala was the most socially important event of the season. But he would never write a film for him, though Spiegel importuned him for years to write and direct Fitzgerald's *Last Tycoon*. After he became a power and a glory, Sam changed his name to S. P. Eagle.

One day, Mr. Eagle got married. Wilder wired the *Hollywood Reporter:* THE MARRIAGE OF S.P. EAGLE AND LYNN BAGGETT HAS LEFT OUR TOWN S. P. EECHLESS.

# 9

# FALLING IN
# LOVE AGAIN

Molly Haskell, like others, has wondered why the men who made
the wonderful films of the 30s and 40s, portrayed a gallery of fiery,
intelligent, and independent women. The women characters in Wilder's pictures have almost invariably been clever, articulate, bold,
adventurous, and flirtatious, in that uniquely bantering style which
Wilder wrote so well. And Ms. Haskell, like women who are irritated by the absence of interesting women in recent films from Hollywood, has sought many reasons for the vanishing American movie
heroine. I don't know why they vanished. I do know why they were
present once. They were there in the pictures because they had first
been there in the private lives of the men who made the pictures.
These men had known those exciting women and married them or
lived with them. They had admired them. They had experienced
them in all the variety of their humanity. And this had happened to
Billy Wilder. When he conceived the witty and exuberant and intellectual ladies played by Claudette Colbert, Olivia de Havilland, Garbo, and Barbara Stanwyck, he had expressed the nature of his actual
experiences with a woman who had come into his life back in 1935—
Judith . . . Judith Coppicus Iribe. (Charlie Brackett saw women in
a more traditional way as idealized vessels of virtue, noble statues;
he could see them either as pure or soiled. He could not see them as

human.) Billy did not "meet cute" with Judith, any more than he had "met cute" with Hella. He went to dinner at Jacques Théry's. Théry was a screenwriter. He was married to an American. Mrs. Théry said she knew the perfect match for Wilder. He was one of those bachelors who make a crusade of their bachelordom. He was a challenge to Mrs. Théry. Billy went to the dinner in a spirit of resignation. He knew that these blind dates were likely to be boring or painful. For once, he was wrong. By God, she was one hell of a woman. Judith was a tall and voluptuous woman, with long black hair flowing to her shoulders. Her lips were large and her cheekbones high, her eyes were large and dark and penetrating. She was at once sensual and intelligent. She was cultured and she was sophisticated. She spoke French like a native. She had been born in California and came from an old California family. (An uncle had been a lieutenant governor of the state.) Her father was George Coppicus, head of Columbia Artists, famous for having brought Caruso over for his first Metropolitan Opera engagement. She had grown up in an atmosphere of art and music. She was a painter herself. Her parents were divorced. Her mother then married Paul Iribe, a French artist, and later an art director for De Mille. During her adolescent years, Judith Iribe had lived in France. She carried herself like an aristocrat. She was an extremely sharp and provocative woman. She gave Billy Wilder as sarcastic a wisecrack as he gave her. He had met his match. He was conquered. She was—well, *elegant* is the best word to describe Judith in this phase of her existence. She was a political reactionary, but an elegant one; and she wore fine clothes with elegant hauteur. And she, for her part, was captivated by his, (to her) proletarian style, his radicalism, his barbs, his amiable hostility, and his way of jiving the world and her. They looked into each other's eyes across the table. At once there was that marvelous look—what de Maupassant called *le rouge regard*—which passes between a man and woman when they are destined to fall in love. So it began. Soon it became necessary for them to see each other every day. When Wilder went to Paris and Vienna in 1935, she wrote to him every day. She wrote to him by airmail. The transatlantic airmail was just coming into use.

In May 1936—just about the time he was getting married to Charlie Brackett—Billy Wilder married Judith Iribe. They eloped to Yuma, Arizona. They were spliced by a justice of the peace. Billy did not like formal marriages. He felt matrimony was sort of like an

unusual sex perversion which was more exciting if performed co-
vertly. Billy had been living at the Chateau Marmont—in better and
better rooms as his fortunes waxed. Now they moved into a suite.
Then they moved into her mother's house at 8224 de Longpre Avenue in Hollywood. One can chart the rise—and, alas, the fall—of a
Hollywood marriage by the addresses and the geography. From
West Hollywood they moved to an elegant apartment at 136 South
Camden Drive; this is in Beverly Hills, but the "wrong" side of
Beverly Hills, south of Wilshire. Now they thought of buying a
house. First they rented one—a small Tudor on Chevy Chase, in the
"right" side of Beverly Hills.

In April 1939, Mrs. Wilder became pregnant. They bought a house
in Hidden Valley. Hidden Valley is the name of a real street which
veers off Coldwater Canyon towards the summit on Mulholland
Drive. This was in a lovely, bucolic area—with few people and no
traffic. Judith liked spaces and quiet. She had an enormous garden.
She loved flowers and plants. Many of the photographs of her I've
seen show her in her garden, tending flowers, cutting them, holding
garlands of them. She was a person who liked to be with herself and
her quiet luxuries. As time went on, she became more engrossed in
art and quiet, and increasingly disinterested in luxuries and the social clamor. She also liked walking and horseback riding. She had
her own horse. She rode in the Santa Monica mountains every day.
She became more radical with the years. Billy became less radical.
She loved the isolation of Hidden Valley. For Billy it became alto-
gether too hidden. He had a long drive to Paramount. He had a long
drive to get to parties. He loved parties. He loved crowds. She liked
her small circle of friends, which included Lisl and Walter Reisch,
the Jacques Thérys, Chick and Don Hartman, Mia and Joe May.
They rarely saw the Bracketts. Elizabeth and Charlie Brackett now
lived on Bellagio Road in Bel Air. They gave Sunday afternoon parties once a month which were popular among *le tout Hollywood* . . .

When they met and fell in love, Judith had been a woman with an
eye for fashion and a love of exterior and interior decoration. But
now she was blasé. All these aspects of high living were empty. She
was going through a deep moral and spiritual crisis during the war
years. She had been shaken by the war. While the war had made Billy conscious of life's slender thread so that he clung more intensely
to sensual joys, she began seeking new values, different roads. He

was still hung up on the *old* Mrs. Wilder. She complained to writer Lincoln Barnett in 1944 that Billy was always bringing home bolts of cretonne and chintz for her to use in reupholstering. They were stored in the attic. She did not care to repaint and selecting new wallpaper prints was, for her, ennui. She began to go around with Communists. I do not know if she took out membership. But she went to the meetings and became active in the groups. She became a political activist. She and Billy were still friends and lovers and they went around together and shared many experiences—above all, that exciting give and take of repartee—but, although they were not conscious of it at first, there was a split, and the split was widening. . . .

For, to a degree, a difference in values and sensibility between a man and a woman can be stimulating, but when the difference becomes a chasm, the bridge across it is too long to cross over and each one remains on his own side—and this is what happened, as it happened also with Brackett.

Brackett and Wilder had been growing apart. At first, their differences had been stimulating, and then they became the occasions for quarreling. In one sense, Brackett was a Victorian. He was a right-wing Republican. He was a nineteenth-century throwback. He liked heavy Victorian furniture. He had inherited many pieces and he bought new ones. Belter furniture was to his taste—as Bauhaus furniture was to Wilder's. Wilder had already started buying modern paintings. Brackett liked Landseer, Bonheur, Winterhalter. He loved paintings of animals. He simply adored animal paintings if the animals were sheep. He could not resist buying a painting of sheep grazing in a meadow.

Wilder remembers Sunday afternoons on Bellagio Road with the sun slanting on the red plush of the Victorian sofa, the large Tiffany vases, ladies and gentlemen sitting in Belter chairs around Belter card tables playing cribbage with an antique cribbage board. Brackett had attempted to re-create the nineteenth century in Bel Air.

On December 21, 1939, Mrs. Wilder gave birth to twins: Vincent and Victoria. Vincent died in infancy. Victoria flourished. Billy couldn't stand Hidden Valley. They moved to Rexford Drive and Lexington—another rental. Finally, in 1941, they bought a large house at 704 North Beverly Drive, in the heart of the most elegant stretch of Beverly Hills, and here they lived during the next six years, in an atmosphere of rising marital discord and mutual withdrawal, remaining together in the diminishing hope that perhaps their almost extinct emotions might be kindled once again. As they became more estranged, as he remained away from home more and more and she heard rumors of affairs with actresses and screenwriters and demi mondaines and mondaines who were not demi, she completely withdrew. She opened a boutique on Rodeo Drive and sold imported clothes. She painted a great deal. She went to her meetings. She would help to change the world. She would help to make a society in which there was no more war and no more exploitation of the working class.

Once, Billy dreamed of constructing a spectacular house in a contemporary design for Judith and little Vicki. His friend Charles Eames had made a fantastic plan for the house. He bought three acres on Sunset Boulevard and Foothill Drive. It was an unbelievable parcel of the best land in one of the best neighborhoods in the country. It was large enough so Judith could have her gardens. And yet he would be near his friends and parties.

The house was never built.

Two of the acres were sold.

He still owns one acre.

It stands vacant.

# IO

# GOING TO
# A MASQUERADE PARTY

At twenty-nine, Joe Sistrom was one of the rising executives at Paramount. He was a tall, striking-looking man of military bearing. He had a black crew cut and wore thick glasses, and his jaw was rugged. He looked like a young Rudyard Kipling. He found out about the resemblance when he was Pandro Berman's executive assistant at RKO. George Stevens was making *Gunga Din*. He wanted Sistrom to play Kipling, the young journalist. He had pictures which showed Kipling looking amazingly like Sistrom. Sistrom played Kipling. He played contract bridge with Wilder. He was a friend of Billy's. He was always telling him about new books he read and stories in magazines. He was one of these voracious readers who remembered everything he ever read. He had a finely attuned sense for what was cinematic in a published story. Sistrom brought Billy a *Saturday Evening Post* story, "Sunny Goes Home"—from May 7, 1921! He thought Brackett and Wilder could update the theme and they would have a flashy comedy here. Against vehement objections from Charlie, who kept trying to dissuade Wilder from his insane schemes, they started writing this story of a stunning Iowa lady who comes to Manhattan to make a career and returns home because men keep treating her as a sexual object; lacking the train fare she disguises herself as a child under thirteen to get the half fare!

This was the "macguffin" of *The Major and the Minor*, Wilder's maiden voyage as a director. Billy now believes that the front office encouraged him to go ahead because they wanted him to fall on his face and get back to being a full-time writer. He knew, from Sistrom's secret reports to him, that they were snickering at the story idea. Nevertheless, prodded by Wilder, obsessed with revenge against Leisen and Boyer, the two writers completed the screenplay. And now to play Susu Applegate, the beautiful girl who is going to look age twelve on a train, Wilder said he wanted to cast— Ginger Rogers. Ginger *Rogers?* Well, they were really chortling in the front office. Ginger—that quintessence of the magnificent feminine animal, that dancing partner of Fred Astaire, she of the dazzling golden hair and the magnificent breasts and legs and buttocks. How did that idiot think he was ever going to make her look age twelve? And furthermore Miss Rogers had just won the Oscar for her performance in *Kitty Foyle*. She was not about to chuck away her prestige on a neophyte director with an idiotic script. Well, they all forgot, for one thing, that in *Kitty Foyle* there had been several flashbacks to the heroine's youth and she had played a subteen girl from the wrong side of the Philadelphia tracks. She had even demonstrated that she could do other things besides dance. She could speak sophisticated lines. She could play comedy. She could play love scenes. She could, in a word, act. She was Billy Wilder's idea of the all-around woman protagonist, of wit and elegance. And his enemies at Paramount also forgot that Billy's new agent was Leland Hayward and that Hayward was Ginger's agent and soon Ginger Rogers had agreed to play the lead in *The Major and the Minor*.

I asked La Rogers (who is still elegant, witty and gorgeous at sixty-four) not long ago whether she had done this picture as a favor to Leland Hayward or Billy Wilder—you know, a kind of a sympathy gesture to help an aspiring young man try his wings?

"Hell no," she said, full of the old fire, "I didn't do it to help anybody. I did it because it was one hell of a good script and I knew Charlie Brackett and Billy Wilder were the best writers in the picture business and they had written one hell of a part for me."

For the hero, Billy wanted one of Paramount's hottest contract players—Ray Milland, the lean Welshman with the ironic intonations in his lovely baritone. Milland was also a hot property. Why did Milland do the picture? I mean, he wasn't a client of Leland Hayward, for one thing. I accosted Milland in the cocktail lounge of the Bel-Air Hotel while he was here on a visit from his chateau in

France last year. He had come in after a day of sailing. He was wearing a waterproof jacket and sailor's cap. He still had that rakish air about him—oh, it was middle-aged rakishness, but it was there and the rich ironic voice was there. He vividly remembered how it happened:

"I was driving home from Paramount after work. I was exhausted. In the rear window, I saw a green car trailing me for miles. Finally it caught up with me at Melrose and Doheny. I heard somebody yelling at me, 'Would you work in a picture I'm going to direct?' It was Billy. He was grinning. I said, 'Sure.' I was too tired to go into it with him and thought he wasn't serious anyway. A few weeks later I got the script. I liked the story. It didn't bother me that it was Billy's first picture. Hell, in those days you finished one picture on Friday and started a new one on Monday.

"One place where I figured Billy was wrong was in thinking Ginger would look convincing as a twelve-year-old kid. I was wrong. His intuition was right. Like when he put me in *Lost Weekend.* When I saw her in the rushes with her bosom taped down, in bobby sox, no makeup, that white straw sailor hat, sucking a lollipop, she was a delectable little girl."

On the question of the illusion of Ginger Rogers as a "little girl," Wilder also stressed that "we had Ginger's marvelous tits strapped down."

During an interview with Ginger recently at the Polo Lounge, I queried her as to whether it had been painful when her mammaries had been taped down. She exploded: "Taped down, was it? Who the hell told you that, anyway? I can assure you that my tits were absolutely *not* taped down, *not* strapped down, not even a tight brassiere. Don't know why Ray Milland and Billy Wilder say those things. They're out of their cotton-pickin' minds. I am an actress. I just acted a twelve-year-old girl in a middy blouse. Yeah, and I also played me as a mature woman—and as my mother. I played three generations in *The Major and the Minor.* Don't give me this drivel about strapping down tits, old boy. No, I never went ballroom dancing with Billy. Did you know he used to be a gigolo? Oh, you did? I never did it with Billy, by the way, contrary to any gossip. I never understood Billy socially. I never could get close to him. He always kind of avoids me. You think he's afraid of me? If we are at the same large party, which happens often, he seems to linger in another part of the room. I don't know if it's accidental or deliberate.

"And since we're on the subject, I've always been piqued that

Billy has never given me public credit for my making it possible for him to direct his first picture. When I meet him at a social function he just says 'hello' and then disappears, kind of.''

The Sunday before he was to start filming, Billy went over to talk to Lubitsch. He was running a fever, his nerves were shot, and he was suffering from diarrhea. He said to The Master that he dreaded the first day of shooting. He said he was literally crapping in his pants. Lubitsch put an arm around him and said,

"I have directed fifty pictures and I'm still crapping in my pants on the first day."

To lend Billy moral support and technical advice, Lubitsch rounded up all the German directors in Hollywood. They came to the set on March 4, 1942, en masse. E.A. Dupont, William Wyler, William Dieterle, Bobby Koster, and Mike Curtiz. Preston Sturges also came, to boost Wilder's spirits. Sturges had proved that good writers could be good directors. He had done it at Paramount in 1940 with his *Great McGinty*. He now had his own production unit. As a result of all these geniuses on the set, the first day of shooting was a shambles. Billy did not get a single foot of usable film. In his confusion, Wilder turned to his cutter and editor—a lanky, stoop-shouldered, laconic man: Doane Harrison. Harrison had started as a cutter of Mack Sennett comedies. He knew film technique. He became Wilder's right-hand man and was beside him on the set almost every day until he died in 1967. He helped Billy plan the setups and advised on lighting and when to make the cut. By his third picture, Billy knew his own mind, but he always wanted to have Doane Harrison around him just the same.

Following Lubitsch's example, Wilder always shot in sequence as the scenes were written. So he did scene one, which was in Robert Benchley's apartment, where Ginger Rogers comes with her equipment to give him a shampoo. (She anticipated Warren Beatty by thirty-five years.) Benchley's first line became a classic: "No matter what the weather is, I always say—why don't you get out of that wet coat and into a dry martini?"

Ever since, Benchley has been incorrectly quoted as having originated this quip. It was written by Charlie Brackett, who had once heard Charlie Butterworth, the comedian, say it at a party in Manhattan.

Wilder points out that the paradox of Ginger Rogers masquerading as a twelve-year-old was not whether an audience would believe her, but whether the characters in the picture would believe her. Toward the end of the film, Ginger's mama asks her what happened between New York and Iowa to delay her return on the train. Ginger replied, "I went to a masquerade party." The masquerader is a recurrent theme in Wilder's films—sometimes blatant, as in *Some Like It Hot* and *Irma La Douce.* He had been fascinated with the device since he'd first seen Molnar's comedy, *The Guardsman,* which was about an insanely jealous actor who impersonates a Russian guardsman and makes love to his own wife to test her fidelity. Whether or not the wife ever saw through the husband's disguise was left ambiguous. Wilder perceived that the device heightened dramatic tension and created delicious farcical situations. In *Midnight,* Claudette Colbert had to do a bogus Hungarian countess. The audience enjoyed the game of wits. It was on tenterhooks. Moreover, when an actress already acting one role is required by the role itself to play a *second* role, she is able to open herself up, and reach fantasy levels very deep in her nature. As twelve-year-old Susu Applegate, Ginger could express sadness, loneliness, sentimentality, fear of thunder— emotions she kept under wraps when she played a mature career woman grappling with Manhattan seducers like Mr. Benchley.

Wilder also says that the real motif in *The Major and the Minor* was the Lolita element, a decade before Nabokov's novel. "Ray Milland falls in love with Ginger as a twelve-year-old child. We had here the first American movie about pedophilia. The Major is sexually aroused by her. He can't help himself. I was worried that audiences would be shocked by this story, but it seems that they were not."

Had Benchley wanted to rewrite his part? "On the contrary," Wilder says, "he was a lovely man. He did not change his lines. Each morning he came with a large net sack, like a French marketing bag. It was filled with books. He went to his trailer and he read. When he was needed in a scene, we called him and he would do it expertly, on the first take, and then he would go away and read."

In his first film, Wilder had proven to himself he could cope with actors. In his next one, he had to learn to cope with nature. It was *Five Graves to Cairo.* It was about Rommel's conquest and defeat in North Africa. The desert scenes were shot on location in Yuma, Arizona. The opening sequence was a powerful one, without words, and showed a lonely British tank crawling over desert dunes. The tank is full of dead bodies. Billy had found a marvelous dune with a nice background of other dunes and sand slopes. It was clean, virginal sand. He had rehearsed the scene with Franchot Tone. He and cameraman John Seitz had agreed on a setup and had the lights prepared. (Yes, they use lights, even in desert filming, to correct glare and highlights.) They would start filming at five A.M.—at sunrise. In desert shooting you always get going early in the morning.

Billy went out there at four A.M. He got a shock. That beautiful sand dune—and the surrounding terrain—were all tracked up. Nearby there was an army base. Somebody had driven a jeep all over the place. It was the first great crisis he faced as a director. He took action. He sent a dozen men into Yuma. They returned with every broom they could buy or borrow.

Wilder is like an old general recollecting his first cavalry charge. "Well, we had maybe a hundred brooms and everybody was sweeping the sand to look clean. Me, Anne Baxter, Akim Tamiroff, Franchot Tone, people from Yuma, and we cleaned up every goddam tire track and I shot the scene and it was perfect.

"But imagine—to sweep a desert clean like that! I was young and felt confident. I knew everything was possible to me now in films, and that I could not be defeated."

Back in Los Angeles to shoot the interior scenes, Wilder was rather nervous about his first meeting with Erich von Stroheim, who was to play Rommel. Paramount had brought the great actor-director over from France. Billy was in awe of him. He had admired him as a genius when he was a struggling journalist and hopeful screenwriter in Berlin. Why, once he had even written a gushing fan letter to von Stroheim and begged for an autographed picture. He had framed it! Now, his heart beating, he went over to Western Costume Company on Vermont Avenue, where the great man was trying on uniforms and hats.

Billy said it was an honor to be directing him.

"You were always ten years ahead of your time," he said.

"Twenty, Mr. Wilder, twenty," von Stroheim barked.

Wilder gave von Stroheim everything he wanted. He was as shameless as Mitchell Leisen in his coddling of Erich von Stroheim.

As Rommel, von Stroheim had to wear field glasses and a camera, both slung around his neck. He insisted on real German field glasses and a real Leica camera—which had to be loaded with real 35 mm. film! Billy gave him what he wanted, but he wanted to know why *real* film?

Von Stroheim explained: "An audience always senses whether a prop is genuine or false."

I once asked Billy, in view of the fact that much of *Five Graves*, like von Stroheim's masterpiece *Greed*, was filmed in the desert whether they had ever discussed *Greed*.

"No, I did not discuss *Greed* with Mr. Stroheim," Wilder replied. "It would have taken him sixteen hours to explain the eight hours of *Greed*. He had a habit of rambling on forever if you started him on one of his pictures. Mostly we talked about food, about Vienna in the old days, about love and women. This obsession with foot fetishism, underwear fetishism, other sexual perversions which his pictures are filled with, was the *real* Stroheim. He loved to go into details about his own fetishes and how he had satisfied them. The movie he should have made was an adaptation of Krafft-Ebing's *Psychopathia Sexualis*. But he succeeded in slyly getting a lot of sex perversion into those films he shot in 1919, 1920. In regard to sex perversions, Mr. von Stroheim was not only twenty years ahead of his time—he was fifty years ahead of his time."

# II

# THE LISTS OF
# RAYMOND CHANDLER

Joe Sistrom burst into Billy's office one morning. He slapped a stack of *Liberty* magazines on his desk. *Liberty* was a nickel weekly, famous for printing the reading time *to the exact minute* of each article and story. The stack comprised a series of back number issues, dated from February 15 through April 4, 1936. They contained a novelette by James M. Cain in eight installments, illustrated by James Montgomery Flagg. It was *Double Indemnity*. Sistrom said Billy must read it immediately. He said it was a thriller about this dame who kills her husband to collect his insurance. He knew it was just the sort of romantic love story to warm the cockles of Billy's rotten heart. *"Reading time: 2 hours, 50 minutes, and 7 seconds."* Wilder read it in fifty-eight minutes because he did not use his lips. Yes, it certainly possessed a sort of charm, for the murderess entangles an insurance salesman in her web of lust and greed. Charlie Brackett, upon reading the story, told Wilder it was disgusting. He would not write it. He would not produce it. There was a violent dispute, terminating with objects flying at Billy's head. The partnership broke up. Sistrom produced *Double Indemnity*. He tried to get Cain himself to collaborate with Billy. Cain was unavailable. He was working at Twentieth on a treatment of *Western Union* for Fritz Lang. Sistrom said he knew another writer in the Cain style. Raymond Chandler! ("It has always irritated me to be compared with Cain," Chandler wrote in a 1944 letter. "I'm not in the least like Cain. . . . Cain is a writer of the *faux naïf* type, which I particularly dislike.") Wilder never heard of Chandler. Sistrom bought him *The Big Sleep.* I hope you will bear in mind that back in 1943 Chandler was unknown even to mystery novel freaks. Billy read *Big Sleep* in one sitting. (*"Reading time: 2 hours and 14 minutes."*) He loved it. Chandler had a kind of sinuous poetry in his descriptions of Los Angeles. He wrote amusingly vicious dialogue. He had a gut feeling for the killer instincts of a blonde. Yes, this man would be an ideal collaborator. He told Sistrom to make Chandler an offer. Sistrom got in touch with H. N. Swanson, the Hollywood agent who represented authors. Swanson told him Chandler was an eccentric fellow who did not always answer his phone. He lived in a small Spanish-style house on Drexel Avenue in West Hollywood near La Cienega. He gave him the man's phone number. Chandler had been living in and around Los Angeles for twenty-five years. He had never been inside a movie studio. He didn't even know where Paramount was located. Sistrom gave him explicit driving directions. He was to go east to Crescent Heights, left on Crescent, hang a right on Melrose, and he couldn't miss it, just keep going east on Melrose. Chandler sounded like a man who was—well, blurred. Sistrom repeated the directions.

Wilder was always respectful of talent. Chandler had talent. Chandler could write American speech beautifully. He looked forward to starting work with this guy. He pictured him as a sinister guy in a Borsalino hat. He would be packing a Colt .45 in a shoulder holster. He thought he had been a private detective formerly, that's how real *Big Sleep* was. You can imagine his disillusionment when Miss Hernandez showed in this washed-out, pasty-faced, middle-aged man. Chandler was forty-four when he sold his first mystery story to *Black Mask* magazine. He was fifty-five years old when he became a screenwriter. He looked very conventional . . . very petty-bourgeois. Wilder says, "If I was casting a man to play an accountant, I would cast Chandler. He looked like an average CPA. He looked kind of like Porter Hall." (Porter Hall was a stocky man with a rumpled face. He played the man from Medford, Oregon, who starts conversing with Fred MacMurray, masquerading as the crippled husband of Barbara Stanwyck, on the observation platform of the train going up to Stanford for the football game.)

Chandler sat down. Right away, Wilder was suspicious of him. He was smoking a pipe. He was wearing a tweed coat with leather elbows. He was wearing a button-down shirt and regimental striped tie. Chandler, for his part, thought Billy Wilder was a very high-strung, nervous, crazy man, because he kept jumping around the room, talking very fast about how he was going to make this picture from the Cain novel, and he kept snapping his fingers, or lashing the air with a riding crop. And he was wearing a hat. It was a baseball cap. He did not know that Wilder always wore a hat indoors. He thought it rather impolite.

It was a case of hate at first sight.

Chandler was tapped out. He said therefore that he was interested in writing a screenplay. He had never written one before. He thought it might take him as long as two weeks to write one. Maybe three!

Wilder—who usually took upwards of four months to do one with a partner—raised his eyebrows. He laughed.

Chandler had a nervous habit of creasing his forehead so it looked as though he was frowning. There was a twitch about his lower lip. He was a heavy, daily drinker. He was stoned most of the time, but he carried it off well. He was a virtuoso alcoholic.

"As for salary," Chandler mumbled, "I must have at least $150 a week." (His average income from his books and magazine stories had been running around $3,000 a year for a decade.)

"Mr. Chandler," Sistrom said, "we propose to pay you $750 a week."

Chandler returned to his home and his bottle of Old Forester bourbon, his favorite refreshment. He knew that a real writer like himself could knock out a movie fast. But he did not want to make it *too* fast. He had been put on salary at once. It was a fortune they were paying him. He had better stretch it out to four weeks. . . . He started writing pages which he studded with camera directions, the usual ploy of the neophyte, "EXT." and "INT." and "DOLLY IN FOR CU." They had given him a typical movie script—*Hold Back the Dawn*—to study. He wrote long and well-turned speeches for the characters. He wrote descriptions of the murder house in Glendale. He wrote descriptions of Griffith Park. He wrote a beautiful manuscript. He schlepped it in five weeks later. Billy read it at once while Chandler watched.

Then he threw it—yes, *hurled it*—right at Chandler. It hit him in the chest and fell on his lap. "This is shit, Mr. Chandler," he said amiably. He suggested that Chandler use it as a doorstop or contribute it to the scrap paper drive. "I think I have to teach you the facts of life, Mr. Chandler. We are going to write this picture—*together.* We are going to lock ourselves in this room and write a screenplay. It is going to take us a long time. You will be on salary even if it takes a year to write this picture."

Chandler said he had never written in the same room with another person. Wilder said that was how he did it. Chandler had signed the contract. Those $750 checks looked real tasty. He sighed. He frowned. He twitched. He agreed to endure the collaboration.

The first six weeks they just talked it out. Wilder paced. Wilder talked. Wilder listened. Wilder argued. Chandler talked. Chandler suggested scenes. Chandler sat in an upholstered easy chair and smoked his pipe. He smoked and smoked and smoked. The office was thickened by the noxious smoke. Wilder was choking.

"For Chrissakes, Ray, open a window."

This impudent man was giving him orders, was he? And not even asking him with decent manners. And always wearing a different hat. What kind of a boor wears hats? And criticizing his pipe smoking and clothes and knowledge of syntax?

They were calling each other "Ray" and "Billy." Ray was opposed to open windows. He had a theory that Los Angeles fresh air was unhealthful by day and not too salubrious at night.

Chandler was intrigued by the numerous times Wilder went to the toilet. This man would go to the toilet every fifteen minutes. Did he have a bladder problem? Perhaps an enlarged prostate? He did not know that, as Wilder once explained to me, a convenient toilet is necessary in a successful screenwriting collaboration. Whenever he could not stand Chandler, Wilder would beat it to the toilet. He might or might not urinate. But anyway he sat on the toilet seat and smoked a cigarette and wondered why God had imposed these tribulations upon him. Brackett at least, with all his craziness, knew how to write a picture. But this man—he was impossible, he was arrogant, he was a typical book writer. So he had his toilet as a refuge and he would say to himself, *Someday this script will be over and I'll never have to see this crazy Chandler again.*

Now, it happened that Chandler was not idle while Wilder was in the toilet. He had a brown briefcase with him. In it was a writing board, sheets of cut-up legal-sized yellow paper on which he liked to make notes while hanging around seedy bars and decayed hotel lobbies. (The original Chandler briefcase is now in the possession of E. T. "Ned" Guymon, a San Diego collector of mystery novels. He was an acquaintance of Chandler's.) He had a pint bottle in the briefcase. He took a good slug of bourbon. It gave him the strength to bear Billy's abuse. One day he could bear it no longer. He did not show up in Wilder's office. He sent no word. On the third day, as Billy was getting apprehensive, he got a call from Sistrom. Chandler was sitting in Joe's office. He wanted to quit the project. He wanted to get a release from the contract. Sistrom said to come over right away, fast.

In Sistrom's office, Chandler glared at him. He was sucking on his pipe. He had presented Sistrom with a list of complaints about Wilder written out on these cut-up pieces of yellow paper. Unless Wilder apologized, Chandler would not write the movie. It was . . . farewell, my lovely . . .

Sistrom apologized. Wilder apologized. It was the first—and perhaps the only—time on record in which a producer and a director ate humble pie, in which a screenwriter humiliated the big shots. Usually it is the other way around, at least in all those accounts of the sufferings of novelists who become movie writers. Having made Wilder eat humble pie, Chandler now threatened resignation at least once a week. He went through the same charade of the list of grievances and Wilder went through a sincere apology.

Among the complaints on these various lists were the following, as Billy recalls them:

"Mr. Wilder frequently interrupts our work to take phone calls from women. . . . Mr. Wilder ordered me to open the window. He did not say please. . . . He sticks his baton in my eyes. . . . I can't work with a man who wears a hat in the office. I feel he is about to leave momentarily."

The collaboration dragged on for almost six months—with arguments and apologies and tantrums. "Working with Billy Wilder on *Double Indemnity*," Chandler wrote Hamish Hamilton, his British publisher, "was an agonizing experience and has probably shortened my life, but I learned from it about as much about screenwriting as I am capable of learning, which is not very much. Like every writer, or almost every writer, who goes to Hollywood, I was convinced in the beginning that there must be some discoverable method of working in pictures which would not be completely stultifying to whatever creative talent one might happen to possess. But like many others before, I discovered that was a dream. Too many people have too much to say about a writer's work. It ceases to be his own. And after a while he ceases to care about it. He has brief enthusiasms, but they are destroyed before they can flower. People who can't write, tell him how to write. . . ."

Perhaps a good example of how Chandler-Wilder transmuted Cain's story is the moment when, after having dumped Dietrichson's body on the railroad tracks along with the crutches, Neff and Phyllis go to the car, parked in the darkness to make their getaway. Cain's text reads:

> We ran over and climbed in and she started the motor, threw in the gear. "Oh, my—his hat!"
> I took the hat and sailed it out the window, on the tracks. "It's O.K.; a hat can roll—*get going!*"
> She started up. We passed the factories. We came to a street. . . .

In the script, Phyllis cannot start the car. The starter whines and whines and the engine does not turn over.

And now let us see what took place when coauthor Wilder became director Wilder. Fred MacMurray remembers how surprised he was that this turned out to be "the most successful scene in the picture. I remember we did it on a process stage with rear projection for the trees, y'know, the scenery behind us. Barbara and I sat in this dummy car. Just a car seat. No dashboard. No ignition key to turn. We faked it, pantomimed it. When I changed places with her and turned the key I remember I was doing it fast and Billy kept saying, '*Make it longer, make it longer*,' and finally I yelled, '*For Chrissake Billy, it's not going to hold that long*,' and he said, '*Make it longer*,' and he was right. It held. It held—that was how much the audience was involved in the story. By the way, you remember that bit where I fall off the observation car platform? Where I'm pretending to be the husband with the crippled leg and the crutches? I didn't do the fall right. Wilder showed me how to do the fall. That's the only time he demonstrated an action for me by doing it. Usually he just told you what he wanted and expected you to do it.

"Did you know my name was Walter Ness in the first version of the script? Then they found out there was an insurance guy over in Palos Verdes named Walter Ness so Billy changed it to Neff.

"And Mr. Cain, he complimented Billy and said it was the first time any book of his came to the screen in better shape than he had written it. He admired the way I played Neff and he gave me an autographed copy of *Three of a Kind.* . . ."

MacMurray never wanted to play Neff. He knew it would ruin his happy-go-lucky image. Paramount told him he would not be permitted to play in it. In 1943, a hero could not be a man who lusted for blondes and killed for money. Every leading man in Hollywood, including Paramount's Alan Ladd, scorned the role. Wilder begged and wheedled. He could not get an actor of any reputation to risk it. He sent copies of Cain's novella and the Chandler-Wilder story treatment to every agent in town. He was shunned by the agents. They advised their clients that *Double Indemnity* was poison. Wilder was desperate. He even sought to interest George Raft. He phoned Raft. The eminent movie gangster had now purified himself. He was playing good guys in the Warner Bros. slam-bang pictures. He said he would send Raft the first forty pages of the script.

"I don't read scripts," Raft said. "Tell it to me."

Wilder told it to him.

"Let's get to the lapel bit," Raft interrupted. "When comes the lapel?"

"What lapel, Mr. Raft?"

"The lapel," the actor said, annoyed by such stupidity. "You know, when the guy flashes his lapel, you see his badge, you know he's a detective."

"There is no lapel bit, Mr. Raft."

"So long, pal," the actor said. Raft was not an astute judge of roles. He had also turned down Sam Spade in *The Maltese Falcon*!

If the part of Walter Neff was too loathsome even for George Raft, what chance did Billy have? He wanted MacMurray anyway. He wanted a nice, sweet, wisecracking guy who had larceny and lust inside his Rotarian go-getter skin. A guy with a grin. He went after MacMurray. He badgered him every day—every single day, according to MacMurray. He badgered him in the commissary, in his dressing room, at home. He didn't give up. He wore MacMurray down. MacMurray said yes, knowing that the executive head of West Coast Paramount production, Y. Frank Freeman, wouldn't let him. Mr. Freeman hated immoral movies. He considered this a dirty movie. He hated Billy Wilder. He hated the idea of making this picture. MacMurray was having a fight with the studio over his new contract. He figured he would use the threat of playing Neff to get a better deal. To his surprise, they suddenly let him play it. They thought they would punish *him*. It would cut him down to size. Mac-Murray went into it fearful it would wreck his career and destroy his charming, lovable image. "I never dreamed it would be the best picture I ever made," he says.

According to the anti-Hollywood cliché, when a writer completes one assignment, he is shifted immediately to his next job. And if he is an expert in murder stories, they put him on a college musical, say, or a Western, right? Sorry, wrong number, sweetheart. Wilder insisted that Chandler remain *on full salary* during the shooting of *Double Indemnity*. Wilder would not alter a line on the set unless he had Chandler's grudging approval. John Woolfenden, unit publicist on the picture, and now editor-publisher of the *Monterey Peninsula Herald*, remembers Chandler as a quiet and polite gentleman who was on the set each day and seemed to be intently observing every move Wilder and the actors made. He once expressed to Woolfenden his delight at how Robinson memorized long speeches—and did them freshly at every retake. Chandler saw the daily rushes every day. Chandler was given a heavy publicity treatment by the studio. Teet Carle, publicity head, had him giving press interviews and posing for pictures. They sent out a studio biography of Chandler. ("Unlike his detective," this biography tells us, "Chandler rarely touches alcohol at any time, and never while working. When at his work, Chandler stimulates himself continually, and exclusively, with tea.")

As originally filmed, *Double Indemnity* ended with MacMurray dying in the gas chamber at Folsom. It had cost Paramount $150,000 to build a replica of the execution room and it took five days of shooting to make the scene. Billy felt uneasy about it. He had it screened many times. It was too strong. It was out of key. Suddenly he made a decision. He would scrap the entire gas chamber business. He would, with Chandler, write a new ending. He would shoot a new last scene. That was a hard decision for him to make. He had to fight with Sistrom and with Freeman. But he got his way. He was making money for the investors. So, against Chandler's wishes, Wilder made a beautiful conclusion to the film—a quiet and poignant ending. Now Wilder experienced the loneliness, as well as the power, of a director. He stood alone against everyone—even Doane

Harrison. Was his judgment right? He had to believe in himself at all costs. And now it was MacMurray dying—bleeding to death in the corridor by the elevator—and asking Robinson to give him twenty-four hours to flee to Mexico, and Robinson saying, "You'll never make it to the elevator," and lighting a final cigarette for MacMurray, who says that the investigator couldn't figure out this scheme because "the guy you were looking for was too close, right across the desk from you . . . ." And Robinson saying, "Closer than that," as we hear police sirens in the distance.

They faded out on those two faces—the love of a father for his surrogate son. This may well be the most powerful emotional scene Wilder ever wrote. He summed up the film in a few images and in a few words. He went far beyond anything in Cain's novel. In fact, the film as a whole was almost entirely a reconstruction—no, more than that—it was a totally new aesthetic experience, although if you see it on television or in a revival house and you think of Cain's novel (in memory only) you may think the film is a faithful translation of the novel. And, says Wilder, that is just the way it should be.

Now comes a turn of events that is unbelievable, unless you realize that by now Raymond Chandler had become literally insane, and was a well-tempered paranoid. I have read hundreds of his letters to various persons, which are in the Raymond Chandler Collection at the UCLA library of special collections. His letters are brilliant and witty and quite deranged if you know the facts. Chandler would invent incidents and twist facts around to get sympathy from his friends, his editors, his publishers.

Now, in 1945, after Paramount Pictures had treated him so decently, Chandler wrote a slashing attack on Hollywood's treatment of screenwriters. It appeared in the November 1945 issue of the *Atlantic Monthly*, as "Writers in Hollywood."

"The first picture I worked on was nominated for an Academy Award, if that means anything," he wrote, "but I was not even invited to the press review [*sic!*] held right in the studio. An extremely successful picture made by another studio from a story I wrote used verbatim phrases out of the story in its promotional campaign, but my name was never mentioned once in any radio, magazine, billboard, or newspaper advertising that I saw or heard—and I saw and heard a great deal. This neglect is of no consequence to me personally; to a writer of books a Hollywood by-line is trivial. To those whose whole work is in Hollywood, it is not trivial, because it is part of a deliberate and successful plan to reduce the professional screenwriter to the status of an assistant picture-maker, superficially deferred to (if he is in the room), essentially ignored, and even in his most brilliant achievements carefully pushed out of the way of any possible accolade which might otherwise fall to the star, the producer, the director.''

It was a malicious essay, with all the customary tales of how writers were persecuted by Hollywood producers and directors. Chandler had listened sympathetically to his fellow authors at the Writers' Table at Paramount. He had taken note of the thrice-told anecdotes. He loved paranoia. He set down many things for the *Atlantic* but he did not say a word about the respect with which Sistrom had treated him, nor how he had made Wilder apologize to him on a regular basis. He did not say that it was he, Chandler, the man who was published by Knopf, who had wanted to knock off a slapdash screenplay in three weeks; and that it was Wilder, the Hollywood director, who had taken time to painstakingly devise a pattern of images and words. He had not found it necessary to state that he had been kept on salary during the filming and that no script changes were made without his approval. He forgot to tell the readers of the *Atlantic Monthly* how Paramount had put on a publicity campaign for him. He didn't breathe a word about the fact that he was given a nice room and a secretary and that, subsequently, when he was working on a film for producer John Houseman (*The Blue Dahlia*), he was permitted to work at home—and in addition was furnished with three relays of secretaries, chauffeurs, and Cadillacs on a twenty-four-hour-a-day basis—but that is another story. . . .

I once knew a psychoanalyst named Edmond Bergler who specialized in treating neurotic writers. He had a theory that all writers were "psychic masochists." Certainly, Hollywood writers loved sitting around and getting drunk in such hangouts of the 1940s as Musso-Frank's, Victor's, the old Scandia (the one on the north side of Sunset), and the Beverly Hills Tennis Club, and telling sardonic, bitter, hilarious stories about their sufferings at the hands of Cohn, Zanuck, Warner, L. B. Mayer, Sam Goldwyn. There was practically a cottage industry in Harry Cohn stories and Sam Goldwyn stories. It was not that these stories were not based on actual events. They were. They were exaggerated, yes, but true, in the sense that scripts were often mangled and rewritten and screenwriters were often

treated like serfs—rich serfs, but serfs. But there were also crafts-
men who were respected. There were also writers who loved film
and had learned the art and practiced a craft with intensity and love
as Wilder did, and as hundreds of others in the industry did: actors,
producers, directors, cameramen, cutters, editors—all those who
came together at a time and place from about 1929 to 1955 and collectively made innumerable movies which were so finely wrought
that they capture our imaginations to this day and have endured now
to a fourth generation of moviegoers.

Sometimes I get to thinking that the problem isn't that Hollywood
is disrespectful of authors but that authors are disrespectful of Hollywood, by which I mean they have no knowledge and respect for
what it means to structure and create a screenplay and what it means
to make a movie. But Chandler knew—at first hand. Therefore in
writing the above article, I have to say he was a liar—a consummate
liar, a polished and lapidary liar, but a liar.

That *Atlantic* article made a big noise in Hollywood—and screenwriters, though they knew it was as much fantasy as fact, loved it
because Chandler was sticking it to the bosses. Anyway, it was the
talk of the town. Chandler dashed off a postcard to his friend at the
University of Colorado, James Sandoe: "Have been blackballed at
all the best bistros and call houses for my remarks about screenwriters and producers in the November *Atlantic*."

The only time I have seen Billy Wilder get truly mad is when I
quoted some sentences from Chandler's article.

"Hollywood treated him badly?" he said. "We didn't invite him
to the preview? How could we? He was under a table drunk at
Lucey's. It's a wonder they don't say Hollywood drove him to
drink. I've heard people say that I drove him to drink. Don't fall for
that dreck—what Hollywood did to Raymond Chandler. What did
Raymond Chandler do to Hollywood? It reminds me of a curtain line
in *Shanghai Gesture* where Mother Goddam finds out one of the
whores in her brothel is her own daughter. A friend says, 'God will
forgive you.' And Mother Goddam says, 'But will I forgive God?'
That's how I feel about sons of bitches like Chandler. Will Hollywood forgive Raymond Chandler? He gave me more aggravation
than any writer I ever worked with."

One of the few times when Chandler was honest about Hollywood
was in reply to a query from Dale Warren of Houghton, Mifflin, who

wondered how a serious writer survived in Hollywood. Chandler had learned his lessons from Wilder well. He did not write these things for publication in the *Atlantic*. This is part of his letter:

> If you really believe in the art of the film, it is a long-term job and you ought to forget about any other kind of writing. A preoccupation with words for their own sake is fatal to good film making. . . . It is not my cup of tea, but it could have been if I had started twenty years earlier. . . . The best scenes I ever wrote were practically monosyllabic, and the best short scene I ever wrote . . . was one in which a girl said "uh-huh" three times with three different intonations. . . . The hell of good film writing is that the most important part is what is left out. It's left out because the camera and the actors can do it better and quicker, above all quicker, but it had to be there in the beginning. . . .

*Double Indemnity* in its time was an outrageous picture. For the first time a sympathetic man, played by one of those gum-chewing, wisecracking "good guy" actors, portrayed a character who killed for lust and money. The film also broke new ground in its technique of revealing the killer in the opening scene, and telling the story in voice-over flashbacks. *Double Indemnity* has been copied in hundreds of suspense films and television plays.

Chandler and Wilder were nominated for Best Screenplay in the annual Oscar sweepstakes and the picture was nominated for Best Picture. It is customary in Hollywood that during the weeks before the nominations and the final balloting, the studios as well as individual stars stage campaigns for votes. The Hollywood trade papers are thick with advertisements proclaiming the grandeur of the nominees. David O. Selznick's *Since You Went Away* was a contender. He paid for a lavishly designed series of expensive but dignified blurbs in which political and cultural leaders stated they had never seen a movie which so stirred their hearts as *Since You Went Away*. Each leader was identified as "distinguished composer" or "distinguished legislator."

Wilder took out his largest needle, filled it with pure rattlesnake venom, and then gave Selznick a shot in the form of the following advertisement, which appeared in the trades:

THIS IS WHAT A DISTINGUISHED RESTAURATEUR THINKS
Dear Mr. Billy Wilder:

I certainly do appreciate the opportunity you gave me to see your picture *Double Indemnity*. It held my attention, it held my wife's attention, it held my sister-in-law's attention. It certainly was a good picture, one of the best pictures we have seen in several days.

> Sincerely,
> George Oblath [signed]

OBLATHS: The Best Foods for Less Money and Utmost Effort for Service

Selznick was furious at the gag. Selznick had his attorney write formal letters on his behalf to the *Reporter* and *Daily Variety*. He stated that if any more of Mr. Wilder's satires were printed he would take out all Selznick advertising.

Wilder went to Grauman's Chinese on Oscar night expecting to win, though he knew that his own studio had been concentrating on its other hit of the year, Leo McCarey's *Going My Way*. Employees of a studio were expected to vote for that studio's favorite. Well, as the winners were announced, it became evident that it was a *Going My Way* sweep. Leo McCarey, writer-director of it, was looking proud. He beamed as his picture won for special effects, scoring, best original song, best this, and best that. When McCarey was named as Best Director, it was more than Wilder could stand. As McCarey strode down to get his statuette, Wilder, sitting on the aisle, stuck out his foot and tripped up his colleague, who fell flat on his face.

This cheered up Billy Wilder enormously. *The bastard deserved it,* he thought. *He only won it because he had Paramount in his corner.* He was in a black mood when he and Judith went out to wait for their limousine. He finally yelled, so loudly that everybody could hear him, "What the hell does the Academy Award mean, for God's sake? After all—Luise Rainer won it two times. Luise Rainer!"

The *enfant terrible* was becoming the *moyen-âge terrible*.

# 12

# THE LOST MOVIE

Experiencing Raymond Chandler was a wracking experience for Billy Wilder. Beneath his cynical mask, Wilder was a guy who responded to human suffering. He could not make sense of Chandler. He did not know the nature of the alcoholic's madness. I don't think he has ever fully grasped this peculiar disease—as was illustrated in his reaction to my being unable to drink. Perhaps he has resisted knowing. Perhaps he is afraid to know how close to the edge of insanity persons get, because he is so close to that cliff himself. To be in close contact with a man of talent and watch him disintegrating was a sad experience for Wilder. Sometimes Chandler had nice days when he smiled and seemed at peace and worked hard. Chandler, as had always been his wont, would even journey outside and do field work. Because Stanwyck and MacMurray have secret meetings in a supermarket, Chandler (with his writing board and note paper) went to Jerry's Market on Melrose and prowled around studying the scene. He made verbal sketches of Glendale and the Los Feliz area and a Franklin Avenue bachelor flat and the Pasadena railroad station. He drenched himself in the ambiance which enveloped the persons of the movie. He brought it all back to Wilder, and Chandler's acute responsiveness to Los Angeles seeped into the movie. It was not even directly on the paper—which was the stunning fact of it. It was just in Chandler's head—in the back of his imagination—and it seeped into the film, though he and Wilder squabbled incessantly over words and lines and action. Wilder kept him on a tight rein. He made him rewrite and throw away and polish. Look, Wilder was crazy in his own way. A perfectionist is also a driven soul. But he was not a lost one. Chandler was a lost soul. So one day he was living in reality and the next he would fall into a spell of morbid gloom and become incomprehensible to Wilder—frightening.

Wilder wanted to know why. He did not consciously seek the answer. He perhaps was not aware how deeply he had been disturbed by his proximity to this poor, suffering, hostile, crazy bastard.

And that was why, I believe, Billy Wilder made *The Lost Weekend*—to explain Raymond Chandler to himself. Though it was a 1944 best-seller, Charles Jackson's novel had been spurned by every star and studio. It was a "downbeat" story. You did not make a heart-wrenching story about a drunk. That was not entertainment, fellers. Drunks were funny characters, you know. Who wants to pay money to see a guy having the DTs in the Bellevue alcoholic ward?

En route to New York for a holiday, Wilder, during the five hour respite between trains in Chicago, bought four novels to read. *The Lost Weekend* was one of them. He was enthralled by it. He had to make it into a movie. He was up all night and read it twice and started making notes. It was 9 A.M. when they pulled into Grand Central Station. That meant 6 A.M. in Los Angeles. Billy telephoned his old collaborator. He asked Charlie, who was only partly awake, if he wanted to forgive and forget and make another picture together? It was the call Brackett had been waiting for and he said hell, yes, let's go, what did he have in mind? Wilder told him. He struck a sympathetic chord, for reasons which I will divulge later. Brackett asked Bill Dozier to buy the novel for them. Now I have to explain the Paramount hierarchy at that period. At the summit, from the New York Paramount building on Broadway and Forty-third Street, reigned the king—Barney Balaban, a former theatre owner from Chicago and one of those profit-oriented but movie-loving scoundrels who made Hollywood the greatest production center the art has ever known. Under Balaban, was Y. Frank Freeman, titular head of West Coast production, a man of high morals and low intelligence. Under Freeman was the former songwriter, Buddy De Sylva, who was the actual production executive, comparable to Zanuck at Twentieth. Henry Ginsberg and Don Hartman were also powerful executives of the second level. Freeman, a Georgia movie exhibitor, knew theatres and thought he knew moviegoers. He knew very little about how to make pictures and what pictures to make. He was a Baptist. He drank only Coca-Cola. He was an original investor in Coca-Cola. He had cases of it stacked in his office. He also had purebred Boxer dogs in the office. He had a corral outside his office bungalow in which were other Boxers. Much of Chandler's penulti-mate novel, *The Little Sister,* is set on the Paramount lot. In chapter nineteen, there is an accurate description of the elegant goldfish pool and plaza of plants and grass and stone benches which have now been paved over. There is an amusing profile of a "Jules Oppen-heimer," (who is really Y. Frank Freeman) and his Boxers and their pissing patterns.

Freeman was the butt of studio remarks. Crosby and Hope passed him one morning as he was walking his Boxers.

"I wish I had the answer," Hope said.

"To what?" Bing asked.

"Y. Frank Freeman," Hope replied.

When he screened *Going My Way,* Freeman predicted, "Nobody will go see this picture, except Catholics in church basements." Freeman did not like Catholics, Jews, and Negroes. He was not too crazy about Protestants, either, unless they were white Baptists who loved purebred canines.

Freeman had already read a précis of *Lost Weekend.* He said it was garbage. Freeman, however, was out of town, and during his absence De Sylva bought the book. He told Dozier who told me that he bought it because Brackett and Wilder wanted to make it and that was enough for him. He was most anxious to get these two crafts-men into double harness again.

There was a terrible conference when Freeman returned. Wilder and Brackett were present and Freeman raked everybody over the coals. Dozier was there. De Sylva. Ginsberg. They all listened in stony silence. Wilder, who usually spoke up for the team, gave one of his animated monologues about how they were going to make a beautiful picture about love. He was smart enough to make it sound practically like a Janet Gaynor-Charles Farrell four-handkerchief movie. He had them crying as he told of this great love and he im-provised one of his classic "meet cutes"—or "meet coats." You know, that mix-up over coats at the Metropolitan Ope-ra. . . . Yeah, he had them all in the palm of his hand—except Freeman.

Freeman stated that the studio would make this picture only

"over my dead body," and Wilder was ready to accommodate him except that these three Boxers were at point, growling, baring their teeth at him. These dogs hated Billy Wilder. He knew that if they ever got loose they would tear him to pieces. Back in New York, almost all the brass voted against making it, including Russel Holman, who was a power. However, there was only one vote which counted—Balaban's. Balaban said, "Make it." I don't know why. Nobody knows why. Maybe there had been somebody once whom he had loved and who had been destroyed by booze.

When Charlie and Billy began writing, they wrote out of personal experience. It was a story which had a strong personal meaning for them. Neither was a real drinker. Billy liked a martini before dinner and wine during. But, as he confided in me, his body is chemically unable to handle a quantity of alcohol. If he drinks too much, he gets sick and vomits. "I don't know why, but I never tell myself one more drink will make me feel better than I feel after two drinks," he says. As for Brackett, he hardly drank; a glass of sherry was about the limit. But he was one of those who, all their lives, are involved with alcoholics, who become the friends and husbands and allies of alcoholics, the rescuers of them. The Victorian façade of Elizabeth and Charles Brackett's mansion concealed a Victorian tragedy. Mrs. Brackett had lost control of her drinking during the 1930s. She became more and more of a recluse. They rarely went out together because she got plastered. Charlie was a gregarious person. He either went out alone—as when I first met him at the Ambassador Hotel—or he went in the company of certain delicate elderly ladies, such as the fan magazine writer, Ruth Waterbury, or the screenwriter, Dodie Smith. They were wispy, genteel ladies. No breath of sexual scandal was here. The Brackett Sunday afternoons on Bellagio Road were still taking place, but Mrs. Brackett would make only a brief appearance, and vanish. They had tried all the methods—psychiatry, sanitariums, drying-out hospitals. Everything failed.

One of their daughters had also become an alcoholic. She was married to James Larmore, another alcoholic. Mrs. Larmore perished after falling down a flight of stairs drunk. Her husband died in a fire in the Midwest. He also was passed out.

Larmore was a person of charm and talent when he was sober. He became a monster when he drank. Charlie had made him a production assistant. This became one of the sore points between Charlie and Billy. Billy did not want Larmore around him. He liked to play bridge with him and he liked his company—but as soon as Larmore was intoxicated he became truculent. Larmore was an actor. Wilder would not cast him in any picture he directed. Brackett pointed out that Billy put girl friends into their pictures, so why shouldn't Larmore have a chance? Billy stopped going to the Bracketts on Sundays because he did not want to run into Larmore. He never invited the Bracketts over to visit the Wilders because he knew the Larmores would be along. Charlie had been a friend of many alcoholic writers. He was the friend who was there to nurse them through hangovers or rescue them at the end of a spree. He had nursed Scott Fitzgerald and Robert Benchley through many drunken episodes. He had seen Dorothy Parker become a lost soul because she couldn't stop drinking. At Paramount, and later at Twentieth Century-Fox, Charlie always tried to find writing jobs for Parker. She had become a lush—but there was in Charlie some compassion for the lost souls of the world that compelled him to succor them. It was Charlie Brackett, as Lillian Hellman tells us in her memoirs, who nursed Dashiell Hammett through many of· his drunks in Hollywood. And, in 1937, it was Brackett who phoned Hellman in New York and told her how sick Hammett was and put him on a plane to her.

Brackett and Wilder wrote this film with their blood. They completed a rough draft in two months, instead of the usual four to six months to do an incomplete draft. In those days—and until very recently—Wilder never worked from a finished script. He usually started with 60 to 80 pages of a 140-page script and he and Brackett would write while filming got under way. But this one they *had* to write. It is evident to me that Brackett was writing himself in the characters of Don Birnam's brother and Jane Wyman, and that Wilder was writing Wilder in the opposing constellation of sardonic characters—Howard da Silva's bartender, Doris Dowling's hooker, Frank Faylen's homosexual Bellevue Hospital nurse.

Rarely has a Hollywood screenplay told its story with so few words and in such powerfully focused images—from the opening helicopter shots of Manhattan as we zoom in to a whiskey bottle dangling by a string from an open window on a hot summer night, while Milos Rosza's eerie theme plays. Wilder took us on a realistic tour of hell—Third Avenue and Bellevue Hospital, Fifty-second Street jazz joints, neighborhood bars—getting the same feeling for New York streets he had for Berlin in his UFA films.

Who can forget the concentric circles, growing in number, as Don Birnam sets down one glass after another, making wet rings on the bar? He doesn't let Da Silva wipe it up. "Let me have my vicious circle," he says. And he tries to explain his compulsion. When he drinks,

"I'm Horowitz playing the Emperor Concerto, John Barrymore before the movies got him by the throat, and Jesse James and his brothers, all three of them, and William Shakespeare . . . And out there it is not Third Avenue, it is the Nile, man, the Nile, and down comes the barge of Cleopatra . . ."

Until he is beyond rhetoric and must drink to survive. The bottle concealed in the chandelier. He must drink to survive. The great pawning of the typewriter on Yom Kippur, and seeing the wooden Indian, this reminding him of Doris Dowling's flat upstairs. A memory of Wilder's childhood, of his mother's tales of Manhattan, had come back to him to be used. It was the kind of writing with images that Chandler had said screenwriting was. The drunken fall down the stairs, the way Brackett's daughter had fallen. The terrible nightmare scenes at Bellevue's alcoholic ward, which Wilder had filmed right there in Bellevue, after showing the superintendant a bogus script. And then that most unbearable and poignant sequence after the escape from Bellevue and the return to the flat and the DTs—the bat hurtling itself at the gibbering mouse.

As in the case of *Double Indemnity,* the screenplay was not a faithful rendering of the original novel by Charles Jackson. Yet nobody complained. Everybody was sure it was the same. And you imagined that every scene in the film had been derived from the novel. You were sure you had read a scene when you saw it in the movie. This was a trick the mind always played when you liked the novel and liked the movie. But a comparative study, for which I have no space here, would show that *The Lost Weekend* on film was seventy-five percent different from the book in characterization and incident.

Billy wanted José Ferrer to play Birnam. Buddy de Sylva demurred. He argued that an attractive-looking hero would make the audience feel that if he were not an alcoholic he would be a worthwhile human being.

Milland was as loath to play a drunk as MacMurray had been to play a murderer. Milland was not concerned so much about his image. He was concerned about his own technical ability to play the role. He also lacked confidence in Wilder as a dramatic director. He still thought of him as a high-comedy director.

De Sylva ordered him to play Don Birnam. Milland went into it with a deep sense of "my own inadequacy" and being sure that Wilder would "foul it up" and no audience would ever "buy" such a story of human degradation.

As I have said, *The Lost Weekend,* photographically, was a symphony of a city, and most of it was shot on location in New York, where Wilder and the company went in November 1944. Wilder was learning to exercise authority. He had to position his cadre of electricians and sound men and camera operators strategically on the streets. He had to set up police blockades to protect the actors from the crowds. He was at the mercy of the elements. He dreaded filming on location because you could not control sound—there was the droning of planes overhead and passing buses and honking automobiles. You could not control light. You could not control people. A director had to *control.*

Wilder says: "To be a good director, one has to know the script, and then, to be like a general under fire. The screenplay is the battle plan. The filming is when the bullets are flying.

"To know that a day of shooting costs the studio $30,000—this is unsettling to the nerves. If you think about it. So I don't think about it."

They shot exteriors on 55th Street, brownstone houses, and at P. J. Clarke's saloon on Second Avenue, and on various streets, and in Bellevue Hospital—lights and shadows—cinematographer Johnny Seitz employing his expressionistic values as in the best German films of the 1920s. Much of the filming was done by day, using available light and the fastest film available at that time; this enhanced the realistic effect of many scenes. The great sequence of Milland, sick and unshaven, dragging his typewriter up Third Avenue from 55th Street to 110th Street *was filmed in a single day with the actor actually walking all that time,* while a camera, concealed in a bakery truck, followed him. It was shot on Sunday when the pawnshops are closed. New York pedestrians did not know shooting was going on. It was a clear, cold morning with good light. Milland was unrecognizable, and, as they moved uptown, block by block, nobody was aware a film was being made. Somewhere in the eighties, however, as Milland was rattling the gates of a pawnshop, a girl came over—

ruining the take—and said, "Mr. Milland, may I have your autograph?"

Milland turned around and shrugged toward Wilder who was following him at a distance.

"I'm not Mr. Milland," he said, for the hell of it. "I'm just a guy who needs a drink bad and trying to pawn my typewriter."

"Who do you think you're kiddin', wise guy?" the girl said, breathing heavily. "I been a fan of yours from way back. Why'n't you come over to my place—I got a quart of Seagram's Seven—which is looking for a guy like you? The bars don't open till one."

Ray Milland suddenly realized that she thought he was *really* a drunk.

Wilder interrupted this touching pickup. He told the girl that they were making a picture. She didn't believe him. He told her to go away. She would not. He took her over to the truck and showed her the hidden camera. She was skeptical. She was a New Yorker. He finally placated her by taking her name and address and promising to give her a screen test.

When a heavy snowfall ruined the illusion of a Manhattan summer, they returned to Paramount and finished the picture on the lot. Wilder had a faithful replica of P.J.'s built. Nat's Bar is really P. J. Clarke's. Robert Benchley, between takes on another Paramount film, was a regular visitor on the set. He liked to sit at the bar and look in the smudged back-bar mirror. P.J.'s was his favorite watering hole.

One day he told Billy that the setting lacked only one detail. There was always a sleepy black cat at P.J.'s. Where was the cat?

Shooting was completed in December 1944. Rosza scored it. Wilder and Doane Harrison made the final cut. Billy and Charlie Brackett saw it one evening. They believed they had done their best work so far. They felt good.

Then disaster.

Paramount sneak-previewed *The Lost Weekend* in Santa Barbara in a thousand seat theater. The audience reacted with laughter and giggling. They started walking out. At the end, only a handful remained. The preview cards were unanimously of the opinion that the movie was putrid, disgusting, boring.

Wilder was driven back to Hollywood in a studio limousine. Henry Ginsberg sat beside him. They rode in silence.

Finally, Ginsberg patted him on the shoulder. He comforted him:

"They don't all come off, Billy. Maybe the studio will never release it."

Y. Frank Freeman said the film should not be released. It had cost $1,100,000. Better not to spend another $2,000,000 in publicity, promotion and advertising. Buddy de Sylva knew he had made a mistake in backing Wilder. Ginsberg had to agree. Dozier had to agree. Dozier loved the picture but he saw that audiences hated it. In New York, Russell Holman, a Paramount vice-president, took a strong stand against the picture. It was a sure loser. He said it should be put on the shelf—indefinitely.

Wilder was crushed. He went into a state of gloom so profound that nothing could relieve it—not his bridge games nor his tennis nor his amorous amusements. Had his judgment been wrong from the start? He now began hearing rumors—which were accurate—that the distillery industry had secretly raised a fund of several million dollars. Through syndicate overlord Frank Costello, who had interests as a syndicate representative in the fields of Canadian, Scottish, and American distilleries as well as sundry liquor distributorships and restaurants, it was decided to make an under-the-table deal with Paramount. A dummy corporation would be set up to buy the negative and all prints of *Lost Weekend* from Paramount for $5,000,000. The corporation would ostensibly buy the film for distribution overseas. What the liquor interests feared was a resurgence of propaganda against alcohol. Prohibition had been repealed only twelve years previously.

Deeply humiliated by the affair, Wilder could only think of getting away from it all.

# 13

# EUROPE LOST,
# THE MOVIE FOUND

Elmer Davis, OWI chief, had learned about Billy Wilder's Teutonic background from a *Life* magazine article in 1944. He invited Wilder to join the Psychological Warfare Division of the U.S. Army. He would go to Germany and assist in the postwar reconstruction of the German film industry. He would screen out undesirable Nazi types. He would perhaps be able to use his experience in setting the German theater back on its feet. Wilder seized the opportunity to escape from Hollywood. It had suddenly become a bleak city to him. What if Chandler had been right in that article he wrote? What if one were at the mercy of fools and dollar-crazy idiots like Freeman?

In New York, he was interviewed by an OWI accountant who was preparing the papers for his service salary—$6,500 a year. He was asked what his former salary had been.

"Twenty-five hundred—" he started to say and was interrupted by an indignant bureaucrat who was incensed that the U.S. should pay a man thrice his civilian salary.

"It was twenty-five hundred a week," he shouted.

He was in New York on VE Day, May 8, 1945. On May 9, he took the Clipper to Europe, making stops along the way at New Brunswick, Newfoundland, and Ireland. Though he was in a black despair, though he despised Hollywood and was through with motion pictures, he was already seeing a movie as he traversed the Atlantic Ocean, a flight across the Atlantic, Lindbergh's first flight in 1927, for Lindbergh had been one of Billy's heroes at that time and how sad it was that Lindy took a medal from Goering and been an isolationist in 1939 and 1940 when Britain fought the war alone. He could not understand certain men, and Lindbergh disturbed him as Chandler disturbed him. It was the unreason of it that upset him, the madness of it, some hidden psychological drive certain men had which made no sense in their own terms. Wilder was making a movie in his head as he crossed the ocean. He knew this was a movie he would never make for a studio anyway. He could not stop his creative machinery from functioning. He was enslaved by his art—just as he was also a master of it. One sometimes felt as if one were moved by powerful invisible forces.

I forgot to tell you that Wilder never starts a new screenplay without typing two words on the first page: *Cum Deo* ("With God"). He has a pantheistic feeling about the universe. There is a power higher than human beings . . .

He loved Ireland. He wrote to a friend that it was a feast for the eyes and the soul. He forgave James Joyce and Eamonn de Valera. He even, he swore, forgave Leo McCarey.

There were days in London in which he walked the bombed-out streets and marveled at the courage and moral power of the English. "Do you know," he wrote, "that no censor would ever allow a letter to leave England in which a British subject asked a friend in the U.S. for a bar of chocolate or condensed milk or a pair of stockings? They are a proud people and, what is more important, a sound people."

In London he was made a colonel and given a uniform. At a party, a British officer asked him what year he had been graduated from West Point.

Wilder said, "Not West Point. Oblath's Military Academy. Class of thirty-six."

In Paris, he encountered a GI in a bar, who told him, "They got the weirdest gadgets in these French toilets. You piss into it, you push a button, and it pisses right back at you!"

He had loved Paris above all cities and he drank it in from one end of the Champs Elysées to the other and many of the side streets, remembering favorite brothels and favorite *putains*. The city was not changed. The people had changed. He did not like the changes. The

Frenchmen had become corrupted during the years of the occupation. He wrote letters home in which it was clear that his experience stunned him. He sat on the *terrasse* at Fouquet's and had a Pernod and water and watched the women strolling and the women riding bicycles and "a great feeling of happiness came over me that day"—but it was transitory. He was plunged into bitterness as he saw a corrupt, cynical people, "a nation of black marketeers." And what was always disturbing to Wilder when he confronted human depravity was that he felt within himself a secret sharing of the worst in human nature. He knew we were all more human than otherwise, and yet some of us could act with decency when we were tested. The British had behaved honorably. Why was this so?

In Germany, he first made a tour from Bremen and Hamburg in the north as far south as Salzburg.

The director of the famous Passion Play at Oberammergau came to see him about reopening the production. Anton Lang, who had played Christ before the war, had become a member of the SS Elite Corps during the war. The director asked permission for Lang to resume his former role.

"Yes—on one condition," Billy said.

"And what is that?"

"That in the crucifixion scene, you will use real nails."

Wilder was impressed by the energy and hope of the population. He wrote about the bombed out cities: " . . . the destruction is unbelievable . . . Total obliteration . . . block after block after block is rubble—burned out, pulverized! The amazing thing is the German neatness, how the rubble has been built up on both sides of the hastily repaired streets, like snow . . . way up some fifteen or twenty feet . . . so that the traffic moves . . . the people are still living in this rubble . . . in their cellars, in ruins with just two walls standing, in sewers . . . "

And he started writing another movie in his mind.

By plane and jeep, Wilder covered 3,000 miles of occupied Germany and attempted to do his best to help those who were relatively untarnished to begin a new life. He also would remark on the sensual joys. In Heidelberg, he tasted a 1937 Rhine which, he observed, was "far superior to the 1921."

As an expert on the masquerader, Billy, while in Stuttgart, espied a nun walking strangely. She had a face like Hitler. He suddenly decided she was Hitler in disguise. He could visualize a headline: BIL-

LY WILDER CAPTURES ADOLF HITLER. But what if it were an authentic nun? He saw another headline: BILLY WILDER, AMERICAN SEX PERVERT, MOLESTS NUN.

He let the nun go her peaceful way.

In Berlin, he and his driver, a husky redheaded corporal from Georgia, drove out to the Jewish cemetery in Weissensee. He was looking for his father's grave. His mother and grandmother, he had learned through the Red Cross, had perished in Auschwitz. Little remained of the old cemetery. The Russians and Nazis had fought a tank battle here. Headstones were split. No flowers grew and no grass. Only two Jews remained: an Orthodox rabbi and a gravedigger. The gravedigger, a scarecrow hunchback, looked like a character out of an old German expressionist film. He was missing one leg. The rabbi, a tall person, was like a skeleton. His caftan hung loose on him. He talked half-crazily and did not finish sentences. He had survived the Hitler years, somehow, and the war, and the bombardments, and he told how he and his wife had welcomed the invading Soviet soldiers and how they had gang-raped his wife before his eyes.

"And it was in these circumstances we located my father's grave," Wilder remembers. "I stood there numb and I heard somebody crying. I turned around and I saw my driver, a tough guy, and he was sobbing. He couldn't stop himself."

In Berlin, a meeting had been arranged with Colonel Wilder's equivalent in the Soviet army. The occupying armies had decided to coordinate their plans for rehabilitating the German film industry. The meeting was arranged in East Berlin. Colonel Wilder was accompanied by an American lieutenant who spoke Russian. Colonel Wilder met two Russian colonels. One of them was a fierce looking gentleman with a Van Dyke beard and spectacles, who resembled Trotsky. The other, equally formidable, was cradling a submachine gun in his arms. He was cross-eyed. "He was able to look out of the window and at me at the same time," Wilder recalls. "At first, we made polite conversation about the weather and then they asked the American lieutenant, in Russian, what were my qualifications. He told them that I was a writer and director of Hollywood films. Suddenly, one colonel, the Trotsky type, stood up and left. I was fully aware that he now had gone away to investigate my dossier. Was I an enemy of the Soviet Union? Or was I a friend? Suddenly I had a horrible thought. They are going to see my name on the credits of *Ninotchka*. They are going to decide I am a bad person. You know how your mind can, at certain moments, become insane, how it exaggerates, so I started thinking they are going to shoot me for that Garbo picture, and I'll never go home again.

"Then, the colonel with the beard came back. Had a big smile on his face. He whispered something to the other one and they both smiled and put out their arms to me and yelled, '*Meeses Meenevah. . . Bravo . . . Bravo . . . Tovarich Wyler!*"

Colonel Wilder, after emitting a long sigh, smiled wanly. He thanked them and said it had indeed been an honor to direct Greer Garson in *Mrs. Miniver*. Wilder knew what had happened.

They had examined, and approved, William Wyler's credits. Colonel Wilder did not disillusion them. Let them think he was the director of *Dodsworth, Dead End* and *The Little Foxes*.

Billy returned to New York in September, 1945, his mission accomplished. He was met by several representatives of the Paramount publicity and advertising department. There was a sudden reversal. President Barney Balaban had decided to release *The Lost Weekend*.

"I don't make pictures to throw in the toilet," he said.

They had been screening it for the press in New York and the reactions were marvelous. They were going to release it in November! Wilder happily gave a series of interviews. To Tom Pryor of the *New York Times*, he observed that Ray Milland drank a large amount of whiskey during the picture.

"If *To Have and Have Not* has established Lauren Bacall as The Look," he said dryly, quoting Warner Bros. current publicity campaign slogan on Ms. Bacall, "then *The Lost Weekend* should certainly bring Mr. Milland reknown as The Kidney."

Billy Wilder was back in form. Billy Wilder was happy again. Billy Wilder was sarcastic again. Billy Wilder was making unconventional statements to the press.

The picture opened nationwide on November 16, and the critical and public reception was good. The film, the director, the stars were all nominated for Oscars. David O. Selznick's *Spellbound*, directed by Hitchcock, was also in the running. During its run, Selznick featured an advertising campaign which showed Gregory Peck fervantly embracing Ingrid Bergman, while holding an open straight-edged razor behind her back. A most macabre, but effective, layout.

And Warner Bros. featured a slogan in its advertising which stated that Warner pictures combined "Good Citizenship with Fine Motion Picture Making."

Billy thought of an ingenious method of needling Selznick and Jack Warner with one blow. He concocted an ad which showed Wilder and Brackett embracing, while holding knives behind each other's backs. It ran as a double-truck in all trades. The slogan which they used was: "Combining Good Citizenship With Good Cutlery."

On Oscar Night, finally, Billy won his first Academy Award—as cowriter of *The Lost Weekend.* And his second as director of it. And, most unexpectedly of all, the film was voted the best film of the year. Ray Milland won his first Oscar as best actor of the year.

Wilder went to Romanoff's for a glorious celebration and would have gotten as drunk as Don Birnam if he were able to get drunk.

The next morning when he drove his Buick on the lot he saw that from every window of every office of the Writers' Building there was suspended a bottle of whiskey!

On that day, one could say of Billy Wilder, paraphrasing Floria Tosca, "Before him all Hollywood trembled."

# 14

# BILLY'S DAUGHTER

Victoria Settember, Billy's only child, lives in Penn Grove, near Santa Rosa, California, an agricultural community 100 miles north of San Francisco. She and Tony Settember, her second husband, reside in a large ranch house on a country road. The walls are decorated with pictures, many of them painted by her mother: still lifes in bold yellows, greens and reds. Vicki and Tony work for a manufacturer of transmissions. She is car-crazy, like her daddy. Tony, her second husband, is a sports car enthusiast. Tony was a race-car driver until he became sales manager for this transmission company. Tony Settember used to race his own Formula I car. He has raced at Le Mans. He once won the Grand Prix in the Naples road-race. A 1956 classic Mercedes 300 SL sits in their driveway. They will take it to Stuttgart someday and have it overhauled at the Mercedes-Benz plant there. They also had a Porsche 911 which they recently traded for a monoplane. Papa was upset that she and Tony were exchanging the Porsche for a plane. He sought to change her mind. She was stubborn. He said, "At least, do not all fly at once. Don't you dare all go up together." Her family includes a daughter, Julie, by her first marriage to Fiorenzo Gordine, a San Francisco high school teacher.

When Vicki was graduated from Tamalpais High School at sixteen, her daddy gave her a maroon MGA.

Vicki remembers: "Formerly I had been a wallflower, but now I turned into the most popular girl in school, because I had the neatest car. I loved that little MGA. I had it for many years. Even when I outgrew it, I could not bear to sell it. How did I know it would get the proper care? I finally gave it to a friend who would love and cherish it. Later I owned a Corvette, a Peugeot, a Porsche, and this beautiful Mercedes. I can't ever think of a time when I wasn't in love with automobiles. I loved driving very fast with Daddy up the coast highway. I remember the Cadillacs when I was little, playing with the power windows. He didn't mind my playing with the power windows. I remember when Daddy was in his Jaguar XKE period. Now like Tony and me, he has a Mercedes."

She is not called Victoria or Vicki by her husband and their friends. She is called Billi. Her license plate is BILLI.

She adores her father. She always has hungered for signs of his love. She is always pleased when she is told she has a sardonic wit like her father's.

She says: "My daddy is a hard person to get to know. I worship him but I cannot seem to get close to him. He is kind and generous, but he can't say 'I love you.' He never has to me, not once. It embarrasses him. He just *loathes* Christmases and holidays and birthdays and Thanksgivings. You know, he'll send Tony and me and Julie some things at Christmas and the card will say, 'Wishing you Merry Christmas and all that stuff.' He's just, like, afraid you'll think he's sentimental. I don't know why. Do you? He just doesn't touch you. He doesn't hug and kiss you. He isn't a physically expressive man. I don't know why this is, but that doesn't mean he doesn't have deep feelings, you know."

Her favorite Billy Wilder films are *Sunset Boulevard, Love in the Afternoon,* and *Sabrina.* She could identify with Audrey Hepburn in the latter two pictures. And Maurice Chevalier, the hard-boiled private detective guarding the virtue of his daughter from the predatory amorist, Gary Cooper, was a reflection of her father, as she was a reflection of Audrey Hepburn. In *Sabrina,* too, there is an intense father-daughter relationship.

Billy was able to express in his films the emotions he felt for his child. Both the fathers in these films are men of dry wit, somewhat formal with their daughters, only able to express feelings in terms of

their professions. John Williams, who played the father in *Sabrina,*
is the chauffeur of a wealthy family. He is a man who knows automobiles, loves them, repairs them with serene competence, as Maurice Chevalier performs his duties as a detective, as Billy Wilder at-
tends to making pictures.

"But why *Sunset Boulevard?*" I asked Vicki. She said that when
Norma Desmond asks Joe Gillis when he was born he says December 21. "That is my birth date," Vicki said. "I felt as if Daddy was
sending me a personal message."

He would never give her a copy of his screenplays, not even *Sabrina* or *Love in the Afternoon.*

"Since I have grown up," she said, "I have wanted copies of all
my father's scripts. He has always refused to give me any of them.
He would say, 'Movies are to be seen and not read.' He always says
that. To this day, I haven't got a single solitary script which he *gave*
me." Then she grinned. Her beautiful sharp black eyes gleamed
mischievously. "I do have *one.* He didn't *give* it to me. I was in his
office once and I stole a copy of *Seven Year Itch.* I do have his copy
of Claude Anet's novel, *Ariane,* which is the basis of *Love in the Afternoon.* Stole that too."

Vicki came to know her father most intimately after he and her
mother broke up. She said her mother is a complex and interesting
woman, with a penetrating mind and a gift for expressing beauty.
She said she regretted that her mother would not speak to me. She
said I had to understand that her mother had made a new life for herself and that she wanted to put behind her the ten years she had been
married to her father. I said, yes, I could understand that, yes, I was
sorry about it, but I could understand it.

When Billy returned from his tour of duty with the Psychological
Warfare Division in the fall of 1945, he and Judith decided to go
their separate ways. He had, he says, never been ready for marriage. Judith Wilder had undergone an interesting metamorphosis,
rather like a Ninotchka in reverse. When Judith and Billy fell in
love, she was a reactionary and he was a radical. Gradually, she became class-conscious; from liberalism she progressed to radicalism.
She was surfeited with wealth and material possessions, with all the
objects and artifacts which she once prized. Billy Wilder was now
an ardent collector. She now believed that possessions owned the
owner. Had the marriage been good, she would have endured the
pain of living in Beverly Hills and in rooms of great beauty, for she

loved the shape of things and she loved colors. But they had grown apart from each other. By now—after 1942—she knew that Billy was seriously involved with another woman. When she found out it was Doris Dowling, she knew it was the end. Doris Dowling expected to marry Billy.

Judith divorced Billy in 1947. For a time she remained in the house on Beverly Drive. Billy moved in with Ernst Lubitsch. Judith did not stay there long. Her only close friend in their old social circles was "Chick" Hartman. She felt increasingly estranged from the actions and passions which interested the people in the movie industry. She took Vicki to Brooklyn Heights in New York. They lived on Remsen Street. They moved in a circle of bohemian radicals, of painters and sculptors, of poets and novelists. Later, they returned to Los Angeles and lived in Laurel Canyon, which was then an unfashionable, bohemian area in the Hollywood Hills. Then Judith and Vicki moved to Mill Valley, where Vicki went to high school and later to San Francisco State College. She majored in English and anthropology.

Now Mrs. Badner, Judith lives with her third husband, a cabinetmaker, in a simple house on Stinson Beach. She paints seascapes. She leads a simple life, uncluttered by wealth and bourgeois values. So Vicki grew up in two worlds. She took pleasure in the sensations of both. Her own instincts drew her to the simpler life, but she wanted to please her father. He was the fundamental mystery of her life.

When she was young, she remembers him coming to New York and taking her for a month in the summer. He would take her to the shows. They would dine in elegant restaurants. He educated her in *haute cuisine.* She recalls seeing *Finian's Rainbow, Oklahoma!, Brigadoon, Kiss Me Kate.* Then, after a few days of the Manhattan whirl, they boarded the Twentieth Century to Chicago and then the Super Chief to Los Angeles. She had him all to herself for three days and four nights. It was wonderful. On the trips cross-country she wanted the upper berth. They had a bedroom-sized compartment. She loved every moment of the ride. He gave her all his attention. He told her amusing stories. He bought her presents. Once, in Chicago, she saw a pink alarm clock with animals instead of numbers. She wanted it. He bought it for her. The Albuquerque stop was exciting; he bought her kachina dolls at the Fred Harvey shop there.

She was rather a gamin, a tomboy, during her childhood. She did not like to play with dolls, dollhouses, and doll furniture. This puzzled her father. When he gave her dolls, she cut them open to see what made them work. She had to see what was *inside* them. She loved the "wrong" kind of toys; he was an indulgent father and bought her Tinkertoys, erector sets, and, oh yes, the most wonderful childhood present of all, a fantastic set of Lionel electric trains, with switches, signals, watertowers, and coal dumpers. She loved machines. He gave her her first television set and her first encyclopedia. She seems to remember each present he gave her.

She also liked animals, especially horses, as her mother did. Billy did not like horses, but when she was visiting him in Beverly Hills during the summer months, he took her to horse shows, rodeos, and riding academies, patiently waiting while she rode a horse for an hour.

He did not like animals. She liked cats and dogs. Billy could not stand cats but he could abide dogs. When he remarried, she and Audrey became friends. Audrey loved her. Vicki was putting on too much weight. It is hard to believe that she weighed 200 pounds during her adolescence. She is slender now. Audrey would tell her secrets of complexion care, makeup and clothes styling. Her mother by now no longer put on makeup, not even lipstick. Audrey showed her the right shade of face powder for her skin and how to put on mascara and eye shadow. Audrey went shopping with her and chose her lovely skirts and blouses. Vicki adores Audrey. She remembers one trip west when her hair was made up in French braids. These had to be undone at bedtime. Daddy patiently attempted to unravel them as the train roared towards the Midwest. In the morning, try as he might, he could not re-braid her plaits. She "looked a god-awful mess" when Audrey met them at the Union Station in L.A.

Audrey liked pets. The Wilders now had a Yorkshire terrier which Billy barely tolerated. He was a stupid animal and cowardly, Vicki says, and this did not endear him to Billy, though it made Audrey and Vicki want to cuddle him all the more. Once, for Christmas, Vicki gave Billy a toy lion which, when wound up, shook its tail and roared. This terrified the Yorkie and he ran and hid and trembled. He finally died. The next dog was Michelle, a French poodle, who was smart, but Billy could not lose his heart to Michelle either. Once, somebody gave Vicki a piglet. A live baby pig. Michelle disliked this little pig. When nobody was watching, she would bark the piglet out into the street and lead it down Beverly Drive, crossing Santa Monica Boulevard, until she came to the shopping streets.

Here, Michelle would scamper away, leaving the piglet oinking. The police would round up the piglet. Then they called Billy at the studio and told him to come and get his lost pig. This incensed Billy. He said either the piglet or the poodle had to go. The piglet went.

When her parents were still together, though living in a state of quiet desperation, Vicki spent much time at Lisl and Walter Reisch's. They had a daughter about Vicki's age. Vicki learned to swim in the Reisch pool. Another house she went to frequently was her Uncle Willy's. She loved Edna and Willy (or W. Lee, as he had to be called). Their son, Miles, was in her age group. They played together a great deal. She was often at Aunt Edna's for dinner. She remembers that they had a slot machine in the living room which they allowed her to play with nickels. She could play it for hours. She loved machines. When Aunt Edna and Uncle Willy went on trips abroad, Miles would stay with Uncle Billy and Aunt Judith. Miles was impressed, as he was growing up, with his uncle's circle of companions. Once, at dinner, Moss Hart was a guest. Miles Wilder, who grew up to become a successful writer of television comedy, recalls that Uncle Billy did not know how to relate to children. He did not know how to talk to them or listen to them and he could not understand them.

"He was always trying to find me suitable playmates," Miles Wilder says. "Once when my folks were in Europe—oh, I was about thirteen or fourteen then—he brought me together with Edward G. Robinson's son, Eddie Robinson Jr., who was about fourteen. Well, Uncle Billy did not know this, but Eddie Jr. was already a full-fledged sneak thief and before he was sixteen he was living with an older woman, and drinking a bottle of whiskey a day. That was the kind of playmate Uncle Billy got me."

When Vicki was eight, her father took her dining at Romanoff's. She had a Dubonnet with a twist of lemon as an aperitif. He discoursed on the various aperitifs, like Ray Milland explaining thunder and lightning to the little impostor in *The Major and the Minor*. She had her first spinach salad and her first steak tartare, both of which she enjoyed. Recently he took her and her daughter to The Bistro. The Bistro is not accustomed to children. They did not have the usual child seat risers. They had to stack three phone books on a seat so Julie could reach the table.

Daddy took her to Hollywood parties and she met stars.

"My father never tried to make a big deal out of it," she says. "It was like magic to me. . . . It was like coming to a wonderland when I came to Hollywood . . . To be able to see in person Robert Wagner, on whom I had a big crush. The first set I was ever on was the one for *The Emperor Waltz*. I had my picture taken with Bing Crosby and Joan Fontaine. Daddy took me on the *Stalag 17* set. I met William Holden. I was about fifteen but I looked older as I had matured physically. I had a crush on William Holden. He looked at me in that special way, and I had the feeling that he seemed to be interested in me, but did not make a play for me as he did not wish to upset Daddy. I did not know then how valuable his paintings were. Sometimes there would be a blank space on a wall and I asked where was the painting and he said he loaned it to a museum.

"I remember a party where Elizabeth Taylor was there. I just couldn't talk. I was struck dumb. I just stared at her. Natalie Wood was there too. I wanted to be beautiful like Natalie Wood or Elizabeth Taylor. Once Daddy took me to a birthday party which Tony Curtis gave for Janet Leigh, who was then Mrs. Curtis. I remember they had a pool with an electrically operated cover which rolled itself up when you pressed a button. The only one of its kind I ever saw. During the party a plane circled over the party. It had a streamer: HAPPY BIRTHDAY, JANET.

"Oh, he took me to screenings all the time. I once saw and shook hands with Bogart and Bacall. I just flipped. I guess poor Daddy, he had this screaming teenaged fan daughter, and it kind of embarrassed him.

"When I was going to Tamalpais High School, I'd be introduced to somebody and they'd say, 'This is Vicki Wilder. Her father is the movie director—you know, *Some Like It Hot—The Apartment—*'

"I didn't mind that. I was very proud.

"He gave me a nice present when I was twenty-one. A two-and-a-half-month trip in Europe—the Scandinavian countries, England, Germany, France. My mother was touring Leningrad and Moscow and other parts of Russia, and I met my mother in Paris. It was a fantastic trip."

Later, we stood beside the car I had rented at the San Francisco airport. It was a brand-new American Motors Pacer, a fiery red color. She asked me how it handled and I said smooth. I admired her classic gray Mercedes 300 SL. As we were saying good-bye, and making an arrangement to meet a group for dinner later that night, she said,

"I hope your book will explain my father to me. I never could understand him, what makes him go."

One could not take a human being apart like a doll.

# 15

# SUNSET BOULEVARD

The triumph of *Lost Weekend* had vindicated Billy Wilder. In his own eyes, he had always been a genius. Now his opinion had been confirmed. He had power. He had glory. He had money. He loved them all. He had never been what you might call a sweet and gracious person. But now, his ego swollen beyond even the customary Hollywood megalomania, he strode the make-believe streets of Paramount like a conqueror. He trampled roughshod on the sensibilities of any and all persons in his periphery. Of course, he strutted about and shook his scepter with style and cleverness and he was always sure to intersperse his disparaging remarks about others, with cuts at himself. But his wit now knew no boundaries of taste or respect. And his temperament had to dominate. His artistic demands on his studio became boundless. Up till now, he had to some extent compromised with his partner, but now he would no longer heed Charlie Brackett. It had to be done Wilder's way—or no way at all. The animosity festered between these two men, the most brilliant screenwriting collaborators in movie history. They quarreled and they screamed and Brackett got hysterical and threw heavy objects at Wilder's head. Wilder would always throw the last punch, however. He would threaten to break up the partnership. He would threaten to get a divorce. He was in the process of divorcing Judith

Wilder. He was in the throes of a stormy relationship with the dark-haired and beautiful Doris Dowling. Doris and Billy had always had a tempestuous time together but hitherto the insults had been part of the sweet excitement of their love. Now Wilder, who had become an emperor psychologically, acted like King Louis XIV dispensing favors to mistresses. Wilder had become drunk on a substance more poisonous than the alcohol which was destroying Raymond Chandler. This dangerous and intoxicating elixir was power. Hollywood, like all centers of politics or industry or culture, was a place which responded to power. And Billy Wilder, for the time, was wielding a powerful scepter. That crown felt marvelous on his head. He did not feel any uneasiness about it. He liked to wear hats anyway. To him this was the best hat he had ever worn. He forgot those words he always wrote on page one of a screenplay— *Cum Deo.* He had forgotten his mystical sense that his talent and energy derived from God. It was as if he were saying, "I'll take it from here on, God. You have done well up to now. From here on in, I am going to control my life—and the lives of other persons." It was what they used to call the sin of pride, in the old days when there were sins. And, as he had probably forgotten, pride goes just before a fall. But the fall was several years in the future and it never seemed to diminish the pride, even when it came.

Wilder's egomania as a director was illustrated by the first film he made after *Lost Weekend.* This was *The Emperor Waltz,* which Wilder probably wanted to make as a homage to Lubitsch. It would be delicate and subtle. He would show those film critics, who, even while praising him, would shiver at his crassness, his vulgarity, his rich vein of sordid humor. He would show them he could make a sophisticated film, a film in which there was a romance between a commoner and a princess, in which he played the story against the setting of the Austro-Hungarian Empire, and in which that figure of his childhood, the Emperor Franz Josef, would have an important part. Yes, he would make a respectful homage—and not only to Lubitsch: he would remember affectionately the world of his father and mother; he would re-create his memories of the royal parades and the castles. There would be music—waltzes and waltzes and long ballroom gowns—and Bing Crosby would play the commoner, an American phonograph salesman, and Joan Fontaine would play a countess. Singing and dancing and love and innuendos, for Bing would have a nondescript dog who falls in love with Joan's purebred

French poodle and their romance would be counterpointed against those of the human beings. There would even be a dog psychiatrist, for Joan's female poodle becomes neurotic as a result of sex frustration. It was a great scene as played by Sig Rumann. Wilder never forgave Sigmund Freud for having thrown him out when he wanted an interview in Vienna to get his Christmas story. Whenever he had a chance, Wilder gave psychiatrists a knife in the back.

It was Billy's first film in glorious technicolor. Made dizzy by his new power, he went to extremes in spending Paramount's money to achieve tonal nuances in the film. There were several gorgeous sequences taking place in the Tyrolean Alps. For the Alps, Wilder chose to film in Jasper National Park in the Canadian Rockies. Jasper National Park is one of the most breathtakingly beautiful places in North America. But nature was not good enough for Wilder. He went about gilding lilies in a way that can only be described as the self-indulgent spirit of a decadent Roman emperor. For one sequence, he wanted a background of magnificent pine trees. There were hordes of pine trees in Jasper National Park—tall ones, lofty ones, beautiful ones. But they were not quite—well—coniferous enough to suit Wilder's whims. Somehow the green was not green enough and the shapes were not properly formed. At an expense of some $20,000, he imported several dozen suitable pine trees from California, which he had planted exactly where he wanted. The Canadian forest rangers watched this bizarre man giving orders to plant four trees here and eight trees there, and they shook their heads. It confirmed every weird story they heard about Hollywood. He imported 4,000 daisies—also from California—because he had to have daisies arranged just precisely so, in a certain design, for a dance number. But that wasn't enough to suit the Emperor. (Yes, in the making of *The Emperor's Waltz* it was Billy Wilder who played the title role.) He had the daisies painted . . . *blue.* All 4,000 of them—all brushed in a cobalt blue tinge! I know you don't believe it. But, you see, as Wilder explained quite seriously to the Hollywood journalists who were flown up to cover the event, "White photographs too glaringly."

Then, he had a gang of painters brought in to paint all the roads for miles around in a particular shade of ochre which he fancied. (He was like a woman driving a crew of house painters crazy when she is redecorating her home.) He explained that "Canadian roads photograph either too darkly or too palely."

To climax his extravagances, he even built an island in Lake Leach. You see, there's this two-minute scene in which Buttons (that's Crosby's pooch) and Scheherezade (that's Fontaine's) swim out to this little isle and consummate their canine passions. Wilder ordered his technicians to make him one island. They floated oil drums first and then laid rocks and earth upon it and gave him an island, with trees and flowers, a completely new island.

Just this one island cost Paramount $90,000.

As Herman Mankiewicz said, in another connection, "It only goes to show you what God could do if he had money."

Wilder displayed his arrogance in other ways. The company was on location for several months and, as is customary, there were the inevitable flings between the boys and the girls connected with the movie and the natives. There were wild parties. There were orgies. There was happiness. There was love. There was lust. There was the erotic spirit of the Viennese court before World War I.

Suddenly, in what seemed a contradiction of his philosophy of hedonism, Wilder issued an edict that there was to be no more hanky-panky between the foreigners and the natives. A bulletin, signed by him, was posted prominently in many places on the location: WE ARE HERE AS REPRESENTATIVES OF A GREAT AMERICAN INDUSTRY AND A GREAT COUNTRY AND WE ARE JUDGED BY OUR ACTIONS. EVERYONE WILL BEHAVE AS IF YOU WERE AT HOME. According to word passed along by the unit manager, there would be instant dismissal for any person, be he extra, grip, electrician, costumer, whatever, who was caught drinking or making love with the natives.

They all thought that Wilder was some goddam crank and a hypocrite besides. For Doris Dowling had come up from Hollywood to console him after the enervating hours of his working day, and you know life is not easy when you have to worry about the glare of daisies and the aesthetic symmetry of pine trees.

But the movie was popular. It made millions of dollars for Paramount. Brackett was in a good mood because now he and Billy were making the kind of pictures he wanted to make, sheer entertainment, sophisticated comedy, music and dancing, singing. He hoped that Wilder would now understand the importance of not being earnest. The critics found *Emperor's Waltz* a pleasing diversion. Even James Agee, the toughest critic of his time, praised it with faint damns. Reviewing a quantity of Hollywood pictures in an omnibus review in the *Nation* (July 24, 1948), Agee recounted the dual love story, the man for the woman, the dog for the bitch, and remarked, "At its best this semimusical is amusing and well shaped, because Charles Brackett and Billy Wilder have learned a fair amount from the comedies of Ernst Lubitsch. In general it is reasonably good fun. At its worst it yaps and embraces every unguarded leg in sight."

In the same batch of reviews—Agee often lumped in one piece critiques of a dozen Hollywood films, each of which were dissected and dispatched in a few quick cuts of the knife—was an opinion of *A Foreign Affair,* though it was released a year later than the Crosby-Fontaine *strudel.* Agee on *Foreign Affair:* "Brackett and Wilder again, this time in American Berlin. A visiting Congresswoman (Jean Arthur), an ex-girl friend of a ranking Nazi (Marlene Dietrich), an American soldier (John Lund). Some sharp, nasty, funny stuff at the expense of investigatory Americans; then—as in *The Emperor Waltz*—the picture endorses everything it has been kidding and worse. A good bit of it is in rotten taste, and the perfection of that is in Dietrich's song "Black Market." (End of critique.)

Well, I want to call your particular attention to Agee's reference to "rotten taste." If even such a sophisticated critic as Agee felt revulsion at the sight of Wilder's pictures as an exhibition of human vulgarity, greed, lust and ugliness, what would be the reaction of less sophisticated critics and censors, of liberal moralists and tight-lipped conservatives? Wilder was in real trouble. He could not change. He was Wilder. He had to have a rusty sardine can under the buttocks of the lovers. He had the kind of X-ray vision which insisted on seeing skulls beneath skins and rattling the bones in your face. He would first get your respect by his honesty and his wit, and then he would fling the pus of a soul's sickness right in your face, just when you were open-mouthed with laughter. He had to make sure that you did not love him. He had to be the man you hated to love.

Looking back from the perspective of almost thirty years, it is evident that *Foreign Affair* was one of the first realistic and honest post-war films and, in my opinion, was on an artistic level with the works of De Sica and Rossellini. It cut deep and meanly and it told the truth, which was that under pressure men and women do not follow the Ten Commandments. The story took place in occupied Berlin and the film was shot in occupied Berlin and, as always when Wilder filmed in a city, he was a neo-realist, and the film has the authentic look of a Berlin street picture of the 1920s, or of the Siodmak-Wilder

*Menschen am Sonntag*. He put in this film all the things he had seen and felt during his six months as an officer of the occupation. He put into it all the hate and reluctant admiration Wilder felt for the Germans, and especially for the Berliners, for Billy could have said with John F. Kennedy *"Ich bin ein Berliner."* In a certain hard uncompromising quality of his sensibility, his approach to human events, he had that cynical *Weltanschauung* of the Berliner.

This one was conceived, written and filmed against the most strident objections of Charlie Brackett, though he was the line producer. He disliked the premise and he could not stand the unpatriotic description of American soldiers bartering silk stockings for sex from the Fräuleins—of the general mood of corruption and sin portrayed in *Foreign Affair*. He liked the serious and sincere American expressed in Jean Arthur's member of Congress from Iowa. He concentrated on writing her. She was a good woman. She was a Henry James innocent. And like other American innocents, she awoke to her disillusionment and maturing when she was confronted with Europe in its decadence.

It is in this film that, for the first time, Wilder plays a theme which will obsess him from now on: the nature of a woman's love; the nature of the whore; the nature of the woman who does it for money or gifts, the woman who does it for seemingly pure and unsullied motives. The hero is torn between the two women. There were vague intimations of this theme in every film in which Wilder had a hand up till now, but it now emerges nakedly. I think it was his own rude awakening to Europe after the war, combined with his new arrogant confidence in himself, which brought about this emergence.

Wilder saw positive elements in the "whore" and negative sides in the "virgin." And this was a shocking theme which simply did not exist in American films until Billy Wilder put it there in loud, brash colors—yes, in vulgar colors—but then there are persons who think Toulouse-Lautrec's whores are in poor taste, and Picasso's *Demoiselles d'Avignon*.

The Wilder touch—as opposed to the Lubitsch touch—is exemplified in a romantic scene between Lund and his mistress, Marlene Dietrich. We see Lund trading chocolate bars for silk stockings at the Brandenberg Gate, where the black market is in full swing. He trades the chocolate cake which his Iowa fiancée had baked for him and which Congressman Phoebe Frost (dear, wholesome Jean Arthur) had brought over. He gets an old mattress for the cake. He drags the mattress and stockings over to Marlene's pad. She is living in a ruined basement in a bombed-out building. As he picks his way through the rubble, our hero is humming "Isn't It Romantic?", one of the hit songs of the period. As he enters, we see Marlene first reflected in a cracked mirror. Wilder has always adored mirror shots. We see her in her underwear and she is brushing her teeth. He comes near. She rinses her mouth. She turns—and affectionately *sprays a mouthful of water in his face!*

And he loves it.

She likes the mattress. She loves the silk stockings. Her opening line is, "And next time bring me back some sugar and some soap."

Well, Brackett had a fit over this scene. You could not show a woman spitting lovingly in a man's face. It was crazy. It was revolting. It went against everything we know about romance. You did not dare photograph such scenes in a movie. Hell, even Italian and French pictures did not have such nauseating scenes.

"It offends me beyond words, Billy," he kept saying.

"Charlie, that's just how a broad is if she really likes the guy. It's love, Charlie, love. We show how close they are—physically."

"Only a whore does such things," Brackett said, "and only a pervert would find this fun."

"The most interesting women characters in a picture are whores," Billy said, "and every man in love is a sex pervert at heart."

"You're sick, Billy, you're very sick," Charlie said and he threw a telephone directory at Billy's head and missed as usual.

He endured the vicissitudes of *Foreign Affair* only because Wilder had sworn that their next work would be a tender film about a silent-movie star who makes a comeback twenty years after the world has forgotten her . . .

*A Foreign Affair* cast a sardonic eye at Congressmen on an investigating junket in Europe, as well as our military personnel. It was denounced on the floor of the House of Representatives as a rotten movie. The Department of Defense had to issue a statement which said that this picture gave a false picture of our occupation army, who were a noble and celibate company of warriors. Paramount Pictures was under fire from many quarters and it decided to quietly withdraw *Foreign Affair* from release. It is still one of the best political pictures ever made in Hollywood. It is still as good and as true and as entertaining now as it was in 1948. Like Erich von Stroheim, Billy Wilder was sometimes twenty years ahead of his time.

In March 1948, Billy completed the scoring and editing of *Foreign Affair*. Wilder was also winding up several domestic affairs. Judith Wilder was divorcing him. Doris Dowling was telling him, in effect, "Thanks—but no thanks." And he was finally to divorce his partner, Charlie Brackett. Theirs had been the longest collaboration between screenwriters in movie history. Before they divorced, they made one more picture—the best Hollywood movie about Hollywood, *Sunset Boulevard*. For several years, they had been kicking around the idea of such a movie. There had been many good ones before—James Cruze's 1924 silent *Merton of the Movies*, Raoul Walsh's *Going Hollywood* with Marion Davies (1932), George Cukor's *What Price Hollywood?* (1932), Victor Fleming's *Bombshell* with Jean Harlow (1933), William Wellman's original version of *A Star Is Born* (1937) with Janet Gaynor and Fredric March, and Preston Sturges's wonderful *Sullivan's Travels* (1942) with Veronica Lake and Joel McCrea. These films usually showed us a man or woman aspiring to success in Hollywood— still an intriguing springboard for a movie, as witness the recent *Day of the Locust* and *Hearts of the West*. Because Hollywood represents a great fantasy of our time, the dream that one may get everything the heart desires simply by looking photogenic and being "discovered," the situation of the neophyte in Hollywood is always a good springboard.

Brackett first spawned the idea. His idea was to reverse the usual theme of the innocent in Hollywood. He would tell the story of an aged silent movie queen, awaiting her comeback in a Hollywood which has passed her by. She would still be interesting-looking and very rich and she would, after a series of amusing experiences, triumph over her enemies. It was to be a high-spirited comedy. Brackett still liked comedies. Wilder, however, as time went on, was growing more cynical. His experiences in postwar Europe had confirmed his pessimism about the human species.

Wilder was, as he had been for some time, the dominant creative member of the team. So, insidiously, he took over the reins of the Hollywood movie. Brackett became subservient to him after they started elaborating a story. To disguise the real story, they had a fictitious working title, *A Can of Beans*. Nobody was to know they

were planning a movie about Hollywood. Nobody. Not even the
men in the front office. Wilder had become almost paranoid in his
obsession with secrecy. Helen Hernandez had strict orders to lock
up in a special iron drawer all their notes and memoranda at the end
of the day. Not even Henry Ginsberg or Don Hartman or story editor D. A. Doran knew they were writing a sardonic movie about
Hollywood. Nor did anybody among the higher-ups ever see a completed script. They were to go into production with only about forty
pages of script. Wilder was convinced he had to conceal from the
trade papers, the studio executives, and the entire industry the nature of this picture. He feared that if the industry suspected what he
and Brackett were plotting, there would be pressure on Barney Balaban to kill the movie at its inception.

It was customary for each executive producer at Paramount to
make a report every Thursday of work in progress. Wilder and
Brackett no longer had to write eleven pages of script on Thursday.
They could work at their own sweet pace. But Brackett, as line producer, had to produce a report on *A Can of Beans* every Thursday,
so Billy would improvise wild and fascinating notes about a non ex-
istent film, and Hernandez would type these out and transmit them
to the front office. While *Sunset Boulevard* was still in its germinating phase, Wilder was casting. He wanted Mae West to play Norma
Desmond! Yes, he did. Honestly! Of course, Norma Desmond as
she was originally conceived was not the Norma Desmond we have
come to know and love. Billy had always found Mae West's image
irresistible, ever since he had seen her early talking films *I'm No Angel* and *She Done Him Wrong*. West was a Paramount star. She and
Billy often got together in the commissary and over at Lucey's to
swap licentious stories. Billy had a mysterious affinity with Mae
West. She represented a platonic idea of The Whore, whose mystery Wilder was forever trying to unravel. There was about her a
certain superb vulgarity and fleshiness which reminded him of Viennese and Berlin prostitutes.

Wilder put the idea of being Norma Desmond to her one day. She
recoiled in disgust. She was fifty-five years old. She did not consider
herself a faded flower. She was in the prime of her life. (Now eighty-
four, the Divine Miss West still lives a sensually flamboyant life and
is seen around town in the company of rampant studs. Not long ago,
I happened to be sitting not far from her table in Knoll's Black For-

est, a Santa Monica restaurant, and saw her put away a healthy portion of sauerbraten with red cabbage. She was also happily pawing one of her masculine admirers.)

Mae West would not discuss the project. She would not look at an outline. She was insulted. So Wilder went back to elaborating the plot with his partner.

They now occupied a sumptuous corner suite in the Writers' Building. There was an anteroom for Helen Hernandez, two bathrooms and a kitchen. The large office was furnished with antiques. This was Charlie's place. The boys—writers in the studios were always known as "the boys" even when they were over fifty—called this one The Bedroom because they siestaed there an hour after lunch. The smaller office, decorated in bentwood and contemporary, with a few small choice Postimpressionist works, was Billy's. The boys called this The Game Room because many afternoons, when their little gray cells became enervated, they played bridge, cribbage, or gin rummy. These were the sort of fancy quarters in which Paramount producers were domiciled. It was too good for screenwriters. But here resided Brackett and Wilder.

As writers—which was what they still considered themselves—Brackett and Wilder had reached the pinnacle of success. They were at the $5,000-a-week salary level, individually, and that was the highest scale in 1948. They had the run of the studio. They lived and worked in complete autonomy. In the late afternoon, as the sun went below the yardarm, and the goldfish grew cold in the pool out on the plaza by the Writers' Building, and as the studio alcoholics went over to Oblath's for a quick one (Oblath's, the joke went, served the only greasy Tom Collins in town), Brackett and Wilder played host to various writers and actors who liked to play bridge or kibitz. To take a hand, you really had to play bridge well. Wilder was deadly serious about bridge, as he was about tennis, or baseball; in fact, he became a demonically possessed and slightly crazed character when he was interested in anything. Once, a producer on the lot phoned and asked if they needed a fourth in the afternoon bridge game. Wilder barked into the phone: "I'll have lunch with you, I'll have dinner with you, I'll talk to you, but I won't play bridge with you. You're a marvelous guy and I'm an admirer and I'm happy to see you anytime—but I won't play bridge with you because as a bridge player you stink. Good-bye." Among the bridge players who occasionally sat in was a young *Time-Life* reporter and film critic, D.

M. Marshman, Jr. One day, Brackett and Wilder confided their difficulties in getting a handle on the Hollywood story. Marshman had an idea. They liked it. He joined the team. Brackett later explained, "He suggested a relationship between the silent movie star and a young man; she, living in the past, refusing to believe her days as a star are gone and holing up in one of those run-down, immense mansions. We saw the young man as a screenwriter, as a nice guy, maybe from the Middle West, a man who can't make the grade in Hollywood and who is really down on his luck."

The impasse was bridged. They were running now and once it was determined that the young screenwriter becomes a gigolo, the film had to become Wilder's picture. It was, you might say, almost the basic theme of his imagination—the *Eintänzer* motif, the man selling love for money, and the woman buying it with presents. It became an increasingly pessimistic film. They completed the story by the end of 1948 and were now writing the screenplay.

After Mae West, Wilder thought of casting Mary Pickford. At this stage, the character of the faded star was subordinated to that of the gigolo writer. He was the hero and core of the plot. It was his movie. His was the dominating role. He was a man who sold out his love— he was to be in love, in the original draft of the screenplay—with a young actress—for the security an older woman gave him. To play the young writer, Joe Gillis, Wilder had already gotten a commitment from one of the most exciting new actors in the Broadway theater—Montgomery Clift. While they were completing the screenplay Clift was making his first two films, one of which was *Red River* with John Wayne. The plan was for him to make *Sunset Boulevard* as soon as Howard Hawks wrapped up the cattle drive on the Chisholm Trail. Wilder had a meeting with Miss Pickford and her young husband, Buddy Rogers, at the Pickfair estate. The estate, of course, was not fallen into dilapidation like the house and grounds of Norma Desmond. Yet the tale the movie would tell had a resemblance to the events of her life. Wilder read the outline and acted out some scenes. Rogers was enchanted with the story. So was Mary Pickford. However, she would not make her triumphant return to the screen unless Brackett and Wilder completely revised the story and made *her* the center of interest. She was a star. She would always be a star. Nothing had changed since the days of the silent pictures, for Mary Pickford. She was what the movie was about, in one sense, the persistence of a sense of the past so that the present is a pale shadow against those memories. Wilder saw that if he were to cast Miss Pickford, she would become the autocrat on the set. He graciously declined.

You will observe that, from the first, he planned to employ an actress as Norma Desmond whose own career essentially duplicated hers. An audience would be shaken by the double masquerade—a woman playing a part and playing herself playing the part. Now he turned to Pola Negri. Miss Negri threw one of her famous bursts of temperament. She was outraged that Wilder would imply that she had been a has-been. Though Billy sought to pretend that it was all make-believe and that he wanted her because she was a superb actress, she was shrewd enough to see that he was capitalizing on her decline. She did not want to be food for the vultures.

Wilder visited George Cukor, an amiable gentleman and a director correctly known as the finest director of women in Hollywood. Cukor lives in a multilevel mansion on Cordell Drive in the Hollywood Hills, above Sunset Boulevard, in that area known as The Strip, because it is an unincorporated strip of land between Los Angeles and Beverly Hills. Billy sat in the garden and sipped tea amicably with Cukor. He poured out his heart. Now you may imagine Hollywood as a jungle of bloodthirsty animals but there is much kindness and Cukor is the most amicable of men. He listened to Wilder's travails. Cukor said that there was an ideal woman for Norma Desmond. And why had not Wilder mentioned her? Gloria Swanson!

It was strange, wasn't it, how he had somehow blocked Swanson out—it was probably those clinging memories of the aged Swanson vainly trying to recapture her lost youth in *Music in the Air* that had first planted the seed of *Sunset Boulevard* in his subconscious? Well it had been a terrible movie and part of his three awful years in Hollywood as a down-and-out writer, and he had blocked that time out of his awareness.

Yes, Gloria Swanson. Miss Swanson told me recently that she remembered getting a phone call in 1949 from Wilder. He described the role to her. She was the *conferencier* of a TV talk show on WPIX, New York. She was living in New York. She had fled from Hollywood a decade before. She was no Norma Desmond. She was a volatile and vigorous lady. She lived in the present. She lived in an elegant apartment on Fifth Avenue in the Eighties. She asked to see a script. He said it was not completed and he would call her the following week. The following week she was taken to Doctors Hospital. She underwent major surgery. She came home to recuperate for a month. She canceled a Paris trip. She had time on her hands. She had not received a Brackett and Wilder screenplay.

"I had forgotten all about it," she says, "when I suddenly got a call from somebody at Paramount—my old studio, you know, the one you might say I built—and some nauseating little creep said they wanted me to fly out to the coast at once—*at once,* mind you—and take a screen test for the role in this movie. Test for a part in a picture? Me? Test? I was revolted. Never made a test in my life. Then Mr. Wilder called. I was rude to him. I said what the hell do you have to test me for? You want to see if I'm still alive, do you? Or do you doubt I can act? And I asked him to send me some goddam pages of script. So far all I heard was talk. So he sent some pages, I don't know, about twenty pages. I liked what I read. I was intrigued by the character, yes, but I was also horrified by this element of it being anti-Hollywood. I took it as an attack on the movie industry. No, it was twenty-six pages. I remember.

"Well, I absolutely refused to be tested. I told Mr. Wilder I would never, *never* be tested.

"Then I got a phone call from darling George Cukor. Oh, he is so persuasive, charm the birds out of the trees, that dear man. He said this was the greatest part of my career and I'd be remembered for this part and that Billy Wilder had become the number one director of Hollywood. He swore that Mr. Wilder would do justice to me. He said I had to come out and test for it and I did and we started shooting without a completed script and sometimes we were working only one day ahead. And Mr. Wilder shot it in continuity and it was the first time in my many years in pictures, the very first, I was in a film done like this."

Two weeks before the first day of shooting, April 11, 1949, Wilder faced disaster. Montgomery Clift broke his contract! Suddenly he would not play Joe Gillis. No. He would not listen to Wilder's pleas and he would give no explanation except that his agent told Billy he suddenly felt unable technically to give a convincing performance as a young man in love with a woman twice as old as he! He was incommunicado. The truth—as we all knew back in New York and Connecticut—was the opposite. Not only could Clift, an actor of great subtlety and power, portray a young man in love with an old woman, but he was—and had been for some years—in the grip of a romantic obsession with a woman about thirty years older than he was—Libby Holman, the famous torch singer of the 1920s, the lady who had married an heir to the R. J. Reynolds tobacco fortune and who had shot and killed him in what was ruled an accident by the coroner. Holman became an alcoholic and Clift became part of her dark alcoholic world. They were inseparable. They lived most of the year on her large estate in Connecticut. I remember a visit there once in the spring and seeing a field with thousands of daffodils. Libby Holman had threatened to kill herself if Montgomery played such a role in this movie. To her it was so obviously a pastiche of the romance of Montgomery Clift and Libby Holman!

Strangely enough, if the theme reflected any private secret it was a mirror image of a fear haunting Billy Wilder while he was filming *Sunset Boulevard.* For he could have paraphrased Flaubert and cried, "Norma Desmond, *c'est moi.*" Yes, he identified with the gigolo of Joe Gillis, having been a paid dancing partner or *Eintänzer* in his Berlin years, but the real drama of his life in 1948 was that he was in love with a woman who was twenty years younger than himself. He lived in the fear that he would not hold her love. He dreaded marrying her and yet he wanted to marry her. He hated to be emotionally dependent on any other person, and he found himself almost a sentimental adorer of her personality. He was crazy about Audrey Young and he didn't want to be. Norma Desmond's enslavement by her heart was his own enslavement, and try as he might, with sneers and wisecracks, he could not disguise from himself his obsession with Audrey. As with artistic works in painting or literature, we can be sure that if a film moves us deeply and continues to move us, on each experience, then it undoubtedly corresponds to a deep emotion which its creator felt. *Sunset Boulevard,* more than any other Brackett-Wilder film, was Billy Wilder's. It is almost his love story. For Norma Desmond and Joe Gillis are Billy and Audrey. And Joe Gillis' Nancy Olson, the young story analyst and aspiring screenwriter, is a portrait of Audrey Young—yes, in many small details as well as the general shape. He was telling both love stories at once.

And now he had no Joe Gillis. Billy went to Fred MacMurray. MacMurray, now under contract to Twentieth Century-Fox, was grateful to Wilder because *Double Indemnity* had brought him recognition. Wilder had to have an answer quickly. Regretfully, MacMurray said, "No." He had read the script. A strange thing had happened when Gloria Swanson took her screen test. For she exuded such savagery and madness from the screen that Brackett and Wilder shifted the story radically and now made Norma Desmond the central role in the film. MacMurray, who was now a superstar, believed it would set him back if he were to play this demeaning role, though he excused himself to Billy by saying this whole conception of a "kept man" was abhorrent to his moral values. The days were ticking by and now, in desperation, Billy submitted the partial script to William Holden. Holden was a Paramount contract player and had been one for almost ten years. He had been shunted into boring roles in action pictures and musicals. He had not played a solid part since his prizefighter in *Golden Boy* (1943). He was almost as desperate as Wilder but he was not desperate enough to risk his "image" on a secondary role to a woman who was, after all, a forgotten has-been. Would they consider fattening his part? And now Wilder did something that went against his grain. He asked Henry Ginsberg, the executive head of Paramount, to intervene. Ginsberg ordered Holden to play Joe Gillis—and it was not only the making of Holden as a major actor, but led to an interesting friendship with Wilder. Pauline Kael once wrote a cruel interpretation of Holden's work in this film. She praised him for his acting and added, "When in a mixture of piety and guilt, he makes love to the crazy, demanding old woman, he expresses a nausea so acute that we can almost forgive Holden his career during the last decade: this man knows the full self-disgust of prostitution." But Holden had never wanted to impersonate these pasteboard characters in B pictures. He was under contract. He had never had the clout to make demands. He had to speak the lines they told him to speak in the films they told him to make. *Sunset Boulevard* gave him the power to stand up for his convictions.

Brackett engaged Wilder in many furious encounters during the making of *Sunset Boulevard*. One of the most violent was over a montage of Norma Desmond rejuvenating herself by means of steam cabinets, electric massages, mud masks, emollients, cosmetics, adhesive skin-tightening patches. "An army of beauty experts invaded her house on Sunset Boulevard," says Holden off-camera.

Brackett said it was vulgar and offensive. William Schorr, who became Wilder's associate with this film, remembers a screening of the rushes during which the two men came to blows. Brackett, as producer, insisted it must be cut. Wilder said it had to go in. It was ugly, yes, but he wanted to show the torment an old woman would go through to hold a young lover.

Schorr was asked to referee the dispute. He had been a Broadway director and producer. This was his first film. He had made Billy's acquaintance as a tennis player at the Beverly Hills Tennis Club. There were mean persons who said Wilder had put Schorr on the payroll so he could have a tennis partner. Wilder did have a new tennis court put on the location and he and Schorr did play several sets of tennis during the lunch break daily.

Schorr voted in favor of retaining the montage.

Brackett stood up and shouted curses at both men. He stamped out of the screening room.

It was at this time that Wilder confided that this was the last film he would ever make with Charlie Brackett. . . .

Norman Desmond's flamboyant castle on a hill in *Sunset Boulevard* was not located on this avenue—nor was it in those curving streets around Beachwood Drive in the old precincts of Hollywood above Franklin Avenue, where the silent movie stars had resided, nor in the Los Feliz area. It was in the mid-Wilshire district. It had been built in 1924 for $250,000 by a William Jenkins. It was a Renaissance-style castle. Jenkins had spared no expense. He had surrounded his mansion with high cement walls. There were two acres of landscaped grounds. There were staircases and wrought-iron doors and that fantastic ballroom and fourteen rooms. It was a palace. Jenkins deserted his palace after a year and went to Mexico. For over a decade the house stood there empty at the intersection of Wilshire Boulevard and Western. Then J. Paul Getty purchased it as a residence for himself and the second Mrs. Getty. When they were divorced, she received custody of the house. Her representative agreed to rent the house to Paramount for a reasonable amount on one condition. The studio was to make a swimming pool—which was essential to the story as Holden is shot and killed and falls into the swimming pool—but if Mrs. Getty did not like the pool, the studio agreed to pave over the pool and landscape it back to its original shrubbery. Tom Wood, unit publicist on the film, tells us in his book on Wilder that "the studio spared no expense in turning the silent star's home into a monstrosity. It added stained-glass windows in the front hall, filled the conservatory with palm trees, crowded the living room with overstuffed furniture . . . hung velvet drapes that looked as if they had been gathering dust for a quarter of a century. . . ." An Isotta Fraschini was rented for $500 a week. The swan-shaped vessel of a bed in which Norma Desmond sleeps had once belonged to the legendary Gaby de Lys, the famous dancer and courtesan.

In 1957, the Desmond mansion was torn down by the wreckers. In its place, Getty put up a twenty-two-story business structure, which is now the home of the Getty Oil Company and its subsidiaries. The address is 3810 Wilshire Boulevard.

The opening and ghoulish sequence of *Sunset Boulevard* was written entirely by Wilder. Brackett washed his hands of it. He said it was disgustingly morbid. Wilder filmed it, not over Charlie's dead body, but over the "dead" bodies of thirty-six others, in the receiving room of the Los Angeles County Morgue. The event was described in a communiqué from the Paramount publicity department: "Some three dozen extra players were called to portray corpses. They stretched out on the metal slabs which had been equipped with headrests to keep their heads from moving, and, paradoxically, *froze into immobility* the moment Wilder called 'Action!'" The corpses were covered with sheets—which became transparent and then the dead started talking.

William Holden still relishes describing the lurid scene: "The corpse lying next to me asks me how I died and I say I drowned and he asks how can a young guy like you drown and I say, 'Well, first I was shot in the back,' and then he says, yeah, he was shot also. He was a Chicago gangster killed in Los Angeles. Then a little kid on a slab across from me says 'I drowned too,—swimming with my friend off the Santa Monica pier. I bet him I could hold my breath two minutes.' Some dame is over by the kid and she says he shouldn't be unhappy as his parents will come and take him to a nice place. Then from way down there's this great big Negro corpse and he says, 'Hey, man, did you get the final score on the Dodger game before you got it?' And I say no, I died before the morning papers came out."

And the picture concluded in the morgue. After Gloria Swanson has finally gone stark, staring mad, and is playing her dramatic scene as she sweeps down the staircase in an imaginary De Mille film, Wilder cut to the morgue, and the last image was of a weeping Nancy Olson hovering over Holden's corpse like Robinson over MacMurray's.

Willie Schorr didn't like the finale. It went against the tragedy. The tragedy was not in the young woman—but in the old woman, and the film must end with Swanson's madness. Wilder concurred and he rounded out the scene with Swanson and the newsreel cameramen, whom she mistakes for cinematographers.

One of the difficult scenes to light and play was the scene in which Swanson, von Stroheim, and a man from an undertaking parlor bury the star's pet chimpanzee in the garden. John F. Seitz, the great cameraman, asked Wilder how he wanted him to film this scene. Billy gave him an insouciant shrug, and said,

"Oh, just your usual monkey funeral shot, Johnny!"

Many of the scenes walked a narrow line between farce and tragedy like this monkey funeral shot and it was very hard to be sure one was in balance. But, as always, Wilder made sure he did not communicate his anxiety to the players. He always tried to be amusing on the set. Miss Swanson remembers it as "a happy picture. There was love and excitement on the set. All were excited, even the gaffers, the juicers, the prop men. I cried when we finished it because I'd been so happy while we were shooting that I wished we could have started it all over again.

"You know, there was that lovely scene where I do a Chaplin imitation with a cane and derby; well, the next morning when I came on the set and everybody—all the cast and crew and even the dead chimpanzee—was wearing a derby, and the little monkey, he had a miniature derby on his stuffed head.

"I thought it was the sweetest tribute in my life."

Planned for a spring 1950 release, *Sunset Boulevard* was sneak-previewed in Evanston, Illinois, in January. This city, according to a Paramount demographer, was a cross section of America. Wilder went to Evanston. Wilder was regarded as something of a heroic figure in Evanston because of *The Lost Weekend*. Evanston was the place where the WCTU was founded. It is still illegal to serve alcoholic beverages there. Maybe that was the problem. Everybody in town had to see *Sunset Boulevard* cold sober. Oh, it was a terrible hour for Billy. There he was, sitting in the audience. He was nervous. He was tense. He had not had any martinis. And now the credits roll and you hear Franz Waxman's ominous theme music and—ah, we are now in the morgue and we see a numbered tag on the big toe of a corpse, and—what is this? *In Gottes Willen*, the whole goddam audience is laughing: first they are giggling, then they are laughing, then they are screaming. What do they think they are seeing, a Marx Brothers picture? They are rolling in the aisles. *Oh, where did I go wrong, Mr. Lubitsch?*

Wilder slunk out during the screening. He was not the only one. Customers were drifting out by the score. Wilder had that sensation of the blunt instrument on the head. He wiped his face. He *plotzed* himself on the bottom step of a staircase. Nearby was a powder room. A well-dressed lady, who looked keen and smart, sauntered out. He asked her—hoping against hope. "How do you like the picture so far, madam?"

"I never saw such a pile of shit in all my life," she replied.

Wilder accused Evanston of being an atypical American city. How could you take seriously a place where they drink ginger ale and apple juice? This was a sophisticated movie for intelligent people. So Paramount next sneaked it in the town their demon demographer stated was your average American ultrasophisticated hamlet— Great Neck, Long Island. The reaction was even more extreme. There was not only sneering laughter but boos, hisses, and raucous blubbery noises made by blowing through one's lips in an especially hideous manner which New Yorkers have developed. Oh, it was more than flesh and blood could bear. And they were a sophisticated audience, many of whom had gargled with wine and whiskey before going to the picture show.

The release of *Sunset Boulevard* was delayed for six months. During this time, Wilder scrapped the opening sequence. The film now began with police cars racing down Sunset as their sirens screamed and Holden's voice, off camera, telling about how he died and that great image of the floating corpse in the swimming pool and the camera looking up through the water seeing the distorted faces of cops and news photographers. They tested it in Poughkeepsie, New York. It passed. The audience, like pupils requiring an instructor with a ruler and a blackboard, now was informed they were to see a black tragedy and they were silent and emotionally stirred by it and the preview cards cheered the film and the stars.

Before opening *Sunset Boulevard* in the summer of 1950, Paramount screened it on the lot in their largest theater. They invited the elite of the movie colony to see a movie about the movie colony. The screenwriters present were enthralled to see themselves as sexy heroes. The rest of the audience, with a few exceptions, was shocked. Louis B. Mayer, then the single most powerful force in

Hollywood, was enraged. Outside the theater, he held court and, in a loud voice, he cursed Paramount for allowing Wilder to make such a picture. Billy walked over to him.

"You bastard," Mayer shouted, "you have disgraced the industry that made you and fed you." He shook his fist at Billy. "You should be tarred and feathered and run out of Hollywood."

Wilder looked him in the eye. He pulled his homburg down tightly. "Fuck you," he cleverly riposted.

I tell you—and I have been assured of this by several witnesses to the confrontation—a deathly stillness fell upon the crowd, almost as if they knew that a bolt of lightning would flash and strike Billy Wilder dead.

Mayer turned his back and strode away.

An equally dramatic scene was being played by Barbara Stanwyck. She had been moved by the film. She saw the small figure of Gloria Swanson standing with her entourage. Miss Swanson is small of stature—less than five feet high—but on a screen she becomes a tall and imposing presence, suggesting grandeur, with eyes that burn into you. Several of her lines, spoken with a deadly intensity, would become classic lines and often be quoted and requoted when scholars spoke of silent movies. When Holden says, on first meeting her in the decayed mansion, "You used to be very big," her reply was, "I am big. It's the pictures that got small." And when she screened an old film of hers for Holden, she said, "We had *faces* then!"

Stanwyck stood before Swanson. Stanwyck was speechless. She was weeping copiously. She suddenly knelt down. She seized and crumpled some of Swanson's silver lamé gown in her fingers. Suddenly—her head came close and her lips touched the gown. She was kissing it. Then Stanwyck arose. Swanson was also weeping now. They embraced.

Yes, I know that both ladies were enjoying the attention, and inventing a moment for the photographers and the columnists, but were they not also telling us that they knew how true was this film, that it was reverberating in them now, for fame and beauty in Hollywood were so temporary, so fleeting?

As one wag put it, the idea of the movie was "Sic transit Gloria Swanson."

Wilder still is rueful about the final cut of *Sunset Boulevard*. "The public never saw the two best scenes I ever shot," he once remarked to me. "This morgue sequence in *Sunset* and that gas chamber sequence in *Double Indemnity*."

Among some other scenes and images the public never saw were several of Erich von Stroheim's ideas. Some of them were good. He suggested Wilder use a few scraps from his *Queen Kelly,* made with Gloria Swanson and, at that time, never released. Wilder did so to good effect. He suggested the business of von Stroheim (as a former husband and great European director, now Swanson's butler) writing fan letters to her to help her maintain the delusion that she is not forgotten. He also suggested that he as a butler be shown washing out Norma Desmond's lingerie and experiencing an erotically fetishistic thrill as he dallies with her brassiere and stockings. This scene Wilder did not shoot. Cecil B. De Mille, who was cast as himself, did not make any suggestions. "We made an agreement," Billy says. "He wouldn't tell me how to direct *Sunset Boulevard* and I wouldn't tell him how to direct *Samson and Delilah*." Even Buster Keaton, who was a wonderful idea man and who played one of the bridge players in the weekly bridge game at Swanson's did not tell Billy how to direct the bridge game. Here, as throughout the film, Wilder strove for a pseudodocumentary illusion by casting such famous silent screen stars as Anna Q. Nilsson and H. B. Warner to join the foursome. It is the only bridge game in a Wilder film.

As Axel Madsen, the Swedish writer has pointed out in his Wilder monograph, *Sunset Boulevard* won worldwide acclaim at once, for it "is a rare movie . . . a gnawing, haunting and ruthless film. . . ." It was hailed in the very first number of *Cahiers du Cinema* and Wilder was to be the subject of a long interview there some years later. Georges Sadoul, the eminent French film historian, acclaimed him and the film and it was on the cover of *Newsweek* and James Agee wrote a long essay honoring the film in *Sight and Sound*. It appealed equally to newspaper reviewers and serious critics.

It would, as the years went by, become recognized as the best film ever made about making films in Hollywood. It would finally remain a classic film as a study of madness and love on several levels, which was what the film was most profoundly concerned with. In the Oscar sweepstakes it was nominated for Best Picture. Holden and Swanson were nominated for Best Actor and Best Actress. Von Stroheim for Best Supporting Actor. Wilder for Best Director. Brackett, Wilder and Marshman for Best Original Story and Screenplay. Only the writers were elected. (For those who care, *All About Eve* was chosen Best Picture; José Ferrer was best actor, for his *Cyrano de Bergerac*; Judy Holliday won Best Actress for her *Born Yesterday;* George Sanders, Best Supporting Actor in *All About Eve;* and Joe Manciewicz won as Director for *All About Eve*.)

And now Wilder and Brackett parted after fourteen years of collaboration as a writer-director-producer combination. They were, and still remain, unique in the annals of movie history, for they were, *au fond*, two writers, two screenwriters who did not want to be a producer and a director but were drawn into it against their wishes in order to exercise control over their screenplays. They remained writers and were always to be writers, for though Brackett now became an important producer at Twentieth Century-Fox, he was a cowriter on many screenplays he produced. Wilder, of course, cowrote every screenplay he filmed. Of the two men, Brackett seemed the more dependent. He was, as their secretary Helen Hernandez once put it, a clinging vine. And yet, as Strindberg knew, such persons are often the strongest in a two-part relationship. Somehow their very dependency begins to make the other person always alert to ensure that the clinger is comfortable and safe, and finally Wilder could not stand it any longer. He had, you see, come to be very dependent and very fond of this man. He could not bear to be loved as Brackett loved him. So he became harsher and harsher, as was his wont when he felt too close to a person. Finally he was stifled by Brackett's swarming need of him and he had to end the affair. Remember, it was Wilder who always made metaphors of married love about their collaboration.

"We are Hollywood's happiest married couple," he would say to interviewers. And when the partnership temporarily split during *Double Indemnity,* Wilder later said, "Oh, it was just the usual marital infidelity." They both knew it was a marriage of love and hate, of power and dependency, and that it was Brackett who was the stronger and Wilder who was the weaker—though Wilder concealed his fear of being lonely and deserted under his armor of abrasiveness. . . .

In his book *Hollywood* (1974), Garson Kanin describes a deathbed scene with Brackett. Brackett was seventy-five years old and dying. Brackett confided to Kanin that the divorce had come as a shock to him. "I never knew what happened, never understood it, we were doing so well. . . . But we met one morning, as we always did, and

Billy smiled that sweet smile of his and said, 'You know, Charlie, after this, I don't think we should work together any more. I think it would be better for us if we just split up.' I could say nothing. It was shattering. Don't you think it was odd? What he did? There was no reason. . . . I don't think in all our years together, in all those pictures we made, we ever had a serious quarrel.''

I don't deny that Brackett said these melancholy words as he lay dying. I do deny that they are true—though Kanin believes them. Brackett and Wilder had been squabbling for years with one another. Violently. Insanely. As for it all coming as a "shattering" surprise to Brackett, this was not so, because after Wilder returned from Europe, he made it clear that the partnership would be terminated soon. They both knew *Sunset Boulevard* was to be their last picture as a team. All those close to the team—Helen Hernandez, Walter Reisch, William Dozier, Willie Schorr, Henry Ginsberg—all knew this and expected the divorce.

They never forgave each other. Brackett rarely spoke of Wilder. I had several meetings with him when I was investigating Marilyn Monroe during the '50s. Once, I asked Brackett a question about Billy. He at once froze up. I never mentioned Wilder again and he never referred to his former collaborator.

Wilder, on his part, also spoke as little as possible about his work with Brackett. He wanted to forget Charlie. He had been an admirer of the screenwriter, Richard Breen, who worked on *A Foreign Affair*. When Breen started writing with Brackett, Wilder cut him off and would not see him socially or work with him professionally. Walter Reisch, who had been one of his most intimate cronies since the Berlin years, wrote several films with Brackett. That ended the intimacy with Wilder. They were still friends, in a way, but the former intimacy was over. Reisch never worked on another picture with Billy.

Wilder would not trust any man who chose Brackett.

When Kanin's unflattering picture of Wilder as a monster came out, I asked Wilder about the truth of Brackett's deathbed confession. Wilder stopped pacing. He stared out of a window. Do you know what he said?

Nothing.

Absolutely nothing. And I changed the subject.

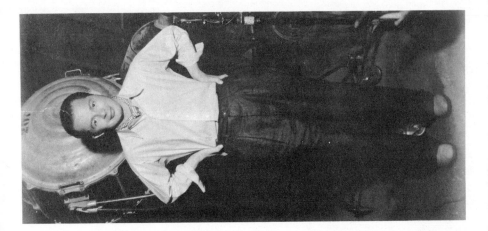

Billy Wilder, age three, might have been singing "Now we don our gay apparel" as he faced the camera for the first time in Vienna in 1909, with (from left) older brother, Willie; mother, Eugenia Baldinger Wilder; and father, Max Wilder. Little did the infant phenomenon realize that in his future there lay *Some Like It Hot*, with Tony Curtis and Jack Lemmon in drag.

In Paris while directing his first film, *Mauvaise Graine*, in a Neuilly garage converted to a movie set. He was 27 years old. He decided he would never direct a picture again.

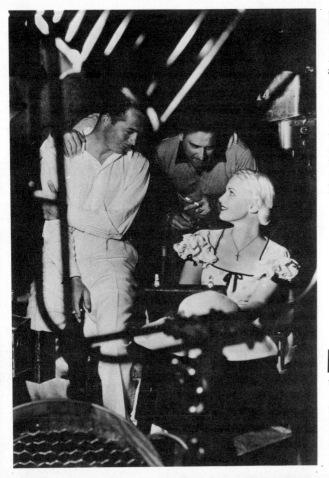

In 1934 Billy cowrote *Music in the Air,* his first Hollywood credit. It was directed by his great Berlin friend Joe May and produced by Erich Pommer. On the 20th Century Fox set we see Billy, director May and studio contract player June Lang. I do not know why the name of a then obscure Georgia town was chalked on the box, nor can I identify the owner of the disembodied hand on Billy's shoulder.

Mr. and Mrs. Wilder poolside at Joe May's place in the Hollywood Hills, about 1940. From left, Hanni Lowenstein (secretary to May), Billy, Judith Wilder, Joe May and the fabulous Mia May. The canines are named Inga and Chrystal.

A birthday party for Vicki Wilder—her fifth. Flanking the birthday girl are Michelle, a French poodle; and Johnny Waxman, an American boy, son of the composer Franz Waxman. The beautiful lady behind Vicki is her mama, and that adorable creature, with the blond bangs, staring up at you is Maureen Reagan, child of a certain Ronald.

Vicki Wilder sits in daddy's tall director's chair. Though he was a doting father, Billy found it hard to express his most tender emotions.

A beautiful lady herself, Vicki (now Mrs. Settember) visits daddy on the set of *Irma La Douce*. The child in grandfather's arms is her daughter, Julie Ann.

The old Eintänzer had not forgotten how to lull older women into a state of rapture as he danced them around a floor. In this glimpse of the director at work, we see Billy rehearsing Gloria Swanson for her New Year's Eve tango with William Holden in *Sunset Boulevard.*

Joyce Haber, an *arbiter elegantiarum* of the movie colony, once defined an "A" party as one at which Billy Wilder dances and Audrey Wilder sings. This one, a private party upstairs at the Bistro in 1976, was definitely an "A" party. The lady happily swept up in the old Eintänzer's practiced hands is Audrey Wilder. Later she sang a medley of swing tunes from the 1940s.

Ernst Lubitsch checks over the hand props in one of the suitcases Ninotchka has brought from Moscow. Greta Garbo's photo—an unposed shot—is extremely rare and has never before been published. *Ninotchka* was Garbo's penultimate film.

Ray Milland, starring in *The Lost Weekend*.
Wilder is pointing out that for an alcoholic "one drink is too many."

A still from the deleted sequence of the Brackett-Wilder classic *Double Indemnity*. Fred MacMurray is about to die in the Folsom Prison gas chamber while Edward G. Robinson's heart breaks as he watches. Wilder says it is one of the two best sequences he ever created.

Yes, that is Ginger Rogers as a twelve-year-old in Billy's first flight as an American director. We see him here as he positions the actors and makes some suggestions to Rita Johnson, who played the hero's fiancée, Ray Milland, and Ginger herself. The film: *The Major and the Minor*, a bit of 1942.

Before production on *Sunset Boulevard* started, Gloria Swanson held a conference with Brackett and Wilder in their suite. Perhaps the butterfly on her hat symbolized her hope that after almost a fifteen-year absence from pictures, she was going to leave the cocoon and fly once more. She did. Brackett and Wilder were never to work together again after this picture.

The look of love. At the traditional farewell cast and crew party after the wrap-up of *Sunset Boulevard*, Billy accompanied Audrey Young (right), band vocalist and Paramount contract player, whom he had asked to be his wife. Both their faces were radiant with feeling that afternoon, and even Gloria Swanson caught some of the romantic excitement.

Billy shows cinematographer Johnny Seitz what he has in mind for your typical monkey-funeral shot in *Sunset Boulevard*. The man in the grave is not Seitz; he is the camera operator. Seitz can be seen standing at left, with only his legs visible.

Producer Joe Sistrom, who discovered the stories *Double Indemnity* and *The Major and the Minor*, seen here going over sketches for *Double Indemnity* interiors with art director Hal Pereira.

While shooting *The Apartment* on the Goldwyn lot, Sam Goldwyn came over to see how the picture was going. Billy says, "Sam Goldwyn, so to speak, was the landlord of *The Apartment*." Wilder denies that he had just said to Goldwyn, "Where's the thousand dollars you still owe me?" Goldwyn's thumbing gesture indicates he is saying, "Up yours!"

Vicki Wilder, here eight years old, seizes daddy's bullhorn, while mama beams. Bing Crosby obviously has his mind on other matters, probably white Christmases. This was taken on the set of *The Emperor Waltz* at Paramount.

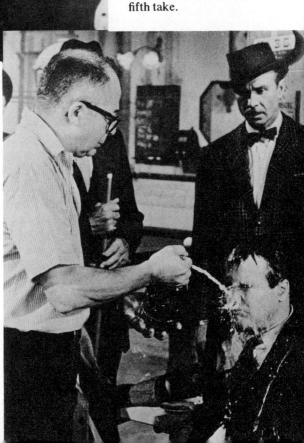

This is the elevator scene which drove Shirley MacLaine crazy during the making of *The Apartment*. She is saying, "But, Billy, for God's sakes, I already did four takes," and he is replying, "We need one more because you didn't read the lines as Iz and I wrote them." Jack Lemmon looks on with great pity. He knows what she is going through. She got it right on the fifth take.

But did Shirley return the sympathy when Wilder spritzed Lemmon in the face to show him how to react in a scene from *Irma La Douce*?

The ocean and a sandy beach and a crowd of admirers always induced euphoria in Marilyn Monroe. Billy Wilder says that the only time Marilyn was no problem was during the weeks they were working on location for *Some Like It Hot* at Coronado Beach, near San Diego, California. At left, the character in a girl's swimsuit, with breasts as big as Marilyn's, is—Jack Lemmon. The gentleman on the right is I. A. L. Diamond.

A rare still from another sequence you never saw. Peter Sellers played Orville J. Spooner in *Kiss Me, Stupid* for six weeks of filming until he suffered a massive coronary and was replaced. Wilder said that the footage he shot with Sellers was magnificent. It all had to be scrapped.

Ray Walston, who replaced Peter Sellers, is told how to impersonate a songwriter. Dean Martin looks up at Kim Novak with authentic lust. Kim Novak is looking at Billy Wilder with authentic fear. Her breasts are authentic, by the way, and larger than Marilyn's, though smaller than Jayne Mansfield's. The author has seen all three sets *en décolletage*.

On location at Loch Ness, Scotland, where Wilder shot *The Private Life of Sherlock Holmes*, he makes a point to French actress Genevieve Page, who played Ilse von Hoffmanstal, the German spy with whom Holmes falls in love. Was Ilse von Hoffmanstal an avatar of Billy Wilder's first love in Vienna? You will notice her black hair. All of Wilder's wives and lovers have been raven-haired.

Jack Lemmon, Wilder, Walter Matthau and Iz Diamond have just left a projection room at the Goldwyn studios on a late afternoon in January, 1966.
They have been looking at *Fortune Cookie* rushes. The rushes were awful.

James Cagney gave an electrifying performance in *One, Two, Three*. Here
Billy demonstrates an arm movement as Cagney flings off his suit coat.
Howard St. John, Pamela Tiffin, Horst Bucholz and Iz Diamond look on.

During the shooting of *The Apartment*, Iz Diamond, Jack Lemmon, Shirley Mac-Laine and Billy Wilder have lunch at the Goldwyn commissary. Raymond Chandler would have disapproved of Billy's wearing a hat during a collation. You will notice that Wilder is eating knockwurst. He loves all varieties of sausage. Also note the pack of Viceroys. At this time he was smoking five packs a day. He kicked cigarettes in 1971 and now chews five packs of gum a day instead.

Felicia Farr married Jack Lemmon in Paris during the filming of *Irma La Douce*. This shot of Diamond, Lemmon (in makeup as the Milord), Felicia and Billy was taken near one of the Seine bridges where Lemmon fakes a suicide.

Arthur Hornblow, Jr., who produced many of the films Wilder and Brackett wrote at Paramount, is seen with Billy during the shooting of *Witness for the Prosecution*, a Hornblow production. It was Hornblow who refereed the violent fights between Wilder and director Mitchell Leisen *(Midnight, Arise My Love, Hold Back the Dawn)*.

While filming on location in Paris, Wilder forgot to bring a hat one afternoon and Audrey Hepburn was teasing him about it and finally she took one of the props, a pannier, and put it on his head. Chandler would have disapproved of breadbaskets as headgear.

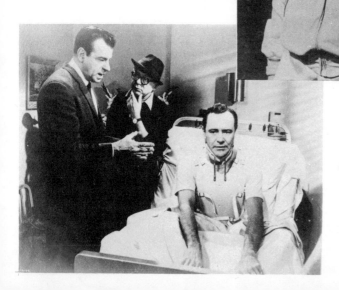

Walter Matthau is telling Billy Wilder how he thinks the scene between him and Jack Lemmon in *The Fortune Cookie* should be directed and photographed. Wilder listened. Then he did it his way.

To win a $50 bet with producer Leland Hayward and Jimmy Stewart, during filming of an aerial-circus sequence in *The Spirit of St. Louis*, Wilder did a wing-standing stunt. He flew at an elevation of 800 feet and at a speed of 65 miles an hour, and he was in the air about 10 minutes.

Hollywood's Happiest Writer-Director-Producer. Billy Wilder is being congratulated by Bob Hope on the night he became the first person to win three Oscars in one evening. He won them as screenwriter, director, and producer of *The Apartment*. Hope, who has never won an Oscar, is attempting to repress his envy.

Hollywood's Happiest Couple. Here, Audrey and Billy arrive at the Santa Monica Auditorium on Oscar night.

In the Wilder stateroom, autumn of 1975, aboard the *France* during her last voyage, are Leonard Gershe, Audrey and Billy.

# 16

# THE SONS
# OF BILLY WILDER

For seven years, Billy wrote with a varied succession of writers. Some were young and unknown. Some were old and well known. He had to have somebody there in the room. He could not write alone in the room. He had to have sons and I think that is what his cowriters became—his sons, his surrogate sons. He found in them what a father finds in his son—a miniature replica of himself and he would treat his surrogate sons as wet clay whom he wanted to mould into Billy Wilders. He would populate Hollywood with Billy Wilder clones. Naturally he would favor writers who were new to the screenwriting game and who were still raw in character. He had to be the teacher of the sons. He would show them how to live as well as to write. He would educate them. He would pass on his wisdom and subtle tastes to his heirs. He was, like some fathers, a stern taskmaster. He was hard. He was even harsh and cruel. He had to show them how to survive in the jungle out there. He was severe with his sons because he loved them so much. And his sons, as sons will do, rebelled and hated him and resented his authority, but always loved him and respected him. None of them was the same after experiencing Wilder's scourging discipline, and witty tongue-lashings. For better or for worse, he changed every one of them—except the last man. The first one was Walter Brown Newman, a twenty-year-old radio writer. Billy heard one of his plays one night on his car radio. He summoned Newman to a conference. Newman was goggle-eyed. He remembers Wilder in a black Tyrolean velour hat which he did not remove, and that Wilder did not stand still and did not sit. He strode nervously back and forth, swinging a malacca cane. Newman recognized it. It was the cane Gloria Swanson used in her Chaplin routine in *Sunset Boulevard.*

Billy sized Newman up. Newman was, and is, a quiet and polite gentleman, a listener, a sensitive absorber. He listened as Billy told him about an idea he had. A leading gangster, a sort of Frank Costello type, starts going to a psychoanalyst to treat an embarrassing condition for a Mafia *capo*, namely, that he suddenly breaks out crying. He naturally has to divulge his secrets to the analyst. This worries his fellow gangsters. "Do not worry, boys," he says, "as soon as I am cured, I will *kill him.*"

Newman was laughing. It was a perfectly marvelous weenie. Billy asked him if he wanted to collaborate. Yes. They started working the following morning. After three weeks, they abandoned the weeping gangster. They could not lick the story. Billy had another idea. There was in England, a Tory gentleman, a Lord Something, an imposing nobleman of the old school. All his fellow squires are being taxed out of existence but this lord, he still lives as though in the past—with his servants and paintings and antiques and horses. How does he do this? The secret is that when he tells them he is going to his ranch in Canada—he is *really* a television wrestler in the United States and is making a fortune as the "Masked Marvel."

Walter Newman was in stitches. After they had been discussing the story for several days, Billy said he thought they were making progress and now he wanted them to write it for Charles Laughton. He said the great actor was to be here at 5:30. Laughton arrived punctually. He brought Wilder a Hokusai print as a gift. Wilder now told the story of the Masked Marvel who was a British nobleman.

Newman told me, "I witnessed a sight which was, well, quite unbelievable. I never saw such a sight in my life."

For as Wilder recounted some of the wrestler's adventures, Laughton literally fell apart. He shook with spasms of laughter. He became hysterical with laughter. He—*literally*, Newman assures me—tumbled out of his chair and lay on the floor, his 250-pound body shaking like jelly. Then he started crawling on his hands and knees across the floor. Billy stopped pacing.

"Oh, genius," Laughton moaned, "oh, genius."

He took one of Billy's hands and kissed it—and kissed it—as if Wilder were some kind of a religious dignitary, a pope or cardinal.

But Wilder and Newman could not develop the Masked Marvel macguffin and they severed the partnership. As he was leaving, Newman remarked that the Floyd Collins story was a good premise for a picture. What was that? Wilder never heard of Collins. Newman told him about this man in Kentucky trapped in a cave for many days while the whole country prayed for him.

"So long and good luck," Wilder said.

Newman forgot about it, until suddenly, some weeks later, he found a message to call Wilder and to hurry over to Paramount. He was at once back on the payroll and cowriting *Ace in the Hole* with Billy and Lesser Samuels, an ex-newspaperman and Paramount contract writer. The trio composed a harsh and pitiless study of human beings at their worst. Wilder gave his misanthropy a wild ride. It was a movie unrelieved by laughter. It was cold and hard. It was the first public dissection of one of those hypes we have come to know as "the media event." Wilder not only savaged the average American who smacked his lips at tragedy and made a carnival with popcorn and carousels, but he ridiculed the press and radio and television for exploiting misery. Kirk Douglas, portraying a vicious alcoholic reporter from a big town, who is down on his luck and takes a job on an Albuquerque paper, made journalists into a species of hustler and hypocrite. Billy had very little good to say about those who flourished under the First Amendment, or anybody else— except the victim's parents, who were honest and religious and simpleminded, good people. Filmed almost entirely on location in New Mexico, it is a vivid piece of cinema, authentic in its images and events, and it has the sheen of *cinéma vérité*. It was a totally uncompromising film at a time when the movies were said to be totally compromised. It is shocking even now. Imagine how much more shocking it was in 1951. You felt as if you had been violently beaten up when you walked out of the movie theater. We had never seen an American film like this before.

*Ace in the Hole* was castigated by the critics and shunned by the public. Wilder was called a cynical man. The film was denounced as an untruthful attack on the integrity of American newspapers and on the new medium of television.

Wilder, formerly king of the Paramount hill, now felt like an outcast in the commissary. People looked the other way. He was losing friends all over the place.

Besides his other troubles, he and the studio were sued for plagiarism by a Victor Desny. Desny was an actor. Desny had made an agreement with Homer Collins, brother of Floyd Collins, for the rights to the Collins story. He asserted—and proved—that he had vainly attempted to sell this idea to Paramount. He proved he had submitted a story on the Collins entombment!

Now it happens that Billy and his sons were already writing their screenplay when Desny phoned Wilder one day. But Rosella Stewart, his new secretary (Helen Hernandez had chosen to cast her lot with Charlie Brackett at Twentieth), was always instructed to keep mum on any project in work. So when Desny had phoned and spoke to her about his Floyd Collins story she did not tell him they were already writing on a similar theme. She was forbidden to tell these secrets.

As a result of Wilder's penchant for secrecy, Desny had a good case and a good lawyer—Jerry Giesler. Giesler got a $25,000 settlement out of Paramount.

With *Ace in the Hole,* Billy's relationship with Paramount became strained. His contract gave him the right of final cut and choice of title. "Without my consent and without consulting me even, Mr. Y. Frank Freeman, having decided it was a bad title, changed it to *The Big Carnival,*" Wilder says.

Several years later, Newman ran into Wilder on the Goldwyn lot. They were ambling along when Wilder suddenly said, "You know that picture we made—*Ace in the Hole*—that lost me power at the studio."

Then he shouted, "Fuck them all—it is the best picture I ever made."

Newman was to become a great screenwriter, his credits including *Man with the Golden Arm* and *Cat Ballou. Ace in the Hole* was nominated for Best Screenplay by the Academy members. In his definitive book on the craft, *Screenwriters Look at Screenwriting,* William Froug states that among the "Hollywood cognoscenti" Newman is considered one of the "half-dozen best screenwriters working in American films today."

Newman believes his training under Wilder made this possible. He recalls two Wilder aphorisms. Discussing women characters in films, Wilder vouchsafed,

"Unless she's a whore, she's a bore."

Dissecting a scene written by Newman and Samuel, he said it was dull. "Now"—he posed a rhetorical question—"what is it which makes a scene interesting? If you see a man coming through a door-way, it means nothing. If you see him coming through a window—that is at once interesting. Please bear this in mind in every scene."

At their last meeting, Newman saw the malacca cane amongst other canes and umbrellas in an umbrella rack. He said it looked like the cane used in *Sunset Boulevard*. Was it? It was. Wilder asked him if he liked it. He did. Wilder gave it to him.

Sometimes Newman likes to take long walks in downtown Los Angeles, around Main and Fifth where there are shuffling crowds of pedestrians like in New York, and he swings the malacca cane, Gloria Swanson's cane. He never wrote with Wilder again.

Billy's next filial selection fell on Norman Krasna, who was hard-ly a neophyte. Krasna was a master of the wisecrack movie. He and Wilder had first met at Columbia when both men were new to Holly-wood. They enjoyed each other's company. They could volley these clever jibes back and forth. Krasna was a fast man with a verbal punch. He was a fast man in general. It is believed that he—and Jer-ry Wald—were models for the hero of *What Makes Sammy Run?* He had written a score of commercial films and won an Oscar as writer for a film he also directed, *Princess O'Rourke*. Even so, he was flattered to be asked to lunch at Romanoff's, and asked to write a movie with a man he considered a master. Wilder was now toying with the notion of a screwball comedy with . . . Laurel and Hardy! He pointed out that their features were popular in Europe, though forgotten in the states. Europe was providing about fifty percent of the gross of Hollywood films, as the American box office, feeling the pressure of television, was starting its slow decline. Wilder told how they would open with a longshot of that famous HOLLYWOOD sign and zoom in for a close-up, very tight, and we'd see Stan sleeping in an O and Ollie sleeping in another O. They are movie extras. Oh, yes, the story was about Hollywood during the Mack Sennett cus-tard-pie comedy era. They lived in a cemetery. A rich widow, com-ing to pay her respects to her late husband, falls in love with Ollie—but hates Laurel. . . A triangle, *n'est-ce pas?*

Krasna found it irresistible. Wouldn't you?

They started writing. Before a month was out, Krasna resigned. He says if he had not, he would have murdered Billy. He says Billy insisted on doing all the talking. It was becoming a Wilder film, not a Krasna-Wilder film. He said he felt like a $150,000-a-year stenographer.

Q: Was that why you walked out, Norman?

A: Not entirely. It was really his insults. He would say these terrible things to me. Ridiculing me. He knew where I was vulnerable—and he stuck me in these places. They were sharp wisecracks. What kind of cracks? I wouldn't repeat them to you. They could still be used against me. I just couldn't take the abuse. The funny thing about it is, he loved me. We remained friends. When I was hung up on a story, I would phone him and get his ideas and when he was in some trouble with *Avanti!* I went over to Italy a few weeks and helped him out. But sit in the same room with this lovable monster and write a script? Never, never, never—

Edwin Blum, also a veteran screenwriter, was the next person to be tapped by the Emperor's baton. They knew each other from the Beverly Hills Tennis Club. They played bridge together. They played tennis together. Blum started collaborating with him on the Laurel and Hardy movie. Then Oliver Hardy got sick. The movie was discarded. Blum was still on salary at Paramount.

Billy now proposed a black version of *Camille.* The setting would be Harlem. It would become a musical. The love affair would be between a high-yellow courtesan from Sugar Hill and a lieutenant in the U.S. Navy—a handsome young white man—whose real father, though he does not know it, is a black man. The lieutenant is passing! The father would reveal the truth to the courtesan and ask her to give up his son to protect his career. Well, all this seems like an awfully amiable idea for a film in 1977—but this was 1951—and it was unconventional, to say the least, to have a white man, even if he is really a light-skinned Negro, enamored of a black woman, even if she is a mulatto. Wilder was excited by the possibilities. He saw a score written by Duke Ellington, who was his favorite black composer of jazz. He had already spoken to Lena Horne and she would be Camille. Paul Robeson had agreed to be the father. And Tyrone Power was excited at the prospect of playing opposite Miss Horne in a Billy Wilder musical extravaganza.

Wilder and Blum struggled with the black *Camille* for about six weeks. They could not resolve the structural and character problems of the story. It was an idea whose time had not come.

Billy went to New York. He saw *Stalag 17.* It was a Broadway hit. No studio would buy it and independent producers wouldn't touch it. It was a play about prisoners in a Nazi camp. There were no women in it. Wilder purchased it with his own money. He paid $50,000 for it. This was an incredible bargain for a Broadway hit. It was like picking up a Matisse *odalisque* for—well, for $50,000. Blum read the play. The drama was wound around a situation in which the prisoners try to trap a Nazi informer disguised as an American soldier in their midst. Blum couldn't see a movie in this. He asked Billy why he had bought the play.

"Guys in underwear," Billy said.

"Huh?"

"You didn't see it so you don't appreciate it. There are guys running around in underwear. That's what I bought. You want to write it with me?"

At $2,000 a week, Blum was not disposed to argue the aesthetic merits of *Stalag 17*. He figured if worst came to the worst he would get to improve his tennis with Billy and would win some money at bridge. Some of Billy's enemies, and they were now as common as snails in California gardens, were saying that Blum got the job because he was a good bridge player.

Now the hero of this little drama was a man called Sefton, and Wilder had Charlton Heston in mind for the part, as Sefton was a noble person—not quite as noble as Moses, but fairly noble for a prisoner of war. However, as Wilder began reconverting the play into a movie, his baser impulses took over once more and Sefton became as sly and conniving and wicked a character as Kirk Douglas had played in *Ace,* except that Sefton was an amusing hustler. I would like to digress here for a few sentences and remind the reader that the anti-hero in films, about which we heard so many trumpetings during the 1960s and 1970s, when Dustin Hoffman, Jack Nicholson and other naturalistic stars came into view, was an old story with Wilder, except that nobody praised him for his anti-heroes and they hadn't even thought up this phrase. But the original anti-heroes in American films were: Walter Neff *(Double Indemnity),* Don Birnam *(Lost Weekend),* Joe Gillis *(Sunset Boulevard),* Chuck Tatum *(Ace in the Hole.)*

Wilder was wretched when his work was not only misunderstood and reviled, but lost money. He concealed his misery by attacking our movie critics—the daily reviewers and the highbrow essayists. Asked once for whom he made pictures, he snorted, "I make movies for six people in Bel Air."

He would not identify these persons.

Having transformed Sefton into a hustler who sneered at patriotism and thought war an absurdity, Wilder had to forget Charlton Heston. How could Heston possibly impersonate a man who makes alcohol out of prunes and sells it to his fellow prisoners for cigarettes—which he trades with the Nazi jailers for contraband cameras and silk stockings? He puts on races at his Stalag 17 Turf Club using live mice and booking cigarette bets. He charges two cigarettes for a twenty-second look at Russian women prisoners through a telescope he's bartered. Please allow me to remind you once again all these dreadfully anti-American, antiwar sentiments appeared in a—yes—*Paramount* picture in 1953, fifteen years before *M*A*S*H* and *Catch 22*.

And now Wilder went through the usual obstacle course in securing a leading man. Nobody wanted to play Sefton. He finally resorted to William Holden, who was now already an important star, and only by playing on Holden's guilt feelings and his debt to Wilder was he able to secure him.

But Holden was not happy, and all during the filming he pestered Wilder to rewrite his role and to at least insert a few anti-Nazi lines and make him basically a good human being. Wilder urged him to have faith. Holden skulked around the set grumbling under his breath and predicting disaster for *Stalag 17* and a setback in his own career.

Lo and behold, on Oscar night, William Holden received the golden statue for Best Performance by an Actor—beating out Burt Lancaster, Marlon Brando, Richard Burton, and Montgomery Clift. There was a party at Romanoff's later. Holden raised high a glass of Dom Perignon and quieted the group at the large table.

"To Billy Wilder," he said grinning, and added, "Of course I knew it all the time."

In dollar terms, *Stalag 17* was his biggest Paramount hit, grossing over $10,000,000 in its first year of release, a formidable return in a period when ticket prices were about half of today's prices.

Billy retrieved his power at the studio. He was in for a substantial share of the profits. His dreams of perhaps raking in a million dollars above his salary vanished as the Paramount accountants and lawyers found a method of applying the profits on this one against the losses of *Ace in the Hole*. The way it wound up he practically owed the studio money.

Blum regarded himself, as do most of the Wilder cowriters, as "little more than his butler. It was his screenplay. My name is on the credits but I don't think of it as mine. Oh, I made important contributions, especially in developing Sefton. When you work with Billy he rules you a thousand percent. I couldn't take insults. I wouldn't work with him on another picture. I know he is a man that the more he likes you, the more sarcastic he gets, but I couldn't take it. Yet he treated me as nobody had ever treated me before."

After they finished the script and it was time to go into production Wilder told him:

"You will continue on the payroll as my associate—through the directing, editing, scoring and final cut. Anything you want to say at any point, say it—any suggestions, any criticisms, I want to hear it."

Puffing on his pipe, Blum says, "In my experience—forty years of screenwriting, I have never been able to talk to a single director about anything—I mean, *anything*—except for this one experience with Billy."

Q: Was it then worthwhile, Eddie?

A *(after a long pause):* No.

Q: How come?

A: I just couldn't take his insults.

Among Wilder aphorisms were: "When you and I *write* something, we are *directing* it at the same time. When you write in this office with me, always remember you are also directing the film. Everything that goes on paper is final. That is the picture. We create it right here—the whole complete film, right here in this room.

"Don't be too clever for an audience. *Make it obvious.*"

Blum asked, "But, Billy, how about subtleties?"

"Make the subtleties obvious also," Billy snapped.

Ernest Lehman remembers his first encounter with Billy Wilder. It was 1951. His *Cosmopolitan* novella, *The Sweet Smell of Success,* was a success. Paramount signed him to a one-year contract. John Mock, the new head of the writers department, brought him over to the writers table one day. Lehman was wearing conservative habiliments—striped tie, button-down shirt, J. Press suit. He remembers being introduced to Sid Boehm, Ed Hartman, Norman Panama, Mel Frank, Ben Hecht—and Billy Wilder.

Billy's opening line was: "I have heard such nice things about you. You are the best-dressed writer in Hollywood since Casey Robinson."

Lehman didn't know what this implied. He knew from the snickers he was being put down. He later asked Mock what about this Casey Robinson crack. Mock said Robinson, a veteran screenwriter, always dressed like an Easterner.

After a year at Paramount, Lehman's option was dropped. John Houseman, producing *Executive Suite* at MGM, hired him to write it. He did. He wrote a fine script for this all-star picture. Among the stars was William Holden. Holden praised Lehman's dialogue to Wilder. Wilder was now working on an adaptation of *Sabrina Fair,* a Broadway hit by Sam Taylor. Taylor was also a screenwriter with many credits. Taylor's most famous credit was on Warner Bros.' *Midsummer Night's Dream.* The writer credits read: "By William Shakespeare. Additional Dialogue by Sam Taylor."

Taylor who had, after all, collaborated with Shakespeare, withdrew after several weeks of taking Wilder's abuse. Lehman was brought in. He now began the grueling existence of a Wilder collaborator. He went to Billy's house for breakfast. They talked all morning, at home and in the studio. Then they lunched and then he usually remained for cocktails and dinner. Wilder's propensity for jibes at those he loved was something Ernie never got used to, even though he knew that Billy did it with everybody. He used to make cracks at Audrey and even at Audrey's father, once saying, "Her father is so stingy he goes to a Chinese dentist who fills his teeth with rice." Lehman's dietary habits drove Wilder crazy. For instance, he could not get over the fact that Ernie hated caviar. He recalls an argument he and Billy had over headcheese.

"If you serve headcheese," Ernie said, "forget it."

"What do you mean, forget it?"

"It is that simple, Billy. I don't eat it. I never have eaten it. I never will eat it."

"Who brought you up, King Kong?" he yelled.

He regarded Lehman's eating habits with contempt, though Audrey Wilder catered to them. What Ernie liked for a repast was sandwiches—peanut butter and jelly, cream cheese and jelly, white meat of turkey with Russian dressing, bacon and tomato on toast, melted American cheese on toast. He drank milk instead of champagne.

"It made him angry that I wanted to eat like I was getting a quick lunch at a drugstore counter," Lehman recalls. "I think it pained him to be working with a man of plebian tastes. Billy has to take over your whole life. You don't just collaborate on a script with him. He has to change what you wear and what you eat. Well, I just couldn't stomach the sight of headcheese or caviar."

For Ernie, Billy Wilder was exhilarating, exasperating and, ultimately, exhausting. There was his perfectionism. "I would make a suggestion—for instance, throw him a line. He would say, 'That is very good.' Pause . . . one beat. 'But we can do better.' Or: 'Very good' . . . (beat) . . . 'but let us make it better.' Make it better—that to a great extent is his credo."

In September 1953, they entrained for New York. The exteriors and interiors of the Larrabee estate were shot on Barney Balaban's Glen Cove, Long Island, estate. Lehman and Wilder were still writing the script.

Lehman: "That was when I realized the quality of desperation in this situation. Billy must have brought this upon himself, and upon those who worked with him, out of some unconscious need for crises. I found out he rarely started a picture with a completed script. This is not done in Hollywood. It is dangerous."

Wilder got himself trapped as a result of dawdling over the script. To start filming with an unfinished screenplay was supremely dangerous when the director was also a writer. Wilder set himself a physically impossible task. He would not let Lehman write by himself. Lehman wrote all day. Wilder directed all day. Then he sat up with Lehman most of the night and they rewrote. Wilder survived on two, three hours of sleep and endless cigarettes and coffee. Lehman's nerves got more ragged. They soon reached the point where they were only one day ahead of the shooting and then they fell behind.

Wilder suddenly asked cinematographer Charles Lang to make a most peculiar arrangement of lighting for the next camera setup.

"And take your time about it," he told him. "I want it to be perfect. Give me a Murnau feel. Give me a Sternberg effect." Doane Harrison wondered why this sudden surge of impressionism?

"I'll tell you why, Doane," Wilder snapped, "it's because Ernie and I, we ain't got the goddam dialogue finished for the next scene." He was stalling for time.

While the cinematographer and crew spent hours lighting the set, Wilder raced back to the studio bungalow where Lehman was feverishly typing. By now it was time for the cast to go home. He and Lehman had the whole night to polish the pages. In the last weeks of filming, Lehman collapsed. One morning he started weeping uncontrollably. Billy put his arm around him and tenderly murmured, "Nobody ever worked harder than you did, Ernie. Now you must go home and rest and do not worry."

Billy shut down the production for two days, while Ernie rested. Ernie's physician, Dr. Ray Spritzler, gave him a shot which put him out for thirteen hours. He was ordered to stay in bed and cease working on the screenplay.

Wilder thought this revealed a shocking medical ignorance of the picture business. So the next night, he arrived at Lehman's house. Lehman, in pajamas, sat up in bed and, somewhat weakly, argued with Billy about a certain sequence which had given them more trouble than any other. It is the one in which Audrey Hepburn, having switched her affections from the younger playboy Larrabee brother (Holden) to the older and stuffier Larrabee (Bogart) comes to his office at night and, like Ninotchka, makes him an omelette. Billy and Ernie saw this scene differently.

"We had many fights about it," Lehman remembers. "Now at that time I had no authority in Hollywood. I was still an unproduced screenwriter. Billy wanted Bogey to sleep with Audrey Hepburn. I said we can't do it, no dice, people don't want that, particularly for Audrey Hepburn. She was just a slip of a girl, nineteen years old then, gentle and sweet. She had won the Academy Award for *Roman Holiday*. He was furious at me for insisting they don't sleep with each other. I wouldn't give in on this point. He called me all kinds of names, eunuch, fag, didn't know women, hated sex, was afraid of women, but in this vile and vicious manner he has when he's insulting you.

"What we would do at night, after the day's shooting, we would hang around on the set of Bogart's office, trying to get the feeling of the scene. The omelette was his idea. As you know he worked out some beautiful touches for the scene with Audrey. And of course she did *not* sleep with him finally.

"Yet, Gawd, that one scene seemed so hopeless. It was just hopeless. We could not write it. We tried it one way. We tried it another way. It was hopeless. We did not know what the hell to do with it. I remember one night after Billy had been on the set all day, and then we were at his house working on this scene and we couldn't think indoors. We started walking the streets of Beverly Hills together and it was two, three in the morning; absolutely crazy we were, and we were panicked, as he had to start shooting that scene in the morning, in a few hours, and we did not have a word on paper. Finally we went back in his house. I put a sheet of paper in the roller and started typing lines, lines we had framed as we walked. Then I read it to him."

Billy snarled. At four-thirty in the *morning*, Billy phoned C. C. Coleman, assistant director. He said cancel the calls for Bogart and Hepburn. No shooting tomorrow!

Ernie got worse. Dr. Spritzler said *no work for two weeks*. Billy came around anyway for an hour or two in the evening to debate whether or not Bogart and Hepburn should copulate. One evening, Jacqueline (Mrs. Lehman) burst into the bedroom and said Dr. Spritzler had unexpectedly dropped in to look at his patient.

Billy Wilder scuttled into a closet.

Dr. Spritzler examined his patient. He pronounced him normal.

"Well, Doc," Ernie said, "I guess I can tell Mr. Wilder to come out now."

Wilder bounded out of the closet. He wore a pleased expression on his face. He had outfoxed the medical profession.

Lehman's antipathy to caviar was challenged by Wilder when the twain were going to New York. Irving Lazar had sent Billy a gift basket including a one-pound tin of unsalted beluga caviar. The first night on the Super Chief, Ernie and Billy were talking script in Billy's compartment and Billy insisted he eat caviar. Ernie refused. During the next few days of the cross-country trip, Wilder never let up badgering him.

As they were pulling into New York's Grand Central Station, Wilder asked Ernie to tuck in his suitcase several train towels, on which were stitched "New York Central R.R." Ernie did. Laden with their baggage, they taxied to the St. Regis Hotel. A valet and two bellmen took Wilder and Lehman up to their interconnecting suites.

Suddenly some impulse made Ernie ask, very loudly, "Oh, Billy, what do you want me to do with those towels you asked me to *steal* from the train?"

He did not know why he said this—in front of the servants, yet. Wilder looked crushed. After he tipped the bellman, he said sadly to Ernie, "That is the sort of thing I expect my wife to say to me."

Wilder could never understand why his amiable wisecracks were misunderstood by his friends. He was so vulnerable to retorts himself. That was the paradox in him.

Wilder was going through physical hell while making *Sabrina*. His back hurt so badly he sometimes fell down in agony, while directing. He went in to Manhattan one day to get treated by his old Berlin friend, Dr. "Maxi" Jacobson, the notorious Dr. Feelgood. Ernie drove in from Long Island with him. He waited outside the consulting room. He could hear Billy screaming in pain. Screaming and screaming.

And Ernie found himself exulting in Wilder's screams. He was ashamed of himself for feeling happy, but he could not help himself. Billy Wilder deserved to suffer!

In November, Don Hartman (now executive head of production) gave Wilder an ultimatum. Shooting must end the following Saturday night. Wilder and Lehman still had not written the crucial scene in which Audrey Hepburn's father is driving her to the pier to take a boat to France.

Saturday morning came. The scene was not written yet. Lehman was in Wilder's office. He was trying to concentrate on the father-and-daughter scene. He could not. There was noise outside. Dean Martin and Jerry Lewis and some friends were playing a loud game of touch football.

Lehman pulled up his window and yelled, "Shut up, you creeps, I'm trying to work."

They ignored him. Billy returned at noon. Ernie said he couldn't write with that racket outside.

Wilder called the Paramount security officer and asked that Martin and Lewis stop. The officer stated that the comedians, who were then the hottest property at the studio, could not be touched. Wilder phoned D. A. Doran, executive assistant to Hartman. Doran dared not interfere, either. Martin and Lewis were sacred. John Mock finally let Ernie use his office. Ernie finished the scene.

Billy started shooting at two P.M. John Williams, the father, kept blowing his takes. He had a lengthy speech. He would get it right—and then stumble on a word or a phrase. They broke for supper at eight P.M. without a printable take. They resumed at nine. Williams was still blowing his lines.

On the seventy-fourth take, he got it right.

Billy sighed. He shouted, "Cut—print—*this is it.*"

Then he did a strange thing. He looked at the heavens and screeched, *"Fuck you."*

It was, Ernie figured, a victory cry, as if he were calling out to God and saying, "I completed this picture despite everything you did to make me surrender."

In the course of a long colloquy between Lehman and me, we had the following exchange:

Q: Well, Ernie, now there's a kind of what you might call sophisticated tenderness that's typical of your dialogue, I'd say, in *North by Northwest* and *Sweet Smell of Success;* and when I recently watched *Sabrina* I couldn't help but feel that this romanticism came from you, more than Billy, as his sophistication is harder—harsher in tone.

A: Well, thank you, but I must tell you that in those days Billy was most romantic. He could write a romantic line or a romantic scene. All his movies have a romantic flavor because he is a romantic person. And it's a kind of an American romantic feel, an F. Scott Fitzgerald feel about love. It comes out in his love of American popular love songs. As I got to know Billy, I was always surprised by how deeply he was immersed in American life. For instance, he isn't just a casual Dodger fan. He knows all the names and statistics and he feels the feelings that go with the names. That's it—the feelings. He feels like an American feels. I never think of Billy as being a European—not at all, not at all. You get Billy on a political subject, hell, he won't sound like a guy remote from the American scene. I have this feeling he was conscious of people thinking of him as European and I think he wanted to do the *Spirit of St. Louis* because it was a very American subject. He wanted to take the most American of all subjects—and make it his.

*Sabrina* was a hit in this country and even bigger in Europe. Wilder had a strong following in England, France, Italy, Germany. He got a letter from George Weltner, a Paramount executive who masterminded worldwide distribution. Weltner wanted to make a special dubbed version of *Stalag 17* for German release. Germany was now a rich market for Hollywood pictures. Weltner suggested that Wilder change the Nazi spy into a *Polish prisoner of war who has sold out to the Nazis!*

Wilder dictated a letter in white heat. He told about his own background in Galicia, and about what the Nazis had done to the Jews. He was proud of the Jewish resistance in Warsaw. Not only would he not make this change but unless he received an apology he would sever his connection with Paramount.

He got no apology. He walked out on the best contract a writer-director ever had. He walked out on complete autonomy as to story, casting, final cut, total power, a high salary as writer and director, a percentage of the profits. His honor had been impugned.

And so, after twenty years, he drove his Jaguar XKE through the Bronson Gate, never to return.

He never forgave a reference, even jocular, suggesting he had a Prussian streak or strutted like a Nazi officer. Wilder would have forgiven Humphrey Bogart every insult except this one, quoting Bogart in *Time:* "Wilder is the kind of Prussian German with a riding crop. He's the type of director I don't like to work with. This picture *Sabrina* is a crock of shit anyway."

John Huston was directing *The Roots of Heaven.* He asked Wilder to give him an opinion on Romain Gary's script. Wilder criticized it harshly. Visiting Huston at his hotel one evening, Billy noticed a letter from M. Gary to Darryl Zanuck. It was a nasty letter and it ended with these words: "I cannot understand why you and Huston would ask a well-known Nazi like Wilder for advice on this script."

Gary entered. Wilder leaped on him. He might have killed the Frenchman, according to Huston's story, if Huston hadn't pulled him off.

Romain Gary later was appointed French consul in Los Angeles. About fifteen years ago, Wilder received word from the French ambassador that he had been awarded the Legion of Honor. Wilder prized this recognition highly. Informed however that the red ribbon would be pinned on him at a ceremony in Los Angeles by consul Romain Gary, he refused the coveted ribbon.

Billy resents slurs not only on his own reputation, but on that of his friends. He admired the reporting of Murray Schumach, who for some years covered the Hollywood scene for the *New York Times.* He was a friend of Schumach's. Schumach was attacked in *Close-Up. Close-Up* is a weekly scandal sheet put out by Jaik Rosenstein, a former press agent. As a result of Rosenstein's innuendos that Schumach accepted gifts in return for favorable studio stories, Schumach was recalled to New York, where he is still a valued staff member.

Now we dissolve to 1971. Rosenstein was being sued for libel. He did not have many friends in Hollywood. He called several character witnesses. Among them was Otto Preminger.

Wilder considered this a personal insult. Rosenstein had insulted his friend Schumach. Preminger was helping Rosenstein. Ergo, Wilder could no longer be Preminger's friend.

From that day to this, Wilder has refused to have any social intercourse with Otto Preminger, whom he had known well for so many years.

One of Billy's close friends is that aggressive little agent, Irving Paul Lazar, known as "Swifty," because of his speed in making moves when he smells money. He is not Billy's agent, as he handles only writers. He has represented such authors as Irwin Shaw, Moss Hart, Noel Coward, Cole Porter, George S. Kaufman, and Richard M. Nixon. It was Lazar who set up the recent $2,000,000 deal for Nixon's memoirs.

Lazar was attending a cocktail party in Bel Air. About ten feet away, he overheard Kenneth MacKenna, of MGM, say that his studio was about to close a deal for *Seven Year Itch*. This was the biggest hit on Broadway. It was written by the unknown George Axelrod. MacKenna remarked that Axelrod had the audacity to ask for Billy Wilder as his director!

Lazar inhaled the intoxicating aroma of large sums of money. Lazar asked Wilder whether he would like to direct *Seven Year Itch*. Swifty said he would maneuver so Wilder got to direct this smash Broadway sensation. By the way, could he be Wilder's agent on the deal? Certainly, said Billy. Lazar at once flew to New York. He whispered to Axelrod that he would be able to get—honestly—none other than that brilliant master of comedy, Mr. Wilder, to direct George's fine play. How would George like that? George loved that. By the way, added Lazar as an afterthought, he would of course like to represent Axelrod on this deal.

So now, Swifty had ten percent of Billy's end and ten percent of George's end. Then Charles K. Feldman, who was Marilyn Monroe's agent, came to Lazar. He wanted *Itch* for his blonde client. Could Lazar somehow arrange this matter? Of course, he would have to persuade Billy—who had personally bought the play with his own money, for $255,000—to sell the property to Twentieth Century Fox, Marilyn's studio. How about it? Oh, my, it was hard, but leave it to Lazar. One little thing, though—why shouldn't Feldman become *producer* of the picture and let Lazar agent his producer's deal with Twentieth? Sure, why not? So now, in one of the brilliant strokes in agent history, Lazar got ten percent of Feldman's salary. He also resold the play rights to Twentieth—for $500,000.

Axelrod was collaborating on the script. He brought his play to the first meeting. He handed it to Billy, who said, "This we forget right away, Mr. Axelrod?"

"What'll we do with it?"

"Well, we could use it as a doorstop."

They worked either at Billy's office at Twentieth or Billy's office at Warner's. Billy was preparing a movie for Warner's, simultaneously with *Itch.* He was driving back and forth with George. In between Wilder would stop in bookshops, antique stores, galleries, men's boutiques, and browse. He browsed and he bought. Axelrod had never known a compulsive collector before. He remembers Wilder being obsessed with thin neckties, which were just coming into vogue. Billy would go into a shop and buy a dozen narrow cravats in all colors. He did not wear ties as a rule so Axelrod could not make sense of this.

They usually started their mornings with warm-ups, inventing "meet-cutes" for imaginary movies.

"One of them," Axelrod says, "was about two psychiatrists, a man and a woman, and they send out their couches to be reupholstered and, by mistake, they get each other's couches—and so they meet and fall in love. This was so good that I used it as the second act curtain speech in *Will Success Spoil Rock Hunter?* Our best was a cold war romantic comedy. We fade in on an exterior, night, the Russian embassy in Washington, camera dollies in to a colonel working at a desk. He is played by Yul Brynner. Phone rings across the office. Camera trucks with Yul as he answers phone. Cut to Audrey Hepburn in bed. Audrey is wife of the British ambassador. She is doing the Sunday *London Times* crossword puzzle. She has called to find out what Lenin's middle name is, for the puzzle. Yul is very angry and tells her she has insulted Soviet Russia. She laughs in her charming way. Yul slams down phone. Now we cut to a State Department ball. Yul Brynner is there. He is a military attaché. He hears that same beautiful laughter across the room. He crosses over. Clicks his heels. Bows. Says one word: "Ilyitch." Audrey looks puzzled. Then she remembers. Why it's Lenin's middle name and this must be . . . And so they meet and fall in love.

"Billy Wilder is the greatest authority on meet-cutes who has ever lived. He is also the most consummate film craftsman I have ever known. Everything I know about writing films I learned during these five terrible months I was writing with him. To this day, when I get into a quandary on a script, I ask myself, *What would Billy Wilder do in this situation?*"

Axelrod went on to write such marvelous pictures as *Bus Stop, Breakfast at Tiffany's, The Manchurian Candidate,* and that cult black comedy, *Lord Love a Duck.*

Sometimes, during a warm-up, Billy improvises story ideas. He once had an idea for a historical film, which took place in Paris during the Middle Ages. The knights in shining armor prepare to depart for the crusade. There is a gripping montage of the crusaders as they secure their wives in chastity belts. Closeups of hands locking the belts. The crusaders mount their horses and are seen galloping down the broad highway, the sun reflected in their shields and lances. Now we cut to a shop on a cobblestoned lane. A wooden sign waves in the twilight: PIERRE COEUR DE LION, LOCKSMITH. For the Parisian locksmith, Wilder planned to cast Cary Grant.

"I've often thought I might make a porno-horror picture and capitalize on two of the big trends," he said recently. "The plot would have a sloppy hooker who gives all of her innocent customers crabs. The crabs grow into giant octopuses and eat New Orleans. The beauty of this idea is that we get both nudity and animal horror in the same picture. I might call it *Deep Jaws.*"

During one of his intermittent periods of creative frustration, Wilder was disgusted when the two big box-office hits of the season were John Wayne's *Fort Apache* and Red Skelton's *The Fuller Brush Man.* Wilder detests westerns and he shuns comedies with low gags and one-liners. "I think in my next picture," he said, "I will combine two angles. My hero will go out on the road selling tomahawks."

For a twist on the Oedipal theme, he came up with: "This boy falls in love with his mother and he marries her. They live together quite happily until one day he learns that she isn't really his mother. So he commits suicide."

His idea for a spy movie is "about this scientist who has a formula for blowing up the whole world. The formula is tattooed on his prick. It can only be read when he has a hard-on. Since the scientist is gay, the government has to train our heterosexual agents to become homosexuals."

Wilder was writing *Spirit of St. Louis* with his old friend and veteran scriptwriter and raconteur Charles Lederer. Lederer suddenly resigned. He couldn't stand Wilder's insults. While perusing the *Los Angeles Times* one morning, Billy read a favorable review by television critic John Crosby of a teleplay about a midwestern family by a new writer, a Wendell Mayes. On this basis, Billy told Leland Hayward, producer of the picture, to hire Mayes for $1,000 a week. Mayes had never been in Hollywood. He had never seen a Wilder movie. He had not heard of Billy Wilder. He was a Broadway actor. He was a complete theater man. He had only written this teleplay hoping to get a good part for himself.

His life was transformed by one newspaper review.

I recently enjoyed a pleasant afternoon with Wendell Mayes, a handsome guy with the courtly presence of an ambassador. He lives in a shining palace on the Bel Air heights. It is not true that rich and successful writers are unhappy, frustrated persons. Mayes is a happy and fulfilled human being. He loves luxury and the good life. He loves writing movies. Perhaps it was because he was not a professional writer—with all the turmoil which this introverted way of living brings to its votaries—Mayes found the experience with Wilder invigorating. He enjoyed every moment of it. He did not resent the barbs. He was amused by them. He regarded Billy Wilder as quite the most fascinating human being he had ever met and the year with Wilder was a magnificent year. He himself had come out of a flat and uneventful background in Missouri and he thought these events now happening to him were like an Arabian Night's adventure.

The problem the writers faced was this: most of the film occurred in a narrow cockpit and only one man was in the camera's eye. The drama of it was one man against the elements.

Wilder felt as though he was in a straitjacket. He could not invent episodes or characters. He had to confine himself to the facts of the Pulitzer prize-winning book by Lindbergh himself. Lindbergh was now a figure in history. The book ended with the arrival in Paris in 1927. Wilder was not permitted to flash forward to Lindbergh's love for Anne Morrow and he could not, obviously, deal with the kidnapping of the baby, nor his notorious excursion to Nazi Germany.

Wilder says: "I had a slight suspicion that he was a secret agent for U.S. army intelligence. But I couldn't even *ask* him about these matters. I couldn't get into his private life. He had become a Scandinavian Viking hero, without flesh and blood."

During his inquiries into Lindbergh, Wilder had heard an interesting story. One of the reporters assigned to cover the flight from Long Island learned that Lindbergh at twenty-seven was still a virgin. He couldn't let this guy go to his death without tasting of love. The reporter paid a friendly waitress to go up to the Lone Eagle's room the night before the flight and that was why he had a sleepless but concupiscent night. There was no romance in the picture. There were none of the usual rivalries between rival aviators for a girl's favors, which was the subplot of most aviation pictures since the time of *Wings* and *Dawn Patrol*. There were no characters fighting against Lindy, no conflict—just one man against the elements.

During the period when Wilder and Mayes were composing the script, Lindbergh came out to California for several meetings. He came to dinner at Billy's home. He was in a downtown hotel. He never took taxis. He would take a bus to Beverly Hills and then walk those long blocks from Santa Monica Boulevard up to Billy's house at 704 North Beverly—almost a mile's walk.

"Mr. Lindbergh was an imposing man," Billy recalls. "An authentic presence. He spoke very little. He was a dry, factual man. He was intensely patriotic and proud of his family. I remember him speaking proudly of his wife's books and her character. He also had a son who was studying at the Oceanographic Institute in San Diego. Mr. Lindbergh was a very difficult man to make into a movie hero. He was an aristocrat by nature. It was there. I never dared to make a wisecrack in his presence and I was embarrassed to ask him about his personal life, his sexual experiences, that sort of thing. I didn't even dare ask him about his meetings with Goering and what he had seen of the Luftwaffe.

"Later we were in New York together and once I remember walking up Fifth Avenue with him. He was not recognized by one person. *Not one.* Remembering the newsreels, how he was mobbed, and now nobody knew him, he was just another face in the crowd, I had a strange feeling.

"Then we flew down together to Washington on a commercial

flight. We were to go to the Smithsonian. He would show me the original Spirit of St. Louis. During the flight, we ran into rough weather. The plane was shaking. I leaned over toward him and said, 'Mr. Lindbergh, would it not be embarrassing if we crashed and the headlines said, "Lone Eagle and Jewish Friend in Plane Crash"? He just smiled. He knew exactly what I had in my mind.''

Months had gone by. Jack Warner had already spent over $2,000,000 on the writing and preparation and he had not seen a single page of screenplay. Wilder ordered a duplicate of the Spirit of St. Louis, which had originally cost $13,000. The Warner Bros. replica plane cost $1,300,000. Warner was getting nervous. He insisted on seeing the script, already. He hectored Wilder. Wilder was not about to start showing screenplays to *anybody*—even Jack Warner. After forty pages were done, he consented to—well, read them aloud. Wilder, Mayes, and Leland Hayward came to Warner's office. There were four of Warner's top executives present, besides Jack Warner.

Wilder had assigned Mayes to read the narration and all the dialogue. Hayward, who had an ear for music, would hum appropriate underscoring themes. *And Billy himself would do all the sound effects!* For about two hours, the trio went through a weird performance. Wilder snorted and clicked and clacked and made whirring propeller sounds and did revving engines. He did trains, automobiles, airplanes taking off and landing, engines in trouble, cold winds over the Atlantic . . .

Jack Warner was hypnotized. "Great, great," he said. Wilder went on to spend $6,000,000 of his money, as he shot expensive aerial footage following Lindbergh's route—from Long Island, Nova Scotia, Newfoundland, over the Atlantic, over Ireland, to Le Bourget in Paris.

To whom would Lindbergh talk during his thirty-three hours in the monoplane? There would be flashbacks, of course. But goddammit, something dramatic had to happen *in* the plane. Wendell Mayes suggested a little mouse in the cockpit to whom Lindy could speak. Billy flinched. No mice. He had used one of them in *The Lost Weekend.* How about an insect? Or a bird? They considered small birds, moths, butterflies, and houseflies. Billy did not like houseflies. They were associated with garbage. They finally used a fly. The excuse was that Lindy had taken sandwiches and this attracted the fly.

I once remarked to Wilder that in this scene between a man and an insect he had disproved Boyer.

"I didn't see the connection until you brought it up," Billy said. "To me, the fly and Lindbergh were like two fellow aviators."

Had Stewart objected to talking to a fly?

"Mr. Stewart does not object to talking to insects," Wilder snapped. "After all, he has had to deal all his life with agents and producers."

Among the aphorisms of Wilder imprinted on Wendell's mind were these:

"You must remember as a screenwriter that nobody is going to read what you write. That is why I became a director—because no one was reading my scripts."

"You must never take an assignment seriously, because few persons in this business know anything about it and you have to endure the fools and the scoundrels. And the only way to endure it is, do not take them too seriously or your work too seriously."

With Lehman it was caviar, with Axelrod it was thin ties, with Mayes it was *pyrogenes. Pyrogenes* are large, beautiful French ashtrays—which are no longer produced. They consist of a heavy tray base, in the center of which is a corrugated hollow cone, that holds the large kitchen matches to be struck on the corrugations. These handsome artifacts bear the names of beers and aperitifs. Billy's new mania was collecting *pyrogènes*. During their three weeks of shooting in Paris, he would entice Mayes away from the typewriter for an hour or two, and they strolled the boulevards of Paris, as he taught the young man some of what he knew and loved about Paris. He always had his eye out for a *pyrogène,* and whenever he spotted one in an antique shop or secondhand junk store, he would dart in and buy. He acquired hundreds of them—no, thousands of them. He started Mayes off in the *pyrogène* collecting business.

Though they never collaborated again, Billy Wilder followed the young man's career and was always there to advise him on a script or a career problem. When Otto Preminger sought a writer for *Anatomy of a Murder,* Billy recommended Mayes. Mayes wrote the script. It got an Academy nomination and made Wendell Mayes, who went on to write many box-office hits—*Advise and Consent, Von Ryan's Express, Hotel, In Harm's Way, Poseidon Adventure,* and *Death Wish.* Within a decade, Mayes had reached the highest level of screenwriting income. He was in the $5,000 a week category.

Once he ran into Wilder at the annual banquet and show of the Writers Guild of America.

"Why don't we collaborate on a movie again, Billy?" Mayes asked.

"I would like to very much, Wendell," Billy said, "but I no longer can afford your prices."

Jerry Wald, now executive producer at Columbia, invited him to meet Harry Cohn and discuss the prospect of Wilder writing and directing *Pal Joey*. Wilder was agreeable. He moved into a suite of offices at the Gower Street studios, in which he had been a $150 a week junior writer a scant twenty years before. Now he was one of the most powerful figures in Hollywood. He brought his own secretary with him. He had a three-room suite. He hung up some of his works of art. He decorated the offices in his usual good taste—with many *pyrogènes* on desks and tables and some fine examples of bentwood furniture. He had latterly also gotten into collecting bentwood chairs.

Wilder's idea for filming *Pal Joey* was that there must be a strong age difference between the hero and the lady who is keeping him. It would be Bill Holden and Norma Desmond—in another variation. This was how it was in the original John O'Hara tales and how it was in the Rodgers and Hart Broadway show, in which a matronly Vivienne Segal was bewitched, bothered and bewildered by a rutting young Gene Kelly.

Billy envisioned Marlon Brando for Joey. He knew Brando loved jazz music, that he played the bongo drums and that he was a flashy ballroom dancer in the best *Eintänzer* tradition. And for the woman? Ah, he had a coup in mind: he would secure Mae West. Mae West and Marlon Brando.

Billy talked to Brando and to West. They were agreeable.

Now he had two long and lengthy parleys with Harry Cohn at the Columbia commissary. He remembers Cohn being furious when a waitress accidentally brought him a carbon copy menu at one of their lunches. Cohn was always to be handed the original *ribbon* copy! Anyway, Billy described how he saw *Pal Joey* and how he wanted to cast the leads. Cohn looked at him apprehensively. Didn't that idiot realize that Rita Hayworth had to play the woman? Didn't this *dummkopf* know that there had to be equality of ages between the boy and the girl? How had a *schmuck* like this ever won Academy Awards? Cohn chewed his steak and grumbled at the idiocy of writers.

"After ten days," Wilder says, "I got a call from Jerry Wald. He said my conception is turned down. Harry Cohn hates it. Alright, I said to Jerry, no harm done. I packed my bags and typewriter and pictures and *pyrogènes* and secretary and left.

"Two weeks later, I got a bill from Columbia Pictures, for two lunches—*five dollars,* can you believe this?"

In 1954, Allied Artists, which specialized in low-budget cowboy pictures, made a big splash. They signed contracts with William Wyler, John Huston, and Billy Wilder. These giants would make high quality A pictures for Allied. Steve Broidy was the new president of Allied. He was allied with Harold, Walter, Marvin, and Irving Mirisch. Broidy's company would produce pictures of serious content and noble purposes. In return for signing, Wilder got stock in the company and options to buy more stock, as well as his usual high percentage of the profits on a film, and total freedom. Before the deal was announced, Allied stock was fluctuating between seven and eight. When the news broke, shares plummeted to three and a half!

"Those stockholders were no fools," Billy remarks. "They knew guys like Willy, me, and John would spend a million or two on a movie. They wanted Allied to make cheap pictures, surefire money makers." Wyler started *Friendly Persuasion,* which he soon finished. Huston started *The Man Who Would Be King*—which he did not finish until—1975! And Wilder, ruminating over stories, remembered a scene from a 1931 German film, starring Elisabeth Bergner (directed by her husband, Paul Czinner) about a girl cello player in Czarist Russia and her French lover, an older man. All he remembered was a tearful farewell scene between the lovers at the railroad station, while the train made hissing sounds and steam flowed from under wheels. He would see if he could not fashion something contemporary and entertaining from Claude Anet's *Ariane,* on which Czinner's film was based.

Casting about for a collaborator, he interviewed a certain I.A.L. Diamond, a Lazar client. He was still a Pygmalion looking for fresh Galateas. Wilder was intrigued by the fact that Diamond's real name was Itek Domnici and that he was Rumanian born. Rumanians had a mysterious gypsylike flair about them. He was fascinated that the "I.A.L." stood for Interscholastic Algebra League, as Iz Diamond had been a young mathematics wizard. Aside from this, he was not impressed by this diamond in the rough. Iz was a quiet, tall, shambling, remote sort of guy. He talked slowly and witticisms did not fall from his lips. He looked like a college professor—too serious. Not his cup of Darjeeling, thank you, Mr. Lazar.

In April that year, 1955 it was, Audrey and Billy attended the annual clambake of the Writers Guild. In the show, were two sketches Wilder thought were good. The writer of either of these sketches might be a possible cowriter. One sketch was about two screenwriters seeking *le mot juste* for a parenthetical description indicating the tone in which a line is spoken. The other was a parody of the Fugue for Tinhorns from *Guys and Dolls*—three agents touting three different writers to Sam Goldwyn. Wilder inquired who were the writers of these sketches. They had both been written by that scholarly Rumanian, I.A.L. Diamond.

Not a man to ignore destiny, Wilder started working with Diamond, though he was still completing *Spirit of St. Louis*. Diamond was to outline a structure based on *Ariane.* He told Iz to write the story with a Paris setting and to make the elderly lover a sort of roué, but a charming roué, who would be, he hoped, acted by Cary Grant. Like everybody else in pictures, Wilder revered Grant's talent for comedy. The role of Leon in *Ninotchka* had been written for Cary Grant, but he had not been available. More recently, Wilder had conceived the role of Linus Larrabee in *Sabrina* for Cary Grant. He was not available. Once again, though Cary Grant admired Billy and wanted to work in this *Ariane* film, he was already committed to two future projects.

So now Billy decided to write it for Yul Brynner. (Audrey Hepburn had agreed to play the young girl, who remained a cellist.) He sent Iz Diamond over to talk to one of our leading Beverly Hills hostesses, the charming Doris Vidor, one of the daughters of Jack Warner. Billy was going to model Yul's character on Aly Khan's. Aly Khan had frequently been a guest *chez* Vidor. So Mrs. Vidor would describe an international playboy to Iz Diamond, and they would transform him into the hero of *Love in the Afternoon* (a title suggested by Diamond).

Mrs. Vidor said that Aly Khan was "charming." In what way, wondered Iz? Well, he was charming in many ways. He could tell you about the latest Paris styles, women's clothes, very charming . . . horses—oh, yes, he was charming on the subject of horses . . . and . . .

Suddenly, she paused. Iz Diamond's pencil was suspended in the air. He waited for the crystallization.

"To tell you the truth, Mr. Diamond," she said at last, "Aly Khan is really a fucking bore."

Billy now struck out in another direction. He would model his hero after an American playboy millionaire, make him a Howard Hughes type, a billionaire industrialist, and get Gary Cooper for this. Sure, there was a real-life disparity of thirty years between Audrey Hepburn and Coop—but who would notice with makeup and the proper lighting and Cooper's ageless virility? He knew Cooper could play high comedy. He could play sophisticated lovers. He could play lean gunslingers, mouthing his "yups"; but he could also speak amusing lines; as in *Bluebeard's Eighth Wife.*

The picture was finished. Much of the intrigue took place in Cooper's suite in the Ritz Hotel, Wilder's favorite Paris hotel. One day, Billy was summoned by Steve Broidy to a title conference. Present also were *les frères* Mirisch. Broidy did not like the title *Love in the Afternoon.* It was too dull. He wanted either a violent title along the lines of *Gunfight at the O.K. Corral* or a real socko one-word title like *Panhandle* or *Wichita.* Allied's *Wichita* had been a smash.

Billy patiently listened to Broidy's lecture on the theory and practice of correctly titling pictures. Then he could take no more. He stood up.

He said with a perceptible sneer, "Why don't we just call it *Meanwhile, Back at the Ritz?*"

Wilder thinks it is typical of a certain breed of movie executive to think there is something significant in the choice of a title.

Billy says, "Joan Crawford got an Oscar for *Mildred Pierce.* Warners' decided a woman's name is the perfect title for a Crawford picture. Her next picture they called *Daisy Kenyon.* It bombed."

Billy Wilder chose Harry Kurnitz as his partner on *Witness for the Prosecution,* he told me, because Kurnitz was an anglophile and had written several mystery novels under the *nom de plume* of Marco Page. Kurnitz was a tall and gangling person, fifty years old, loose of limb and lip, a charmer, a superb raconteur, an international-setter, with a snob's disdain for Hollywood and movies, though he wrote many and got rich therefrom. Wilder undertook to reshape him. Kurnitz just wasn't serious about work. He hated hard work. He hated work. He liked coffee-housing. He liked flirting with women. He liked being a Parisian *flâneur*. Kurnitz proved to be as intractable a Galatea as Raymond Chandler or Ernest Lehman. Nor could Wilder even jangle Kurnitz's nerves with insults, which was a tactic he used to shake up the emotional molecules of his collaborators, and thus make them amenable to his requirements. Kurnitz was impervious to insults. He laughed at them. He bounded back with amusing stories of his adventures with ladies. He was marvelous company. He was just lazy.

Kurnitz had known Billy a decade and found him excellent of wit and sharp of mind. But to work with this obsessed man—impossible. He did it. They wrote a good script which made a superb film. But never again. Kurnitz set down some of his observations on Wilder the collaborator in 1964. One was covered with Band-Aids after being lacerated by a day's work with Wilder. His collaborators "have a hunted look, shuffle nervously, and have been known to break into tears if a door slams anywhere in the same building . . . Though I kept no day-to-day record, interested persons who open Twentieth-Century-Fox[e]'s *Book of Martyrs* more or less at random are likely to come on text or pictures conveying the nature of my experience. . . . He is a fiend for work." Fiendish—that's what Wilder was—a monomaniac, a raving lunatic, always saying "Let's make it better."

Summing it all up, Kurnitz said: "Billy Wilder at work is actually two people—Mr. Hyde and Mr. Hyde."

Nineteen-fifty-eight was a milestone year professionally for Billy Wilder.

The four Mirisch brothers had left Allied Artists to form an independent production company releasing through United Artists. Wilder signed a deal with them which gave him complete freedom of subject, screenplay, casting, direction, final cut, a munificent salary as writer and as director—and a twenty-five percent share of the net profits on each of his films. He was to work under the Mirisch banner for sixteen years.

In that same year of 1958, Billy also got out of the Galatea business as far as writers were concerned. He chose I.A.L. Diamond as coauthor of his next film, *Some Like It Hot*. He had already known that Diamond—like the mineral for which he was named—glittered but was harder than steel. Iz Diamond could not be transformed. He had his own tastes in clothes, food, and art, and was rigorously monogamistic libido-wise. He was a doting father. He was a quiet, soft-spoken, scholarly person, nondescript in appearance, almost invisible on a set, uninterested in verbal sparring with Wilder or anybody else, a hard worker but not a compulsive worker, as intensely devoted to the art of film as Wilder, as knowledgeable about it as Wilder. Unlike Brackett, he was not frustrated. He did not throw temper tantrums. He withdrew into himself when there was a crisis. He had the habit of waiting out Billy during a cantankerous spasm. Soon it would pass, he knew. The depth of Diamond's respect for Wilder was great. It was there. It did not need to be spoken.

Wilder has remained married, as it were, to Diamond from that day to the present. Apart from their work, both men lead separate lives, with separate friends and separate interests. Diamond, in the area of writing and moviemaking, has the same feeling for structure, for integral wholeness of story, as does Wilder, and the same convictions as to film technique. Diamond already had fifteen years of training in screenwriting and had written at Paramount, Warners, MGM and Twentieth Century Fox. He knew how to fit the pipes together. He knew how to make the clockwork mechanism which operated the laughter machine.

*Some Like It Hot* had its remote origins in an old UFA musical film (1932) with a German depression setting. Two unemployed musicians put on a series of costumes to get different jobs with different types of bands. They black their faces to play with Negro bands. They put rings in their ears and bandannas on their heads to work as gypsies. They dress up as girls to play in a women's orchestra. The gags were broad—taking a shave or smoking cigars while in drag. Getting kissed by men while in dresses. There were implications of lesbianism and sadism in some scenes.

The original had been written by Robert Thoeren, who was a Hollywood screenwriter now. Wilder would make it a story about two American musicians of the present—i.e., 1958—and they would be playing hit songs of the 1950s.

*Some Like It Hot* is not in technicolor for two reasons. One, it would have become a "flaming faggot" picture in color. Two, Wilder hated color. Since 1949, almost all major pictures were in color. Wilder bucked the trend. He made *Emperor Waltz* in color. He had made *Seven Year Itch* in color only because Monroe's contract demanded color. Wilder finally surrendered to color after 1969 because black-and-white films became unsaleable to television.

Even in black and white, Wilder was afraid that men masquerading as women would look cheap. Diamond said they should do it as a period piece because all clothes of a former period looked "funny." *Charley's Aunt* being the classic example of a transvestite hero/heroine who was in good taste because he/she cavorted in the late Victorian era. What period should it be?

One morning, Wilder got that gleam in his eye: "It comes to me what period we should make this. 1929. Prohibition. Al Capone, Chicago. The St. Valentine's Day massacre . . ."

They started inventing the plot and the scenes. Wilder was casting the men. He right away wanted Tony Curtis and Jack Lemmon. The women roles were not going to be important. United Artists wanted a heavyweight. They wanted Frank Sinatra. Billy drove over to Palm Springs and explained the story to Old Blue Eyes. He liked it. They made an appointment to meet the following week in Los Angeles. Sinatra did not appear. He did not telephone. That was the end of Sinatra. Then, suddenly, Marilyn Monroe became available and interested. She was now married to Arthur Miller. She was in a state of depression after a miscarriage. Her husband felt it would raise her spirits to make another comedy with Billy Wilder. Billy sent them a five page précis of the Diamond-Wilder story. He approved. Now that UA had Monroe, they didn't care if he hired Lemmon. At that time, Lemmon was an obscure actor, strictly a nice-guy, clean-cut comic foil. Wilder knew there was greatness there. Nobody else did. Except Harry Cohn was suspicious. Maybe Lemmon was good. Who knows? Lemmon owed Columbia *one* more picture. In order to get his release for *Some Like It Hot,* he had to promise Columbia *four* more pictures.

And so Lemmon's great career as superstar began—through the fluke of Sinatra missing a dinner engagement, and Marilyn Monroe miscarrying, and a husband who cared enough about her to want her to return to the movies. When Marilyn and Arthur Miller came out, Harold Mirisch gave a dinner party in thir honor, with some eighty persons of moviedom royalty invited. Seven P.M. for cocktails. Dinner at nine. Marilyn, a notorious latecomer, was late, though for her, it was almost early. She arrived at 11:20, when the party was breaking up. It got unbroken when they saw her. She was magic—even to moviedom royalty. Like Garbo had been. Like Gable. Like Chaplin. Wilder took the couple around to the tables and made the introductions. At the table where Iz Diamond was seated, they lingered. Iz Diamond knew her from her starlet days at Twentieth. He had been a contract writer and had written most of her dialogue in her early pictures, *Love Nest, Monkey Business, Love Happy.*

Arthur Miller put one arm around Billy and one arm around Iz as Marilyn looked at the trio apprehensively. Then Miller said, in a pedantic tone, "The difference between comedy and tragedy is . . ."

He spoke for several minutes. He was impressive. He was profound. Wilder doesn't remember a word he said. Diamond remembers. He did not wish to tell me . . .

At this soireé, Billy told David O. Selznick that his opening scene was going to be the St. Valentine's Day massacre, which Tony Curtis and Jack Lemmon would witness. They would thus be compelled to flee in women's clothes and join the All-Girl Band.

"You mean," Selznick said, "you're going to have machine guns, bullets, dead bodies—and then gags?"

"Sure, David, baby," Wilder said.

"You can't make it work, Billy. Blood and jokes do not mix."

They mixed beautifully, in this case. It did not seem so at the first preview. Billy has been through some ghastly sneak previews in his time—viz., *Lost Weekend, Double Indemnity, Sunset Boulevard.* But they were not amusing films. For comedy—he had the sure touch, didn't he? Well, he sneak-previewed *Some Like It Hot* at the Bay Theatre in Pacific Palisades in December 1958. It was preceded by Joe Mankiewicz's grim version of Tennessee Williams' *Suddenly Last Summer,* a melodrama of homosexuals and cannibalism.

Perhaps this conjured up the wrong expectations in the audience. Perhaps they thought Tony Curtis would chop up Marilyn Monroe for dinner.

It was a total disaster. Only one person in that entire audience of 800 persons laughed. Only one. He laughed loudly and continually. When the lights went on, Billy rushed down the aisle to shake the hand of the one person with intelligence in the audience. It was none other than Steve Allen! Wilder knew there were not enough Steverinos in the United States to make a profit for the picture. Something had gone wrong? What? How could he change the picture? Was Selznick right?

Joe Manckiewicz, an old friend, had been invited to the sneak. He had made that Tennessee Williams picture shown ahead of *Some Like It Hot.* As a fellow writer-director, Joe felt great sympathy for Billy's plight. He put his arm around his old friend. He murmured, "It is all right, Billy; it happens to all of us."

Billy hates sympathy. He lashed back at Manckiewicz. "I was thinking, Joe, that with *Suddenly Last Summer* you violated one of the basic rules of the movie business—not to offend big pressure groups. This picture will offend the vegetarians!"

Before recutting *Some Like It Hot,* he sneaked it at a theater in Westwood. The audience started laughing at scene one and never stopped for the two hours duration and audiences have never stopped laughing at it since.

Wilder and Diamond both have a strict rule against divulging who wrote which line. Wilder makes one exception. The celebrated curtain line of this picture ("Nobody's perfect!") was not his.

"This line is entirely from the brain of I.A.L. Diamond," he says. "I had nothing to do with it. Not even the exclamation point!"

Around this time the Black Muslims, who were wont to change their names into letters, came into prominence. Wilder said, "It will be interesting if Iz ever becomes a Black Muslim. He will have to change his name to I.A.L. X."

# 17

# AUDREY
# AND BILLY

Wilder gave a rare interview to the *Los Angeles Times* in December 1944, rare because it is his only explicit reference to symbolic imagery in his films. The film is *The Lost Weekend.*

"Birnam's hallucination is a result of his schizophrenic, or split, personality," he said. "The mouse represents the everyday Birnam; the bat—or mouse with wings—the artist he dreams of being. The bat, of course, destroys the mouse."

Of course? Yes, of course. That was how his own obsession with artistic perfection destroyed his everyday life.

In 1946, Billy wrote the only essay he has ever written about movies. It was called *The Case for the American Film* and it appeared in *America*, a publication of the State Department, for overseas propaganda. He defended the "happy ending" in *Lost Weekend*. In Jackson's novel the hero is already thinking of his next drunk as the story ends. In the picture, Don Birnam slides a blank sheet of paper into the typewriter to begin a novel about his alcoholism.

"We don't say that the man is cured," Billy wrote. "We just try to suggest that if he can lick his illness long enough to put some coherent words down on paper, then there must be hope."

Hope! For Wilder lived this paradox of an artist whose obsession with beauty destroys him, while his compulsion to impart symmetry and wholeness to the chaos of his experiences is all that makes it possible to go on day after day. But he was also denying that it was a "happy ending," a fraudulent Hollywood walking-hand-in-hand-into-the-sunset fade-out. For he knew that to put the paper in the typewriter and to get some coherent words on it was not a euphoric resolution of man's dilemma, but another, though sublimated, event in the same struggle.

One more quotation. It is from a long tape-recorded interview in *Cahiers du Cinema*, August 1962:

> In making a picture there's only one rule and that is to do only what's good for the picture. You must never start out with the idea of pleasing this one or that one. You don't cast an actress in a certain part because you want to go to bed with her. From the moment you start making the picture, you have to think only *is it good for the picture?* I adore my wife—but if it's a matter of a picture I'm shooting, and she wants me to put something in, or take something out, to please her, and which is not good for the picture, well, I would refuse to do it—*even if this would lead to the end of my marriage*. I would even refuse my own mother, if she were alive, but she died at Auschwitz. It is the picture which interests me—and what is not good for the picture, I will not use in the picture.*

In 1944, Audrey Young was twenty-two years old. She was a tall and willowy dark-haired woman, with an ivory skin and dark eyes and a hauntingly beautiful face, resembling Merle Oberon's. Miss Young was a contract player at Paramount. She was a Los Angeles native. She was born way downtown on Main Street. Her father, Stafford Young, practiced what is perhaps the quintessential southern California profession: he was a used-car dealer. Her mother was a wardrobe woman and worked at various movie studios. Later they moved a little farther west and she grew up in the La Brea and Washington Boulevard area of southeast Los Angeles. She attended

*This is my colloquial translation of "La grande règle est de ne jamais rien prendre que de ce qui convient au film. Pas question de faire d'abord plaisir à un tel, ou de prendre telle actrice parce qu'on veut coucher avec. A partir du moment où le film est en jeu, il ne faut plus penser qu'à lui. J'aime beaucoup ma femme, mais si à propos d'un film je dois faire quelque chose pour elle qui ne soit pas bon pour le film, je le refuserais, même si ça devait amener à la fin de mon mariage. Et je refuserais aussi à ma mère, si elle ètait vivante, mais elle est morte à Auschwitz. C'est le film qui m'intéresse; ce qui n'est pas bon pour le film, je ne l'utilise pas."

L.A. High School. She did not go to college. When she was a child, her mother sometimes took her with her to the studio. The character of Betty Schaefer in *Sunset Boulevard* is a thinly veiled portrait of Audrey Young as she was when Billy first looked into her eyes. And his most tender love scene is the one in which Joe Gillis and Betty— Holden and Nancy Olson—stroll the darkened streets of the Paramount lot. They have been sweating to get those "coherent words down on paper" and now they wander down the "Western" street of the lot. They find an apple machine and slip in the coins and eat apples. From "Western Street" they meander to "Boston Street" (and Billy and Audrey had taken just such strolls) and she says "Look at that street. All cardboard, all phony, all done with mirrors. You know, I like it better than any street in the world. Maybe because I used to play here when I was a kid." She tells him how she came from a movie family and how she was expected to be a star and had years of "dramatic lessons, diction, dancing. Then the studio made a test. Well, they didn't like my nose. So I went to a doctor and had it fixed. They made more tests and they were crazy about my nose, only now they didn't like my acting."

Like Betty Schaefer, Audrey Young had studied tap dancing, acrobatic toe dancing, singing, and diction. She had studied at the famous Fanchon and Marco school. Unlike Betty Schaefer, Audrey Young started her career at eighteen as a chorus girl in a touring company of George White's *Scandals.* She escaped the puritanical restrictions of her family. She always had to wear simple dresses with Peter Pan collars; her mother, severe though she was about Audrey's personal life, did not mind it when "I came out on stage with only three sequins and a G-string, but that was all right with mother because I was now a professional performer." She toured with the *Scandals* a season and then danced in Broadway cabarets. In 1944, she was signed by Paramount.

Those were the days when all the studios were grinding out wartime musicals; singers and dancers were in demand. Paramount gave her the usual treatment: glamorous makeup and coiffure, exercises and posture training in the studio gymnasium, acting and singing lessons. She was tested for many parts. She looked fine in full face or three-quarters but her profile, right or left, was bad and so, like Betty Schaefer, she had her nose changed. Like Betty's, her new nose cost her $300. But now, like Betty, she found out that, even with a new nose, she could not act. She enrolled in the acting classes of Josephine Hutchinson—a famous stage actress who had been a costar and intimate of Eva Le Gallienne in the Civic Repertory Theater of New York. She worked hard at her acting but it did not get better. She just could not make imaginary girls come to life. She took private singing lessons with coach Glenn Raikes. Like other contract girls, Audrey was given walk-ons and bits, scenes where you just had to look beautiful in a beautiful dress; but most of her work was in the musicals. She says "we used to have a lot of fun on those kinds of pictures. The directors were slaphappy guys and there was lots of horsing around and laughs. There were three directors that we would get calls for sometimes and they said, 'No horsing around on a Wilder set, a De Mille set, or a Preston Sturges set.' When I got this call to do a bit in *The Lost Weekend,* the casting director warned me that he is a very serious guy when he's shooting. 'Don't make jokes,' he told me." He was shooting the sequence in the Fifty-second Street club in which Ray Milland steals a woman's purse. Audrey was playing the hatcheck girl. Her big moment would come when Milland would present his check and she handed him his hat. She had no lines. The scene opened with Harry Barris at the piano playing and singing "You are so beautiful, so wonderful, so gorgeous, so divine, and you are mine, and you are mine." Wilder had known Barris for years. He was one of the original Rhythm Boys vocal trio with the Whiteman band, the others being Al Rinker and Bing Crosby.

It was October 18, 1944. She walked on the set and reported to the production manager. It was to be two days' work. The cameras had not yet started turning. Audrey had known many Manhattan clubs like this one. It looked real. She walked up and down it and leaned on the piano, while Barris was running through his number.

Just then she became aware that somebody was standing there. She turned around. It was the fearsome Billy Wilder. A narrow-brimmed velour hat on his head, a feather sticking in the brim. Cigarette in the corner of his mouth. Script under an arm. A black, unbuttoned cardigan sweater with a white matelot-collar lisle shirt underneath it. He looked into her eyes. She shivered slightly. She did not fall in love at first sight. She sensed something, however, as one always senses in these first strange and fateful meetings between a man and a woman, and this was indeed the first "meet-cute" in Billy Wilder's love life.

Brackett and Wilder could have written a more sparkling and sophisticated opening gambit than the one he used. He asked, "What's your name?" She told him.

His next line was equally flat, "Isn't the set nice?" She said it was very nice. There was, so far, not an intimation of the famous Wilder persiflage. There was, in fact, a prolonged silence, which made her nervous and finally, just to make conversation, she said, apropos of the song "It was so wonderful, so marvelous," that "I love it. It always makes me cry."

Wilder cocked his head at her. He said, "I have to walk over there to do something and when I come back I want to see if you are crying."

He went over and parleyed with Johnny Seitz, the cameraman. Then he sauntered back. He regarded her. There were tears dripping down her face.

"Believe me," Audrey says, "I can't act worth a damn. I just have no talent in that direction, but when Billy came back, there I was crying and I just couldn't stop."

Billy was so impressed that he asked her to dine with him later in the week. He sent her a dozen roses on that night. They went to a friend's house for dinner. They had to be discreet, as Billy was still married. But it was not the first Mrs. Wilder who was the chief obstacle to love's flowering. It was the fact that Billy was infatuated with Doris Dowling. It was one of the hottest romances in Hollywood and the subject of much gossip. Constance Dowling, Doris's sister, was having an equally passionate romance with another director, Elia ("Gadge") Kazan. The sisters, both breathtakingly beautiful, both brunettes, both kinetic and dramatic, were known, in Hollywood's bachelor colony, to be fabulously exciting companions. It was more or less expected that Constance would eventually swing into matrimony with Gadge and that Doris would capture Billy after his divorce, which was already in the talking stages.

Billy himself—whatever Doris's plans might have been—had made up his mind that he was not the sort of person who could be a husband. He was, he had come to realize in the process of filming *The Lost Weekend*, a man hopelessly enslaved to his art. A woman, any woman, would be only a distraction from his obsession with making pictures.

Yet this Audrey was so calm and sweet, so artless and charming, so—well, so unsophisticated. She began to arouse the Pygmalion instinct in him. There was another supper and one or two more dates and then their relationship drifted into a casualness. He had now adopted a kind of bantering, avuncular tone when he was with her.

One time, he took her home. She was still living with her parents in the house at La Brea Avenue and Washington Boulevard.

"I would worship the ground you walk on, Audrey," Billy cracked, "if you only lived in a better neighborhood."

"Can't you think of it as East Beverly Hills, Billy?" she riposted.

She had a sharp mind, this girl. Ah, if only one had world enough and time, one could make something of her. . . .

Most of her *Lost Weekend* scene wound up on the cutting room floor. All that is visible of her is an arm handing a hat to Milland. She did better in a later picture, an Abbott and Costello epic, *The Wistful Widow of Wagon Gap,* in which she played Marjorie Main's daughter, which may have been Paramount's attempt to disprove Mendel's theory of heredity. Abbott and Costello liked her and hired her as a singer in a stage show they were doing at the Roxy in New York. She worked about two months here, and then started playing nightclub gigs as a solo chanteuse. By now Billy Wilder was in Germany helping to cleanse the German film industry. Now and then she thought of him but she did not imagine anything would come of it. She had heard that he was still deeply involved with Doris Dowling. The Dowling relationship survived until 1947.

By now, through the efforts of the late Marie McDonald, the blonde actress and wife of the shoe manufacturer, Harry Karl, later a spouse of Debbie Reynolds, Audrey was introduced to Tommy Dorsey. She was hired as the successor to Jo Stafford and Connie Haines. It looked as if she was really going places finally. Audrey remembers joining the Dorsey orchestra in South Dakota and playing long engagements in Minneapolis and Chicago and other midwestern cities. She started to get lonely.

Wilder had completed *Emperor Waltz.* He was now making *A Foreign Affair.* In January 1948, Audrey went on a tour of one-nighters with the band. One night she was alone in a small hotel room in an old hotel in some Pennsylvania mountain city. She had to talk to him. She had his home telephone number.

"I just picked up the phone and called him collect," she says. "He accepted the call. He was in the middle of directing *A Foreign Affair.* We talked about everything—and nothing. He was very kind. We had previously dated only a very few times. I don't know why, when I went on tour, I had the nerve to pick up the phone and call him collect but I did it, and more and more often. He always took the call. Often he'd be asleep when I called, as it was two or three in the morning in Los Angeles. He was always very charming about it. He didn't talk about the picture. I knew Marlene Dietrich was in it and Jean Arthur; that's about all. Like he would say, 'Where are you?' and I'd say, 'Buffalo,'—really clever dialogue like that—and he'd say, 'When are you coming back?' and I'd say, 'In a couple of months.' But it felt good, hearing the sound of his voice, his accent, all that charm and kindness. He used to laugh at how I was talking now. You know, when you travel with a band, your language changes. Musicians are hip, always on to the latest slang expressions. Without even thinking of it, I had started using some of these expressions. I remember once using the phrases 'gone' and 'real gone,' in the sense of terrific, and he had not heard this yet and he stopped me and said, 'Now wait a minute, what does this mean? 'Gone?'

"Then the tour with the Dorsey band, it ended the end of January and I came back to Hollywood in February and I phoned Billy and we went out and it was then I fell madly in love with him."

Billy, on his part, seems to have been torn between his increasing affection for this sweet creature, and the tempestuous Miss Dowling. He was not even sure that he wanted to embark on a serious relationship. Love, after all, despite its emotional climaxes, was also wearing on one's nervous system and made it hard to concentrate on his films. Like any artist, Wilder's screenplays and the films therefrom, have always had a personal substructure. Was John Lund, in *A Foreign Affair*, faced with the contrast between Marlene and Jean Arthur, really Billy, between two loves?

Audrey did not reveal to him how much she wanted him. She sensed that he was the kind of man who would withdraw. She was playing it cool. And it was hard. She could not bear to be apart from him. After completing the editing and scoring of *A Foreign Affair*, he was planning his usual holiday—a European trip. He was going to go with his old friend, the director Anatole Litvak. In April 1948. It was as painful as hell for her.

"I remember telling him, 'Please go, don't worry about me, go and have a wonderful time, how marvelous that you can go with dear Anatole'—and all the time I wanted to kill myself. I felt so vulnerable. I felt deserted and lonely when he left for Europe but I did not show it to him. I was going to play it very cool even if it killed me. He was playing it cool too, I guess.'' But, it must have been like that Cole Porter line which speaks of a love affair as being too hot to cool down, for when he returned from Europe, he told her, for the first time, he had missed her very much and now they were inseparable. She knew that he loved her as she loved him. She wanted now to get married and make a new life together. Audrey and Billy. He flinched at the very idea of such a connubial partnership. She went on a determined campaign in favor of holy matrimony.

"I started begging him constantly,'' she says, smiling wryly, " 'Let's get married, let's get married.' I didn't give up on it. I have to tell you that he was not exactly crazy about this idea of mine. He said, 'I have been married.' He seemed to feel that this was the sort of idiotic thing which a person did once and that was sufficient. He tried to convince me that marriage was just not that overwhelming an institution by giving instances of how marriage ruined some marvelous friendships between people he knew. He argued that we had too nice a friendship going to spoil it with marriage.

"This was in the spring of 1949. I really just couldn't live without him. I just wanted him all the way in every way. I was terrible, nagging him and nagging him to get married. Well, he was into *Sunset Boulevard* by now and he was worried about it and things not going so well with Charlie Brackett and all, but I couldn't stop nagging.''

One evening, after a hectic day at the studio, Billy suddenly turned to her as they were sharing a brandy-and-soda and exploded, "Aud, I give you this promise. When the picture is finished in a few weeks, I will let you know whether we will get married. But, please, do me this one favor: do not bring up the subject any more, because it is driving me crazy.''

She said, "That is fine.''

She refrained from all references to wedlock, though it took every bit of willpower she had.

Meanwhile, Billy, between the agonies of getting *Sunset Boulevard* on film and rewriting the script with Charlie, was searching his soul. Willie Schorr, who had become Billy's confidant as well as the uncredited associate producer of the film, remembers an evening when—after the day's shooting was done, after Charlie and Billy had revised tomorrow's pages, after they had had sandwiches and coffee in the offices, after all this and so much more, after Brackett had departed and it was past midnight—he and Billy started "taking a walk on the Paramount back lot, just like Holden and Nancy Olson. It was on this walk that Billy saw this real apple machine, a coin machine that sold apples instead of candy, right there on New York Street or Western Street, one of those. We bought apples. This gave him the idea for that little touch. That night, for the first time, I saw a side of Billy I did not know before. This sophisticated guy, this man of the world, well he just amazed me. He confessed that he was thinking of getting married and he was scared shitless. He was like a young guy of twenty-one. He loved Aud. He started talking about her and, knowing how he hates sentimentality, I guess he hated telling me how crazy he was about her and he was afraid maybe he was not cut out for marriage. I don't think he was worried about the age difference between them so much. He was worried whether he would be a good husband. Aud came to the set every day. He wanted her on the set every day. She wanted to be near him every day. It was so obvious that they were in love and like it was first love for both of them. She did not remain on the lot when they went overtime and were shooting at night. I would drive her home. Strange thing—but she was not afraid of the marriage. She had faith that 'it would be good'."

A biographer has to be leery of reading personal references into his subject's imaginative productions—be they novels or films—though we all do it, suspecting that there is a substratum of fact behind every fiction. In the case of Billy Wilder, I have no doubt that *Sunset Boulevard,* like *Lost Weekend,* is, on one level, an objective correlative of the emotional crisis in which he found himself in that period. In terms of story, *Sunset Boulevard* shows us a hero torn between his love for a young girl and his pity and dependency on an older woman, who is almost choking him to death spiritually with her overwhelming possessiveness. Now Billy has told me that he drew upon his life and Audrey's for the Betty Schaefer and Jo Gillis characters. But who was Audrey's rival? Who was the Gloria Swanson character in Wilder's private life?

And here I am impelled to make a wild leap and suggest that Norma Desmond—long-nailed, raging, insane—personifies the bat who bleeds the mouse; she personifies art and the insane dedication to pictures, that same obsession which drove Billy Wilder, and which in the film results in the art murdering the artist.

So Billy feared that his compulsion would wreck Audrey's life and make a good marriage impossible. Was he not married to his studio, to his actors, to his production crew, to the work in progress?

Was not his real wife his collaborator? And now he was divorcing his collaborator and the future looked hopeless at times and he experienced waves of despair that he had not felt for many years. Perhaps, finally, it was his loneliness and his fear of becoming even more lonely, now that Charlie Brackett and he were splitting, that impelled him to make up his mind about Audrey Young; for he did not then know that there would be other collaborators, other men with whom to write the pictures, and he certainly did not then conceive it possible for one so compulsive as he to enjoy the pleasures of a reasonably normal married life.

One evening during the last weeks of filming *Sunset Boulevard*, Audrey and Billy had gone to Romanoff's for a small supper party in honor of D.M. Marshman, Jr.'s, engagement to be married. Billy had pulled his Jaguar XKE up to the curb. He came around to her side to open the door. Then he stuck his head into the car and said, "I have something to ask you, Aud."

"What?"

"Would you do me the honor of becoming my wife?"

"Why, why, Billy, this is . . . so . . . sudden."

There was a pause.

"Well."

"Yes."

He kissed her on her beautiful nose. He did not give her a ring. She never did have an engagement ring. But some kisses, like diamonds, are forever. This kiss was forever.

Wondering what was the nature of the repast on that enchanted evening, I once asked Audrey,

"What did you have that night in Romanoff's?"

"A hell of a good time," she at once shot back.

She remembers that once he had made his proposal, she could hardly wait. She was in constant attendance on the set, badgering him to set the date. "When? When? When?" Finally, after *Sunset Boulevard* was in the can, they went on a trip to Nevada. They went with Ray and Charles Eames, who had become their friends. Somewhere they were going to be married. Billy had not decided whether it would be in Las Vegas or Lake Tahoe. He had not even provided himself with a wedding ring when they started out. They stopped in a small jewelry shop on Ventura Boulevard in Encino and he selected a simple gold band for $17.50. Billy was acting very casual about the whole affair. They drove until noon, when they arrived in Min-

den, Nevada, a town of which she had never heard, though Billy re-
collected that Clark Gable had married one of his wives in Minden.

Suddenly Billy said, "This looks like a good place for a marriage." They found a Justice of the Peace. Mrs. Eames (Ray) went
out in the backyard and made a bouquet of garden flowers, daisies,
and ferns. So they were married. So he placed the ring on her finger.
She has never taken it off and she has never wanted a second wedding ring.

She still has the bouquet of flowers that she held in her arm that
afternoon. It is dried now and in tissue paper and she still has it.

"What really made me so mad," she says, "was that I had bought
such a nice dress, a simple but very nice dress, and I didn't have it
on. I was wearing these old blue jeans and a bandanna on my head. I
wanted to change my costume. But Billy said, 'No.' I said, 'Aw,
come on.' And he said, 'Either you get married like this or you don't
get married at all.' I wasn't about to take any chances with this guy
so I got married in the old blue jeans. We went up to Lake Tahoe
and we had a room that was so terrible in this old hotel. There was
still a pair of old socks under the bed from the previous guest. We
had dinner in the hotel's dining room. It was a tacky dinner. We got
up very early the next morning. We all went out, the four of us, and
Billy and Charlie Eames had their cameras. At that time, Billy was
very much into photography. Eames, of course, is a fantastic photographer. Billy had his Leica around his neck and Eames had his
Nikon. All they were doing was shooting pictures of rock forma-
tions and trees and I finally got irritated and said, 'Let me shoot
something.' And I finally took pictures of Billy, Ray, and Charles,
and finally made Charles take some pictures of me and Billy.

"So I can't say that I really had a romantic time on my honeymoon but it was beautiful, beautiful. We remained there two days
and then we drove home to Los Angeles."

Looking back, she realizes, now, that "Billy was embarrassed at
himself for getting married again. He did not approve of this. So he
did not want to act like it was anything special. He had been saying
cynical things so long about the stupidity of persons who get married
and—well, to find himself in this same position must have been embarrassing to him. So aside from the legal aspect of it—the certifi-
cate, the marriage service—he had to pretend to give it as little recognition as possible. We came home and it was back to his work immediately."

It is the dream of most men to fall in love with women who will truly understand them—and love them with all their shortcomings. Billy Wilder had come upon such a woman and now she was Mrs. Wilder.

She wanted very much to have children. She knew that with such a father they would be geniuses. Her word—geniuses. He said he did not want any more children. He already had one of them. Vicki was twelve years old when she met her stepmother. The new Mrs. Wilder fell in love with the girl and they have been friends since then. She was too much in awe of him to press the issue of progeny, and now she is glad that she did not. Audrey also found, as the years progressed, that she could not only adopt Vicki and Vicki's daughter, but also some of the ladies and gentlemen who played in her husband's pictures, and in several cases, notably those of Felicia and Jack Lemmon and Carol and Walter Matthau, they became good friends.

Philosophical about the whole matter, Audrey recently remarked, after she had cogitated upon the frequency of divorce among couples and the even sadder situations in which unhappy people remain in holy deadlock fearing to traumatize the children: "I do think many unhappily married people stay together because of the children and if you stay together when you don't have children, then you are staying together because you really want to do it and are in love with the person."

She is in love with the person. He is in love with the person. Remarking to Wilder once that I would have a hard time in painting a clear portrait of a lady with so many nuances, he said that Audrey could be summed up in one word: *saint*.

"She is a saint," he said. Then he paused. He cocked his head. He squinted at me. "And I am a shit. The saint and the shit."

Billy simply finds it intolerable to accept the idea that he is—to Audrey and a few other discerning persons—a most lovable and admirable human being, as well as a master in his art. It makes him wretched when people say nice things about him. One hates to ruin his reputation and yet he is, take him for all in all, a lovable man and a good husband.

And, as of June 1974, they had been married twenty-five years.

What did she desire for a silver anniversary gift? Well, she thought a really stylish diamond ring might be a fine thing. It was, after all, high time that she had an engagement ring. Oh, no, no diamonds. They were so bourgeois.

"Well, how about a really long trip to Europe?" she said.

"Now we are getting into a good area for negotiation," he said.

So, on September 4, 1974, they sailed on the last eastward voyage of the S.S. *France,* bound for Southampton, and then a week in London, where they would meet friends, and then another week to a castle outside Amsterdam owned by friends, and then a week in Paris, where Billy, like Gary Cooper in *Love in the Afternoon,* "is always descended" at the Hotel Ritz, and then to Austria and other places. . . .

That the marital alliance of Audrey and Billy has lasted this long never ceases to astonish their old friends. (Their new friends take it for granted and regard them as a single entity with two bodies.)

But when it all started in June 1949, everybody gave "it" six months, if not less. At first, she had no identity and seemed to be swallowed up by his overwhelming presence. Their first year together was a dreadful time for them. It seemed likely that the bonds would be broken. After their queer honeymoon at that Lake Tahoe dump, they came back to inhabit the old house at 714 North Beverly Drive and it was another woman's house—and I guess it is always Manderly for the second wife. But that was not the principle source of tension. It was the work. It was only when she was in close quarters with Billy that she really came to know how enslaved he was to his films. Returning to Hollywood, he was faced with the problem of cutting the beginning and ending of *Sunset Boulevard.* As I have said, the sneak previews had been disastrous. Billy Wilder went through moods when he was convinced that this film was a disaster and would wreck his reputation and power at the studio.

Audrey knew that, like anybody else, Billy had his ups and downs. But she did not know that, just as his exhilaration was immense, so his periods of despondency were cataclysmic. George Axelrod had noticed, during the period of his collaboration and through the many years of their friendship subsequently, that "when Billy has a flop picture he is unbearable. He suffers. During the years I lived in Hollywood the whole town seemed to become unlivable when Billy was suffering. He could not stand setbacks and his black moods would seem to suffuse the whole damn environment in Beverly Hills like the morning fog." And in their first marital year, Billy had much to give him the blues. Wilder has rarely made a picture that did not unconsciously reflect his dominant moods and when he was preparing his first non-Brackett picture, *Ace in the*

*Hole,* the pessimism in which he was steeped penetrated the film. He had told Walter Newman that the most interesting women characters in a movie were always, *au fond,* whores. What if, instead of marrying the sweet innocent all-American Jean Arthur girl, he had really married the hard-boiled, selfish Marlene Dietrich type? How could he be sure, *really* sure, that his naive little Audrey wasn't a golddigger, out to take him for all he was worth? The dismal marriage of Mr. and Mrs. Leo Minosa in *Ace in the Hole* mirrored his miserable feelings. Jan Sterling, as Mrs. Minosa, gave us a classic portrait of the bitch, a variation of the Stanwyck type in *Double Indemnity* or the Dietrich type in *Foreign Affair.*

For Audrey, having to endure the morose moods of her new husband, trying to learn how to manage the big house on Beverly Drive, adjusting to a new circle of friends, and above all, learning that the making of a movie swallowed up the man she loved—all this posed an insurmountable challenge to her. I think nine out of ten women would have given up in the first year.

She not only had these problems with which to contend, but became aware of a social, cultural, and intellectual gap that separated her from Billy.

But Audrey is a rare human being. She set her mind, her body, and her will to conquering what she now saw was enemy territory.

And, gradually, as she changed herself, she altered Billy's perceptions of women, and this is reflected in many of his later films, most interestingly in *Irma La Douce,* whose *leitmotif,* after all, is that a woman may do some of the things done by whores and even, speaking professionally, be one—and yet be a marvelous human being and make a man a lovely wife. Shirley MacLaine interpreted so well the ambivalence Billy was struggling with during these years. Her Irma captured it—and also her Fran Kubelik in *The Apartment.* And he could see the kindness and generosity in the characters Monroe played for him in *Seven Year Itch* and *Some Like It Hot.*

Billy was to hang a series of portraits of wives and lovers in his movie gallery of the 1960s and 1970s, women who were complicated and interesting partners of the men they loved. They were neither the classic Hollywood bad girl (the whore) nor the classic Hollywood Mary Pickford good girl (the virgin), nor were they the good-bad girl of so many of the sophisticated films. Wilder's ladies more and more became neither good nor bad, nor good-bad, but human beings in their own right. Partners. Friends. Interesting characters on the screen. He had found out that a woman could be interesting and not be a "whore." He had found out that a woman could be forever interesting even if she was a "wife."

And it was Audrey Wilder who had educated him by her shining personality. Billy was to teach her many valuable lessons about art, history, literature and the sensual amenities of living, about foreign culture and our European heritage. I think that what she taught him was a more than even exchange, for he profited not only as a moviemaker but as a private person. With her he found personal fulfillment. This new kind of woman, this friend, this partner, emerged in Audrey Hepburn's Sabrina and Ariane, in Monroe's heroines and MacLaine's, and in Felicia Farr's warm, charming wife in *Kiss Me Stupid* (she will play the whore for a night for the husband's sake!), in Lynn Redgrave's simplicity and honesty in *Avanti!*

And when the plot demands, as it did in *The Fortune Cookie,* that the wife be a hardhearted bitch out for money, Billy Wilder's heart is no longer in it; and Judi West's role as the gold-digging Sandy Hinkle is unconvincing and is perhaps the principle reason that the tension sags during the action. Wilder can't do Jan Sterling, Barbara Stanwyck, and Marlene Dietrich any longer. He knows better now. He has gone to the heart of a woman. Likewise his imaginative energy sagged in *The Front Page* because there was no woman of dignity and class to fight Walter Matthau for the love of Jack Lemmon.

Willie Schorr, during the early years of their marriage, had become Audrey's confidant as well as Billy's.

Describing the first years of adjustment, Schorr says, "Look at the situation she faced. Here was Billy: witty, charming, a bachelor, moving in the best circles, the most desirable extra man for a dinner party—hostesses loved to invite him. Suddenly he gets married. And whom does he marry? Somebody from Bel Air or Newport Beach? The Riviera? Who is she? they were asking. A nobody. A singer who once sang for Tommy Dorsey. She must be a social climber.

"Do you think Audrey was accepted so quickly by Billy's friends?

"And Billy, because of the studio pressure, he wasn't aware of her struggle to make a place for herself. He was a man set in his habits. She was sensitive enough to appreciate that she had not married a twenty-two-year-old man out of college. It was hard for Billy to realize that this was a girl who would be unsure of herself for a long time.

"But she is a fine, straight person of high character, an unusual woman. She was at quite a loss how to handle it. How do you become Billy Wilder's wife? That was something she was not prepared for. She saw that it was not easy to move comfortably in his circle. She had to make it on her own and be accepted on her own.

"It was a strain on them both and at times the strain became so great that they both were convinced that the marriage would crack up. It was hard for her to adjust to the situation but she worked at it and he came around also and worked at it."

One area of conflict, for example, was politics. It seemed to be Billy's fate to marry women who were conservative. Audrey was as antiliberal and reactionary as Judith had been at first. Audrey and Billy would get into the most heated arguments about world problems and the Republicans and Democrats. Billy accused her of being ignorant and unlettered. He demanded that she back up her viewpoint with knowledge.

"What do *you* know about it?" he would sneer.

So she started reading—books on history, economics, and politics, and serious magazines of public affairs. Now she had ammunition when he came home from the studio. Did he want to get her into a discussion on the Suez crisis, on the federal bureaucracy, on Gandhi, Roosevelt, or Eisenhower, the stock market and its relation to the inflationary process?—she was ready for him. They went at it hammer and tongs. Instead of finding this repelling, Billy became more intrigued by her and began to respect her mind. Now when she would make a statement opposing one of his views and he wanted to know where the hell she got that idea, she was able to cite chapter and verse from Galbraith or Toynbee.

She made herself a woman of independent ideas and soon became bold enough to engage in repartee with Billy. They loved having their fights out in public and their friends began to see that even these public arguments had a romantic tinge.

Aexelrod sums it up nicely as follows: "Their marriage is like a 1930s romantic comedy. They are playing Cary Grant and Roz Russell, Lombard and MacMurray, Gable and Colbert, Powell and Loy, Katherine Hepburn and Spencer Tracy. They are putting each other on all the time. I began to see they were serious in their role playing. I was at the house one time when Billy was in a meeting with his business manager, Rex Cole, now deceased. An argument about money ensued. She was playing her role as the much put-upon wife in a Leo McCarey comedy. Rex Cole was the villain. All the money came through Rex Cole. She was given $100 a week to run the house and buy her clothes. Rex had made out the checks and Billy was signing them. Audrey was on the other side of the room, mixing martinis and waiting for the business meeting to be over. She was getting worked up more and more against Rex Cole. She was growling and muttering that Cole was her enemy and he kept money out of her hands. Then she started on the life insurance. It seems that they had a joint policy for $100,000.''

(It did not carry a double indemnity clause.)

''Well, she yelled at me, 'Can you believe I have only a hundred thousand dollars worth of life insurance?' Finally she stormed over and shouted, 'I have only a hundred thousand dollars worth of life insurance.' Billy smiled sweetly and said, 'I have a solution, darling. You die and see what I do with the hundred thousand.' ''

The epitome of their stylized dialogue was a famous interchange at breakfast.

Audrey said, ''Good morning, dearest. Do you know what day it is?''

''No, darling.''

''It is our anniversary.''

''Please, Audrey, not while I'm eating,'' he replied acidly.

Axelrod observed: ''I would feel I was watching *It Happened One Night* or *Bringing Up Baby* when I was around them. And yet, do you know, it is one of the happiest marriages I have ever known. Billy, God love him, like any creative man, is not easy to live with. For one thing, he is compulsive, not only in making pictures, but everything. Everything must be in its place and you only eat certain things, like the black bread must come from a certain stall at the Farmer's Market and the shoes must be arranged in a certain way in the closets.''

Actually, one of the things which Audrey had to live with was that her husband had an utterly irrational craving for shoes. He was not a shoe fetishist, in the sense that the shoes she wore were erotically stimulating. No, it was *his* shoes. His daughter, Vicki, recalls that on a visit to the Beverly Drive home she was amazed to find that her father had an entire *walk-in* closet filled with shoes—rack after rack of shoes. Many of the shoes in the closet were loafers. Billy has embarked on a lifelong search for the Perfect Loafer. He accumulates loafers as other men accumulate restaurant matchboxes. He has them by the dozens. Audrey once told me that when she'd gone to

Billy's office at the Goldwyn studio, after the disastrous fire in 1974, she was heartsick to see the many art objects and signed photographs and antique pieces burned. But, in a corner of a closet, "in absolutely perfect condition," were eight pairs of Bass Weejuns, Billy's favorite loafer. Now to you and me, one pair of Bass Weejuns looks pretty much like the next. Not to Billy. He believes that each Bass Weejuns has its own individual quality. Once, while I was accompanying him on a shopping tour in San Francisco, we stopped at the famous Cable Car Emporium. Wilder at once headed for the shoe department. So help me. He started trying on moccasins and loafers. He purchased a pair. Weejuns.

Just as Audrey set herself to learning about politics and economics, she studied literature, the fine arts, and foreign languages. She became adept in French—reading it, comprehending it, and speaking it passably. By the second year, Billy was beginning to be impressed with her mind and her self-discipline. Then she applied herself to cooking. She went to cooking school. She studied recipes. She experimented. In time, she became a superb cook, perhaps one of the best nonprofessional *cuisinières* in Hollywood. Was it the old-fashioned notion that the shortest way to a man's heart is through his stomach? I do not think so. She liked to eat interesting food herself. Her developing liaison with Billy had opened up to her new worlds of culture and also new sensations. For her it was a new adventure in living. From a woman who had been strictly a fried-hamburger cook, she mastered French cooking, and also could whip up a Mexican dinner, a Japanese dinner, a Chinese banquet, and even the down-home Viennese dishes so dear to Billy.

Swifty Lazar, a part of their inner circle, is one of Audrey's many worshippers in the movie colony. "She is the best cook in Hollywood," he states. "She is very good with hot, spicy foods. Billy loves her cooking, as why should he not? Billy's favorite pleasure is a highly spiced meal—followed by an intense heartburn. I know and admire many of the wives of Beverly Hills, Bel Air, Brentwood and similar neighborhoods, dear boy, and I tell you she is the most competent, exquisite, and beautiful hostess and cook I have ever known." (For a long time, Lazar was a defiant bachelor and prior to his marriage, he had made a will in which he left his fortune to his favorite wives, among whom was Audrey Wilder. Lazar's marriage several years ago must have been a very upsetting thing to any of those women who had dreamed avariciously of his death.) "To give you an idea—she makes very fine chicken paprika—and she grinds the paprika herself. Imagine—grinding paprika. She found out that Billy adores kashe dishes. Now kasha—that is really a most boring type of food—sort of like oatmeal. But Audrey started working with kashe and now can prepare it in many different ways, using sauces and blending it with mushrooms and eggplant and well, she is unbelievable. Out at their beach house, out at Trancas, she won't have a servant. I've seen her serve drinks and prepare a meal of many courses for eight people—and all by herself. I call her the champion chorus girl of the world. A treasure of a girl. And she is still a hell of a good singer."

Playwright Leonard Gershe (*Butterflies Are Free,* among many others) is a part of their circle, which also includes, besides the Lazars, the Lemmons, the Matthaus, the Freddie de Cordovas (he is the director of the Johnny Carson program), the Armand Deutsches, and until his death in 1975, Jack Benny and his wife Mary. Gershe believes that the soundness of the Audrey and Billy ménage rests on a mutual recognition of the division of labor. Billy runs things at the studio. She runs things at home.

"When Billy is home, everything must be done for him," Gershe has noticed. "I remember once up at the beach, there were a lot of guests, and everyone was doing something, if only to clean an ashtray—except Billy. He was watching a baseball game, as I recall. If it is a Sunday, well, he plants himself before three television sets and watches various games and that is that, and you bring him whatever he wants, be it a sandwich, a beer, a Gelusil. He just holds out his hand and the person nearby fills it up for him. Once he was sitting with Audrey in the kitchen. It is an open kitchen. She was trying to lift a heavy roast on to a rotisserie. She was having trouble. He was right next to her but he looked out of the kitchen, there were a crowd of us in the living room, and said, quite seriously, 'Won't *anybody* help her?' He was only an arm's length away but it wouldn't occur to him to do this. Perhaps according to his reckoning, he works hard at the studio so he shouldn't lift a finger at home. Perhaps it is his Austro-Hungarian attitude to women. But Audrey does not mind. Now you know they could have a lot of cooks and servants but they don't because they don't like too many strangers cluttering up their place. So all they have is this cleaning woman, a day cleaner, and a maid, who has her own quarters in their apartment building.

"Tell you what kind of a woman she is. When Billy is shooting, he gets up around six. She makes it her business to get up a half hour *before* him and fix him a big breakfast. He isn't one of your toast and coffee guys. He likes a big breakfast, with all sorts of things, like for instance some kind of imported Irish bacon that comes in large pieces and has to be sliced and he gets it from some secret place he knows in town, like his black bread; and he loves German sausages, of which there are many varieties. She sees to it that when he comes to the table everything is ready for him.

"Now there are not too many wives in Hollywood or anywhere else who get up at five-thirty to make their husbands a big breakfast and it would be nice enough if she did it out of duty, but she does it out of love. She expresses her love this way and she wants to have the pleasure of sharing his company at breakfast."

Formerly Wilder had started the day by breakfasting with his collaborators, but by the sixth year of their marriage, he wanted to have the morning hours of the day alone with Audrey. He never made a sentimental point about it. He just ceased inviting his collaborators to the house for breakfast. Lunch he eats away from home, but dinners they eat together. Often they both satisfy their whims at the last minute. She always cooks dinner.

"Billy might suddenly be in the mood for Mexican food, so I just make Mexican food or Chinese or Japanese," she says. "We both like every kind of food. We drink beer or a *vin ordinaire* as often as not. I love saké. I love its taste. We often have a sashimi, beef teriyaki, and several bottles of hot saké. You see life is much simpler if you don't go out every night and you cook yourself. You are not dependent on servants. I never have caterers. I hate having strange waiters milling around our apartment. Billy and I both would rather dine *chez nous* than go out. We both hate to get involved in elaborate social planning. Most of it is last-minute dates with what I call our shaggy group of friends, the kind you can call up at five in the afternoon and come over for dinner tonight. When we go out, the places I like are Chasen's, Mr. Chow's, and Dominick's. That is a terrific place, Dominick's—a husband and wife run it and she is in the kitchen and he waits on the tables. My favorite place of all is The Bistro. That is when I can get all dressed up and it is just about the only place in town where you don't feel foolish if you are all done up."

The Bistro, the most elegant restaurant in Los Angeles at present, was in a sense the creation of Audrey and Billy. The Bistro (which has recently become notorious as the scene of a drunken election-night party at which Julie Christie delights Warren Beatty with a dash of fellatio), had been an old idea of Billy's. He had always wanted to put money into a simple French restaurant with *cuisine bourgeoise,* like the one in *Ninotchka* where Melvyn Douglas falls off a chair and Garbo laughs. For a long time, whenever he went to Romanoff's, one of his favorite hangouts, he would get into a conversation with the maitre d'hôtel, Kurt Niklaus, and tell him that if he ever wanted to open a restaurant on his own, he, Wilder, had a clever idea for a restaurant. Kurt had heard this often from exuberant patrons. When Romanoff's folded in 1962, he called several of them and reminded them of their promises and said he wanted to open a restaurant of his own. Only Wilder came through. "I went to see him," Kurt once told *Saturday Evening Post* reporter Richard Lemon, "and within twenty-four hours he had checks in the mail for ninety thousand dollars." In all there were sixty stockholders, each of whom had to put in a minimum of $3,000. The Wilders put in $20,000. Audrey helped round up some of the investors. Billy's original conception had been for the decor to be simple-looking (though expensive), like a neighborhood Parisian brasserie, with red-checked tablecloths, house wine served in liter carafes, sawdust on the floor, fresh fruit in paniers on the table—that sort of thing, though tastefully done. The wives, led by Audrey, wanted *haute cuisine* dishes and a *grande luxe* ambiance. So it was modeled after the famous Grand Vefour in Paris—an 1890s rococo place of mirrored walls and beveled paneling and crystal chandeliers and on the second floor private dining rooms for private parties. (It was upstairs where the bacchanalian revelries of *Shampoo* occurred.) One of the many subjects on which Audrey and Billy have violent disputes— the sort that lead people who do not know them well (and do not realize that their prose style is flavored with the amorous counterpoint of movie lovers of the 1930s) to fear that the Wilders are headed for a divorce—is her taste in clothes. He attempts to carry his directorial authority into every phase of his personal life. He even wants to direct her wardrobe. Because she was compelled to wear boring clothes until she was eighteen, Audrey has always had a penchant for flamboyant costumes. She loves sequins. She has a sequin pant-suit. She loves feathers. She has a feather jacket which he detests. She has a full-length white fox coat which he believes to be an abomination and he tells her so. He doesn't like the froufrou and marabou and glitter she adores. And she has a fondness for the most ornamented and dramatic hats. Sometimes, when they were going out to dine at The Bistro, and she fitted one of these flamboyant cha-peaux on her head, he would shudder. Then he told her, one night, that he would pay her $100 not to wear a hat that night. She asked him if he was serious. He peeled a century note from his bankroll. She went out bareheaded. This got to be a game and she was soon spending $275 for a hat just to get $100 out of him.

One night when they were going out with a group of couples to a party, and she had gotten into her feather jacket—in which she looked marvelous, by the way—Billy said, "When Aud gets dressed up, I am embarrassed to go out with her. I feel like she is going on Sesame Street."

He has often accused her of deliberately dressing up to look like Big Bird.

One of the most endearing qualities of the Audrey and Billy con-nection is that they enjoy everything they do together, and it is obvi-ous that they particularly enjoy their quarrels, and perhaps this is one of the secrets of an enduring marriage. As to his mixture of good and bad, she once remarked to me that it was like that line in the song—"You may have been a headache but you never were a bore." She finds him endlessly fascinating—even when he is hector-ing her about hats and sequin pantsuits.

He has changed her life—in deeper ways than most lives are changed in marriage. But it is not her life only. She says: "Every-body who has come into contact with Billy for any length of time is changed. How? You become more aware. Your tastes get shar-pened. You respond to so many facets of life with your mind and senses you never did before. Your mind is opened. Your eyes are opened. It is done with humor. He doesn't lecture you or bore you with theories about art. He helped me love paintings. You see, Billy believes in a beauty in everything, in the everyday things. He changes your eyes. He sees aesthetic quality in everything. Not just in paintings. A salad, for instance. How you arrange a salad. That is why, if some simple object that might cost fifteen dollars has form, he will consider it beautiful even if it is not by Henry Moore."

As to his negative aspects, there is his tendency to keep his problems bottled up inside him. "He is most secretive. He doesn't think out loud. He doesn't bring studio problems home with him. He just broods. The result is that his tension builds. He acts very calm, but when he's aggravated inside about an actor, let's say, his back will start hurting him. He just won't see that sometimes other persons or situations are making him sick, but Billy will think he is physically ill, and of course he *is* at that moment, but it is not physical as much as it is stress and strain.

"What was hard for me to accept is this total commitment when he's making a picture. He gets absentminded. His head is somewhere else. It's annoying. He doesn't hear what I'm saying. He also nags. 'Don't forget to do this today!' 'Did you call the plumber.' 'Will you get over to the Coffee Bean for two pounds of Vienna Roast?' He even used to make out lists of things for me to do which I was going to do anyway, but now he doesn't make out the lists."

Eddie Blum was privy to one of their rare public moments of tenderness. He and Billy had gone down to Palm Springs to get away from the phone and try to resolve the final sequences of *Stalag 17*. Audrey, who accompanied them, kept to herself for the two weeks during which the collaborators awakened at dawn and walked and walked and finally completed the structure of the film. Then the three of them started the drive home after lunch. Billy was driving. Audrey sat beside him, her arm fondling his shoulder. Eddie was drowsing in the back seat. Billy was in an exuberant mood. He started singing old songs from Viennese operettas in German and songs he remembered from the Berlin cabaret nights, which was a big surprise to Blum as he had never known that Wilder sang. Eddie did not say a word. He pretended to be sleeping. He felt as if it would be an intrusion on a very private moment if he said anything.

Interspersed with the European songs, were popular tunes, of the '20s, '30s and '40s, for Audrey Young Wilder still could swing the mellow classics.

"He and she were singing all the way home," Blum recalls.

When one thinks of that young writer in Vienna and Berlin, admiring Whiteman's type of jazz, remembering *Whispering* and *Japanese Sandman,* and his crush on America and the Lone Eagle and popular music, syncopation and dance bands, and knowing the lyrics of the Tin Pan Alley songs, one can see that Billy had wrapped America in his arms when he found Audrey, who was so American and who, though he had contrived to impart to her certain attitudes of sophistication, would always remain a very American woman and one who knew every standard American song that he could possibly request.

He had found, in John Donne's line, his America, his New Found Land.

# 18

# WILDER THE WIT

Hollywood prizes humor as a weapon against one's oppressors—
the ability to score points in repartee. Actors ridicule directors, directors ridicule producers and actors, agents ridicule producers and
actors and studio heads. Writers ridicule everybody. Billy Wilder is
one of the most caustic of Hollywood wits, in a class with such masters as Charlie Lederer, Charlie MacArthur, Herman Mankiewicz,
Ben Hecht, Nunnally Johnson, George Axelrod, Groucho Marx,
and George Burns.

Billy scored his points at Romanoff's, at the Beverly Hills Tennis
Club, in the Paramount commissary, and at various parties around
town. Many jibes were ascribed to Wilder which may have originated with somebody else. When the much feared head of MGM, Louis
B. Mayer, died in 1957, during a period of dwindling box-office re-
ceipts, there was a vast outpouring of spectators for the funeral
services at Rabbi Magnin's famous temple on Wilshire Boulevard.

Billy cracked, "It shows that if you give the public what they
want, they will come out for it!"

(The same joke was appropriated for Harry Cohn's demise. It has
been credited to various wits. Iz Diamond clearly remembers hearing Wilder say it at Mayer's funeral.)

Speaking of a well-known independent producer, Billy is said to have said, "I saw his last three pictures. I don't know what he's got to be so independent about."

His definition of an associate producer: "The only guy who will associate with a producer."

When veteran producers Leo Spitz and William Goetz were heads of Universal-International, one of their top executives was a Bob Goldstein, whose duties were vague. Someone loudly wondered, "What does Goldstein do anyway?"

Billy promptly said, "He gets for Spitz and spits for Goetz."

Billy was having a late-afternoon libation at the Tennis Club with some friends when a waiter brought over the late edition of the paper which headlined the news that Mike Todd had crashed to death in a plane accident. Art Cohn, a screenwriter who had been working on an adaptation of *Don Quixote* to star Mrs. Todd (Elizabeth Taylor), also died in that crash. Wilder began reading the story. Two columns on page one, telling of Todd's stage and movie triumphs, his wives, his rise from poverty. The story, with pictures, ran over to several more columns on page ten. At the bottom of the story were three lines about Art Cohn's credits. Wilder pointed out the disparity to fellow director Rouben Mamoulian, bitterly observing, "Additional Dying by Art Cohn."

The conversation concerned an obnoxious studio head. Someone defended him on the grounds that the talented Sam Goldwyn was also obnoxious.

Wilder snorted: "Just because Sam Goldwyn is a shit, does not mean that being a shit makes you Sam Goldwyn."

Once, at a party, they were talking about the brilliant director of plays and films, Josh Logan, a moody man, given to morbid depressions, and suffering from a neurotic craving for reassurance.

"All of us," remarked Billy, "need a little praise, a little admiration now and then, but Josh—he must liberate Paris every morning!"

A congregation of wealthy and orthodox Sephardic Jews several years ago put up a magnificent contemporary synagogue on Wilshire Boulevard in Westwood. Walter Matthau asked Billy to what architectural school this edifice belonged.

"Mishigothic," snapped Wilder.

(*Mishigoss* is a Yiddish word meaning "crazy.")

Once, while in Paris, Billy was trying to recall the name of a United Artists executive, formerly headquartered in Paris and now back in Hollywood.

"His name was Mo . . . Mo . . . Steinman?" Billy said, fumbling. "Or . . . Mo . . . Leibman. . . . Or . . . Mo . . ."

"Mo Rothman?" someone suggested.

"Yes, that is the Mo *juste*," Billy cracked.

Once, the Irving Lazars gave a dinner party for Claudette Colbert. The guests were seated at small round tables, four to a table. Ms. Colbert had been placed between Billy and Leonard Gershe. The conversation turned to hors d'oeuvres. Claudette described a tempting appetizer which her cook had invented. She explained: "She takes ordinary soda crackers and puts them in ice water and they swell up and then she puts them in the oven and they get big and crisp and hard—"

"That sounds so good, I'd like to try it on my cock!" Billy cried.

The late Jack Benny, who became very close to Billy in the last years of his life, told me, in an interview just a few weeks before his death: "Billy always has the right answer and gives it to you fast. We were discussing golf one day and somebody asked, 'Who would you consider the greatest golfer today?' So I said Sam Snead and then I gave the reason. 'Sam Snead, because of his age, that he can play the kind of golf that he is playing and he is up front with everybody, and so I must say that Sam Snead is the greatest.'

"So Billy said, 'In that case, Grandma Moses is the greatest lay in the world.' "

East Berlin was the locale of two fine Wilder jokes—one by Mrs. Wilder. Around 1961, after United Artists closed a deal to exhibit *The Apartment* in Rumania, Poland, and Czechoslovakia, the Diamonds and the Wilders were touring Europe. They went over to East Berlin, and visited a dreary basement cabaret where three musicians in faded tuxedos played folk songs on a violin, piano, and accordion. Being apprised that there were *Amerikaner* present, the band launched into a rendition of the latest American hit song in their repertoire, which was *Alexander's Ragtime Band*.

"Which of course was composed by Irving East Berlin," cracked Audrey Wilder.

The Communist filmmakers saw *The Apartment* as a thinly veiled indictment of capitalism, influenced by Marxism-Leninism. (*New York* magazine recently reported on the opinions of another well-known movie critic, Fidel Castro. In a conversation with Francis Ford Coppola, Castro said that *Jaws* was a good Marxist picture inasmuch as "it shows that businessmen are ready to sell out the safety of citizens rather than close down against the invasion of sharks." Coppola sagely replied, "Oh.")

Billy was guest of honor at a dinner given by the East Berlin moviemakers.

Introducing Wilder, the spokesman for the East German film industry said that the incidents of *The Apartment* could only happen in an American capitalistic city like New York.

Wilder spoke in German to his hosts and said that he believed that the theme of *The Apartment* was universal.

"It could happen anywhere," he said, "in Hong Kong, in Tokyo, Rome, Paris, London. But there is one place where it could not have happened, and that is Moscow."

He was interrupted by prolonged applause and cries of the Bolshevik equivalent of "right on."

When the ovation died down, Billy moved in for the kill:

"And, my friends, the reason this picture could not have taken place in Moscow is that in Moscow nobody has his own apartment."

There was grim silence. Hoping to lighten matters, Wilder said that he would be happy to give East Germany the rights "to *The Apartment* in exchange for that documentary film about the Stalin-Hitler nonaggression pact which started World War II."

Arriving at the Ahmanson Theatre to see a revival of *The King and I* not long ago, Billy Wilder was surprised to see that a producer had brought as a guest the director William Wyler, who has been quite deaf. "Taking Willie Wyler to a musical," he murmured to Audrey, "is about as smart as taking Stevie Wonder to the art museum."

Apropos of Willie Wyler, Leland Hayward suggested once to Billy that he change his surname to avoid confusion. Billy refused.

"It's like in painting, Leland," he said shrugging, "Monet . . . Manet . . . who cares?"

* * *

Much of Billy's conversational humor takes the form of long, exaggerated first-person stories in which he ridicules—Billy Wilder! For instance, we were talking once about the new freedom of films and literature in the U.S. We recalled how one had to smuggle *Tropic of Cancer, Lady Chatterley's Lover,* and *Lolita* in those famous green bindings of the "Travelers Library" which we bought in Paris.

"My favorite bookstore in Paris was across the street from the George Cinq," Billy recalls. "That was where I got my pornographic books, usually. One of my favorite writers in this genre, because he was the dirtiest of all, had a name I will never forget. He always would start his books with opening lines like 'Xavier Duplessis had just come for the third time.' I may forget the name of Marcel Proust, I may forget Thomas Mann, I may even forget Harold Robbins, but this writer's name I will never forget—*Akbar Del Piombo!* As soon as I got settled, I would rush over to the bookstore, with my tongue hanging out, and yell, 'Have you any new Akbar del Piombos?' I would grab one or two and go back to the hotel. But now it is different. What do you think is the first thing I do in Paris now? Between the airport and the hotel, in the months with an R, I stop at a seafood restaurant and I have two dozen oysters and a little bottle of white wine, a Muscadet. I'm crazy about French oysters, especially the tiny Belons. I am getting too old to be amused by pornographic books, but tiny French oysters and a Muscadet are lovely, and when I finish the oysters and the last drops of wine in the glass, I take a deep breath and I begin to breathe the soul of Paris."

Wilder once summed up France as "a country where the money falls apart but you can't tear the toilet paper."

Most of *Irma La Douce* was filmed on the back lot of the Goldwyn studio. They had put up a beautiful reproduction of a street near Les Halles—the shops, the bistros, the *louche* hotels. The most gorgeous starlets in town were cast as the whores. Filming the street scenes, Billy became aware that every day the set was jammed with reporters. He turned on them one day and snarled,

"Where were you bastards when I was making *Stalag 17?*"

Expatiating on one's obsession with a film in progress, he said he had a great opening scene for a movie about a screenwriter. "The camera," he said, "dollies toward a house in Brentwood. It is night.

An open bedroom window. The screenwriter and his wife in bed—both fast asleep. He sits up in bed, suddenly. Claps his hand to his head. Screams. His wife wakes up. 'What is it, Henry?' she cries. Talking in his sleep, he says, 'I tell you, Darryl, it just can't be done with flashbacks!' "

Wilder had an idea for a movie about a screenwriter during the period when left-wing writers were blacklisted by the studios. "This writer can't get an assignment because he has no talent. He is ashamed to admit to his wife that he can't get a job because he is a terrible writer. So he makes up a story that he is on the blacklist because he is a Communist. To carry this out he has to pretend he is a Communist and soon he really becomes a Communist and then he gets into many situations and I thought it would make a funny picture at that time but I could not work out the story."

At one time, the studios were infested with Hungarian writers: Lajos Biro, Ladislaus Bus-Fekete, Geza Herczeg, Alfred Sarra, Nikolaus Laszlo, Ladislaus Vadja, Melchior Lengyel, and others. There was so many Magyars at Metro, that somebody once posted a sign by the directory in the Thalberg Building, where writers were quartered: YOU MUST WORK HERE. IT IS NOT ENOUGH TO BE HUNGARIAN. Hungarian-haters told such jokes as "Hungarians are enemy aliens—even in peacetime"; "A Hungarian will sell out his country—but he won't deliver it," and, the most famous of all, "If you have a Hungarian for a friend, you don't need an enemy."

In recent years, Wilder's anal disorders have been treated by a medical specialist who hails from Budapest: Dr. Richard Peterfy.

One night, while Billy was dining with Audrey and friends at The Bistro, and putting away his usual prodigious repast, he observed that he had an early morning appointment with Dr. Peterfy tomorrow. Someone said that when he went to *his* proctologist he was not permitted to eat the night before, and had also to take an enema.

Wilder cracked: "If you have a Hungarian for a proctologist, you don't need an enema."

Not long after the Columbia Pictures version of *The Mysterious Island* was out in 1961, Billy arrived at a posh Beverly Hills soirée in his recently acquired Rolls-Royce. As one of the parking boys opened the door, Billy was chagrined to see that the driveway and the streets were littered with innumerable Rolls-Royces.

"To get any status around here," he remarked to Audrey, "you have to drive around in Captain Nemo's submarine."

Much of *Love in the Afternoon* was filmed on location in Paris. While Billy was over there, Audrey suddenly got the most irresistible craving for a . . . bidet! She had to have a bidet. She could not live without her very own bidet in the master bedroom. She cabled Billy to purchase a bidet and ship it to their Westwood apartment. Unable to locate a French plumbing supply firm which exported bidets, Wilder replied: IMPOSSIBLE TO OBTAIN BIDET STOP SUGGEST YOU DO HANDSTANDS IN SHOWER.

At a dinner party during the holiday season of 1976, the conversation got around to connubial sex. Walter Matthau, who loves to improvise wildly exaggerated tales of his troubles, began complaining of his romantic difficulties with his wife, Carol. (Carol Grace Matthau was previously married to William Saroyan and is consequently accustomed to the vivid imaginations of great men. She is a beautiful and talented writer and actress.) Matthau said that in order to go to bed with his wife he had to be sweet and attentive and amiable for a week before. "If I lose my temper and say something nasty," he moaned, "there goes my fuck for the week."
Tita Cahn, wife of songwriter Sammy Cahn, was among those present. She turned to Mrs. Matthau and asked, "Is that true, Carol?"
"Yes," Mrs. Matthau said, shrugging, "I can't be dishonest in bed."
"And not only that," rasped Matthau, "she watches television while we do it."
Wilder cut in to state, "Did you know that according to the latest research, 60% of American couples are now screwing dog fashion—so both parties can watch television in bed!"
While Billy was writing *Stalag 17,* De Mille phoned and invited him to a screening of his latest epic, *The Greatest Show on Earth.* Billy hated this type of movie but he could not refuse. He went with Eddie Blum. There were just the three of them—he, Eddie, and De Mille. Wilder squirmed nervously through the interminably overblown spectacle film. Blum wondered how Wilder was going to get out of this dilemma, as he would have to give De Mille a reaction.
Finally the picture ended. The lights came on. Billy leaped up. He

bowed. "Cecil," he said, "you have made *The Greatest Show on Earth.*"

De Mille smiled. "Thank you so much, Billy," he murmured. De Mille thought he said, "You have made the greatest show on earth."

After Judith Wilder divorced him, receiving the usual generous settlement to which she was entitled, Wilder was dining at the Ray Millands. Billy said how he longed to once more possess such a large house as Milland had so he could have ample room to hang his pictures.

"What is stopping you?" Milland asked.

"I could not afford it unless I married a very rich woman."

"Don't you know any rich women, Billy?"

"Only one—my ex-wife," he sighed.

Colin Blakely played Dr. Watson in *The Private Life of Sherlock Holmes.* There was a scene during a ballet at Covent Garden. The action called for Blakely to do an impromptu dance with six ballet girls.

Wilder instructed the corpulent Blakely: "I want you to act like Laughton and dance like Nijinsky."

They rehearsed.

"How was I?" Blakely asked.

"Ah," sighed Billy, "why did you act like Nijinsky and dance like Laughton?"

Once, Wilder proposed to write a film about Nijinsky for Sam Goldwyn. He told Goldwyn some of the great dancer's history and how he cracked up and ended his life in a French mental hospital under the delusion that he was a horse.

"What kind of a picture is this?" Goldwyn cried. "A man who thinks he's a horse?"

"In my version there's a happy ending, Sam," Wilder said. "In the final scene we show Nijinsky winning the Kentucky Derby!"

In 1963, screenwriter Abby Mann went to the Moscow Film Festival with a Hollywood delegation. In a speech, Mann criticized satiric films and wanted films of more dignity and positive idealism. He said, "Some of us will resolve to give you less films like *Manchurian Candidate* and *One, Two, Three,* and try to give you more films in the manner of *All Quiet on the Western Front, The Grapes of Wrath,* and *The Oxbow Incident.*"

Wilder dashed off one of his telegrams to *Daily Variety:*

"I shall skip the fact that his remarks were both sophomoric and sycophantic. However, I should like to ask one question: who appointed Abby Mann as spokesman for the American Film industry in Moscow? Personally I'd rather be represented by Abbey Rents."

("Abbey Rents" is the name of a Los Angeles chain which rents everything from wheelchairs to tents for outdoor events.)

Several years previously, Wilder held a press conference at the L.A. Press Club, in the course of which he made several observations concerning the decline of the star as a box-office attraction. Dean Martin—or his publicists—seized on this and attacked Wilder for being unfair to actors. Wilder sent another wire to *Daily Variety:*

> As an old friend and fan of Dean Martin's, I am surprised to find myself in the midst of a public feud with him. But knowing that Dino is neither a reader, nor a writer, nor a feuder, I detect in *Daily Variety* the fine Italian hand of Rogers and Cowan. What I actually said is "if a picture is no good, the stars don't mean a thing." By quoting only the second half of the statement, I have been made to sound like an arrogant dummkopf.
>
> This is like quoting Dean Martin as saying, "I never drink" when what he really said was "while brushing my teeth I never drink."

After the disastrous fire on the Goldwyn lot in 1974, in which Wilder lost priceless personal possessions as well as works of art, I observed that, in forty-eight hours, he was his old serene wisecracking self. I remarked to him how impressed I was by the rapid recovery of his composure. He shrugged and said,

"What I have learned to do when such things happen to me is to think of a bigger tragedy . . ." He paused. "For instance—*Hitler might have won World War II.*"

# 19

# PLEASE DON'T
# SCARE THE PIGEONS

A director's life is one of prolonged anxiety. Wilder insists the screenplay is eighty-five percent of a movie. Maybe. But he was so . . . so . . . dependent on the actors. And actors are flighty, temperamental, oversensitive, and sometimes crazy. He had to learn to live with a kind of knife-sharp worry every hour he was shooting—until the picture was in the can.

Billy Wilder once talked to me about the *angst*. "A director's life is all worry," he murmured, frowning as Charles Durning, playing a reporter in *The Front Page*, stumbled and almost fell while crossing the sound stage. "There are five thousand worries. Not only the photography, not only the camera angles, not only do they understand the script, not only the cutting, the scoring—but *what is happening to each and every one of my actors?* I have to worry about Charles Durning on the freeway and will Walter Matthau lose too much money at the track and will Carol Burnett have a fight with her husband or Jack Lemmon break a leg in the shower."

For a long time, Billy had led a charmed life. He was seemingly protected from the vagaries of a director's existence. None of his stars gave him serious trouble. And, to put it crudely, *nobody died until he finished his pictures.* The death of a star or a disabling injury or illness in the middle of a picture is the unthinkable horror.

Then the gods turned on him.

It started with Marilyn Monroe. Because of her aberrations, *Some Like It Hot* took six weeks longer to shoot and cost almost a million dollars over the budget.

Iz Diamond and Wilder customarily tailored their scripts to their stars. *The Apartment* was being written for Shirley MacLaine, Jack Lemmon, and Paul Douglas. Two weeks before the starting date, Douglas collapsed and died of a heart attack. Billy cajoled Fred MacMurray into taking over the role of the corporation lecher. The dialogue had to be completely revised.

Horst Bucholz, portraying the young Communist lover in *One, Two, Three,* was racing his Porsche one Sunday morning when he cracked up. He didn't die. Wilder was within three days of finishing the movie. He needed Horst for a long final sequence at Templehof Airdrome. He had no alternative but to wait until Horst was on his feet again. He could not substitute another actor. Too late. He closed down production in Berlin. He had to build Templehof on a Hollywood sound stage. He had to transport Bucholz and six German actors to Hollywood. He made the final sequence at an additional cost of approximately $250,000. He got it in the can. Close— but he made it.

Charles Laughton was slated to play Moustache, the philosophical *patron* of the bistro in *Irma La Douce.* Then, late in 1961, Laughton was felled by cancer. He had only a few months to live. Billy did a beautiful thing. He pretended that Laughton was going to recover. He came to his house several times a week and sat by his bed. He brought him pages of the script. He discussed the film and exchanged ideas with Laughton on the way Moustache might be played. Both men pretended Laughton was suffering from an ulcer. Both men knew better. Elsa Lanchester, Laughton's wife, says that he knew he was dying. He also knew Wilder knew he was dying. But he never let on to Billy during these six months. Billy never suspected he knew.

Laughton gave many brilliant performances in his lifetime. I don't think he ever gave a better one than when he would meet with Billy and rehearse lines which he knew he would never be able to play to a camera.

Peter Sellers was to play the hero of *Kiss Me Stupid,* and then Dr. Watson to Peter O'Toole's Sherlock Holmes in Billy's planned fantasy about the great detective. Wilder had great plans for *Kiss Me*

*Stupid* which would have the elegant bawdiness of a Restoration comedy, though it was set in a small Nevada town. Sellers would play an insanely jealous husband who is an amateur songwriter and piano teacher. Dean Martin, who would be played by Dean Martin, is stuck in this little town. This gives Sellers, and his lyric writing partner, a scheming auto mechanic played by Cliff Osmond, the idea of foisting one of their tunes on Dean Martin. They will use Sellers's wife as a lure—except that the "wife" will be the town hooker pretending to be the wife, while the wife pretends to be the town hooker. Sellers is one of those rare actors who can play Everyman, with touches of the bizarre but also sympathetically. The theme of *Kiss Me Stupid* was so indelicate that it required a star of Sellers's aptitudes. For six weeks they filmed. Peter Sellers was superb. Osmond was superb. Kim Novak, as the hooker, and Felicia Farr, as the wife, were superb. Everything was going well—on the surface. It was such a happy set, such a crowded and happy set, visitors came by the dozens, friends of the actors, intimates of Wilder, knowing that Wilder loves an open set, loves to have onlookers, loves to create a festival of happy noise around his actors.

Billy did not know that this was most painful to Peter Sellers. He was almost a Garbo. Sellers was tensed up because he had just married a beautiful young wife, some eighteen years his junior. He was involved in litigation with Twentieth Century-Fox, which was suing Mrs. Sellers (Britt Eckland) because she had deserted a film she was making for Twentieth in London to come to Hollywood with Peter. Sellers was exhausted—he made three major films the year before. He wanted peace and quiet on the set. He resented Billy Wilder's gregarious personality. He didn't know how to talk to him. He was getting more and more uncomfortable. But he concealed it.

Now Billy usually picks up storm signals on a set. He is aware of a slight mood change in his actors. Even when they are birds. He was shooting a scene in *Front Page,* for instance, which required pigeons to fly and roost on cue. There was a pigeon trainer and a dozen trained-pigeon actors. One morning, the visitors on the set surged around the birds and disturbed them.

Wilder ordered the visitors not to go near the pigeons any more. He shouted, *"Please don't scare the pigeons."*

Somehow, though, he had failed to catch Sellers's anxiety. Sellers sought advice from Jack Lemmon, who had made three Wilder pictures by then. "How did you handle the problem?" Lemmon listened and said Wilder was a nice guy and just see him and tell him the problem and he'll understand.

Sellers did so. He found Wilder in a contrary mood. Billy said, "Why don't you do like Jack Lemmon does? When we're ready to do a scene, he closes his eyes. He says, 'It's magic time.' Then he forgets everybody on the set."

"Lemmon says, 'It's magic time'?" Sellers croaked, his lips twitching. "And that's all?"

"Yes, he says that and it works," Billy said.

Sellers said it. He said it was magic time, many times. It did not work. He hated Billy Wilder with the quiet intensity of a Dr. Strangelove.

On April 6, 1974—a Sunday—Sellers had taken his children, by his first marriage, to Disneyland. When he got home, he suffered a massive coronary thrombosis. An ambulance took him to Cedars of Lebanon. His heart stopped! It was revived. On that day, his heart stopped—and was artificially started—*six times!* He made a miraculous recovery and soon was convalescing at home. The specialists told him, and told Wilder, that he would possibly, even probably, be able to resume work on *Kiss Me Stupid* in six months.

Wilder had to make a decision. Should he scrap six weeks of wonderful film and start anew with another star? Should he close down production for six months on the vague possibility that Sellers might be able to finish the picture? He debated for many anguished hours. He could not postpone a decision because each day cost the studio another $30,000. He finally decided to replace Peter Sellers with Ray Walston.

Back home in England, Peter Sellers exposed his discontents to film critic Alexander Walker of the *London Evening Standard*.

"I have had Hollywood, luv," he told Walker. "At the studios they give you every creature comfort, except the satisfaction of being able to get the best work out of yourself. I used to go down on the set of *Kiss Me Stupid* with Billy Wilder and find a Cook's Tour of hangers-on and sightseers standing just off the set, right in my line of vision. Friends and relatives of people in the front office came to kibitz on Peter Sellers, actor. . . . I should have ridden to the set on horseback . . . and bawled out, 'Who are all these damn civilians? Get them out of the range of my cannons!' "

Another near-catastrophe happened during the filming of *The Fortune Cookie*. In the eighth week of production, Walter Matthau suffered a heart attack of such severity that he came close to death. It happened early on a Sunday morning, as had the accidents of Bucholz and Sellers.

Billy told Iz Diamond: "I wonder if it isn't a mistake to give actors a day off. They always get in trouble on Sundays."

Wilder had learned his lesson. He did not replace Matthau. He shut down the production until Matthau recovered. That was a five months delay. The picture was completed with some anomalies. The last scene shot before suspending showed Matthau rushing up the stairs to Lemmon's apartment with the settlement check for $249,000.02. The first scene they shot afterwards showed Matthau opening the door. The shots did not match as he had lost much weight.

"You see me going upstairs weighing a hundred and ninety-eight pounds," Matthau remarked. "I walk in and I'm a hundred and sixty pounds."

Having recently seen *The Fortune Cookie,* I said I hadn't noticed the discrepancy.

"Neither did anybody else," he said.

"How did you do it?"

He shrugged. "Billy told me to act heavier."

Matthau won his first Oscar as the shyster lawyer in this picture. He picked up his award with his right arm in a cast and a sling. He had fallen off his bicycle while riding on the Pacific Coast Highway—the previous Sunday!

Billy had come to think of the seventh day as Sunday, Bloody Sunday, from the picture of the same name . . .

Wilder believes in the inviolable sanctity of the screenplay. He did not abide actors rewriting this dialogue. He was a tyrant in this respect. The script was Holy Writ.

On the first day of filming *Stalag 17,* Wilder called a meeting of the actors. He had given them the uncompleted script. He asked them if they had read it. They chorused yes. He then announced:

"Gentlemen, if you have something to tell me about your lines or anything else in the script—tell me now. Because once we start shooting not a sentence, not a word, *not a syllable,* will be changed. Is that clear?"

William Holden started to open his mouth and he got very red in the face and then he said nothing.

Matthau feels constricted also by Billy's slavish adherence to a script. He wants to act more spontaneously. He can't. He thinks that to Wilder "actors are a necessary evil. I think he wishes there were some way he could make pictures without actors. He once told me that he envied Walt Disney. Donald Duck and Mickey Mouse didn't make trouble. I studied with the great Erwin Piscator. I have heard Piscator say he wished he could put on plays with just turntables, screens, projection machines, light effects—without one actor, because—my God—*actors got in his way!*"

Joe La Shelle, who was cinematographer on many of Wilder's great films of the 1960s, says that Wilder never worried about an actor's "opinions, how he looked, how he should be lighted, and what his best profile was. Billy felt these were not things for an actor to know about. If I, as cameraman, and Billy, thought a certain angle was right for him and it was right for the story, we would not be concerned whether the actor had a shadow on the nose or a bad highlight on the forehead."

On a "pickup," Billy likes to take it from wherever the action stopped, rather than go back to the beginning of the scene. Actors always want to start from the top, to gain an emotional momentum. Billy can't see it. To him, they're wasting time.

He is a fanatic about changing lines.

Shirley MacLaine was startled when she did her first Wilder picture. She didn't think it made much difference if she skipped a few words or changed a phrase here and there. It had not bothered her previous directors. She learned it bothered Billy. In *The Apartment* she was playing a difficult scene in which she's running her elevator and greeting people getting on and off and she had many pieces of business, as well as many lines, and she got it beautifully on the fourth take. Billy said, "Print it." And then Iz loped over. He whispered something to Billy.

Billy said, "Shirley, we'll have to try it again. Those were not the exact words."

*Actually, she had missed only one word!*

But Billy insisted on absolute fidelity to the sacred text.

An even more complicated scene had to be played by Jimmy Cagney in *One, Two, Three.* In a fast and furious tempo, Cagney, who had to completely refurbish the frowsy Communist lover, was examining shoes, shirts, suits, ties, ordering this, sneering at that—fast, fast, fast. On the line, "Where is the morning coat and striped trousers?'', he said, "Where is the coat and striped trousers?''

He went up in this line many times and each time Billy yelled, *"Cut,"* although it really made not a hell of a lot of difference. It had to be "morning coat" and "striped trousers."

Cagney finally did it on the fifty-second take.

He told correspondent John Crosby that this was his all-time record for takes in his long movie career!

Some part of him, some stubborn pride in his authorship, blinds Wilder to the mysterious powers of movie actors and actresses; they are words made flesh on celluloid. There is no comparison between a screenplay and a stage play. A stage play, like the score of a symphony, exists apart from the artists who interpret the roles or play the instruments. The interpreters vary from one season to another. But in a movie, the actors and the screenplay are fused into one entity *forever.* We shall never know how Peter Sellers could have interpreted Orville J. Spooner. Nor can we expect to find each new generation of actors reinterpreting the great screenplays of the past, even of the recent past, as each generation of American performers plays the classics of Shaw and Shakespeare or modern works by Tennessee Williams and O'Neill.

The photoplay is subordinate to the performer in a way that a stage play is not. In his heart of hearts, Wilder believes that a truly competent actor should be able to play his words exactly as he wrote them and play them beautifully. His ideal of an actor is somebody like Charles Laughton. Wilder recalls a day, during the filming of *Witness for the Prosecution,* set aside just for reaction shots of the jury. This meant that the extras were hired for only one day. The assistant director would read various scenes to which they would react. The AD would read the lines of all the stars. Then the reaction shots would be intercut at relevant moments in the already completed film. Laughton begged Wilder to let him read *all* the off-camera speeches. It was his day off, of course. He just wanted to act. He said the jury would react better if he read it. So he came and read all the parts—the judge, prosecutor, defense counsel, Marlene Dietrich, Tyrone Power, Una O'Connor—with different voices, with gestures. It was an exhibition of craftsmanship such as Wilder had never seen. He believes that Charles Laughton had the greatest technical range and power of any actor, man or woman, whom he has known.

He becomes irritated when actors tell him they feel uncomfortable about a line, and want to know motivations. Shirley MacLaine didn't like some dialogue in a scene.

She asked, "Why should I say this?"

Billy replied, "Number one, because I wrote it."

"I know, I know," she said, "but it just doesn't seem to be right, somehow. I mean, this girl saying this. No girl would say a thing like that to a man like him."

"I'll give you another reason, Shirley," he said coldly. "You'll say it because I tell you to say it."

"Oh sure, oh sure," she said, "but I just don't feel it."

"Oh, horseshit," Billy said. She did it.

His way.

Nevertheless, actors love to work for Wilder. His sets are happy places. He is a director who rarely permits his cast to lapse into the ennui engendered by the long hours of sitting around a sound stage, waiting for the next setup to be lighted. He teases his actors, he listens to their problems, he tells them amusing stories. He creates an atmosphere of carnival. He is aware of the need for small details which make an actor feel secure. For instance, to enhance MacMurray's own sense of the character, he had memo pads and stationery printed with "J. D. Sheldrake" though nobody but the actor himself would ever see them.

MacMurray, conditioned by an early life of privation, is tight with a dollar—even a half-dollar. In *The Apartment,* the script called for him to get his shoes shined and flip a fifty-cent piece as a tip to the shiner. He couldn't do it. He pleaded with Wilder that it was against his nature to do this. Couldn't he just this once, please, be himself, and do it his own way? Wilder conceded. MacMurray tipped a dime.

Later, Wilder got his revenge when MacMurray gives Shirley MacLaine a hundred-dollar bill for a Christmas present. Wilder hates stage money. He peeled off a genuine century note from his thick bankroll and gave it to MacMurray to use in the scene. After the take, the actor, lovingly caressing the bill, returned it to Wilder. At the end of the day Billy—having conspired with the crew and the cast—demanded his money back. MacMurray said he had returned it. Wilder argued so persuasively that MacMurray finally became uncertain and, beads of sweat breaking out on his face, he slowly opened his wallet and took out a hundred-dollar bill. Everybody on the set swore they had not seen him return Wilder's bill. So he handed it over.

Only then did Billy reveal the prank.

Another example of Wilder's attention to detail is in a scene in which Lemmon returns from his date with Joe E. Brown in *Some Like It Hot*. They have been tangoing all night. He is dreamily stretched out on the bed, still in drag. Curtis comes in. Then Lemmon had a scene that played almost five minutes. It was his favorite scene. He worked very hard on it. He prepared himself emotionally for it. He walked on the set in costume.

Billy handed him a pair of maracas.

"Get used to these."

"Why?"

"Because you'll be playing with them all through that scene. You say a line and then give these maracas a shake. Every time you say a line, you do a little dance and shake the maracas. See?"

Lemmon was thinking: *My God, it's happened, he's finally flipped, he's crazy, this has got to be the worst piece of shit direction I've ever gotten in my life.*

Aloud he said, "You . . . uh . . . I mean . . . this is crazy . . . I can't . . . that is . . . Billy, please let me do it my way . . ."

Wilder replied, "You know I'll always let you try out your ideas—but there's just no way you're going to talk me out of using those maracas!"

He did it Wilder's way.

Lemmon: "I was upset by these crazy maracas when we started the first take. Well, the long and short of it was that it was a brilliant stroke. If he had not given me something legitimate to do after each of my lines, most of the audience would never have heard the dialogue after I said my first line to Tony, 'I'm engaged.' They would have been laughing through the best lines ever written for me. Like Tony says, 'Why would a guy wanna marry a guy?' and I look at him incredulously and say 'Security!' And Tony says, 'But there's a problem,' and I say, 'I know there's a problem—I smoke. His mother doesn't like that.' Every single line was a laugh and we now could fill in the laugh with the maracas gag. As they came out of one laugh, I hit them with the next line. And then the maracas and then the next line.

"It wasn't until I saw it with an audience that I knew how wise Billy was. In all my advance homework on the scene, I had not made allowance for the laughs. Of course, you can't time laughs exactly in a picture. No two audiences react the same length to the same joke. Now Billy had filled up the space between the jokes with legitimate business, something was going on whether or not they laughed or how long they laughed, and musically it connected with the dancing sequence, reminding the audience of Joe E. Brown holding me in his arms and tangoing. The way Billy paced that scene with the maracas was brilliant.''

With only a few exceptions most of the actors found it a joy to work with Wilder. It was an exhilarating experience. However despondent or fatigued he might be feeling, Wilder never showed it to his actors. He was a fountain of energy, of ideas and enthusiasm, of persiflage and sarcastic banter, of compliments and anecdotes, and he seemed to blossom when he stood by the camera, a baton in his hand, a hat perched on his head, a cigarette between his lips, a slight crouch as he empathized physically with each actor, shouting *'Go . . . Hit it . . . Roll 'em . . . Faster.'* He did not slow down during the working day. Hardly ever. His *élan vital* was so powerful that it surged through the sound stage. His own supernormal kinetic energy became converted into the energy of the actors, of the crew, and ultimately of the film itself. He did not stand still on a set— except for the few moments the camera was rolling. Otherwise he was in perpetual motion (and emotion) on the set—dancing around, moving back and forth, humming old songs to himself, muttering under his breath, sometimes dancing with invisible dancing partners to his secret inner rhythms, restless, nervous, high-strung, striding, striding, striding, forth and back, back and forth, thinking, worrying, planning, inventing all the time, laughing with his actors and making them cherish each moment of their work, never letting them languish into boredom.

GLORIA SWANSON: "He reminded me of Toscanini conducting an orchestra. Many musicians playing different instruments and one man in absolute control. He has such an authority, does Billy Wilder; but he conducts in a sort of very light, delicate, polite manner— but madly irreverent. I never saw him give a line reading, to me or anyone. And he never showed you how to play a scene. He would discuss a character but he expected you to know how to do the character, speak the words. He is like Mr. De Mille. I remember an actor once asking him, 'Would you show me how to play this?' and Mr. De Mille replied, 'I am not running an acting school.' It went for thirteen weeks, *Sunset Boulevard,* and all of it full of love and excitement, the crew full of enthusiasm. I wept when it was over for I was so happy during the making of it. I was so unhappy when we finished, I wished we could have started all over again. The whole experience was magical.''

Holden grew close to Wilder during the making of *Sunset Boulevard.* A simple, untutored lad from Pasadena, he says that Billy opened up the world of culture and travel to him. He had been troubled how to play Joe Gillis. He was afraid of projecting a vulgar, pimpish, gigolo type. He couldn't relate to the Norma Desmond character. He revealed his confusions to Wilder, who told him simply that he had to visualize a garage mechanic who was living in Des Moines. ''And when he goes to see this picture, I want him to say 'There but for the grace of God, go I.' '' Somehow this brought Holden close to that corruption in us all.

In *Sabrina,* Holden speaks of an inspired piece of direction. He had to leap over a tennis-court net. He did it. He did it well. He was in splendid physical condition. Wilder told him to do it over again, and this time, as he was vaulting over, to *stop for a split second in midair.* This is impossible. But Wilder implanted the idea in his mind. Wilder wanted him to impart a sort of casualness to his leap. On the next leap, Holden mentally ''stopped'' in midair, and the leap was an arabesque.

Sometimes it is only a word or a suggestion to stir an actor's imagination. Cliff Osmond asked Billy in what mode he wanted him to play Purkey, the private investigator, in *Fortune Cookie.*

''Incessant pursuit. Relentless. Play Javert,'' Billy said. Osmond reread *Les Miserables.* Now he had the psychological nature of the character, on which he could put his own flesh.

Kim Novak's tantrums and arrogance were notorious in Hollywood. Prior to shooting, he laid down the law to her. He knew he must not lose the upper hand or she would tear him apart. He intimidated her. He also knew that beneath her toughness there was concealed a shy little girl. He saw he had terrified her—too much. He had asserted his authority but perhaps at the cost of stifling her emotions. He therefore requested Osmond to help her ''run her lines'' in her dressing room. Osmond found a very scared Ms. Novak. He reassured her. They didn't ''run lines.'' She spoke of her fears. He spoke of his. She was comforted. On her first scene—with Osmond in a bar—Wilder cleared the set of everybody but her and Cliff and himself, for a little run-through.

Wilder decided to approach her as if she were Garbo.

After this, she became virtually his slavish admirer. She never complained—not even during an evening when they had to work overtime and didn't break until two A.M. She then invited Wilder and the principals to her dressing room. She laid out trays of finger sandwiches and her own home-baked cookies. She stirred fifteen-to-one martinis for Wilder and Dean Martin. She served Billy with a look of worshipful admiration.

They yearned for his approval. They were jealous of one another. They watched nervously for signs of favoritism.

Billy had known Marlene Dietrich since his Berlin days. They were old personal friends. *Foreign Affair* was her first film for him. It was also Jean Arthur's first Wilder picture. Ms. Arthur observed, with jealous twinges, that Wilder would be engaged in animated German conversations with Dietrich. Sometimes he went to her dressing room and partook of her cooking. Billy did not know Ms. Arthur was seething over this. One night, after midnight, the front doorbell rang. Outside stood Jean Arthur, accompanied by her husband, producer Frank Ross. Her eyes were red from weeping.

"What is it, Jean?" Billy asked.

"What—what did you do with my close-up?" she cried.

"What close-up?"

"The one where I looked so beautiful."

"What do you mean, what did I do with it?"

"You burned it, Billy. Marlene made you burn that close-up. She doesn't want me to look good."

He took her with him alone into a projection room the next day and showed her the rushes, including her unburned close-up. Thereafter, he ceased talking German to Marlene and taking refreshments with her in her trailer. He made certain that Jean Arthur knew she was loved and appreciated by her director.

Marlene Dietrich loves to cook. She loved cooking elaborate Viennese and German dishes for Billy. She prepared many lunches when they made *Witness*. But Billy had learned his lesson. He would not dine with her, unless Laughton and Tyrone Power were included.

Marlene regarded Billy as a saintlike individual. She praises his charity, a characteristic of Wilder which he never mentions. The biographer Charles Higham, interviewing Marlene, once asked about Billy. Instead of the usual hard-boiled anecdotes, Marlene revealed that Wilder had worked harder than almost any other member of the European Refugee Rescue Fund in Hollywood. He had given generously of his money and his time and his organizing ability. He had found jobs for screenwriters and actors. She said he was the kindest, sweetest man she had ever known!

One of his collaborators told me that he found out, quite inadvertently from a lawyer he had met at a party, that Wilder was sending several black and Mexican-American students of talent through college. The sole condition was that they must never know the name of their benefactor.

In 1946, Humphrey Bogart signed a new contract with Warners'. He submitted a list of five "acceptable directors." In 1955, Marilyn Monroe handed to Twentieth Century-Fox a list of sixteen "acceptable directors."

Billy Wilder's name was on both lists.

Subsequently both stars made pictures for him.

Both came to hate Wilder with a passion.

He detested them with an equally intense passion.

In confronting Bogart and Monroe—two persons of great charismatic presence on the screen—Wilder had also to confront the truth that the movies were not a writer's medium. He needed these mysterious, powerful presences more than they needed him.

Bogart was a nervous little man, an immaculate dresser in slacks of knife-sharp creases and a bow tie and a navy blue blazer. He was a drunk. He was a needler. He beat up strangers. He beat up wives. He fought in bars and at parties. He was barred from many of the fashionable watering holes in Los Angeles and New York. He liked trouble. He married Lauren Bacall in 1945, his third wife. She was twenty-five years younger. He took testosterone shots to induce potency. He had two children by Mrs. Bogart. The hormones made him bald. He wore a toupee in all his films after *The Big Sleep*.

Bogart was induced to play Linus Larrabee in *Sabrina* by his friend Irving Lazar. Lazar thought it would enhance his career to prove he could play high comedy. Bogart started the picture with a grudge. He knew the part was originally written for Cary Grant and that Grant was unable to do it. He resented the fact that Bill Holden and Wilder were old friends. He resented Audrey Hepburn. He resented the world. Resentment was his way of life. He needled and needled. Wilder started needling back. He was a virtuoso at it.

"Y'see," explained Swifty Lazar in his little office on South Beverly Drive one afternoon, "Bogart was a man of caprices, which Billy did not find amusing. Bogart thought that a director must humble himself before Bogart. On a Billy Wilder picture, there is no star but Billy Wilder."

By the second week, Bogart knew that Hepburn, Holden, Wilder, and Ernest Lehman were in a conspiracy against him. After working hours, he observed that they all retired to Holden's trailer. They never invited him to join the party. Oh, no, they were making plans against him. The idea of that snip, Audrey Hepburn, thinking she could act. He started giving out some of his blunt quotes to interviewers and gossip columnists. He said Audrey couldn't take a scene in less than twelve takes; that Holden was a dumb prick; and that Ernest Lehman, he had learned, was a guy who attended the City College of New York. CCNY! And that Hun, that Prussian with a whip, that kraut, Wilder, that Nazi, he was the leader of the gang.

Perhaps Bogart identified too strongly with Queeg while filming *The Caine Mutiny*. He had gone straight from that picture to *Sabrina*. His delusions of persecution seized on anything. He knew that Holden was deliberately smoking cigarettes to make him cough during his lines. He complained to Billy.

"That fucking Holden over there, waving cigarettes around, crumpling papers, blowing smoke in my face. I want this sabotage ended, Mr. Wilder."

Most people found Billy's Viennese accent charming. Billy was ashamed of it. Bogie, who had a needler's flair for sensing a weakness in an opponent, learned this. He made fun of Billy's accent. He also believed—or made believe—that Wilder was not Jewish but a Nazi. Sometimes when Wilder was tense, his accent got worse. He gave Bogie a direction: "Giff me here, blease, a little more faster."

"Hey, Vilhelm," Bogie said in a nasty tone, "vould you mind translating that into English? I don't schpeak so good the Cherman, *jawohl*."

"One more crack like that, *mein Herr*," Wilder snapped, "and I'll get Dick Brooks in here to direct you."

Wilder rarely lost an opportunity to throw Brooks and Nicholas

Ray, another young director, in Bogart's face. Both of them had done two pictures each with Bogie. Wilder claimed that they sucked around Bogart and meekly accepted his insults. Wilder told Ezra Goodman, who was researching a cover story on Bogie for *Time*, that "he surrounds himself with whipping boys, aspiring young directors like Nick Ray and Dick Brooks. . . . He exposes them to ridicule and they have to take it because it is part of the business. They want to direct him in a picture.

"But Huston, Mankiewicz, and I don't take that from him."

Sometimes when he couldn't think of any retort, Bogie would say, "You're still a Nazi son of a bitch in your heart," or call him a "kraut bastard."

On one such occasion, Billy looked him over slowly and then said, "I examine your face, Bogie. I look at the valleys, the crevices, and the pits of your ugly face—and I know that somewhere underneath the sickening face of a shit—is a *real* shit."

That was how it went day after day. Sometimes Bogie lunged at Holden or Hepburn. Sometimes he shot at Lehman.

Once, Lehman came on the set with two copies of a scene he had just revised. He gave one to Billy and one to Holden.

"Where's mine?" Bogie snarled.

"I–I don't have another copy," Ernie said.

Aha! Another proof they were ganging up on him. He went berserk, Lehman remembers. He raged and screamed at the top of his lungs. His eyes rolled. Spittle came out of his lips.

"Get this City College bum out of my sight," he ranted. "Send him back to Monogram where he belongs."

Wilder folded his arms. He called a break.

"There will be no further shooting on this picture until Mr. Bogart has apologized to Mr. Lehman," he stated.

Lehman, embarrassed, moved away. After a long silence during which not a person on the set uttered a sound, Bogart finally slouched over to Lehman and whispered, "Come on into my dressing room, kid."

They had a drink.

Wilder resumed shooting.

Working as they were under pressure, some days a page or two ahead of the shooting, Wilder wanted to work late. Bogey refused to lift a finger after 6:00 P.M. That was his strict rule. He had to start his drinking at 6:00 P.M. Billy did not know what it meant to have to drink. He did not—he could not—know how hard it was for Bogart to go long hours without his alcohol. There was an unvarying ritual in the late afternoon. His secretary, Vera Petersen, whom he called "Pete," brought him, promptly at 5:45, a tumbler of Scotch and soda, with a handkerchief over it. He did not drink it until 6:00—but it was comforting to know that it was waiting there for him.

Wilder could not help but think that Bogie was taunting him with these tricks. "You're all set up for a shot," he said, "and it's exactly six P.M. Maybe it took you three hours to light the shot. He will not stay on for ten minutes to finish the shot; he will walk out."

Bogie gave him trouble every step of the way. He said he didn't feel authentic wearing a homburg hat and striped trousers and stiff collars. He decided Lazar had given him a bum steer. Lazar was in the plot against him also. A big-shot Wall Street businessman—that was no role for Humphrey Bogart. Bogart ridiculed every aspect of the screenplay and his costume. Wilder says he came on the set without knowing his lines. He came on time but he did not study his lines until the scene was ready to go.

Wilder said Bogart was essentially a sadist, an evil man, and a physical coward, who never dared to back up his insults with his fists and ran away from a fight and hid behind waiters and police when there was real trouble.

On one occasion, recalls Lehman, he and Billy went to Bogart's home in Holmby Hills. They wanted to reassure him. Lauren Bacall sat in the living room. She did not say anything. She was knitting. Bogart said that Wilder was favoring Audrey Hepburn and that he was giving her too many close-ups. He complained about Holden's getting so much attention. Wilder tried to placate him with all the politeness he could muster. They parted in a mood of amiability.

The next morning they were firing insults at each other again.

Hepburn, a sweet and gentle woman, regarded all these events with large eyes.

Wilder had promised Bogart that, though the last third of the script was not yet written, he would get the girl—not Holden. Then rumors—probably started by Wilder—began circulating around the set. Lehman and Wilder were going to write it so that Audrey Hepburn would fall into the arms of Holden. Bogart went around muttering, "I'm gonna get fucked . . . I'm not gonna get the girl . . . Billy's going to throw it to his buddy, Holden. . . ."

This was Wilder's most effective thrust. He deliberately kept Bogart in suspense, torturing him, until the last few days of the filming.

Billy Wilder made up his mind that he would never again put up with such insanity from an actor. He would never again make films with monsters, even if they were geniuses, even if they were transcendent images on the screen. He would make films with men and women who were human, who were rational, who were responsible. Oh, yes, a star—well, he or she could be difficult and temperamental, but not, for God's sake, insane. He was not a psychiatrist. He was a movie director. Never again . . .

So his next film was *The Seven Year Itch*, starring Marilyn Monroe, and, three years after that, he made *Some Like It Hot*, again with Marilyn. There were many times during the course of these films when he looked back nostalgically to his fights with Bogart. Why, *Sabrina* was a piece of cake compared to *Some Like It Hot*. At least, Bogart was *there*. He got there on *time*. He was there all day. So what if he left at six P.M.? A man got tired, he had to go home, he had a dear woman at home waiting for him, he was not a bad sort, really, Bogart, just a vulnerable guy, yeah . . . But Marilyn . . . ah, there—there was a monster of monsters.

Wilder experienced such agonies in the course of making two films with Marilyn that, in retrospect, not only Bogart but also Charles Boyer came to seem amiable human beings. *Sabrina* was the last film he did for Paramount. He had moved his pictures and little statues and books and his small collection of batons and whips from his office suite in the Writers Building and it was good-bye to the Marathon gate and it was good-bye to the logo of the snow-capped mountain. Eighteen years of his life there. Eighteen years of Oblath's and Lucey's and working with Brackett and hating Y. Frank Freeman's boxer dogs. It had been, take it for all in all, one of the most productive periods any serious moviemaker had ever had in Hollywood. As a writer, he had coauthored *Midnight, Ninotchka,* and *Ball of Fire*—three classic films of the 1930s. And *Bluebird's Eighth Wife* and *Hold Back the Dawn* would be equally well established if they were as available to us as novels are, by the simple act of going to a library and taking them out.

As a writer-director, Wilder had been responsible for ten films in eleven years. Of these ten films only *Emperor Waltz* was a clinker.

From the time of *Niagara*, Wilder knew that Monroe projected "flesh impact," that is, her image on the screen did not look like a reflection of flesh, but like *real flesh!* He told me once that when she was on the screen "there was never a hole." She was never lost nor invisible. You could not take your eyes away from her. When she played a two-shot or a group scene, she was the one you had to watch. You did not know why, but you had to watch her. She was compelling the way Garbo was compelling, the way Bogart was compelling. It was a mystery, but there it was. She told him in their first discussion about the film that she did not wear girdles nor brassieres.

So what if one went back to the voluptuous nudes of Rubens and Renoir? And did not the odalisques of Ingres make one's libido quiver? Monroe possessed a quality of vulnerable innocence which contrasted with her flaunting, flashing bosoms and behind. Her look of naiveté at the havoc her body caused, reminded Billy of another painting, a small-sized canvas in Munich's Alte Pinakothek museum: Boucher's *Miss O'Murphy*, the subject an eighteen-year-old concubine of Louis XIV. She was painted sprawled out on a sofa, head looking upwards, her naked *derrière* on display, a look of sweetness in her eyes.

On the whole, Wilder remembered the shooting of *Seven Year Itch* with satisfaction. Yes, Marilyn had often been late on the set, but not too late. She had trouble remembering her lines—but did get them on the eighth or tenth take. He did not mind her coach, Natasha Lytess, giving her signals. What she gave you on film was so transcendent that it was worth the agonizing process of working with her. Yes, *Itch* had run three weeks late, and cost $1,800,000 because of Marilyn's procrastinations—and in those days that was very high for a comedy. But she had given such a delicate, finespun performance and it was a money-maker, which was all that counted in the front offices.

Marilyn told Axelrod, when she met him at a party in Hollywood, "Billy's a wonderful director. I want him to direct me again. But he's doing the Lindbergh story next. And he won't let me play Lindbergh." Billy had danced with her that night. She loved ballroom dancing. She was enchanted with Wilder's mastery of swoops and glides. Where had he learned to dance? Oh, he said, he had been a gigolo in Berlin. She thought he was such a cute man with his funny little stories.

Between *Seven Year Itch* and *Some Like It Hot* only four years elapsed, but her world had changed. She had become one of the most celebrated personalities in the world. She had divorced Joe Di Maggio. She had married Arthur Miller. She had become a disciple of Lee Strasberg. She was seriously studying acting. She was reading good books. For one year, there was an interregnum in her work, while she was on suspension from Twentieth Century-Fox. It was at this time that I came to know Marilyn Monroe and had the first of several lengthy interviews with her. I was destined, after all, to write that book about her which Charles Brackett had suggested to me several years before.

At my first meeting with Billy Wilder, he took a critical, even hostile attitude toward her New York circle of sophisticates.

He said: "Here you have this poor girl and all of a sudden she becomes a famous star. So now these people tell her she has to be a great actress. It is like a man writes a stupid jingle, 'How Much Is That Doggie in the Window,' and it becomes a hit"—there actually was a silly tune with this name that was a big hit—"and he is forced to write symphonies for Toscanini. They're trying to elevate Marilyn to a level where she can't exist. She will lose her audience. She is a calendar girl with warmth, with charm. And she's being compared, my God, to Duse. Duse! They tell her she is a deep emotional actress. I don't know who's to blame. Kazan? Strasberg? Milton Green?" Like most of us who were deceived by Marilyn's air of injured innocence, Wilder thought that Marilyn was being exploited, when actually she was the manipulator. "It's like herring à la mode. Put chocolate ice cream on marinated herring and you ruin the ice cream and the herring tastes terrible.

"I don't say Lee Strasberg is a bad teacher. But, *um Gottes Willen*, if she has to go to school, why doesn't she go to Patek Phillippe in Switzerland and learn to run on time? Marilyn's whole success is she *can't* act. She's going through a bad evolution. If she takes it seriously, it is the end of Monroe. She is being taught acting by the kind of people who don't believe in underarm deodorants. They believe in sitting on the floor even if there are six comfortable chairs. They'll make her into another Julie Harris. She'll lose everything of her own. She'll make herself ugly. The crowd in the bleachers will hate her."

We spoke of her temporal disorientation, which seemed to get worse. What Billy could not understand when he was shooting *Sev-*

*en Year Itch*, and what he still cannot grasp to this day, is how she could be so irresponsible about coming to work on time.

"She was never on time once," he told me then. "It is a terrible thing for an acting company, the director, the cameraman. You sit there and wait. You can't start without her. Thousands of dollars you see going into the hole. You can always figure a Monroe picture runs an extra few hundred thousand because she's coming late. It demoralizes the whole company. It's like trench warfare. You sit and sit, waiting for something to happen. When are the shells going to explode?"

Then he sighed. He was examining Schieles in a gallery. Perhaps that reminded him of the old country. "On the other hand, I have an Aunt Ida in Vienna who is always on time, but I wouldn't put her in a movie."

He was confused by Marilyn's quirks. He had known many actors and actresses with violent tempers and massive egos. He thought he knew how to coddle them and pamper them and play jocosely with them. Yet he had never known anyone as disorganized, in all aspects of her life, as Marilyn; nor had he ever run into a performer who was as unreliable in her working habits.

"What is it? Is she late on purpose? No. Perhaps her idea of time is deranged, *nicht wahr*? You think maybe there's a little watchmaker in Zurich he's got a *mishigoss* and he makes a living producing special watches only for Marilyn?

"Once when my car was in overhaul she gave me a lift from Fox to my house. She is driving this black Cadillac of hers. She received it from Jack Benny. She was a guest on his television program and this was her salary. I looked in the back of the car. Such a mess you wouldn't believe. It is like she threw everything in the back helter-skelter because there's an invasion and the enemy is already in Pasadena. There's blouses lying there, and slacks, girdles, skirts, shoes, old plane tickets, old lovers, for all I know—you never saw such a filthy mess in your life. On top of the mess is a whole bunch of traffic tickets. I ask her about them. Tickets for parking. Tickets for speeding, passing lights, who knows what? Is she worried about them? Am I worried about the sun rising tomorrow?"

How was Wilder to know her inner torments? How was he to know that she had always been a self-absorbed person, a narcissist of narcissists, given to almost schizophrenic states of withdrawal? How was he to know that she lived with a powerful fear inside her guts—a fear of people, a fear of work, a fear of living, a fear of involvement, a fear of intimacy—while also needing love and acting and friendship? The disorder in the back of her Cadillac reflected the disorder in her personality. And how was he to know, how was anybody to know, unless he was married to her or was one of her small circle of confidants, that she had become increasingly disoriented and disorganized and was relying more and more and more on champagne and vodka to get her through the day and on increasingly heavier dosages of Nembutal to get her through the dreadful nights? And that she lived in a stupor most of the time but would come out of that state suddenly and become a radiant and charming self, and so you felt as if you were driving up the Pacific Coast Highway on a night of dense fog so thick your car was crawling and you could hardly see ten feet in front of you and then, as coastal fogs will do, suddenly the fog lifts for a hundred yards and everything is luminous and sharper than it was before—until the fog closes in again.

After he had made his second picture with her, I saw Wilder again and asked him whether he still thought that Strasberg's influence had been baneful.

"No, there I was wrong," he replied. "She has become a better actress, a deeper actress, since Strasberg. But I still believe she was developing herself naturally and would have become greater even without him. I still say she was encouraged in her bad habits. Strasberg doesn't have to stand on a set and direct her. Now it takes longer to get a scene done. If she were working alone, it would be all right. But she's playing with others—and she wears them out.

"Before she was like a tightrope walker who doesn't know there's a pit below she can fall into. Now she knows. She is more careful on the tightrope. She's more self-conscious.

"I'm still not convinced she needed training. God gave her everything. The first day a photographer took a picture of her, she was a genius."

Wilder was correct; morbid introspection was feeding Marilyn's insanity. But it was not only the Strasbergian approach of using oneself and one's own personal experiences as the raw material out of which you made a character, it was also her adventures in psychoanalysis. She had been seeing Dr. Marianne Kris, a New York therapist, and Dr. Ralph Romeo Greenson, a Beverly Hills analyst. They knew of her compulsive drinking and addiction to sleeping pills. They believed these were a neurotic reaction to underlying problems. They would assist her in resolving her problems, and then she would not have to seek release in drugs. But they opened a Pandora's box of long-buried resentments and ancient injuries and Marilyn was unable to patiently "work through" these. As these confusing events were brought to the surface, she felt pain and went immediately to her painkillers. More and more, her sense of herself and of other persons became blurred. She became lost in her narcissism. She was an unfortunate doped-up woman most of the time.

The first *Some Like It Hot* clash happened during a day of tests for makeup, coiffure, and wardrobe. It took place several weeks before the start of shooting. Knowing her procrastinating tendencies, Billy scheduled Lemmon and Curtis for an 11:00 A.M. call and Marilyn for 1:00 P.M.

She arrived at 3:30.

By the time her handmaidens had prepared her for the camera tests, it was 6:10 P.M. She flounced over to the stage. It was deserted. Wilder had dismissed the crew at six. He had left at the same time. The first of many anguished telephone calls came from Arthur Miller at his home. Miller was to be placed in the embarrassing position of being a go-between. It was a humiliating position for him— but he bore it gracefully and never criticized Marilyn. He always defended her to Billy. He found excuses for her. She put Miller through literal hell. He knew no peaceful hours either awake or asleep. *After the Fall*, which Miller was criticized for writing, was an artist's way of purging himself of the guilt he had felt, for even though she was a destroyer of those around her, she made them feel guilty. She did not make Wilder feel guilty. He felt angry. He felt frustrated and helpless. He had to get harsh with Miller. He told him he would condone an hour's lateness, maybe a little more, but surely Miller knew it was impossible to make a film with a person who was four and five hours late. The standard union hours were nine to six. The supporting actors and technicians went on double time after six. Every day that he did not film, it cost the studio at least $30,000. Would Miller make it his responsibility to get her to the stage on time? He vowed it would not happen again. But it happened. Again and again and again.

One day, Willie Schorr returned from Europe on a Kirk Douglas film. He visited Wilder on the set. Wilder was sitting in his director's chair. He was not swinging a baton. He was not striding about nervously. He did not look like Billy Wilder. He looked emaciated and lackluster.

"Willie, did you ever see me drink two martinis at lunch?" he asked in a beaten voice.

"Never," Schorr said.

"Today I had four."

"My God," Schorr said.

"And I cannot get drunk," Billy said. "I want to get drunk but I cannot. Now it is already"—he glanced at his wrist—"almost three o'clock. She still has not arrived. I have not shot a foot of film today."

"How long has this been going on?"

"From day one, Willie; I don't know what to do with her. If only she was not so beautiful when she is playing. We have made footage of her that is . . . like . . . well, she looks like Garbo. But I do not know if I will be able to live through this."

Never had his old friend seen him in such despair. He was not able to get a good night's sleep. His bursitis, which always troubled him when he became tense, was now tearing his shoulders apart, and his lower back was in agony. He was taking strong doses of painkiller. He told Schorr that he thought *Sabrina* had been a headache but that was as nothing compared to this. He did not know what to do; he just did not know. Schorr remained there all day and later they had dinner. Wilder drank four more martinis with dinner. They did nothing for him.

During this time, Wilder did not make a single joke. It had taken Marilyn Monroe to drive all the laughter out of him.

Yet he never once berated her on the set, for he knew this would disrupt whatever small shreds of responsibility still clung to her. His calmness astonished Tony Curtis. Curtis had to play many scenes opposite her, including certain love scenes, when he removed his feminine disguise and appeared as a millionaire playboy and yachtsman and did his Cary Grant number. Jane Wilkie, a Hollywood writer, assisted me in the research when I wrote my biography of Marilyn some years ago. Ms. Wilkie interviewed Curtis on several occasions. He made no bones about his contempt for Marilyn. He described the torment of waiting interminably for her. On her good days, he said, she would come at eleven A.M. when there was a nine A.M. call. On her bad days, which was most of the time, she did not appear until after the lunch break. He was impressed by how Wilder controlled himself. He never blew up, though she drove him to drink. Once, recalled Curtis, Billy made a suggestion about a line reading. He spoke in a tactful voice.

And she snarled at him, "Don't talk to me now. I'm thinking about how I'm going to play the scene."

And it was like a slap in his face, but Wilder took it.

Another time, he wanted a look of surprise on her face when she is discovered concealing bourbon in her ukelele case. He asked her to do it over. She thought she was doing it well. She walked away from the camera and went into a long conference with Paula Strasberg, who was on the sidelines, as Natasha used to be. Wilder was left standing there with the other actors in the scene. She talked and talked with Mrs. Strasberg, ignoring everybody else. Miller, also, was in pain. He sympathized with Billy's distress. He started blaming Paula. He had gotten to dislike both Strasbergs. Wilder regarded Paula Strasberg as an ally—he had no other alternative—and he tried to convey his ideas for Marilyn to her. He knew that after hours they went off together and delved into the nuances of Sugar Kane.

There was a moment when she was reading a certain block speech too languidly. He wanted her to hurry it up.

She said she couldn't. She was a disciple of Stanislavsky. She had to (she explained) "make contact with Sugar Kane."

"Go ahead and make contact with Sugar Kane," Billy said, in a pleading tone, "but for God's sake, could you contact her a little faster?"

Curtis is a disciplined actor who comes to the set on time and knows his lines and gives you a good show on the first or second take. Monroe didn't start warming up until the tenth take. On many scenes, she needed thirty, forty, fifty takes. One went to fifty-nine takes! Curtis was strong in the early takes and then began weakening. She got more expressive. What made it harder was that he had to stand in high heels and padded costumes for many hours. And when Wilder saw the rushes he would see how good Curtis looked on the early takes and how bad he looked on the later ones. But he had to choose Monroe's takes, as "you have to go with Monroe, even if other actors suffer, because when Monroe is on the screen the audience cannot keep their eyes off her."

She had no compassion either for Curtis, for Lemmon, or for her director. When Wilder happened to mention to her that his back was killing him, she told Paula Strasberg that he was inventing stories about ailments just to make her feel sorry for him. He didn't have any back problems. He was a liar! Only Marilyn Monroe was supposed to feel pain.

Marilyn was reading Paine's *Rights of Man* while she was on the set. Hal Polaire, assistant director, went to her dressing room, knocked on the door, and said they were ready for her.

"Fuck you," she screamed, turning another page.

To Wilder, this incident summed up the insanity of Marilyn. She loved humanity—but hated people. How could one be like that? He already knew that the thermos she carried to the set contained vodka and orange juice and that she frequently refreshed herself from its contents. But he could not know how stoned she was most of the time. And that it was the drugs which had transformed her into a monster.

She blew up in her lines all the time and for no reason. There is a scene in which she enters the room in which are Lemmon and Curtis, in their dresses. She had to say, "Where's the bourbon?" and open and close drawers looking for an enema bag containing whiskey. She just could not get this simple line clear. She'd say, "Where's the whiskey?" "Where's the bonbon?" "Where's the bottle?" Take after take after take.

Wilder did not have much hair but he was tearing it out. And you could not plead with her or coax her because she would look at you innocently as if nothing were the matter. He finally had strips of paper with the words WHERE'S THE BOURBON on them and had them pasted into every bureau drawer—and she still couldn't get it straight!

On the other hand when they went for location work on the beach at the Coronado Hotel near San Diego, a situation which Billy felt was fraught with trouble, she came through beautifully. She didn't fluff her lines and she was lovely on the first or second take. How do you figure that? Billy was bewildered. He felt like he was on a transatlantic flight and "they suddenly discover there's a nut on board and he's got a bomb." There was no consistency, or was there? There was, in the sense that Marilyn felt more secure with the impersonal mass, with those strangers standing behind the ropes on the beach and watching her do her make-believe.

One evening as they watched the rushes somebody told Curtis that he looked as if he had really enjoyed kissing Marilyn.

He said loudly, "It's like kissing Hitler." His sentence made Paula Strasberg weep. Monroe was not in the projection room. But Tony's bitterness was relayed to her. She began to suspect that they were all in a conspiracy against her.

Iz Diamond says that on the whole Miller conducted himself with reasonable dignity. He did not make suggestions as to dialogue changes. He never criticized the rushes. He only tried to be a peacemaker. Once, he came to Wilder—this was around November 1— and said, "My wife is pregnant. Would you go easy with her, Billy, please? Could you let her go at four-thirty every day?"

Wilder was incensed. "Look, Arthur," he said curtly, "it is now four o'clock. I still don't have a take. She didn't come on the set till half past eleven. She wasn't ready to work until one. I tell you this, Arthur, you get her here at nine, ready to work and I'll let her go— no, not at four-thirty—I'll let her go at noon."

Arthur rubbed his chin and started to say something. Then he swallowed. He walked away quietly and slowly. He looked crestfallen. She had sent one of the country's most distinguished authors on the sort of errand on which an actress sends her agent or her secretary.

*Some Like It Hot* was completed on November 6, 1958. Audrey Wilder laid on a magnificent dinner party in honor of her husband having survived the ordeal by Marilyn. There was a guest list of about twenty close friends. Tony Curtis and Jack Lemmon were among those present.

Marilyn Monroe and Arthur Miller were not invited.

And Marilyn could not understand why this was so, except that Wilder had set up shop as an enemy of Marilyn Monroe. It did not occur to her that the picture had run about $500,000 over the budget and was many weeks late in completion. The production cost was $2,800,000—which at that time was an extremely high cost for a comedy. It could have bankrupted the Mirisches.

Any ambiguities which Monroe may have felt in Billy's attitude towards her were clarified when Joe Hyams, Hollywood columnist for the *New York Herald Tribune* and student of the great Bogart-Wilder battle, interviewed Wilder. Wilder openly discussed Marilyn's lateness and line blowing. He said,

"I'm the only director who ever made two pictures with Monroe. It behooves the Screen Directors Guild to award me a Purple Heart."

How was he feeling, healthwise, these days?

"I am eating better," he told Hyams. "My back doesn't ache anymore. I am able to sleep for the first time in months. I can look at my wife without wanting to hit her because she's a woman."

Would he like to do another project with Marilyn?

"Well, I have discussed this project with my doctor and my psychiatrist and they tell me I'm too old and too rich to go through this again."

Shortly after this interview was published, Wilder got the following telegram from Arthur Miller, who was now forced into the role of challenging Wilder, in effect, to a duel:

DEAR BILLY: I CANNOT LET YOUR VICIOUS ATTACK ON MARILYN GO UNCHALLENGED. YOU WERE OFFICIALLY INFORMED BY MARILYN'S PHYSICIAN THAT DUE TO HER PREGNANCY SHE WAS NOT ABLE TO WORK A FULL DAY, YOU CHOSE TO IGNORE THIS FACT DURING THE MAKING OF THE PICTURE AND WORSE YET, ASSIDUOUSLY AVOIDED MENTIONING IT IN YOUR ATTACK ON HER. FACT IS, SHE WENT ON WITH THE PICTURE OUT OF A SENSE OF RESPONSIBILITY NOT ONLY TO HERSELF BUT TO YOU AND THE CAST AND PRODUCER. TWELVE HOURS AFTER THE LAST SHOOTING DAY HER MISCARRIAGE BEGAN. NOW THAT THE HIT FOR WHICH SHE IS SO LARGELY RESPONSIBLE IS IN YOUR HANDS AND ITS INCOME TO YOU ASSURED, THIS ATTACK UPON HER IS CONTEMPTIBLE. I WILL ADD ONLY THAT SHE BEGAN THIS PICTURE WITH A THROAT INFECTION SO SERIOUS THAT A SPECIALIST FORBADE HER TO WORK AT ALL UNTIL IT WAS CURED. SHE WENT ON NEVERTHELESS. YOUR JOKES, BILLY, ARE NOT QUITE HILARIOUS ENOUGH TO CONCEAL THE FACT. YOU ARE AN UNJUST MAN AND A CRUEL ONE. MY ONLY SOLACE IS THAT DESPITE YOU HER BEAUTY AND HER HUMANITY SHINE THROUGH AS THEY ALWAYS HAVE.

Wilder assumed that this telegram had been written under duress, that Miller was just bearing his uxorious burden. Nevertheless, he wanted to get the facts on the record. And his reply minced no words:

DEAR ARTHUR: THIS IS A SMALL WORLD WITH VERY SHARP EARS. EVER SINCE THE EARLY DAYS OF SHOOTING, WHEN RUMORS OF MARILYN'S UNPROFESSIONAL CONDUCT FIRST LEAKED OUT, I HAVE BEEN BESIEGED BY NEWSPAPERMEN FROM AS FAR AS LONDON, PARIS AND BERLIN FOR A STATEMENT. I HAVE STAVED THEM OFF, I HAVE AVOIDED THEM, I HAVE LIED TO THEM. AS FOR THE

STORY IN THE NEW YORK HERALD TRIBUNE THE CONCLUSIONS REACHED BY THE COLUMNIST FROM HIS OWN RESEARCH WOULD HAVE BEEN TWICE AS VICIOUS HAD I NOT SUBMITTED TO THE INTERVIEW. OF COURSE I AM DEEPLY SORRY THAT SHE LOST HER BABY BUT I MUST REJECT THE IMPLICATION THAT OVERWORK OR INCONSIDERATE TREATMENT BY ME OR ANYONE ELSE ASSOCIATED WITH THE PRODUCTION WAS IN ANY WAY RESPONSIBLE FOR IT. THE FACT IS THAT THE COMPANY PAMPERED HER, CODDLED HER AND ACCEDED TO ALL HER WHIMS. THE ONLY ONE WHO SHOWED ANY LACK OF CONSIDERATION WAS MARILYN, IN HER TREATMENT OF HER COSTARS AND HER COWORKERS. RIGHT FROM THE FIRST DAY, BEFORE THERE WAS ANY HINT OF PREGNANCY, HER CHRONIC TARDINESS AND UNPREPAREDNESS COST US EIGHTEEN SHOOTING DAYS, HUNDREDS OF THOUSANDS OF DOLLARS, AND COUNTLESS HEARTACHES. THIS HAVING BEEN MY SECOND PICTURE WITH MARILYN, I UNDERSTAND HER PROBLEMS. HER BIGGEST PROBLEM IS THAT SHE DOESN'T UNDERSTAND ANYBODY ELSE'S PROBLEMS. IF YOU TOOK A QUICK POLL AMONG THE CAST AND CREW ON THE SUBJECT OF MARILYN YOU WOULD FIND A POSITIVELY OVERWHELMING LACK OF POPULARITY. HAD YOU, DEAR ARTHUR, BEEN NOT HER HUSBAND BUT HER WRITER AND DIRECTOR, AND BEEN SUBJECTED TO ALL THE INDIGNITIES I WAS, YOU WOULD HAVE THROWN HER OUT ON HER CAN, THERMOS BOTTLE AND ALL, TO AVOID A NERVOUS BREAKDOWN. I DID THE BRAVER THING. I HAD A NERVOUS BREAKDOWN. RESPECTFULLY

Miller insisted that Wilder apologize:

THAT OTHERS WOULD HAVE ATTACKED HER IS HARDLY A JUSTIFICATION FOR YOU TO HAVE DONE SO YOURSELF. THE SIMPLE TRUTH IS THAT WHATEVER THE CIRCUMSTANCES SHE DID HER JOB AND DID IT SUPERBLY, WHILE YOUR PUBLISHED REMARKS CREATE THE CONTRARY IMPRESSION WITHOUT ANY MITIGATION. THAT IS WHAT IS UNFAIR. SHE IS NOT THE FIRST ACTRESS WHO MUST FOLLOW HER OWN PATH TO A PERFORMANCE. GIVEN HER EVIDENT EXCELLENCE IT WAS YOUR JOB AS DIRECTOR NOT TO REJECT HER APPROACH BECAUSE IT WAS UNFAMILIAR TO YOU BUT IN THE LIGHT OF THE RESULTS YOU COULD SEE EVERY DAY ON THE

SCREEN, YOU SHOULD HAVE REALIZED THAT HER WAY OF WORK-
ING WAS VALID FOR HER, COMPLETELY SERIOUS AND NOT A SELF-
INDULGENCE, HAD I BEEN HER DIRECTOR, AS YOU SAY, I WOULD
HAVE RESENTED BUT ONE FAILURE, A FAILURE TO PERFORM AT
HER BEST. SHE HAS GIVEN YOUR PICTURE A DIMENSION IT WOULD
NOT HAVE HAD WITHOUT HER AND THIS IS NO SMALL THING TO BE
BROUGHT DOWN BY A QUIP. SHE WAS NOT THERE TO DEMON-
STRATE HOW OBEDIENT SHE COULD BE BUT HOW EXCELLENT IN
PERFORMANCE. THAT YOU LOST SIGHT OF THIS IS YOUR FAILURE
AND THE BASIC REASON FOR MY PROTEST AT THE INJUSTICE NOT
ONLY TOWARD HER AS MY WIFE BUT AS THE KIND OF ARTIST ONE
DOES NOT COME ON EVERY DAY IN THE WEEK, AFTER ALL. SHE
HAS CREATED SOMETHING EXTRAORDINARY, AND IT IS SIMPLY IM-
PROPER FOR YOU OF ALL PEOPLE TO MOCK IT.

The final shot in the telegram duel was a tongue-in-the-cheek apology:

DEAR ARTHUR. IN ORDER TO HASTEN THE BURIAL OF THE HATCH-
ET I HEREBY ACKNOWLEDGE THAT GOOD WIFE MARILYN IS A
UNIQUE PERSONALITY AND I AM THE BEAST OF BELSEN BUT IN
THE IMMORTAL WORDS OF JOE E. BROWN QUOTE NOBODY IS PER-
FECT END QUOTE.

And then, with the passing of time, the bitter words and the memories of bad events were forgotten, because *Some Like It Hot* was a
magnificent film, a sensation at the box office the whole world over,
a critical triumph for Monroe, a critical triumph for Wilder, an all-
around bonanza. Suddenly, Wilder, that dishonorable cad, became
her favorite director again. Suddenly Monroe, that irresponsible and
arrogant bitch, became the most luminous of all film actresses since
Garbo.

Their first encounter since the terrible days of Sugar Kane and the
boys in drag took place on the Twentieth Century-Fox lot in 1959
during Krushchev's tour of America. He was given a banquet by the
film industry. It took place in the finest of all the movie commissar-
ies at that period, Twentieth's Café de Paris. Only the most luminous of the luminaries received the coveted invitations. They were

asked to be there promptly at noon. Billy Wilder came at 11:45. He saw that Marilyn Monroe was *already* seated at a small round table with Josh Logan.

"At last," cracked Wilder, "a man who can get Marilyn to come on time. Now I know who should direct all her pictures—Nikita Krushchev."

Perhaps he subconsciously wished that he could hire Krushchev to be the producer of his next film, because it was one for which Marilyn Monroe was perfectly suited. He had just bought the movie rights to *Irma La Douce*, the French musical comedy about a Paris whore and her pimp, a soulful *naïf* named Nestor, so jealous of her customers that he disguises himself as an English lord so she shall have no other customers except him. It was another experiment in double disguise like *Some Like It Hot* and this, as well as the whorish ambience, seduced Wilder. *Irma La Douce* had been playing to capacity in Paris for two years and recently had opened in London, where it at once became the reigning hit. Who better than Marilyn to portray Irma the soft and sweet, the tender and sentimental whore?

He knew it. And so did she. She went on a campaign to get the role. As Billy was sauntering away from the banquet, Marilyn ran up to him and embraced him. They kissed. She gave him a good Irma-La-Doucian French kiss. He embraced her. She looked sane and vibrant. Maybe . . . maybe . . . Who knows? . . . Once again into the breach, perhaps . . .

The Monroe-Wilder rapprochement was a big topic of gossip in Hollywood that week. He told reporters that he and Monroe were now "good pals again."

And he was not averse to making another picture with her, he said. But, he was asked, after all you said about no more Marilyn Monroe, how could you?

"Well," Billy explained, "you know how it is. You hate your dentist when he's pulling your teeth. But the next day you're playing golf with him again."

Wilder shelved *Irma La Douce*, as he and Iz had not yet resolved the basic question of how to treat the story. Wilder did not want to make it as a musical. Meanwhile, they had gone on to write *The Apartment* and it was made and they had started sneak-previewing it. There was a sneak at Westwood and the Mirisches had sent out invitations to a circle of Wilder's friends to come and see the film and then break bread at a party at Romanoff's. Doris Warner Vi-

dor—she who had been hostess to Aly Khan, you may remember—
received an invitation. She asked Yves Montand, who was doing
*Let's Make Love* with Marilyn. He said he would like to go—if he
could bring Marilyn along as well. Marilyn, who by now was openly
having affairs with other men, was carrying on with Yves Montand,
who was married to Simone Signoret.

Mrs. Vidor phoned Wilder. He thought it over. He remembered
the New York opening of *Seven Year Itch* at Loew's State, where
Marilyn had made her entrance, with Joe Di Maggio on her arm,
some twenty minutes after the film was on, and right in the middle of
one of Tom Ewell's important monologues. "All right," he said,
"he can bring her, but under one condition, that you're all there on
time and there's going to be none of that business of Marilyn making
a grand entrance and taking everybody's attention away from my
picture."

Mrs. Vidor called Montand and he said boastfully that Marilyn did
what he told her to do, that he had her in the palm of his hand and
that she would be there on time.

She was.

At the party later, Marilyn and Billy did more embracing and kissing. She said how much she wished she could have played the Fran
Kubelik role in *The Apartment* and how much she would like to play
*Irma La Douce*. And indeed Marilyn would have given Fran Kubelik
her own special dimension but there was something, a certain life-
force in Shirley MacLaine, a certain wide-eyed wisdom about love,
which Marilyn could never impart to a role. Anyway, Wilder asked
Marilyn to seriously consider playing Irma if they could come to
terms. By now, though she was still married to Arthur Miller and remained so until she finished *The Misfits*, Miller had also been shoved
into the discard. She started blaming him for all her troubles with
Wilder.

Harold Mirisch, the senior member of the five Mirisches, entered
into negotiations with her while Billy Wilder went to Europe with
Jack Lemmon. During the gruelling weeks of *Some Like It Hot*, he
had drawn very close to Lemmon, a kind and sensitive person, who
came to feel that Billy Wilder was a combination of father figure,
brother, and best friend. He adored Billy's sense of humor and his
grace under pressure, not to speak of his genius as a director. For
Lemmon, Wilder could do no wrong. Wilder was about as perfect a
human being as he had encountered. They shared a love for popular

American music. Jack was delighted by Billy's knowledge of Tin Pan Alley and Billy was pleased to learn that Jack was an excellent jazz pianist and had played in cocktail lounges during his youth. He at once had a piano installed on the sound stage. Lemmon plays a soft and introspective kind of jazz, rather like Art Tatum's or Bill Evans's. Sometimes, Billy's only solace, during the painful hours of waiting for Marilyn, was listening to Lemmon play old songs. And yet, says Lemmon, though it seemed Billy knew every American popular song written since 1900, he could not carry a tune. He was tone-deaf. "Sometimes he'd start singing when I was playing a tune he liked," Lemmon recalls, "and he was always five notes off, but his appreciation of jazz, of pop music, his taste—hell, his genius for selecting music for his films—well, it's uncanny. You know that theme from *The Apartment,* he resurrected that from some old song he remembered, originally done as a piano solo. The music department at United Artists had a hell of a time figuring out the name because Wilder would keep humming it to them and he couldn't hum it straight but they finally located it and now it's a standard, known as the theme from *The Apartment.*"

In Paris he took Lemmon about with him to museums and art galleries and obscure shops that sold interesting objects. He showed him offbeat restaurants and the sights and sounds of every quarter of the city he loved so much. It represented one of the high points of his life, says Lemmon.

During this trip, Wilder had a seance with Art Buchwald, who was then writing his column with a Paris dateline. He told Buchwald he was considering Marilyn for the title role in *Irma La Douce.* After all the mean things he said about her, how was this possible, wondered Buchwald. Why, he thought they weren't even speaking to each other.

"A man has a right to change his mind," Wilder said.

But hadn't he complained about how late she was?

"Exactly, but we didn't waste those hours. We played poker. I managed to read *War and Peace, Les Miserables,* and *Hawaii,* and we all got wonderful suntans . . ."

But hadn't he been heard to complain of her never knowing her lines?

"That's the beauty of working with Monroe," Billy explained. "She's not a parrot. Anyone can remember lines, but it takes a real artist to come on the set and not know her lines and give the performance she did."

How could he reconcile those pejorative remarks about Monroe with his present decision to consider her for the lead in his next picture?

"When I gave the interview I had just finished the picture and I was speaking under duress and the influence of barbiturates and I was suffering from high blood pressure and I had been brainwashed," he said. "Now that I can see it in a clear light I realize that she is worth it all."

And in a strange way, under the banter and the jests, this reflected Wilder's ultimate judgment, and he might perhaps have entered into another collaboration with her.

The article appeared in the *Herald-Tribune* on August 7, 1960. Marilyn did not see anything amusing in Billy's remarks. He was ridiculing her again. He was The Enemy again. She started making vitriolic cracks about him to the reporters. Then she decided that it was more important to appear in *Irma La Douce.* Her psychoanalyst urged her to put her pride aside and telephone Wilder and make peace with him. Her press attache, Patricia Newcomb, put through a call to the Wilder residence. Audrey answered the phone. Ms. Newcomb said that she had Marilyn Monroe there and that she wanted to speak with Billy Wilder. Audrey said that he was not at home. Then Marilyn would like to speak with Mrs. Wilder.

Marilyn came on, breathing as she did, stammering slightly as she did when under tension, "H-hello, Mrs. Wilder. I—I wanted to say that—that—well, about your husband—" (Then, reports Audrey, it was as if a demon took over, and Marilyn's voice got shrill and nasty and she was screaming.) ". . . that he is the worst son of a bitch who ever lived and you tell him he can just go and fuck himself, fuck himself, fuck himself . . ." She stopped for a moment and her voice became amiable again, "And my very best to you, Audrey."

Billy Wilder is the kind of man who will not speak ill of the dead but he makes exceptions in the cases of Bogart and Marilyn Monroe. He has been repelled by the cult which has grown up around what he calls "Saint Marilyn." He resents the imputation that Hollywood somehow "killed" Marilyn Monroe, a theory first .enunciated in *Theatre Arts* magazine by Clifford Odets and frequently echoed by persons who neither knew Marilyn nor Hollywood. She died in the summer of 1962 and Wilder was shocked by her suicide, as all of us were.

And then when the resurrection came, when they started enshrining her, he couldn't hold his tongue. In 1968, he gave an interview to the *Los Angeles Times* in the course of which he touched on the Monroe-mania. "Ah, Marilyn, Hollywood's Joan of Arc, our Ultimate Sacrificial Lamb. Well, let me tell you, she was mean, terribly mean. The meanest woman I have ever known in this town. I am appalled by this Marilyn Monroe cult. Perhaps it's getting to be an act of courage to say the truth about her. Well, let me be courageous. I have never met anyone as utterly mean as Marilyn Monroe. Nor as utterly fabulous on the screen, and that includes Garbo."

And Shirley MacLaine was Irma La Douce, after all.

# 20

# THE OTHER
# REAL BILLY WILDERS

From his first publicity break in that *Life* interview in 1944 to a lengthy 1975 monologue in *New York Magazine,* Billy Wilder has presented himself to the public as a pessimist. Harking back to the cynicism of his Viennese idol, Karl Kraus, echoing American skeptics whom he admired like H. L. Mencken, Mark Twain, and Ring Lardner, Wilder's public utterances, as well as much of the dialogue of his films, have been replete with slurs at himself, the picture business, Hollywood, and humanity. He has reveled in his "bad taste." Often accused of being vulgar, he would say, Isn't life vulgar? But wasn't it also fun—if one could see the humor in it? *One, Two, Three* is the best cold-war comedy, and the only interesting film about communism versus capitalism since *Ninotchka.* Some critics loved it, for all its nastiness. Brendan Gill, in *The New Yorker,* 1962, said, "It is a farce that intentionally mocks and reverses every conventional attitude we have, or think we ought to have; virtue is punished, corruption and stupidity are rewarded, and the whole German people, as if in a trifling aside, are indicted as lickspittles or martinets, and we sit watching and roaring with delight. . . . For this tour de force of fratricidal subversion, we have to thank not only Mr. Cagney, who makes it shamefully attractive, but, again, Mr. Wilder, who produced and directed the picture and who could no doubt wring a hearty yock from the bubonic plague.'' Pauline Kael, recalling the sightseers making merry while a man's dying in a cave, said *Ace in the Hole* had been black enough, but *One, Two, Three,* though more entertaining, of course, was worse. Wilder had ''never before exhibited such a brazen contempt for people.''

Was it possible for him to love the morbidly curious people of *Ace* and the lickspittles of *One, Two, Three*? Yes, it was possible. Yes, he did love them. He loved them because his nature is basically a religious nature. He not only loved the Dr. Schweitzers of the world. He also loved those fat ladies in the balconies, to use J. D. Salinger's metaphor.

But it was really Billy's own fault if the critics saw only the spleen. There is coarseness in his films as there is in his nature. There are other elements in his nature. And in his films. But when he talks to the press it is only cynicism he displays.

Is this the ''real'' Billy Wilder? Yes. Is it the only Billy Wilder? No. There are many ''real'' Billy Wilders. Here are some of the other ''real'' Billy Wilders.

He is a sweet Billy Wilder, a thoughtful Billy Wilder. An example: the exteriors of *Stalag 17* were filmed at a ranch in Calabasas, about forty miles northwest of Hollywood. Hal Pereira and Franz Bachelin designed a realistic prisoner-of-war compound; the Paramount carpenters erected shacks and wooden barracks on the earth, and gun turrets and barbed-wire fences. Then it rained heavily for many days. The earth was mud. The mud in the movie is real mud.

One morning, Billy was getting ready to shoot a scene in which Otto Preminger has the prisoners stand at attention and warns them not to escape. Two ''dead'' prisoners are on display. They have been shot while escaping. Planks were laid for Preminger, the Nazi commandant, to walk from his headquarters to the barracks. Willie Schorr and Eddie Blum—associate producer and cowriter, respectively—came over to Billy's quarters that morning. They were outfitted in warm coats and wore heavy boots. Billy was drinking coffee when they arrived. He put on a cardigan sweater. He studied his array of shoes to make a selection.

''He had a row of shoes,'' Schorr remembers, ''and boots, galoshes, rubbers. Evening shoes. Loafers. They were all shined up. Then he picked out a beautiful pair of custom-made English shoes, which must have cost eighty-five dollars in those days.'' (Blum remembers them as costing $175 and being brand-new cordovan bluchers.) These were the shoes he put on that morning.

Blum asked why these expensive British shoes.

"I can't ask my actors to walk in the mud unless I am willing to get my best shoes dirty," Wilder said.

Out he went and sloshed through the mud, deliberately avoiding the planks. His shoes got wet and caked.

When he was making *Spirit of St. Louis* and filming the sequence in which Lindbergh is a barnstorming aviator, working in flying circuses, there was to be a scene shot with an actor doubling Jimmy Stewart in a wing-walking stunt. Wilder said, hell, you didn't have to use a double. Anybody could do it. Why, he could do it. So Jimmy Stewart bet him $100 he couldn't do it. Wilder got into an aviator's costume. His feet in stirrups, his body tied to the struts of the plane with some cable, he stood on the wings of an ancient World War I monoplane which was flown aloft by Harlan Gurney, a World War I ace. He walked on the wings for ten minutes, an extremely hazardous business, of course. But he knew he would be demanding much of Jimmy Stewart and of the other actors in the months ahead, and he had to show them that he was ready to suffer right along with them.

Wilder transported his company to every location along the route of Lindbergh's original flight. They filmed at the Santa Monica airport in California, at the Long Island airport, and at every place along the way. They filmed in the air above Nova Scotia, Newfoundland, the Irish coast, and the Cornish coast of Britain, and then over the Channel and up the Seine to a reconstructed Le Bourget field in Paris.

"We had unbelievable mechanical problems," Billy recalls. "Well, we could not communicate with a plane when it was up there. So when we had to do another take; it had to land, get the instructions, and take off again. We had other planes in the air to film the plane we were shooting. God, it was horrendous. The weather would change from one minute to the next. I never should have made this picture. It needed a director like John Frankenheimer, a man with an enormous patience for technical details."

It is the only film in which he shot a vast surplus of footage. He shot over 200,000 feet of film, which was finally reduced to about 12,000 feet. Unlike directors like Bill Wellman, who had been aviators themselves and knew how to make aerial photography work, Wilder was lost in the aerial scenes. Artie Schmidt, his film editor on this one, worked on the daily rushes; and finally, when the film was finished, Rudy Fehr, now head of the Warner's cutting department, went over every foot of it with him and they assembled the final film.

At the same time as Wilder was finishing the Lindbergh story, Otto Preminger was making *The Court Martial of Billy Mitchell,* another aviation story, also on the Warner lot. One day, Fehr looked out of his window and saw Wilder and Preminger walking together, conversing in German and arguing.

Fehr chuckles: "I remember saying to myself, Isn't it amazing—here are two boys from Vienna, both making the most typical American stories?"

*Irma La Douce* was not a typical American story. At the splendid luncheon for the press honoring Billy Wilder which the Mirisch brethren laid on at the Villa Capri in December 1961 to announce the start of production, one of the reporters asked him how he would make *Irma La Douce.*

"Dirty," he replied, with the leer of the sensualist.

Most of *Irma La Douce* was shot on the Sam Goldwyn lot, where Alexander Trauner designed and supervised the construction of a winding street in a red-light district of Paris so real it would have deceived Colette. For the exteriors, however, Wilder went to Paris.

Wilder decided it would help Shirley MacLaine play a French whore if she met one. But first he tested. He arranged with Pierre Galante, editor of *Paris-Match,* to conduct an interview with your average French hooker. Wilder heard her story. She was a clever gamine with long black hair. She was smartly dressed in a tailored suit. She lived in an expensive apartment in Neuilly. Her rent was paid by an Air France pilot. Every evening she took a taxi to a bistro in Les Halles. She carried a satchel containing her streetwalker wardrobe. She changed into her working clothes in the ladies WC. She had a regular station at a certain corner. She used the same hot-bed hotel. She said every angel of the pavement had a territory staked out. Sometimes a girl inherited a place from her mother. She planned to work three more years and then she would retire and marry her aviator. So it was with a good conscience that he charged Ms. MacLaine to delve into a whore's psychology. Which she did, asking Jack

Lemmon to accompany her, since he was going to be her *maque-reau*. They had a three-hour session with Marguerite. Lemmon had misgivings about playing *Irma La Douce*. All his friends said he was crazy to do such a low-class part, which would ruin his image. However he remembered that these same people had also urged him not to go into *Some Like It Hot*. They told him it was a five-minute joke. He couldn't sustain interest when he was playing ninety percent of a film in drag. His personal feeling was that it was simply unbelievable that the girls in the band wouldn't find out that "Tony and I, that we were in drag, that we were really guys. I mean, they would get it, wouldn't they?" Just as he was sure that, in this script, Irma would have to know that Nestor and the English Milord were the same; wouldn't she? Lemmon and MacLaine had a marvelous time with Marguerite. Ms. MacLaine had already become an interested observer of people and society. The whore did not interrupt her business while giving the interview. When her name was called, she said, *"Pardonnez moi,"* then dashed upstairs and returned in a few minutes. She worked with lightning speed. She was proud that she was the fastest worker in the house. She said it was a point of honor that she never removed her shoes with a client. She only loved barefoot when she was with her *maq,* her lover. One always had to make a distinction, however slight, in the name of love.

On several occasions, Billy Wilder, in the pursuit of truth-in-cinema, has had to be crooked. Billy had to shoot the alcoholic-ward sequence in Bellevue Hospital. The hospital administrator asked to read the scenes in the script which took place in Bellevue. Wilder stayed up all night. He hurriedly concocted a few scenes in which the Bellevue staff were kindly old Jean Herscholts and Lionel Barrymores. The Bellevue Hospital sequence in *The Lost Weekend* was ghastly. Frank Faylen's sadistic homosexual nurse raised hackles at Bellevue. About a year after the release of *Lost Weekend,* director George Seaton was shooting *Miracle on 34th Street* in New York. The story was a heartwarming tale of a kindly lunatic who believes he is Santa Claus. In one scene, he undergoes a psychiatric test at Bellevue. Seaton called on the Bellevue administrator and explained he wanted to film this lovable scene in the hospital. Seaton says the man was furious and almost "threw me out of his office." Seaton offered to let him read the script and make any reasonable changes.

Then, recalled Seaton, "the roof caved in. 'That's what Billy

Wilder offered to do,' he stormed. 'He showed me one script which I approved. Then he filmed a *different script.* I've had enough of you movie people. Get out of here, fast!' "

The Hungarian gypsy band, who follow Gary Cooper and Audrey Hepburn all over Paris, accepted their roles without approving the script. They could not speak or read English. They were real gypsies. Matty Malneck, the jazz fiddler, was a musical advisor on some of Wilder's films.

Billy and Malneck went to nightclubs and restaurants seeking gypsies. There were at that time many gypsy groups playing in Paris so they had a variety from which to choose. Billy finally selected the ensemble of Gula Kolkasch, which was appearing at the Monsignore in Montmartre. Gula and his boys worked in tuxedos at the Monsignore.

When it was time to start filming, Malneck asked Billy whether he wanted the gypsies in Hungarian blouses to make them look correct.

"No," Billy said, "we'll keep them in the tuxedos—but spray gravy stains on the lapels so they look Hungarian."

Billy Wilder does not like close-ups. He rarely uses them. He says they are like trumps in bridge and you only play them when you have to play them. Joseph LaShelle, who has been his cameraman on many jobs including *The Apartment* and *Irma La Douce,* has sometimes run into heavy weather with Billy. Used to working with other directors—especially those emerging from the television medium—LaShelle wanted to shoot many close-ups, for protection if nothing else. Wilder shoots nothing in excess. He shoots just about what he is going to use. He had developed this technique with Doane Harrison when he started directing and he never changed his *modus operandi* except on the Lindbergh picture.

Executive producers and studio heads want protection shots so they can have room to cut. Wilder uses close-ups only to accentuate a high point. As La Shelle explains it, "You shoot a close-up as a safety measure, so if you want to eliminate part of a scene or even a whole scene in a sequence you just cut to the close-up. I remember when we were shooting *Barefoot in the Park* and it was Gene Saks's first film directing and Hal Wallis was the producer. He came on the set one day and asked me what I was shooting. And I'd tell him like a dolly shot to the window, both people, and then a medium shot, and he'd say, 'What about the close-ups?' and I'd say, 'We don't need any close-ups,'" and he'd always say, 'When I'm running this

in the projection room and I want to cut something out and there's
no close-up, what will I do?' I grumbled and Wallis just ordered me
to get close-ups, which I did; because Wallis, like many executives,
always recuts his films; the director only had the right of first cut.
Zanuck was like that. Cohn was like that. Jack Warner. All of them.
With Billy they couldn't do it. He wouldn't give them these protection shots. There was nothing left on the cutting room floor when he
finished.

"I remember once, early on in *The Apartment,* we were discussing a setup and he said he wanted a low camera angle, right on the
ground almost, and I said, 'No, Billy, no.' He kind of peered at me
over his glasses like an owl. 'What did you say?' So I said, 'No, I
don't think so.' And he said, 'Joseph, you must be a very wealthy
man.' I said, 'I have some savings.' And he said, 'But you do have
to work, don't you?' I said, 'Oh, I don't have to work—not all of the
time.' And he said, 'But Joseph you're *never* going to work.' And I
said, 'Never going to work anymore?' And he said, 'Nobody ever
says no to me. So what do you think about my low setup?' And I said
very loud, *'No.'* And he grinned and said, 'Oh, shit, then do it the
way you want.'

"When we shot it, I said, 'That was right about the setup, wasn't
it?' and he said, 'Don't rub it in, Joseph.'

"Now he was not kidding about his not liking to hear a no. So you
have to be damn sure you are right when you disagree with him. He
is almost always right. But he is not infallible. He is only brilliant
beyond anyone I have known in the film industry. I have so much
admiration for him that I would have to say that I worship Billy
Wilder."

What was it like to be Billy Wilder's friend? It was a great pleasure. Listen to the late Jack Benny on the subject. We spoke together
not long before the great comedian and actor died. We had left his
office on Wilshire Boulevard and walked to the Nibblers Restaurant
at Wilshire and Spaulding Drive. It is not a hoity-toity restaurant,
just a pleasant, low-priced, popular place, the kind of place in which
Jack Benny felt most comfortable. He told me that for many weeks
he had lost his appetite. His doctor had told him he simply had to get
something down. Listlessly, he ordered a chicken pot pie and a side
order of mashed potatoes. We started conversing about Wilder. I
turned on my tape recorder. Caught up in his fascination with Wilder, Jack absently forked up pieces of piecrust and creamed chicken

into his mouth. He said they had become very good friends in the last ten years. He said they had a "mutual admiration feeling." Jack Benny had admired Wilder since *Double Indemnity,* the only movie he had remained to see a second time after the first showing. And Wilder regarded *To Be Or Not To Be* as a masterpiece of comedy. Jack Benny was flattered but he really could not understand why this great man loved his company and admired his talents. He shook his head uncomprehendingly at the miracle of Wilder and Noel Coward—who he believed were two of the fastest wits of their time. Both treated him with a sort of reverence. Benny's attitude was, *Why me, of all people?*

JACK BENNY: "It seems as if we are always with the Wilders, and I love that. Out for dinner, meet them at parties, at our house, at their house. We first met after the war when I was touring army camps with Larry Adler and Ingrid Bergman. Billy was a colonel. It was in Berlin. He came backstage. He did not see me as a gagman but as an actor. I was very complimented. He said he used to listen to my radio show on Sunday evenings when he was trying to learn English. How can I describe Billy? He has the fastest mind. If he was sitting here with us, and we were just talking, he would say things, Maurice, that would have you falling right out of the chair. Now Billy's humor is often sarcastic, but he does not mean to hurt you. His timing when he is talking to you is so great because he says things immediately.

"He would always bring a thoughtful and interesting present for me when he traveled. Knowing how much I love the violin, it might be a painting with a violin in it, perhaps a portrait of Sarasate or Paganini; he once gave me a fine painting of a violin on a table with a vase of flowers, a still life."

For Benny's eightieth birthday party, celebrated at the Frank Sinatra compound in Palm Springs, on February 14, 1974, Wilder brought *two* copies of an old best-seller by Walter Pitkin—*Life Begins at Forty!*

BENNY: "I love to go to his house for dinner. I love it when he comes to our house. You know you have friends, certain rare people, and you are sure of a lovely evening with them. Now some people, if they come, all right; if they don't come, all right. Not with Billy. I *always* want him to come because with him I am sure of a great evening . . . My God, I have finished this chicken pie. If my doc-

tor came in and saw me eating like this, he would give you the credit
for it.''

ZOLOTOW: "Any time your doctor says you should eat a good
meal, you call me and we will talk about Billy Wilder and then you
seem to get an appetite. I think Billy should get the credit.''

JACK BENNY: "Well, as I was saying, if I am at a dinner party, I
hope the hostess seats me near Billy Wilder. You don't actually
have to get into funny things. He sees a funny side to every subject
and he is very fast. He has a way of talking; just being with him
makes you feel good. Now he is never trying to be funny. But he is.
I love him as a man, as a director, and as a comedian. He once sent
me a cartoon which was so funny. It shows this couple in a car driving through a small town—let's say, Nibblers, Oklahoma—and
they're looking at the big road sign. It says: 'Population: none of
your business. Altitude: ditto. Just keep driving through.' You see,
Billy would not care if Nibblers, Oklahoma, had five hundred people
or five thousand. He has a disdain for status. He once described how
he's flying in a plane and just getting to sleep and the pilot said 'We
are now over Mt. Nibblers and the altitude is 15,000 feet'—which
you could not see anyway in the clouds—and it woke him up and
that would get him so damn mad. It's all this nonsense people say
and do, that's what gets him mad. He just couldn't stand all this nonsense but, let me tell you, I never met a man with such a real love for
people—which he hides.''

NORMAN KRASNA: "I once happened to complain my razor
blades were not giving me close shaves. Billy, who knows everything, at once said he had the answer for me. It was some obscure
make nobody had ever heard of—except Billy. Another friend might
just have *recommended* his brand. Not that guy. He brought over a
dozen blades, insisted I try it. They were the best blades I ever used.
He knows everything. He asks questions wherever he goes and he
remembers everything. How he has the time and capacity to be interested in so many little things, I do not know—from baseball to art
to razor blades . . . I've been living in Switzerland for fifteen
years, Klosters. I know my way around that country, as you can imagine. Once, he was on a visit to Switzerland. We met in Zurich. He
said, 'Now I'm going to take you to the good restaurants in Switzerland that you don't know about.' And he did, by God. Little obscure
holes-in-the-wall nobody would know about but him. When I am

with him, I eat better. Everything is better. I have such an enjoyable time with him. He has a great capacity for enjoying life. He can phone me and say, 'Meet me at the airport in Basle' (or Zurich), and I'm there, prepared to go anywhere with him he wants to go.

"Did you ever go shopping with him? My God, it's an experience, because of this knowledge he has of everything. I remember once driving with him along Ventura Boulevard in the San Fernando Valley; he suddenly pulled over. He had seen a little secondhand store out of the corner of his eye. It was halfway down on a side street. He went in. By the way, he never bargains. He has a built-in meter that tells him if the price is fair. He saw a weird-looking chair in this shop. It looked like a piece of junk. An old rocking chair with a straw back. He saw something in this piece of junk. He asked how much? They quoted him some inflated price, $200 or something like that. He took it. He paid in cash. He told the owner that it was one of the first handmade bentwood chairs ever made by some bentwood chairmaker in Europe! The first I knew that he was a bentwood collector, which he is. He started rattling off his information about bentwood furniture and I was knocked out by his knowledge."

SAMMY CAHN (to Radie Harris in the *Hollywood Reporter,* August 12, 1974): "This morning I spent four hours with Donald Fine, head of Arbor House, going over the first rough of a book on my life. It is called 'I Should Care, the Sammy Cahn Story, by Sammy Cahn.' I think it will make some news because I do tell it like it is. I am not sure what reception the critics will give it; I only want Billy Wilder to like it. Since I have known Billy, I have wanted him to 'like what I do,' because I admire him more than most of the talents I have met in my life—including mine."

KRASNA: "Not only that, but I heard that Sammy said in London when he was doing his one-man show that he wanted Billy to direct a movie of his life. Well, who wouldn't? But if Wilder decided to write song lyrics then Sammy Cahn would have to worry."

WILLIAM HOLDEN: "In 1952, I went on a three-months' trip to Europe with Wilder and Charlie Lederer. Billy was running both of us ragged sight-seeing, restaurant going, shopping. Even mountain climbing. We were at Bad Ischul, I remember, and the previous day we had taken in two churches and one museum and climbed a difficult mountain. I flopped into bed totally wiped out. I told him I was going to sleep all that night and the next day. Well the next thing I know the phone is ringing. I pick it up. It's him. I looked at my watch. My God, it's six A.M. What does he want at this ungodly hour? He says, 'We're waiting in the lobby, Bill, where are you?' I groaned, 'Hell, Billy, I told you last night I was exhausted. I can't make it.' He got very stern. 'You just have got to come down here and go with us. If you do not come, I will never forgive you.'

"So down I came and Billy had some coffee and brandy waiting for me, and cheese, bread, and ham. I had a breakfast and figured I might live another day.

"Well, we started out sight-seeing and we made four important stops that day and that was one of the most wonderful days in my whole life.

"It isn't just his ebullience, his love for life, but that need he has to share his pleasures with you.

"How can you resist the guy?"

LEONARD GERSHE: "Billy never talks about the picture he's working on—or any other picture of his in the past. He doesn't come to a party and tell you what he shot today, or his problems at the studio. Billy leaves the studio at the studio. What has impressed me about him is that he can skip from talking about football, about which I know nothing and care less, to French novels or the American musical theater, and be as knowledgeable as a specialist."

DAVID ROSE: "I heard about a spa in Austria, Bad Gastein, which nobody in Hollywood as far as I knew had heard of. Right away I had to go there on my next visit to Europe. I did. It was a beautiful place and very small and out-of-the-way. I was there for a week. I took a stroll one day and saw some tasty Sachertorte in the window of a delicatessen. I went in and had some and then the owner asked me, 'You are an American?' I said I was. And he said, 'Do you perhaps know a gentleman of the name of Billy Wilder?' And I said I did. He said that Billy Wilder came to his shop every summer and he came in and would buy a whole salami and eat it right in the store, slicing it while standing up. 'That Herr Wilder, he sure appreciates good salami,' the man said.

"Can you believe it? Not only did Billy beat me to Bad Gastein, he beat me to the delicatessen."

Being an expert in so many areas of living and being prone to criticize, Wilder frequently gets on people's nerves. He can, unwittingly, irritate even people whom he reveres. Groucho Marx is one of those Hollywood personalities for whom Wilder has great love and admiration. He would like to be on good terms with Groucho. But Groucho will not socialize with Billy Wilder. Several years ago, he had the Wilders over to his home for dinner. At cocktail time, he asked Billy what he would like and Billy said he would like a Scotch and soda. Groucho poured him a generous slug of J & B on the rocks and filled it with Canada Dry club soda.

Wilder would not sip it. He said he was surprised that a man like Groucho Marx would have the bad taste to serve such a *petit bourgeois* whisky as J & B. He said that J & B was a blend which included a quantity of neutral grain spirits. He said that the only scotches worth drinking were unblended virgin malt whiskies. He named several brands but said that the best one, which had a long five syllable Scottish name, was only carried by a liquor dealer in Santa Monica. If there was one thing Groucho Marx did not need it was a lecture on Scotch whisky.

"And not only that, Groucho," Billy said. "Perrier water is what you serve it with, y'know. Only soda worth drinking."

Wilder was astonished when Groucho got up and told him to get out of his house at once. He could not understand why Groucho was mad. He had only been trying to be helpful. He had only been trying to enhance Groucho's knowledge of whisky and soda. He never got another invitation to Groucho's house.

Even Leonard Gershe, who is one of their dearest friends and who loves them madly, finally got upset by Billy's critiques. He ceased inviting the Wilders to his lovely dinners in his lovely house high above Coldwater Canyon on Eden Drive.

One evening, Billy suddenly asked Leonard, "Why don't you invite us any more to your house for dinner?"

Gershe, feeling it was a moment of truth, blurted out, "Billy, I just can't take your criticisms. You don't like the bread I serve, my choice of wines, the sauces my cook makes, my coffee, even my butter."

Wilder promised that he would henceforth refrain from criticizing—no matter how awful the bread was and how dubious the wine. He would smile and smile and be gracious. Gershe said that the next dinner party at which Wilder went out of his way to be gracious was a ghastly experience—because Billy was obviously suffering. Gershe finally gave up. He said he would resume asking the Wilders to his house and Billy must go back to being as obnoxious as always.

Billy is terribly selfconscious about his accent. Once, sitting with a group outside his beach house at Trancas, north of Malibu, he mispronounced a slang phrase. His face darkened. He said suddenly, "I wish I did not have this accent."

Janet de Cordova, wife of Freddie de Cordova, director of the Johnny Carson show, cried out, "But you would not be you if you did not have this accent, and we love it."

When anyone makes fun of his speech—as Bogart did—Billy is hurt. At a dinner party at the home of Ruth Gordon and Garson Kanin, Billy was seated next to Barbra Streisand. It was the first time they had met. She was tickled by his accent. She started mimicking him. So many were there, and talking, that at first no one but Billy heard. Then, at one of those pauses, they suddenly heard her voice ring out in a perfect mockery of Billy, "Vill you blease bass de bebber?"

Billy did not utter a joke all evening. He was morosely silent.

Each year, before Oscar night, the Screen Directors Guild hosts a luncheon for the visiting foreign directors. The president of the SDG presides. The 1975 *déjeuner* was at Perino's and Frank Capra was presiding, as president George Cukor was in Leningrad shooting *The Blue Bird*. There was a Hungarian director speaking in German, a Polish director speaking in French, and several Italian and French directors speaking in their native tongues. Wilder was providing a running translation from French, German, and Italian into English and then translating the American comments of the Hollywood directors. They went around the table as one after another joined in the colloquy. Finally it got around to William Wellman, a crusty old gentleman. He stood up and said, "I didn't understand a fucking word—including when the interpreter was talking English."

Billy loathes physical contact. He does not shake hands. In France, which is a nation of violent handshakers, he will keep his hands in his pockets a lot. A visitor to his office, asking to use the toilet, is always told, "Please wash your hands." When he knows you better, he will ask you to rinse out the basin after using! You have to reach a certain intimacy with Wilder before he insults you or manages your personal hygiene. He is squeamish about dust and dirt. He hates to be touched, even on the back or shoulders. He is not a bear-hugger. After he had told me for the hundredth time to wash my hands after using the office toilet, I assured him that I always did. And he said, "But I never see the towels crumpled!"

Startled that he had checked up on the towels to assure himself of my ablutions, I told him that I had wiped my hands anyway.

"Nobody ever leaves the towels rumpled and then the maids do not change the towels," he growled. "I never yet had a collaborator who rumples up the towels. Why is this? How many times have I begged Mr. Diamond to do this and he forgets? If I could find a collaborator who rumpled up towels, I would not care if he could write screenplays."

FRANZ WAXMAN: "He once said to me, 'Franz, why do you wear your hair so long? People know you're a musician—you don't have to advertise it. If you want to advertise you're a musician, take an ad in the *Hollywood Reporter.*' I know him from Berlin and he still makes fun of my hair. If he ever stops making fun of my hair, I will feel terrible."

EDWIN BLUM: "I like wearing sport coats with leather patches at the elbow. I also smoke a pipe. Billy hates my sport coats. He hates my pipe. He was sure I was trying to make believe I was a British author. He said he had the same problem with Raymond Chandler. He said at least Chandler had an excuse. He wrote books. He said a man who wore jackets with leather patches and smoked pipes should write books, not screenplays. He could be very nasty if he didn't approve of your clothes or what your eating preferences were. Sometimes I went to his house for breakfast. He had a German cook then. There were often unpleasant-looking white sausages at breakfast, which this lady or Billy had bought at some German delicatessen. The sight of them made me sick. Billy tried to make me eat them."

WILLIE SCHORR: "He takes over your life. While I was working with him, he chose my socks, shoes, shirts, and suits. Even my hairbrush. I remember there was a little-known type of brush from New Zealand or some place that he said I had to buy. He is a very dominating personality—equally as much in little things as in larger things."

WALTER NEWMAN: "The only time we got into some sort of row concerning food was one morning, as we started working and he said he had had a marvelous *matzoh brei* for his breakfast. I asked him, politely, 'What is *matzoh brei?*' Well, I thought he would jump out of his skin. He went berserk. He shouted, 'What, you, a Jewish boy from New York, Walter, you never ate *matzoh brei*? But this is impossible.' I told him that furthermore I had never even heard of *matzoh brei* until this moment. He could not get over it. He kept muttering for weeks, things like, what could he expect from a schmuck who never heard of *matzoh brei*? Once he zeroes into something like *matzoh brei,* he never lets go."

VICTORIA WILDER SETTEMBER: "I used to make *matzoh brei* for daddy's breakfast. He said I made the best *matzoh brei,* as good as his grandmother made. The idea is to break up the matzoh but not crumble it. Then you have to soak it in warm milk five minutes. You should not soak it too long. And use plenty of butter. And three eggs. Stir up the matzoh with the eggs before pouring into pan. I made it soft rather than as a pancake. Daddy also liked kasha and hot milk at breakfast. I think his favorite was this very black bread, though, and sausages and cheese. He liked his coffee dark but not too dark, what they call Vienna Roast."

He loves dirty talk—hot gossip about sexual escapades. He will describe his own concupiscent episodes with lip-smacking nostalgia.

Walter Newman, who happens to be a card-carrying monogamist, got irritated by these pornographic conversations. "He was talking about some red-hot experience he or somebody else had with two whores at one time. He saw me looking bored, which I was. He said, 'Aren't you interested in fucking?' I said, 'Billy, I get so much of that at home, I don't have to talk about it.' He shut up—first time he did.

"And he never brought up the subject again."

Billy is generous and thoughtful and giving and is a compulsive gift-giver. On the other hand, he is unpredictable. He doesn't give his secretary a list of gifts and a list of names for Christmas shopping. He usually shuns giving gifts at the seasonal periods like the Yuletide. Once Eddie Blum, who felt guilty about all the liquor he had consumed while collaborating with Billy, thought it would be nice to return the kindness at Christmastime. He brought a case of Chivas Regal scotch and a case of Stolichnaya vodka over to Wilder's house when he lived on Beverly Drive.

Billy looked at the liquor reproachfully.

"It all goes to the servants," he said.

BLUM: "I realized I had made a *faux pas.* He wasn't giving presents that Christmas. He wasn't giving me anything. He was put out that I had given him the liquor. Sometimes you could never figure him out, at least I couldn't sometimes."

SWIFTY LAZAR: "I believe that I see more of Billy Wilder than any other person that I know excepting my wife and secretary, and I know every interesting person in the Western Hemisphere. He is interesting to be with. I go to auctions with him. I often go to Europe with him. I remember, this is now twenty years back, maybe twenty-five, and the first time he took me to the Maeght Gallery in Paris. He was starting my education in art. He was in love with an ugly piece of iron sculpture, small piece it was, by an artist I had never heard of, nor had anybody else. I don't think Billy had either. It was a Giacometti. They asked a thousand for it. And Billy bought it. He told me to buy a piece too. I said they were ugly. He said I did not know enough to tell the difference between ugly and beautiful. I wish I had listened to him. The piece he bought is worth about fifty thousand dollars. He has such confidence in his taste that he will back it up with his money. Did you know that many of the Beverly Hills dealers will start buying artists when they hear Billy is collecting a certain artist?

"And he is a shy person. Not about his knowledge in art. About his importance in making pictures. He doesn't realize how the *nouvelle vague* directors, Truffaut, Lelouch, Godard admire him. Their admiration for him is extraordinary. Yet he was reluctant to accept invitations to parties in Paris and in London. He actually thinks he would be imposing on other people.

"He does not realize what an enchanting man he is. I remember once on a London visit, my phone was ringing all the time, people like Sir Laurence Olivier, Sir John Gielgud, Sir Emlyn Williams—I'm not sure if Emlyn Williams is a Sir or not a Sir—and they all wanted to dine with Billy Wilder and he would look embarrassed when I wanted to make an appointment. He thought they were being polite or I was forcing them to meet him. He is most shy and ill at ease except with close friends and among familiar faces.

"He rarely goes to New York because so many people invite him out that he is convinced that he is imposing on them. In point of fact, they would be enchanted to see him. When he is in Rome or Paris, he is reluctant to phone his friends who live there for the same reason.

"Appearances to the contrary, Billy is a modest man and would rather be a recluse."

LENNY GERSHE: "It is true about Billy's modesty. That does not mean that Billy has no sense of his own achievements. I think he does. But he has no pride or arrogance about them. He does not dwell upon them. He doesn't convey to a roomful of people, 'Look at me, how important I am.' Now Swifty Lazar doesn't understand that, because he is used to being around these inflated egos. A star lets you know he is a star so often, constantly. Now Billy does not do that. Perhaps he does not have to."

NORMAN KRASNA: "His generosity is embarrassing. I have shoes he gave me because I admired them on him. We wear the same size. Once I complimented him on a tie he had on. Within a few days, I received seventy—that is right, seventy!—ties from him, made by the same maker, Charvet or Countess Mara or Sulka or one of that ilk. Once, I saw a Foujita hanging on his walls. I remarked that I had a Foujita. He said, 'Ah, you like Foujita?' He took it down and gave it to me. Right off the wall. I couldn't have made him happier than by liking Foujita. A while later, Erle [Mrs. Krasna] was at a Paris auction and saw another Foujita, not as good as ours, go for $17,000. When I told him this the next time we met, instead of being upset at his reckless generosity, his face lighted up and he just beamed at me."

About his eye, his intuitive sense of beauty, his taste, Jack Lemmon remarks: "You could put him in a junkyard of five thousand pieces and he would spot the one piece that was beautiful in that junkpile. Don't ask me how."

His generosity has limits. He will part with shoes and paintings and ties. But not hats. In a town where nobody wears hats, even in foul weather, Wilder almost always wears a hat—usually a narrow-brimmed English hat, a Lock or a Herbert Johnson, though he has an enormous collection of hats, hundreds of them in all patterns and tones. He loves hats. He looks well in hats. He wears hats when he is writing. He wears hats when he is directing. He wears hats when he is at home, dining or watching television. He would wear a hat when he went to sleep except that Mrs. Wilder draws the line. Wilder and Bing Crosby are the most fervent hat-wearers in Hollywood.

He has never given away one of his hats; that's how much he cherishes them.

There is a paradoxical streak of deep religious feeling in him. It is a sense of the mystery and terror of life, of the unknown, of death, of the conflicting human impulses to good and evil. It is a sense of man's finite nature and God's infinity. It is a sense that we are all in God's hands whether we believe or do not believe. Wilder's bitterness is in the spirit of Ecclesiastes. His is not the pessimism of a totally agnostic humorist like Mark Twain. Rarely does he show his emotions, but when people he loves die he is torn apart. The passing of Charlie Feldman, whom he adored, left him inconsolable for a long time, as did the death of Jack Benny. Without advertising it, he goes to the synagogue often to pray and meditate. He will not discuss this aspect of his life and few persons know about it. The day after Robert Kennedy was assassinated, Billy was in a house of worship most of that day. The next quotation is one that I heard in one way or another from many persons and all who told it to me said that I must not use their names because it would make Billy angry.

ANONYMOUS: "I was going through a very hard period about ten years ago. I had not had a writing assignment in two years. Every project I tried to get off the ground failed. I saw him at a function. He took me aside. He said, 'Do you need any money?' It happened that I had saved up from my good years so I wasn't starving but I think Billy didn't have any money for so long that when he thinks anyone is not working, he thinks they do not have money. So I told him it was all right. And he said, 'Promise you will tell me if you need it?' I said yes, yes, I would, but right now I was all right. And he said, 'Because I have a lot of money, you see. Money is good for only two things. One, so that you can tell producers to go fuck themselves, and the other is to help your friends.'

"I don't think Billy wants this side of him known. I think he relishes people thinking of him as an ogre."

When Audrey and Billy saw *Cabaret* on Broadway originally they both liked it, especially she did, and she said that it was the perfect vehicle for his next picture. She said, "You could make it so beautifully. You could use those things that happened to you in Berlin."

He said, "I'm not interested in it. There are Nazis in it."

Well, there were Nazis in *Stalag 17* and *A Foreign Affair* and *One, Two, Three.* Why did the Nazis, shadows of vultures swooping over Berlin just before Hitler, stand in the way of his directing *Cabaret*? It was because Berlin, his adopted city, the shining city of his glorious youth, had been sacked by the vandals, and the basic idea of the

Isherwood stories, as of the play and musical based on them, was the murder of the city he loved. That wound was never healed. He could never reconcile himself to the end of the Berlin in which he had found his spirit, his language, his art, his first good friends, his second love . . .

AUDREY WILDER: "He feels the pain of that terrible loss but he won't ever show how deeply he feels about anything. He will tell funny stories about Berlin in the 1920s. I feel maybe he doesn't want that ever to have been spoiled by the Nazis. When we saw Bob Fosse's treatment of it, Billy thought it was magnificent and true to life.

"But I always believed that Billy should have made this picture, he really knew the world, he knew it so well, but he was not interested in doing it."

# 21

# DIVERSIONS

$B$illy Wilder is as compulsive in his pastimes as in his moviemaking. He requires great distractions, lest his pictures swallow him up entirely. I have mentioned his devotion to photography, which almost ruined his honeymoon. Billy calls these temporary interests his "spells." One day, he was suddenly bored by light meters, lenses, and film speeds. He never took another picture. Once, he drank only red wine for two years. Once, he read Prescott's *Conquest of Mexico*. He became fascinated by the Spanish invasions of Central and South America. For a year he immersed himself in the adventures of Pizarro, Cortez and De Soto. Then ennui. Next, a "spell" of Napoleon. During such spells he loses himself in the subject—becoming almost a scholar, hardly thinking and talking about any other topic but Napoleon or vintage red Bordeaux or the conquistadors. He thinks art is one of the few cultural diversions to which he has clung over a long period. He not only buys those lavishly illustrated volumes of art reproductions, but he reads the texts—Rewald on the impressionists, Kenneth Clark on the nude, Canaday on modern art. For a long time, he was a collector of studies of murderers and great criminals. George Axelrod, also a murder connoisseur, would spend hours with Billy gossiping about classical Victorian crimes. Axelrod had purchased a complete set of the British Notable Trials Series.

Wilder knew all of the classic American crimes, in detail. He once told me that though the *Double Indemnity* framework came from Cain, the inspiration for the murders came from Ruth Snyder and Judd Gray. Once, he got on the subject of German murderers and was so carried away we hardly spoke of movies that day. He loves a certain Fritz Haarmann, the Hanover mass murderer. Fritz was a homosexual who picked up homeless lads at railroad stations, took them home, had sex with them, killed them, dressed them, and sold parts of their anatomies to housewives as "veal" or "lamb." He murdered many. Asked by the examining magistrate how many, he replied, "Es können dreisig, es können vierzig sein; ich weiss das nicht." ("Could be thirty, could be forty, who counts?")

Billy recalled that a pal of Haarmann's came around one morning. He asked, "Have you had breakfast yet, Fritz?"

"No," was the reply, "he's still sleeping."

I think Wilder would have made more pictures of crime and punishment than he has made, except that he was loath to risk unfavorable comparisons with Hitchcock.

He went through a spell of making the Los Angeles jazz scene. You would see him with Doris Dowling, Matty Malneck, and later Audrey Young, at clubs like Haig's, near the Ambassador Hotel, and the hip black joints way down south on Central Avenue or Main or Eighth. He liked small groups, which swung to a solid beat, and vocalists who sang in the suggestive style of Whispering Jack Smith. He loved Nat King Cole, the Cole of the first period, when he worked with a trio and played mostly in black cabarets. Billy's favorite song was "I'm Through With Love, I'll Never Fall Again." Maybe he was conveying a message to Audrey, but she did not pay attention. He would ask Cole to play and sing it often. He pounded his hands on the table to its rhythms and swayed his body. When he heard this news, Matty Malneck confided that he had written the music. Wilder looked at him as if he was W. C. Handy or Gershwin. He later chose it as one of Marilyn's numbers in *Some Like It Hot*.

Billy lost interest in jazz clubs when the postwar bop revolution came in. He could not attune his ears to progressive jazz. He did not dig Charlie Parker, Dizzy Gillespie, Thelonius Monk and the others. You never see him at Donte's.

Tennis and bridge were two obsessions which lasted a long time. He played both for twenty-five years at the same place: the Beverly Hills Tennis Club, a gorgeous four-acre walled retreat on Third

Street and Maple Drive. The club was started in 1929 by two tennis pros, Fred Alexander and Milton Holmes; later Ellsworth Vines and Fred Perry became copresidents. Towards 1936, the club became a meeting place of the movie celebrities. A beautiful two-story contemporary structure with a sweeping staircase was erected. There was a superb restaurant, a great bar, and six championship courts. There were terraces, sun rooms and two separate card rooms—one exclusively for bridge and another for gin rummy. It was and is hard to become a member. The roster is limited to 155. There is a long waiting list panting to pay the $10,000 initiation fee and the $1,000 a year dues. (Several years ago, the modernistic building was torn down and a ranch-style club put up. The restaurant is smaller and the bar is tiny. Two courts were abolished to make room for a swimming pool.) In the old days, there were fabulous parties at the Tennis Club. The ones on Thanksgiving, Christmas, and New Year's Eve were outstanding. The BHTC was for a time the most *recherché* center of the good life in Hollywood. Among those who you could watch swinging racquets were Ginger Rogers, Gary Cooper, Carole Lombard, Ann Sothern, Laurence Olivier, Charlie Chaplin, Barbara Stanwyck, Clark Gable, and Paulette Goddard. Billy Wilder joined the club in 1938. In that era, Harry Cohn played tennis there, as did Sam Goldwyn, Jack Warner, Frank Capra, and Willy Wyler. Among those who occasionally came was an aspiring young actress named Doris Dowling. She was a friend of a member. One afternoon, she sat beneath a striped umbrella and was sipping a Cuba Libre, as she watched Gilbert Roland playing Don Budge. Wilder did not know her. He was bowled over by her figure, which naturally showed off gloriously in her white shorts and blouse. Her tanned skin. Her sultry expression. Her raven hair. He approached her. He came on with the classical Hollywood overture, "My dear, would you like to be in pictures? I think I can make you a star."

Dowling looked him up and down. She lighted a cigarette. "Why don't you screw off, you crumbum?" she said in a loud voice.

At this, Wilder became enamored of her, forgetting that he was through with love and would never fall again. He pursued her with a passionate single-mindedness that eventually won her heart. However, it was to be one of those violent loves which require the total consecration of a man. Dowling, in the words of another popular song, was always inquiring, "all of me, why not take all of me?" Wilder's heart was in another place, alas, so as Cole Porter observed, it became "just one of those things, one of those crazy flings." But she did carve herself a lovely vignette as the hooker in *Lost Weekend,* and her "Thanks—but no thanks," became a national cliché for a season. She did other American films and finally found herself in Italian postwar films. An interesting lady who later was the fifth Mrs. Artie Shaw, she was one of the many women in Wilder's life who did not desire to reminisce about her days and nights with Billy. Another lady who did not care to summon up remembrance of things Wilderian was the first Mrs. Wilder—Judith Badner. My fruitless delvings into his amorous past also included a screenwriter and another actress who later played a supporting role in *The Apartment.* I had the definite feeling that all of these ladies still hated Billy Wilder, or carried a torch for him or, most likely of all, couldn't understand him and were still troubled by his contradictions. . .

Wilder played poker, bridge and gin rummy. His bridge was good, his poker sad, and his gin rummy a disaster. Hollywood is a country of ferocious gin players. Billy was outclassed. Once, after a succession of games in which his opponent had knocked while he was holding a mess of high cards, he flung his cards on the table and cried, "I'm going to join Alcoholics Anonymous."

He was asked why.

"You see," he cracked, "I have this terrible problem with gin."

One time, Krasna was beating Billy's brains out at gin rummy, when Harry Cohn sauntered over to kibitz. "Where do you think I was last night?" Cohn inquired.

"Night school?" Krasna remarked innocently.

A rich and aging actress, though still a box-office personality, was keeping a handsome young stud. She was sitting around the terrace at dusk once and belting Scotch and soda and whining about her *chéri.* It was a situation analagous to that of Norma Desmond and Joe Gillis in *Sunset Boulevard.* She was complaining about his expensive tastes in sports cars, jewelry, clothes, and so forth. "In one year," she complained to Wilder and Barbara Stanwyck, "that stinker's run through a hundred thousand dollars of my money."

Barbara looked at her intently, and said, "Tell me, darling, is the screwing you're getting worth the screwing you're getting?"

Sam Goldwyn was so impressed by Frank Shields's grace and beauty that he signed him to a contract. He also made an arrange-

ment for Shields to study acting with a coach. Shields forgot his acting lessons and was at the club hitting balls over nets every afternoon. Once Goldwyn got so mad he stalked over, grabbed Shields's
racquet, and shouted, "Tennis you *know*—practice acting!"

Wilder would hear tennis pro and club founder Holmes telling stories about his experiences, and one day, Wilder, who was always
trying to encourage talent as in the case of Doris Dowling, told him
he should be a writer. He gave him some advice. Holmes began writing and publishing pieces on how to improve one's tennis game.
Then, with Billy coaching from the sidelines, he began writing
fiction. One of his stories, "Mr. Lucky," was published in *Cosmopolitan* and later became a vehicle for Cary Grant. Holmes became a full-time writer.

Wilder played a fair game of rubber bridge. He played with,
among others, John Huston, Sam Spiegel, Malneck, Peter Lorre,
and Paul Lukas. Visiting New York bridge players often took a
hand—including Howard Dietz, George S. Kaufman, and Jack
Goodman (editor at Simon and Schuster.) Tournament pros like
Goren, Jacoby, Sheinwold, Schenken, and the then youthful Don
Krauss also sat in. The nucleus of what came to be known as the
BHTC's "A Game" comprised Charlie Lederer, F. Hugh Herbert,
Eddie Blum, Willie Schorr, and Wilder. The game started in a back
room at Chasen's. Then it moved on to a back room at Romanoff's.
Then for a long while it lived at the Tennis Club and finally ended its
career at Lederer's house in Malibu.

The "A Game" was serious bridge, but the wits could never resist
making wisecracks. This threw some grand masters quite off their
form. Ely Culbertson once sat in for a dozen rubbers. He was so dis-
concerted by the wisecracks flying around that he played badly. He
lost several hundred dollars. He threw down his cards, settled his
debts, and never played bridge at the BHTC again. Nor would he
ever speak to Billy Wilder again. He suspected Wilder had deliberately made jokes to ruin his concentration.

Sometimes a rich sucker was inveigled into the game. The stakes
were then raised to a nickel a game. Lew Wasserman, head of MCA,
then a talent agency, sat in one night explaining he hadn't played in a
while and his game was rusty. The three others said that was fine—it
was just a friendly game. They played rotation, so Wasserman was
everyone's partner in turn. Billy was a big winner, Wasserman a big

loser. As he counted up his profit, Billy grinned and said, "Lew, for a guy who hasn't played bridge for a year, you certainly played badly."

Another loser was the millionaire realtor Lawrence Block. He thought he lost because of bad luck. He made side bets with Billy when he went out of town. He would keep the score of all the bridge games he played on cruises and business trips. The agreement was that if he won Billy would pay him, and if he lost he paid Billy. Block was a most honorable person. He always returned with the scores of his game. He usually lost—and paid.

What kind of a bridge player was Billy? He was good, at least as compared to Lew Wasserman or the average player. With bridge players, real ones, he was just passable, just above the *potzer* class. His playing improved later and the consensus of those who've played with him is that he was a sound bidder and had learned to make a count of the cards and to play them well. He had one of the most desirable traits in a bridge player: he had the instinct to go for the jugular and kill his opponents. Freddy Sheinwold once tried to find something nice to say about Wilder's game: "Billy is a regular winner in that A game, and not because he's a great technician. He can't be bothered with that—he plays the people. He always knows where the queen of spades is, as the old expression goes. He just looks at the people and knows." As a bridge player, Wilder was not in a class with writer-director George S. Kaufman, who played at championship level. Nor did Wilder utter any deathless bridge jokes. Not that Kaufman talked as much during bridge games as legend has it. Kaufman is credited with the line, "I'd like to have a review of the bidding—with the original intonations!"

Once when partner Herman Mankiewicz butchered a hand, Kaufman said, "When did you learn this game, Mank? I know it was this afternoon—but what *time* this afternoon?"

I don't say that Kaufman never uttered these cracks. I can only state that I kibitzed quite a few games at the Cavendish and Regency in New York during that period. I was a friend of the bridge writer and champion, Albert H. Morehead. We often dined at these clubs and then I watched the experts play. I watched Kaufman play several times. Not once did he say anything cutting. He played bridge with deadly earnestness—at least when I was kibitzing. On the other hand, it may just have been my hard luck to be around at the wrong times. When Moss Hart's *Light Up The Sky* was trying out in New

Haven, I went up to see it. By chance, I was seated beside George Kaufman. The audience was laughing happily. I now and then glanced sideways at Kaufman to watch his reaction. He was deadpan. He did not laugh. During the intermissions he did not say anything clever. Another time I was hanging around rehearsals of *Guys and Dolls* while gathering material for a story about Abe Burrows. I never saw Kaufman laugh. I never heard him say anything clever.

As I say, it may just have been my George S. Kaufman rotten luck.

Wilder was a more excitable bridge player than Kaufman. Once when Billy bid and made a grand slam, doubled, and redoubled, he got so elated he fell out of his chair, hit a stone urn, and fractured his arm.

He played much bridge with Charlie Brackett. Brackett was a good bridge player, but mulled over each bid for an inordinately long time. Wilder would say, ironically, "Take your time, Charlie, don't hurry, take your time."

Then Billy leaned back, and took a book out of his coat pocket. It was usually something complex like John Maynard Keynes's *Economic Consequences of the Peace*. Billy would say he was always happy to play with Brackett because it enabled him to catch up on his serious reading. He would sit at the bridge table pretending to be absorbed in the book—which drove Charlie up the wall.

One of the memorable incidents at the club occurred when Charlie Lederer came to the card table and announced, "This afternoon I'm not playing bridge. I'm playing tennis. I'm going up against George Toley [Toley was the tennis coach at USC and a top-seeded professional] and I got a bet of a hundred bucks with him. Would any of you bums like a piece of the action?" Now Lederer was a small, slender guy who, even on his best days, played only a passable game of tennis. Billy knew there was a trick in it somewhere. But he bet Lederer $100. Lederer roped in other suckers for similar amounts. Then they marched to one of the courts. Toley was waiting for him. Toley was chained to a baby elephant. Lederer had not mentioned the elephant. A bet was a bet, however. The match started. According to the conditions, Toley served first. He could hardly move two feet in any direction. He hit the ball over the net. He aced Lederer. He aced him over and over again. Charlie never got a chance to return the ball. Toley killed Charlie.

Billy hated to play with persons who grimaced as they contemplated their cards. He felt this was a form of giving information which was unethical. He called these grimaces "Ouspenskayas," after Maria Ouspenskaya, a Russian character actress with a wizened face that she contorted in dramatic expressions.

One day he was playing against an opponent who made a face as he announced his bid.

Billy said, "Ouspenskayas are not allowed at this table."

It was a tense three-cent-a-point game.

On the next hand, the same player—who happened to be a man of whom Wilder was fond—again grimaced while bidding. Billy said, "That's your last Ouspenskaya—you're out of the game."

In cold silence the man, red-faced, stumbled away and another player took his seat.

Eddie Blum asked him, "Billy, I don't understand this—why do you attack a guy you so obviously love when he so obviously admires you?"

Billy said, "That's a good question. I'll think about it and give you the answer tomorrow."

The next day he told Blum: "I got my answer for you, Blum. If I were a horse thief, being chased through a town, I could go to his house. He would hide me, but you would not. That is why he is my trusted friend and not you."

Blum still had not figured out this arcane explanation. "It could be that the better Billy likes you, the more he attacks you. When we were working on *Stalag* I would sit at the Writers Table playing the word game."

Lizbeth Scott, a tough actress who talked loudly in a raucous voice, started sitting at a nearby table and yacking incessantly, which disturbed Billy's concentration. He once called out loudly, *"Has anybody noticed that you never see Ben Blue before six, and you never see Lizbeth Scott after six?"*

Nobody knew what this meant but it had overtones which scared Scott. She never again sat near Billy Wilder. Blum annoyed him also. Blum annoyed him because he won a word game once in a while. Billy seized on the fact that his words were trite. But they were in the dictionary, Blum would say. Wilder was the king of the word game. Nobody won a game against him. He couldn't stand Blum's occasional wins.

"Dictionary?" he repeated, throwing up his hands. "My God, I have this cretin collaborating with me. Listen to the rotten words he uses." He repeated the dull, everyday words and Blum would insist they were in the dictionary and Billy would say,

"That is not good enough, Eddie. When I had Charlie Brackett as my partner, he came up with exquisite words."

"But, Billy, did he win?" Blum said.

"Who cares if he won or not? He was literate. That is the kind of writer I was working with. A literate man. Not an ignoramus like you."

Blum was taking these insults day after day in front of the other writers. Finally, Blum turned on Wilder: "Billy, I got you figured out. You roar like a lion—but you got no teeth. All I feel is gums. Soft . . . flabby . . . gums . . ."

For some reason, this riposte quieted Billy.

Subsequently, whenever Billy worked him over, Eddie would shout, "Gums." And it shut up Billy.

Blum was in the bridge game and would now and then resort to the talismanic word, "Gums," when he felt Billy's sarcasm was getting out of hand.

Billy can be impulsive at times. He quit bridge on an impulse. About seven, eight years ago, he was playing in a rubber game with Block. Block was making psychic bids and he made an unusually wild one. Billy was his partner. They went down four tricks doubled as Block was holding a virtual Yarborough.

Billy got up. He announced. "I'm through with bridge."

And he was. He never played anymore.

He remained a member of the Tennis Club, however. He loved tennis. He played tennis, often, after a day at the studio, coming in the early evening for a few sets. He played often on Saturdays and Sundays—except when he was in the final throes of composing a screenplay. He was a good tennis player—probably a better tennis player than card player. Billy was too violent a man to exercise the cold self-control required of a topflight bridge player. On the other hand, on a court, his dash and will to win gave him an edge on all but the pros. He liked to play against the pros, in tennis as well as bridge.

"The only way to improve your game is to play with the experts for big stakes," was his philosophy.

It is this viewpoint that has kept the great bridge and tennis players in the lap of luxury. Morehead once told me about rich men who knew they would lose and lose heavily but budgeted, say, $50,000 a year for bridge losses for the pleasure of playing with Oswald Jacoby or Johnny Crawford. Wilder wasn't quite that profligate but his bridge education probably cost him $2,000 a year.

His tennis game was unique. For most players, backhand is the hardest. For Billy it is the easiest. He runs around his forehand and swats his backhand shots with the nonchalant grace of a Jimmy Connors. Over the years he played against Vines, Perry, Don Budge, Pancho Segura, Don Riggs and others of that ilk. He never beat them but he held his own. He was somewhat of a klutz at playing the net. He could never master a good serve, but his backhand was superb. He was always in a fine, relaxed mood after a good tennis match. Somehow, playing a physical game seemed to have a spiritual effect on him. He became serene—even when he lost. After he had showered and changed into a pair of Daks slacks and a pair of his Bass Weejuns, one could observe peace fall upon him.

A tennis player of semipro stature who knew Billy Wilder in his racquet period did not agree with others that he was a good player. "He was a very poor player, what we call a hacker," this still active sportsman told me, requesting anonymity. "Oh, he ran around a lot and he sweated a lot and he put on a show—one of those heavy-breathing guys. But he sweated too much to be a really good player. He wasn't even a fair tennis player. I think a lot of the guys at the Beverly Hills Tennis Club were just favoring him, hoping to be cast in a Billy Wilder picture."

Billy sometimes played tennis with Paul Lukas, the great Hungarian actor. Wilder had become very hostile to certain members of the club whom he thought were bad sports. Lukas was the worst of them. He took advantage of every close play and always called it in his favor. Any time any player made what Billy considered an unethical call, Billy would say, "That's a Lukas." It got to be an expression around the BHTC. Any kind of crookedness or unethical corner-cutting became known as a "Lukas." Late one Saturday afternoon, Wilder was sitting with a group of eminent members that included Mrs. Louis B. Mayer. They were watching Paul Lukas playing and, as usual, giving himself the benefit of every doubtful situation. It was just one "Lukas" after another "Lukas." Billy started reviling Lukas, then went on to disparage other members whom he considered equally dishonorable.

Mrs. Mayer said, "If you feel this way, why do you remain in the club?"

Wilder stood up. "You are right," he said. "I am quitting." He wrote out his resignation and would not reconsider it, not even when Lukas died.

Arthur Marx, one of my fellow Hollywood historians, has a different version of the Wilder resignation, which is amusing and which illustrates Billy's way of decorating reality with rococo swirls. Wrote Marx in *Los Angeles Magazine:*

> The specific thing that drove Wilder out was a Christmas card he received every holiday season from a doctor who was a regular in his bridge game. . . . It was one of those Christmas cards that feature a color photograph of the sender's family: the doctor, his wife, a cross-eyed son, and a little girl with a long nose. "Every year, as they grew older, the monsters would get uglier," recalls the acerbic Wilder. "It depressed me more than Nixon. But there was no way I could get them to stop sending me cards unless I told them the truth and hurt them. So my only choice was to quit the club. Now I can look forward to Christmas again."

Billy Wilder is one of those crazed sports fans. He is loyal to our home teams—to the Los Angeles Rams, Lakers, and Dodgers—and of these the Dodgers is his deepest love. When the Dodgers moved from Brooklyn to Los Angeles in 1959, Wilder fell in love with the team. For a time he stopped wearing any other head covering but a Dodger baseball cap, a real one. When they played night games, he carried a battery-operated miniature radio with him to every party and screening he attended.

"He offended many people in Hollywood," a hostess informed me. "People didn't mind being insulted by Billy—they rather looked forward to it. But they resented his keeping his ears to a radio and clucking to himself and moaning and that sort of thing—yes, even at black-tie dinner parties. I had the temerity to mention this gaucherie to Billy once, and he said to me, as if explaining to a little idiot, that absolutely nothing, nothing, transcended the importance of a Dodger game."

Reisch confirms this: "This is a man who is easily bored, you must realize. I have known of only one thing that never bores him. Baseball, American baseball. He completely understands it, which, as you know, is impossible, for a European cannot understand baseball, but he does. His old enthusiasm for tennis is gone. Once he would go to every important tennis match in the world—Forest Hills, Wimbledon, anywhere. But no more tennis. Once in a while a soccer game; a few weeks ago we went to the international soccer matches at the Forum, but it did not mean much to him. It is baseball now which is his first love and, more and more, football.''

Billy's closest friends—Jack Lemmon, Walter Matthau, Armand Deutsch, Freddie de Cordova—are all as emotional about these games as Billy. One exception is writer Leonard Gershe. Gershe says, "I don't play cards and I don't know ballgames. What I do is fill his Gelusil glass. These games get his stomach on edge. Sometimes, to annoy him, I'll say, 'Who are the people in the red sweaters, Billy? Who are the people in green? Why is he arguing with that man?' Sometimes, weekends at the beach, I sit alongside him and heckle him.''

Audrey Wilder has acquired a taste for viewing sports. The Wilders watch Monday night football on ABC and usually have friends over to share the thrills. They watch two games on Saturday and two games on Sunday—sometimes three games on Sunday. She believes that a wife who does not share her husband's interest in sports is a fool. She says a wife can get "huffy about it and go in the other room and read a book and sulk, or learn to enjoy it, because it is fun to do and fun to talk about. Most people like it, most men like it, so why not join them? I don't believe in the old Hollywood tradition of the men in one room and the women in another. I don't believe in separating husbands and wives.''

The Matthaus share this concept. Walter says that if "the boys" are invited, then "the girls" are invited.

"I would never go any place they wouldn't ask my wife," Matthau says. "I'm different from Billy as to sports, in that I do not root for any team unless I have money on them. As you may have heard, I am a betting man. I am no longer a compulsive gambler. I now gamble willingly and place lower wagers. I will bet a hundred dollars a game with Billy. The Los Angeles Dodgers don't mean a damn thing to me, or the Rams, unless I have money on them.

"Now this reputation I have for betting on anything, that is absolutely fallacious. Like which of two flies will climb a wall faster. I don't make fly-on-the-wall bets. I don't make will-it-rain-tomorrow bets. I bet on baseball, football, basketball, and horses.

"I have dragged Billy out to the racetrack many times. He hates horse racing. I love to go to the races. Will go every afternoon unless work interferes. The thing about a track is there is a long pause between races, you know, fifteen, twenty minutes, and Billy can't stand this. But I love this. Billy is not a gambler. You see, it's the time between races that gets a gambler going. You study your form sheets. You walk around trying to get some inside dope. You go to the clubhouse, look the horses over. Best of all, you try to run into Marty Ritt. [Martin Ritt, the director, is the best handicapper in the movie colony.] Ritt you cannot call a gambler. He wins too many bets. He always has the edge.

"Oh, I like to win. It is not true that the real gambler wants to lose—but losing, it hurts more than winning, and a pain is a more dramatic emotion than a pleasure. For losing to give you this drama, it has to be unbearable, and you have to make sure you lose enough to hurt. Billy is not a gambler in this sense, not even in the Marty Ritt sense.

"Billy bets fifty or a hundred, just to be sociable.

"No, I have never played poker with him. I don't think he would play in a game with my kind of stakes."

Among Wilder's hobbies have been restaurants and bonsai trees. His infatuation with miniature Japanese trees lasted about as long as his Napoleon craze—two years, during which time he accumulated 120 rare lilliputian trees, and a storehouse of bonsai books in many languages including the Japanese. Most of these were illustrated with color plates and some were collectors' items. Having spent much money and time on the books and trees, he suddenly became bored by them and put his books away in storage. He gave most of the trees to friends, though he still has a few which sit on the terrace of his town apartment in Westwood.

Billy's fling with bonsai was a seeming anomaly in his character. He loathes gardening, flower growing, and nature in the raw. Hiking and exploring are not his life-style, which verges on *fin de siècle* decadence.

I think Billy's bonsai period was just free-floating collector's mania. He is one of those persons who collects anything just because it is there to be collected.

For instance, driving along Ventura Boulevard, en route to Universal, he noticed a shop he had never seen before: Basically Butterflies. He pulled his Mercedes over. Basically Butterflies stocked only butterflies under glass—all sorts of specimens, some exquisitely framed and quite rare. He started collecting dead butterflies. He went crazy over dead butterflies. Audrey Wilder said, "I give butterflies six months." It was over in three. It is part of Billy's nature that he has to get others interested in his latest collecting mania, as he got Wendell Mayes intrigued with *pyrogènes*. His greatest failure was Tony Curtis. He tried to start Curtis collecting bentwood furniture, pre-Columbian artifacts, bonsais, anything, to no avail.

"Mr. Curtis," he said (when he uses "Mister" before a surname it indicates disapproval), "Mr. Curtis has only two interests: the size of his billing and the tightness of his pants."

I am told by astrological believers that passionate collectors are likely to be persons born under the sign of Cancer the Crab, noted for their predilection for retaining a clawlike grip on objects and people. Wilder, a June 22 birthday boy, is of course right in the heart of the Cancer period. I am a Sagittarian myself (November 23, on the cusp of Scorpio) and several of the most significant persons in my life, including my first and only wife, have been Cancer persons. I have found that they do, indeed, have this propensity to collect and save beautiful objects. They also—and this too is one of their astrological attributes—tend to be home-loving and devoted to furnishing their abodes. For years, Wilder has collected Swiss, Austrian, and German peasant baroque furniture. He once planned to build a Swiss chalet in Gstaad to house these pieces. He has had a "spell" of early American furniture collecting. And bentwood, of course. He had a rattan furniture phase. And a marine instrument period. I suspect he built the house at Trancas Beach to find a home for his rattan pieces and antique compasses and astrolabes.

(Parenthetically, it is interesting to note that Charlie Brackett was another Sagittarian. As is Victoria Wilder Settember. In *Sunset Boulevard,* Norma Desmond wants to know Joe Gillis's birthday. He tells her. And she says, ah, now nice—a Sagittarian. "You can always trust Sagittarians," she observes. This is true. We Sagittarians are trustworthy.)

Billy is a collector of good restaurants, which certainly seems fitting for the son of the Fred Harvey of the Austro-Hungarian Empire. He knows the best and most interesting and out-of-the-way restaurants everywhere. One of his first questions to me, when I began ferreting out information for this book, was: "Tell me—what are your favorite restaurants in West Hollywood." I did not then realize that this was a Rorschach test. I flunked it. I had to admit I had never dined at Dominick's, a small place on Beverly Boulevard, in my quarter. Dominick's is so snobbish it has a neon-script electric sign—*which is never turned on.* One reason I never repaired to Dominick's was I could never get in. It is small and expensive and Mr. Dominick is capricious as to whom he seats. Audrey and Billy Wilder are probably the only couple in town who can walk in without a reservation and be served. They have been patrons since he started the place. Billy probably put some money into it. He likes to put money into restaurants. His first investment was in The Blue Danube, a *Mittel-European* joint operated by Mia and Joe May, former movie star and movie director. It was, I am told, a fantastic place— with zither music and elegant Hungarian food. You would see Willy Wyler and Billy Wilder and Ernst Lubitsch and Peter Lorre and Dietrich and Conrad (or Konni) Veidt there regularly. The whole refugee colony, and Joe Pasternak, Felix Jackson, Paul Kohner, Bobby Koster . . . The strudel was so felicitous that Gregory Ratoff came in each night for several pieces of strudel—no matter where else he had dined. Billy Wilder was also one of the founding fathers of The Saloon, a new and successful joint in Beverly Hills.

To be a truly compulsive collector, you have to be a determined shopper. Billy loves shopping, as I've previously suggested. He loves it as an activity in and of itself, without any specific goal. He loves window-shopping. He loves counter shopping. He loves wandering through interesting bazaars and gazing at objects until he feels a stirring within him and then he buys something. And he always pays cash! He carries a thick wad of $50 and $100 bills. I have watched him exchange these pieces of paper for concrete merchandise and I have seen a certain look in his eyes, the look of a man who has put over a scam on a victim, for his nerve endings still tingle from the Austrian inflation of the 1920s.

Wilder's senses are acute. All of them. Including smell. Once during one of those agonizing hours they were working on *Stalag 17,* Billy and Eddie Blum were tramping around the rear lawn of his Beverly Drive house. They were arguing violently over a scene. Suddenly Billy stopped. He said he smelled smoke. Eddie said there was no smoke. Billy insisted there was and he sniffed all over the lawn like a pointer until he found a *burnt match*—which Eddie had flipped away after relighting his pipe. Billy picked up the match. "Do you have to be such a slob, Eddie?" he asked.

Now that is an abnormal acuteness of smell.

The visual is the most acute of all his senses. He experiences the universe most of all in terms of what he sees. He is what the Germans call an *augenmensch*. It is why screenwriting comes naturally to him for he translates human drama into images by instinct, as much as by training. The screenwriter writes actions, not words, which was always the fundamental problem with good novelists and playwrights like Fitzgerald, Faulkner, S. N. Behrman, or Arthur Miller when they set their hand to writing films. Wilder's addiction to shopping and his *augenmenschkeit* have joined to make him the foremost art collector in the movie colony. He has been acquiring works of art for forty years. He purchases the things he likes and he goes by what he sees. Henry J. Seldis, art critic of the *Los Angeles Times,* said once that Wilder, unlike other rich art buyers, "collects by eye rather than by ear." He meant that Wilder does not buy reputations or what is in vogue. He buys by what he sees and likes. For instance, he bought several Joseph Cornell boxes about twenty-five years ago when few had heard of Cornell and fewer still were collecting him. He was buying Schieles and Klimts when they were unwanted. He began collecting Saul Steinberg ages ago—and has, according to University of California at Santa Barbara art historian David Beghard, "one of the largest and certainly one of the finest collections of Saul Steinberg." He has many Klees in his collection and a ravishing group of Henry Moore pieces. He started collecting Moore in 1941. He has Picasso, Braque, Rouault in his collection and Bombois primitives, Calder stabiles and mobiles, Dubuffet, and De Stael.

To give you an idea—he heard about this mad *collagiste* by the name of Cornell, a reclusive fellow who lived out in Queens. He heard rumors that he was doing unusual work. Billy went out to see him. He was ravished by these boxes in which were combined strange objects with a vague eroticism. He purchased one for $400— and was sneered at by the art dealers. Recently, Wilder told me, he refused $50,000 for that same box. I asked Billy how much it was insured for. He replied;

"I wish you wouldn't mention insurance in connection with my collection. It becomes a target for burglars. Most smart collectors, who have less ego than I have, when they loan a painting or sculpture to a show, they loan it anonymously. I like to have it say, 'From the collection of Mr. and Mrs. Billy Wilder,' but really this is a bad idea. We American collectors are more fortunate than the European. In Paris or London, they kidnap your paintings and hold them for ransom. A friend had to pay many thousands of pounds to ransom his collection. Many of my English friends have been what they call 'silvered,' meaning that crooks have broken in and stolen their silver. These are experts; they go for the hallmarks and they know exactly what to steal—only Paul Storr silver and the first-class paintings. Oh, they are very selective. Here in the United States we are lucky—our burglars are so poorly educated that Picasso means nothing to them. They go for the Zenith twenty-five-inch television set, the Marantz stereo, the Mr. Coffee coffeemaker, and the GE can opener. Thank God, we have uncultured thieves in America. I was much relieved when I read recently that many students entering college are unable to read and write.''

Wilder has incorporated paintings in several films. In *The Apartment,* there's a print of Rousseau's *Sleeping Gypsy,* in the bedroom in which Shirley MacLaine almost dies from an overdose of sleeping pills. The shot of her in a coma on the bed was inspired by the composition in the painting. There is a subliminal overtone of meaning, for the sleeping lady is saved in the jungle by a friendly animal, namely, Jack Lemmon. Subtly, perhaps too subtly, Wilder was saying that even in the New York corporate jungle one could find a friend.

In *The Fortune Cookie,* Wilder, less subtly, showed a print of Whistler's *Composition in Black and White* on a wall of Lemmon's apartment. No attention is called to the print. You become aware of it in a peripheral fashion, and, gradually, as Lemmon rolls around in his wheelchair, you get the point.

In general, Wilder takes great care with the details of his interiors, more than do most directors, as he knows furniture and periods and he has this great sense of style. Many props in a scene were either selected by him, or come from one of his collections. Cameraman LaShelle remembers that Billy had to approve every prop, no matter how small. "I could only change the position of a prop if I convinced him it made the composition better," he says. "Billy has a painter's sense of composition."

Because of his perfect sense of form, Wilder is able to, as they say, "cut in the camera." He knows when a scene can be cut and does not let it run on and on as do many directors. He is economical in his use of film. He more or less shoots only what will be used in the final cut. La Shelle: "I used to kid the cutter. *All you got to do,* I tell him, *is cut off the slates and paste the ends together.* You don't need editors with Wilder pictures. All you need is pasters.''

Billy Wilder wrote the screenplays with his collaborators. When he came to film these screenplays, he picked up a brush and palette. He painted moving pictures.

# 22

# UNHEEDED ADVICE
# FROM MOSS HART

In 1961, members of the Academy of Motion Picture Arts and Sciences convened for the annual ritual. For the first time in thirty-three years, they assembled outside of the Los Angeles city limits, in the newly built Civic Auditorium in Santa Monica. A dense fog was rolling in from the Pacific Ocean. The klieg lights beamed through the fog on the auditorium, on the stars arriving in their limousines, and on thousands of hysterical fans crowded into hastily erected stands. It was a wild evening. Elizabeth Taylor came direct from a hospital bed. She had almost died from double pneumonia. She looked wan and fragile. She was leaning on Eddie Fisher. She had never won an Oscar—though nominated thrice before. There was a short in the ignition of Bobby Darin's custom-made $97,000 limousine—it started burning suddenly, just as Audrey and Billy Wilder were driven up in a rented $20,000 limousine. It was the first Oscar night ever televised on ABC and it was to run two hours and thirty-three minutes. An impressive red carpet stretched from the curb to the entrance. The world was in a dither at that time over Cuba. The headlines on the Los Angeles papers were in 120-point type: CASTRO JAILS ALL YANKS IN CUBA and CRISIS FIGHT NEAR, CUBA EXILES CLAIM.

Billy Wilder had been nominated in two categories (coauthor and

*311*

director); also, as producer of *The Apartment,* he might receive the one for Best Picture.

The roll call began, and finally came to "Best Story and Screen-play—Written Directly for the Screen." Moss Hart and Kitty Carlisle (Mrs. Hart) were the presenters. Moss read the five nominations. Kitty tore open the envelope and cried, "The winner is—I.A.L. Diamond and Billy Wilder."

They went on the stage. Kitty handed Iz Diamond his statuette and Moss handed Billy his. Moss embraced Billy. He whispered in his ear. Billy was seen to shake his head and grin.

Gina Lollobrigida awarded Billy Wilder a second Oscar for Best Director.

And then Audrey Hepburn spoke the sentences which climaxed the evening: "And now, for Best Picture of the year—Billy Wilder for *The Apartment.*"

It was the first time one individual had won three Oscars in one night.

Wilder was to long remember what Moss Hart had murmured in his ear. "This is the moment to stop, Billy," he had advised. "And how right he was," Billy told me fifteen years later. "If only I had listened to him." But Moss Hart knew that Wilder would not stop. Hart had not stopped. You could not stop. Your work became your life. Now there was not any sudden and precipitous decline in Wilder's fortunes after that historic triumph. On the contrary, *Irma La Douce,* released two years later, was the biggest money-maker in his career—grossing over $25,000,000, becoming the highest grossing nonmusical comedy in Hollywood annals. And he made a series of exciting and interesting films after *The Apartment.* He was working out, in terms of symbol and film language, the conflicts of his heart. He was writing a veiled autobiography in the films he made, starting with *The Apartment* and through a sequence of films that is still not over and will not be over until he is too feeble to go out on a sound stage and bark, "Action." The films were superlative. But he came under sharper and sharper critical attack. He began to experience the peculiar sensation that movie critics had a moral revulsion only for his pictures, even sophisticated critics like Pauline Kael, Andrew Sarris, Dwight MacDonald, Brendan Gill, Hollis Alpert. He began to feel like a victim of a conspiracy. He was being singled out, raked over the coals, not on aesthetic grounds, but as if he were a defiler of good taste and moral decency. He was bewildered by the attack, for these same critics praised films by Ingmar Bergman, Antonioni, Bertolucci, Louis Malle, Alain Resnais, Kurosawa, and others which expressed similar moral ambiguities and moods of cynicism and despair, which portrayed men and women as cruel, lustful, and mean-spirited little animals. Was it because these films were in a foreign tongue? Was it some kind of a snobbism? Why was it these elitist critics were forever panning American pictures for being naive and simplistic and oh-so-happy-endingish, and then picking on Billy Wilder pictures for being grim and cynical? He had been taking this kind of a critical beating since *Ace in the Hole.* He would get it again and again, and he did not know why. Sometimes his pain was assuaged by the esteem of his colleagues and the public, as with *The Apartment* and *Irma La Douce.* But then, after *Irma,* the public did not flock to his pictures. He could quip about making pictures for six friends in Bel Air, but he was making pictures for one billion strangers around the globe. He wanted to please the masses. He also wanted to be loved by Kael and Sarris and Alpert.

I am about to reveal a terrible secret about Billy Wilder, which he will deny is true, and at which all those who have brushed against him and been either offended or enchanted by his sharp tongue and cruel japes will scoff, and this is that he is an oversensitive person who is quick to feel rejection, who is easily hurt, and who suffers great anguish—which it has been the principal business of his life to conceal from all other persons, including the woman he has loved longer than any other human being: Audrey Wilder.

This, to paraphrase Oscar Wilde, might be called the virtue that dares not speak its name. It is vulnerability. It is a fear of not being loved. When you are out there showing your dreams in public, your dreams have to be loved, and if they are not loved you feel as if *you* are not loved. It is impossible to convince most people that persons as successful and powerful and seemingly so marvelously integrated and wise as Billy Wilder, can be as scared, deep down, as you and I, especially when they are clever and smart and disdain your pity by setting a distance between you and them through sarcasm. He had to be the man you hate to love. He could not exist in any other style. He could not cry. He could not even cry to his Aud. After *Kiss Me Stupid,* the great debacle of his career, he and Audrey fled to Europe for two months, most of the time being spent at Bad Gastein, that spa with the lovely waterfall that reminded him of the leaky toilet in a Berlin apartment.

He had not told anybody in Hollywood where he was going. He remained in total seclusion, even in Europe, and did not look up any friends. Had he withdrawn to lick his wounds? I asked him, once, "Did you go away to put Hollywood out of your mind?"

There was a long pause. He looked at me. "Yes, Hollywood—and also suicide," he said in a rare—in fact, in the *only*—moment in which he dared to reveal his vulnerability. "I thought of killing myself. I thought I would never make another movie. I did not know what to do with my life. I did not want to live."

"In Hollywood, it is now common to hear Billy Wilder called the world's greatest movie director," Pauline Kael wrote in 1961. She was then an obscure critic. She wrote for an academic journal, *Film Quarterly*. She did not share Hollywood's opinion. To her, Wilder was "a clever, lively director whose work lacks feeling or passion or grace or beauty or elegance. His eye is on the dollar, or rather on success, on the entertainment values that bring in dollars. But he has never before, except perhaps in a different way in *Ace in the Hole*, exhibited such a brazen contempt for people. Is it possibly life in Hollywood that is so conducive to this extreme materialist position?" This was written apropos of *One, Two, Three* (1961).

Coming from a serious, intelligent critic, who was a true film freak, this keenly hurt Wilder; and though he would sound off at Kael and Sarris, he simply couldn't see how she thought he was a dollar-hungry, success-driven, materialistic moviemaker. Neither can I. It just doesn't fit Wilder. Never did. He always marched to his own drum. He had made the film about Lindbergh's flight because Lindbergh was a hero of his imagination. He knew it would not make millions. He knew it would be one hell of a rough story to lick. He did it because he had to do it. It was not a safe, commercial, Hollywood-type genre film. Warners lost six million dollars on it. Jack Warner once said it was "the most disastrous failure we ever had . . . I have never been able to figure out why it flopped." Wilder had gone through hell in casting it. John Kerr, the young stage actor, was the original choice. He turned it down because he did not like Lindbergh's politics during World War II. Kerr, like other young actors who were approached, would not impersonate Lindbergh. Jimmy Stewart had been lobbying to get the part, though he knew he was too old—he was now forty-eight and he had been the pilot of a bomber during World War II. Even makeup could not disguise his age. Lindbergh was twenty-five when he flew the Atlantic.

Yes, it was a challenge to make the picture. Wilder got no laurels for this triumph. Anne Morrow Lindbergh once told Jimmy Stewart that the family had gone to see the film at the Radio City Music Hall. She said, "The youngest of our children said something that might interest you. When you were in trouble over the Atlantic and got into ice clouds and ice started forming on the wings and you started losing altitude and drifted near the waves, the youngest child pulled my sleeve and said, 'Daddy does make it, doesn't he?'" Of Billy Wilder's singular writing and directing feat of sustaining interest in such a difficult film, and Stewart's feat of carrying off what was essentially a two-hour-and-fifteen-minute monologue, Lindbergh himself was impressed only by one touch. He wrote Stewart a thank-you note in which he complimented him for "tapping the oil gauge when you were starting the engine." This had been Stewart's own idea. "When you were flying a reciprocating engine, that was a natural thing to do," Stewart told me. "The oil pressure gauge is of vital importance when the engine is turning over, because if the oil pressure gauge isn't rising, it means the pistons aren't getting lubricated." (I still don't know what the hell this all means but it impressed Colonel Lindbergh.) Aside from this touch, Stewart said that Wilder never permitted him to improvise lines or action for the camera. You could never change a single word with Wilder. Stewart has made several fine films with Hitchcock, another proponent of following the script religiously. But Hitch, he said, would sometimes let you get away with a slip of the tongue or a little verbal invention as long as it looked right on film—Wilder never, but *never.* "He wants you to say the words the way he wrote them," Stewart said, in a tone of sneaking admiration.

It seems hard to believe, now that we are living in a period of freedom of language and theme in pictures that anybody—especially hard-boiled critics—could have been shocked by *The Apartment.* They were. Only sixteen years ago, and they were. To reread reviews and critiques is surely one of the dreariest of literary experiences and so I will not quote in detail. McCarten of the *New Yorker* dismissed this satirical masterpiece of upward mobility through corporate pandering in fifty-five words. That was the entire review, fifty-five words; he called it a "thing." Granted that writer-director Wilder was skating on thin ice when his heroine makes a suicide attempt in a comedy and his hero lets his superiors use his flat as a place of assignation—but we are talking about the *New Yorker*, for God's sakes, not the little old magazine from Dubuque. We are also talking about Dwight MacDonald, writing then about films for *Esquire*, who was disgusted by the film, so much so he suggested that Wilder's collaborator change his name to I.A.L. Zircon! I could see Sadie Glutz of the Oshkosh *Gazette* being wounded when she saw Santa Claus drunk in a bar on Christmas Eve, or Lemmon catering to his happy-go-fucky corporation president, or drunken Lemmon picking up a drunken broad in a sleazy bar—but Kael, Sarris, McCarten, MacDonald, Hollis Alpert? Alpert, the *Saturday Review*'s critic, scorned it as a "dirty fairy tale." Can you blame Billy Wilder for getting paranoid? And then—a decade later—Kael turns around and sings hosannas to *Last Tango in Paris*. Now it is true that distinguished film critics like Charles Champlin and Bosley Crowther were in sympathy with Wilder's sophistication and regarded him as a film master on a par with European moviemakers. Crowther said of *The Apartment* that it followed "a line of extremely sophisticated balancing between cynicism and sentiment, between irony and pity, that has run through most of the best of American comedies, from those of Charlie Chaplin through the fine Frank Capra and Gregory La Cava films. It is a line that Mr. Wilder now follows with superior effect." It was not a total conspiracy. There were two or three friends on the flanks.

Whatever it was, *The Apartment* was not tasteless, though it laid out some aspects of modern life which were, if you like, on the sordid side; but aren't films supposed to deal with life as it is? Aren't we forever being told that Hollywood doesn't face life as it is?

Now, how could Kael possibly construe a film like this (with its hard-edge realism) or *Some Like It Hot* which Wilder had made the year before) as being the products of a cold, calculating, dollar-hungry, movie merchant? They were both daring and unusual films and extremely risky to make and exhibit. Two men dressing up in women's clothes and playing in an all-girl band? Jack Lemmon, in drag, and Joe E. Brown, dancing cheek-to-cheek and murmuring sweet nothings to each other? This was not your run-of-the-mill American comedy. But there was not one critic to salute Wilder's courage. Nobody cried, "Hail, the noble pathfinder." I just can't explain the phenomenon. It is there. Perhaps there is something about Wilder's personality and his insulting manners which offends critics. Who knows? Maybe he had insulted them at parties?

There have been many Wilder movies which were never written—
or being written, were never filmed. My favorite Wilder unfilmed
film is one with the Marx Brothers. While shooting *The Apartment*
on location in New York, Billy stayed at the Ritz Towers, on East
Fifty-seventh Street, not far from United Nations Plaza. It was a
time of world drama, when Krushchev was banging his shoe on the
UN lectern, and Castro was in town with his entourage, and Nasser,
and pickets and counterpickets were marching and police sirens
went on all night long. As Wilder and Iz Diamond were driving out
to the airport, Billy said, "Do you think it would be funny to do a
picture with the Marx Brothers at the United Nations?"

Diamond thought it would be funny.

By the time they arrived at Los Angeles, they had a story. Groucho Marx is the brains behind a heist mob. Their scheme is that
since the New York police are so occupied with protecting the United Nations delegates, the rest of Manhattan is unguarded. They plan
to pull a Tiffany caper! Chico would play the strong-arm guy of the
mob. Harpo would be the safecracker. One scene would show Harpo unable to open a can of sardines. Using sewers as a passage, they
blast their way into Tiffany's and steal four suitcases of diamonds.
They plan a getaway on a tramp steamer going to Brazil. At the
docks, there is an anti-Communist picket line. The police think the
Marx Brothers are the Latvian delegation and take them by police
escort to the Latvian embassy uptown. As the climax of a mad adventure, Wilder saw a scene in which Harpo addressed the UN in
pantomime—tooting the horn, lunging at adjacent blond delegates—
while four simultaneous and different translations interpreted him!

Billy informed Groucho Marx of the story. Groucho loved it.
(This was prior to the argument over Scotch.) He told Billy to phone
Gummo Marx, who agented the brothers, and make a deal. "Just tell
him Groucho sent you," said Groucho. Gummo said if Groucho
loved it, then Harpo would do it for Groucho. I should explain here
that the Marx Brothers had not made a film for a decade and had resisted every movie overture. They had said they were through with
pictures. Pictures were too exhausting. And now . . .

"How about Chico?" Wilder asked.

"No sweat," Gummo said. "Chico'll do it. He always needs
money." Chico was a loser-type gambler like Matthau.

Iz and Billy elaborated a forty-page treatment. The Mirisch Brothers were ecstatic over the prospect of the Marx Brothers.

Then Harpo Marx collapsed during a rehearsal of a television special. He had a heart attack. He recovered. But the adverse publicity made the Marx Brothers uninsurable. No studio starts a film if the stars can't pass a physical examination by an insurance company doctor. This picture would be a four-million picture. Could the Tiffany caper film be a vehicle for another set of comedians? Billy decided it would not work with any other comedians. He abandoned it.

The political energy of *A Day at the United Nations*, the tentative title, was transmuted into Wilder's great political film, *One, Two, Three*, based on a Molnar one-act comedy he had seen in Berlin. Billy persuaded Cagney to come out of retirement and play the lead in what is perhaps the fastest comedy ever shot, Cagney spitting out gags like a machine gun. It was a controversial film, but, for once, Wilder won the hearts of all the New York-based critics. Brendan Gill threw garlands in a long *causerie* in the *New Yorker*. He sat "watching and roaring with delight" at this audacious farce, which ventured to mock every conventional value. One found oneself guffawing at jokes "based on events that, when they are reported in the daily papers, suffice to freeze our hearts." He said *merci mille fois* to Mr. Wilder, the writer-director-producer of *One, Two, Three*, "who could no doubt wring a hearty yock from bubonic plague." Such "breathtaking speed," gag after gag, you were exhausted with laughter, you were riding a giddy roller coaster. Dwight MacDonald, too, though it was against his better judgment, laughed and laughed and laughed. He even apologized for his joke about Zircons, and said that I.A.L. was a true blue-white Diamond, after all. He asked the question, what could be "more vulgar, more tasteless than a farce laid in West Berlin?" And yet, "the tempo is so fast and the invention so prodigal" that one laughed and laughed and laughed, though "there are some things like lung cancer that just can't be joked about . . ." Wilder had done the impossible and made us laugh about them.

What was this about "bubonic plague" and "lung cancer?" Was Gill afraid of rats? Did MacDonald smoke too much? Arthur Schlesinger, Jr. (who became the film critic for Huntington Hartford's *Show* magazine), by God, said the picture was "an irresistible evocation of the mood of Mark Twain." *Time* said Wilder was the avatar of Twain and also of Mack Sennett. Even Stanley Kauffman, of The *New Republic*, a man of extremely high standards, loved it.

But not Pauline Kael. She not only hated the picture—but she hated all the critics who loved the picture. It was tasteless. It was offensive. Wilder saw life as a blocked bladder and *One, Two, Three* was a "comedy that pulls out laughs the way a catheter draws urine." Pauline Kael is a critic of elegance and style and I have always enjoyed her writings. It is a small personal ache to me that she has a blind spot about Billy Wilder. Andrew Sarris is another critic I admire. He also has this Wilder blind spot. He was very bitter about Wilder's political pictures. He wrote that Wilder's Berlin films, the Cagney picture and Dietrich's *A Foreign Affair* "have been wrongly criticized for social irresponsibility. This is too serious a charge to level at a series of tasteless gags, half anti-Left and half anti-Right, adding up to Wilder's conception of political sophistication."

With *Irma La Douce,* Brendan Gill was dislodged from his previous Disease Theory of Wilder's humor. He found this picture about a French whore and her pimp extremely vulgar and he did not laugh. "As a source of comedy I find prostitution about as hilarious as muscular dystrophy," he wrote. What—Wilder could not wring yocks from muscular dystrophy? Sarris grumbled about the "superficial nastiness of Wilder's personality." I love that "superficial." My friend Sarris—I call him my friend because we had a lengthy conversation about Marilyn Monroe at the first Lincoln Center film festival and he said he admired my writing—will not even grant Billy Wilder the honor of having an *authentic* nasty streak. Even his nastiness is "superficial."

The roof was about to fall in on Billy Wilder. However, following the old biblical plan, pride goeth before a fall. He had first to be proud of something. On December 13, 1964, the film library of the Museum of Modern Art presented a Billy Wilder retrospective. Surely, he had, at long last, arrived. It was the first Wilder retrospective—though there would be later ones in Paris, Berlin and a twenty-four-hour marathon at the Los Angeles Film Festival in 1974. The MOMA retrospective played to capacity audiences (which included this writer and his children) for two months. The Museum screened sixteen films, from *People on Sunday* to *Irma La Douce.*

Five days after the Wilder retrospective opened amidst all the glitter of a fashionable Manhattan champagne and hors d'oeuvres party, *Kiss Me Stupid* opened nationally. The praises of museum film curator Richard Griffith were still ringing in his ears: "Wilder is the most precise, indeed relentless, chronicler of the postwar American, in shade as well as light, that the motion picture has produced."

And now he read the notices of *Kiss Me Stupid*. The *New York Herald-Tribune* said it was "the slimiest movie of the year." The *New York Daily News* said it was "coarse and smutty." Liz Smith, in *Cosmopolitan,* reviled the film and said a group of worldly New Yorkers watching it at a press screening had "gasped at such crudity." Bosley Crowther turned on Wilder: "A coarse dissection of double adultery," he wrote in the *New York Times*. "It is obvious, plodding, short on laughs and performances and long on vulgarity . . . *sleazy.*" They forgot all about the relentless chronicler of Americans and the avatar of Mark Twain. Brendan Gill would have no part of Wilder, for it was "*squalid.*" Squalid, did you hear? And "most of the blame for this repellent oversized trifle can safely be placed on Mr. Wilder's shoulders."

An Indiana minister, Dr. Lycurgus M. Starkey, Jr.—a name straight out of a Sinclair Lewis novel—attacked Wilder over the NBC network: "His movies have overturned all the sexual mores, glorified promiscuity, glamorized prostitution and elevated adultery to a virtue."

Throughout the South and Middle West, theaters cancelled the run of *Kiss Me Stupid*. Wilder was denounced from pulpits by regional Savonarolas. The Legion of Decency condemned it as indecent, immoral, and an insult to "Judaeo-Christian sensibilities." The Legion gave it a C rating. It was the second film by an important director from a major studio to receive a C rating. The first had been Kazan's *Baby Doll*, eight years before. The *Kiss Me Stupid* rating was also the last, because, within a very few years we entered upon the era of gross abandon in pictures, the era of *Last Tango in Paris, Carnal Knowledge,* and *The Exorcist*. The Legion gave Wilder's film a hard C. You could get a soft C or a hard C. With a soft C, you got condemned. With a hard C, you got condemned—and you also got berated in Sunday sermons. Parishioners were advised to shun *Kiss Me Stupid* like lung cancer, muscular dystrophy, or the bubonic plague.

Only one critic saw this film in 1964 as I think most of us would see it today. That person was Joan Didion, soon to become a famous novelist and screenwriter. She was then the film critic for *Vogue*. She wrote a perceptive essay about the disillusioned romanticism of Wilder. He was a "moralist, a recorder of human venality. While perhaps half a dozen other people in Hollywood might have made *Some Like It Hot,* only Wilder could have made *Sunset Boulevard* and *Double Indemnity* and *Ace in the Hole. Kiss Me Stupid* shows Wilder doing exactly what only he can do. It is a profoundly affecting film, as witnessed by the number of people who walk out on it. What makes the picture so affecting, what makes people walk out when they will sit through and even applaud the real tastelessness, the true venality of pictures like *The Pink Panther* or *Bedtime Story?* They walk out, I suspect, because they sense that Wilder means it, that he would simply not be interested in pretending, say, that Claudia Cardinale could be a princess. The Wilder world is one seen at dawn through a hangover, a world of cheap *double entendres* and stale smoke, and drinks in which the ice has melted: the true country of despair.''

And she went on to speak of the truth of this bleak landscape which Wilder had painted, the desolation of the Las Vegas glamor, the empty highways and the ugliness of desert towns, of cocktail waitresses in sleazy bars, and frame houses, and the small-town dreamers and illusionists, who are going to make it big with a million-selling record, the jackpot, the slot-machinery of the culture going for the big money in Vegas and Hollywood, the worship of the big stars like Dean Martin, and the sex obsessions so necessary because life is drained of all meaning. "In its feeling for such a world, for such a condition of the heart, *Kiss Me Stupid* is quite a compelling and moving picture. . . .''

Wilder had gone to Bad Gastein in suicidal despair. He returned, still in despair. He wanted to start writing another movie. Every morning he and Iz Diamond would meet in his cluttered upstairs office on the Sam Goldwyn lot. It was a kind of long, rambling wooden structure just like the place where William Holden has story meetings with Nancy Olson in *Sunset Boulevard.* Day after day, Diamond and Wilder sat and tried to prime their pumps. They were drained. They were beaten. Some days, remembers Diamond bitterly, the phone would never ring. Some days they stared glumly at one another in a deathly silence. Wilder did not stalk about the room with a cane in his hand. He sat. He did not coffee-house. He did not crack wise. He did not invent "meet-cutes." He was literally devastated. He was unable to eat and to sleep. He was smoking five packs of cigarettes a day. He was losing weight.

One afternoon, Ernest Lehman, who was on the Goldwyn lot to

discuss a prospective movie, wandered up to Billy's office to say hello. He saw Diamond and Wilder sitting like two waxen figures.

"How are you?" he asked.

Billy sighed. "We feel like parents who have given birth to a mongoloid child," he replied. "Now we keep asking ourselves—*do we dare screw again?*"

It was the first joke he had made in weeks. It was a sign that he was slowly returning to mental health. He now decided to glory in his failure. In Hollywood, one boasted and bragged of success. Wilder began reveling in failure. Richard Lemon, who wrote a long personality piece about him for the *Saturday Evening Post,* said it was the first time a Hollywood celebrity achieved "eminence by catastrophe." This strategy of publicity is unique. I know no other movie celebrity who has cared to follow this public relations technique.

Wilder finally cranked up his machinery and started another picture. He was unrepentant. He would not, he could not, make lovable pictures. His next film focused on the greediness of an ex-wife and the knavery of a crooked lawyer, whose brother-in-law, a decent fellow, is persuaded to get involved in an insurance fraud in order to get back the tramp he still loves. *The Fortune Cookie* was as unremittingly vicious a satire of American sleaziness as *Kiss Me Stupid.* And Walter Matthau performed admirably as Gingrich, the lawyer. He won his first Academy Award. Lemmon impersonated the litigant in magnificent fashion. Cliff Osmond played a private investigator in what I thought was one of the exquisite supporting performances of the year. It was a gorgeous film, an amusing film, a study of good and evil in bold strokes. It was neither a critical nor a public success. On the other hand, Wilder's brains were not bashed in. It was like the man who has spent the day at Santa Anita race track and, upon being asked how he made out, replied, "I had a good day. I broke even."

Wilder had broken even.

Then came his most heartbreaking experience—the Sherlock Holmes movie. *The Private Life of Sherlock Holmes* is Billy's most personal film, his most romantic visually and his most romantic thematially. A lifelong admirer of the adventures of the man in the deerstalker cap, the violin player, the cocaine addict, the intellectual, Wilder became obsessed with the theme when he was writing

*Seven Year Itch* with Axelrod. They talked often about famous crimes and criminals of the Victorian and Edwardian period. When they were not composing "meet-cutes," they were figuring out the Jack-the-Ripper slayings or Wilder was telling gossip about Maria Vetsera and the Crown Prince at Mayerling. They told and retold their favorite Sherlock Holmes solutions. They talked of, perhaps, writing a musical comedy about Holmes. Wilder, in 1955, purchased the rights from the Doyle estate to use the characters of Holmes, Watson, Moriarty, Mycroft Holmes, and so on, in a musical play. Axelrod, by now, was otherwise involved. Billy attempted to collaborate with Loewe and Lerner and Moss Hart—the same team which had created *My Fair Lady.* They were unable to resolve the problems and Wilder let his option lapse for a decade—but his mind returned now and again to the character of Sherlock Holmes. In 1963—though he was now well into the lamentable years of being critically insulted and morally injured—Wilder was granted a temporary remission financially by the gods. *Irma La Douce* was a fantastic world-wide smash. The Mirisch Brothers were rich. United Artists, which distributed their films, regarded Wilder as Mr. Wonderful—though Kael, Sarris, Gill, and Alpert loathed him as an immoral beast, for glamorizing pimps and prostitutes.

Wilder himself was waxing fat with money, and you know how uneasy money made this man get. When he had made his first deal with the Mirisches back in 1957 for *Love in the Afternoon,* he made an agreement in which he received a fee of $250,000 for directing a film, a fee of $100,000 for writing a film, and a ten percent share of the gross profits. He also had complete control over the content of his pictures—the casting, the story, the final cut. He had earned close to $3,000,000 on *Irma La Douce.* Therefore when he proposed a Technicolor musical film about Sherlock Holmes and Dr. Watson, everybody said yes. With a score by Lerner and Loewe. With Peter Sellers as Dr. Watson and Peter O'Toole as Holmes. With a screenplay by I.A.L. Diamond and Billy Wilder. It was the era of the road show musical. *The Sound of Music* was a smasheroo on a two-a-day policy. All the studios were making three- and four-hour musical films. That was what the public wanted, wasn't it?

Well, we know what happened to Peter Sellers, don't we? He wouldn't touch Billy Wilder with a ten-foot pole, not after the way that horrible man ordered him about on the set of *Kiss Me Stupid.*

(Or, as Billy Wilder remarked, when he was asked if he could ever make a film similar to *Rosemary's Baby,* made by the short-statured Roman Polanski: "I wouldn't touch it with a five-foot Pole.")

And Billy couldn't get Peter O'Toole on loan from Sam Spiegel, who had him under contract. You would think Spiegel would have been eternally grateful to Wilder, wouldn't you? After that generous gift of the story for *Tales of Manhattan?* Well, Spiegel apparently belonged to the what-have-you-done-for-me-lately school of gratitude. Wilder hadn't done anything for him lately.

Furthermore, Iz and Billy were not able to build a structure for Sherlock Holmes. They talked and talked and wrote and wrote but naught availed them. They abandoned Sherlock Holmes and went on to Dean Martin and the Adventure of the Hooker Who Changes Places With a Wife. Well, our friends, who you may remember were wondering whether they should ever engage in literary concupiscence again, decided to go to bed once more with Sherlock Holmes. That was in March 1966. The Mirisches had a new option on the Holmes character from the Holmes estate.

When Billy Wilder saw Sherlock Holmes in his mind's eye he saw a character who was almost a mirror reflection of . . . Wilder himself. His intention was to probe the detective's psychology and motivations. He intended to delineate a Holmes who was at once cerebral and passionate; a man with a compulsion to work; a man with a cynical view of the world and human nature, aware of the depravity of the soul and the dark side of life, of murder and deception; a man increasingly prone to boredom and mental fatigue, seeking escape in music and drugs; a man with an ambivalent attitude toward women—attracted to them yet careful to detach himself from them—his most powerful desire having been for that clever and egotistic career lady, Irene Adler, "the most wicked woman in Europe." If we were to substitute an addiction to athletic sports for cocaine, and a predilection for compulsive shopping for violin playing, we would have almost a portrait of Billy Wilder in Sherlock Holmes. In the original planning, Wilder wanted, as he once told me, to show a lonely and troubled side in Holmes. There certainly was one in Wilder. But the fictional hero and the real one disguised their loneliness.

Diamond and Wilder labored strenuously over the screenplay. It resisted them. Once more, they were defeated. Wilder thought now that Iz was the wrong collaborator. Iz went to Universal to write the movie version of *Sweet Charity* for Shirley MacLaine. Wilder started writing Sherlock Holmes with Harry Kurnitz, with whom he had worked so beautifully on *Witness for the Prosecution*. Kurnitz was ideal. He was also a devout Baker Street Irregular, another devotee of the Holmes canon, an anglophile to boot, and wrote amusing mystery novels under the pseudonym of Marco Page. Kurnitz and Wilder churned around in the world of London fogs and hansom cabs. Kurnitz threw in the calabash after five months. The Sherlock Holmes obsession now had Wilder completely in its grip. He could not let it go. The years were passing. He had not started a film since October 1965! His longest hiatus. Desperate, Wilder betook himself to London and started working with a new collaborator, his first British coauthor, the playwright John Mortimer. It did not go. Billy returned to Hollywood. He went to his office every day. He would write the screenplay alone. He racked his brains. He smoked. He paced. He thought and breathed and ate Sherlock Holmes. He could not escape even through shopping or watching football games on television. Sometimes, on Sunday, Barbara and Iz Diamond would come over to the house and Iz would watch football with him. Iz was now finishing up *Cactus Flower* for Goldie Hawn at Columbia. During one of these football games, Billy jumped up and said he had an idea for the Sherlock Holmes film. He would use the Loch Ness monster. What if the monster were really an experimental submarine the British Royal Navy were working on in, say, 1905 up in Scotland? What if the German spies were trying to learn its secret? What if Sherlock Holmes solved the mystery? "Would you like to come back and work on it again, Iz?"

Iz came back and worked on it again. They completed it, finally. It was the longest screenplay Billy ever wrote—260 pages. The film, which he eventually made with Robert Stephens as Holmes, and Richard Attenborough as Dr. Watson, ran for three hours and twenty minutes. It was intended as an opulent road show film, with an intermission after one hour and fifty minutes. Then, after he had finished this $10,000,000 picture, the most expensive he'd ever shot, the public taste veered. A succession of expensive musical films had flopped—*Star, Paint Your Wagon, Hello, Dolly,* among others. United Artists refused to release the full-length version of *The Private Life of Sherlock Holmes*. Billy had the right of final cut, but if he did not cut his movie down to a more compact length, it would never be released. Finally, after eating his heart out, he trimmed the film he loved so much. He cut it down to two hours and twenty minutes. Even in this truncated form, it was exhibited for only a few weeks in this country and then abruptly withdrawn. Few persons have seen the *The Private Life of Sherlock Holmes,* which, even in its chopped up version, is a fascinating movie. But the gods had turned against Billy Wilder. He was to learn humility and frustration. His stars would die or get heart attacks. His films would be demolished by critics or cutter's shears. He had to be taught the use of adversity. He did not think they were sweet.

Four years of his life had been invested in Sherlock Holmes and he had nothing to show for it, not even an appreciative review by Joan Didion.

*The Private Life of Sherlock Holmes* was the worst debacle of his career; in one sense, it was a more bitter defeat than his setbacks with *Ace in the Hole* and *Kiss Me Stupid.* He had been compelled to seriously mangle one of the loveliest films he had ever created. His pride was humbled. He had already gone through a morbid depression over *Kiss Me Stupid.* This time he did not flee to Europe. He did not think of suicide now. He knew he had to bear the hard times. He did not lose faith in himself and in his talent. It was the nature of his work, of the work of the screenwriter and the director, that one had to be circumscribed by a market. You could not simply make a movie out of your own creative urges—the way Renoir or Ingres had painted masterpieces in their old age. In the 1970's, a film, even a simple film, would cost $3,000,000. He tried to understand what had happened to the movie industry and to himself and it was difficult because he had as much to say as he had ever had, and he had matured emotionally and his talent was there. Clay Felker, editor of *New York* magazine, called him in 1975 and asked him if he would sit for a frank interview and he said he would. He had come to know Felker when Pamela Tiffin, then Mrs. Felker, had played the ingenue in *One, Two, Three.* And so, reporter Jon Bradshaw came out to Hollywood in September and Wilder delivered himself of many feelings and observations which were honest and brave and stunned most people in Hollywood, who prefer to lurk in the shadows when things are going badly. At their first meeting in his office at Universal, Wilder saw what he regarded as a look of surprise on Bradshaw's face because he was striding about exuberantly.

"What did you expect to find when you came out here?" Wilder cried. "A broken down director? A wizened myopic boob in his dotage? I guess you thought you'd find me playing with my old Oscars?

In a wheelchair maybe? Poor old Billy Wilder. The great director. Christ, you should see him now. A wreck. A ruin . . . Is that what they told you? Well, they told you wrong. I'm not just functioning in the Motion Picture Relief Home. I feel just as confident and virile as I did 30 years ago . . . I can still hit home runs . . ."

Attempting to unriddle what was happening, he unburdened himself in a way that few persons had ever done in the movie industry. "I'm going through a dry spell . . . a slump . . . You can't figure it . . . I did not suddenly become an idiot. I did not suddenly unlearn my craft . . . Occasionally the vineyards produce a bad vintage . . . But there will always be another harvest. I am the youngest of my generation of directors . . . Ford, Stevens, Hawks, Wyler, Cukor and Hitchcock. My immediate contemporaries are Zinneman, Manciewicz and Huston. They had their dry spells too, y'know. They had slumps. They had bad seasons . . ."

He knew that the historical period through which we are living has affected the industry. "It's a bitch to find a project these days that would both interest me and have a chance in today's market . . . Today we are dealing with an audience that is primarily under 25 and divorced from any literary tradition. They prefer mindless violence to solid plotting; four-letter words to intelligent dialogue; pectoral development to character development. Nobody *listens* anymore. They just sit there, y'know, waiting to be assaulted by a series of shocks and sensations . . .

"It is a difficult time. Ernst Lubitsch, who could do more with a closed door than most of today's directors can do with an open fly, would have had big problems in this market . . ."

Had God made him a novelist or a painter, he could have expressed his dreams and his obsessions to a small audience of thousands or hundreds or even two dozen. As a film maker he could not exist without a mass audience. It was a condition he had always had to live with and until 1964 he had been able to somehow get what he wanted to say on the screen and most of his films had made money, even large amounts of money, and now he had to wonder if he could find a way to still get his pictures made.

*Sherlock Holmes* is a significant chapter in the autobiography of Billy Wilder. In it, for the first time on a serious, even sentimental, level, there is a deep feeling of love and mutual admiration between the cold, cerebral, witty protagonist and a beautiful lady, whose name is Fraulein von Hoffmanstal and who is a German spy. She is an intelligent and crafty lady who is smarter than Sherlock Holmes. She is also a feminine person. She is a woman. She is a person. She is like the best of the woman characters that Wilder was able to write—like Ninotchka most of all. In the course of the episode with Fraulein von Hoffmanstal, Wilder showed us the hero feeling sensuality, tenderness, and respect for a woman of competence and brains. The scenes with her are in lovely pastel-tinged tones. She carries a pink parasol. She has used it to transmit, by Morse code, messages to her spies. After Holmes has finally unriddled the plot and trapped her, he secures her release and he last sees her from an upstairs window as she is riding away in an open carriage; she turns around, and their eyes meet, and she signals to him by opening and closing her parasol a message in code. It is "I love you."

Billy Wilder had finally, after a lifetime of being bedeviled by the riddle of women, mastered the Morse code of the feminine sex. And they were signaling "Love" after all.

Wilder, reminiscing about the film, once told me it made him sad. "I am saddened by so much we had to take out. For instance, there was a flashback to Sherlock Holmes when he was a student at Oxford. He falls in love with a young girl. When he discovers she is a prostitute, he takes this hard, and it makes him always suspicious of women. And yet, I wondered, if this wasn't an excuse he gives himself because he fears to be entrapped by a woman. You see the theme of it is that a man in his profession must be pure reason. He can't let himself be muddled by emotions. And this theme was carried out in the five episodes and many flashbacks of the uncut version. And after the changes—ah, the reasons why I wanted to make this picture so much, they are hardly to be seen after the cuts. What use is it to think about that? It is too late now. I do not like to get into this kind of introspection, yet this is one picture I still can't get out of my system. . . . Perhaps enough of it remains. I hope so. In England it was popular. I wanted to show Holmes as vulnerable, as human. He falls into an emotional dither over a woman and so his mind does not function as well; and actually, you see, in my picture, he does *not* solve the mystery. No, he is deceived. Sherlock Holmes has failed to be Sherlock Holmes precisely because he has fallen in love, and yet he is a better human being than he was ever before."

In the autumn of 1975, through the kindness of Jennings Lang, an old friend and an executive vice-president at Universal, I was able to view, within a time span of two weeks, every film which Wilder had directed and most of the films he had written for other directors. When you see the body of a man's films in this way, you become conscious of certain recurring themes, such as the masquerade. The most intriguing theme, and the one which is of the deepest personal concern to Billy Wilder, is this: what is the true nature of a woman? Why are "hookers" or "whores" the most interesting women in a film? What is a "good woman" and what is a "whore?" These questions agitate him. He is drawn to stories in which these themes and their variations can be performed. They seize his imagination. They capture him. Sometimes there is only the slut, like Jan Sterling in *Ace in the Hole.* Sometimes the slut is opposed to the "decent" woman, like Dietrich vs. Jean Arthur, like Kim Novak vs. Felicia Farr in *Kiss Me Stupid.* But Wilder's "sluts" are invariably good human beings. There are reasons why they engage in sex for cash or presents. It does not change the nature of their essential virtue or their capacity to give honest love. This is hard for Wilder to accept. He seems to be fighting a struggle with himself in film after film. He seems to sometimes suspect that there is a slut crying to get out of every respectable woman's soul, and a respectable woman inside every whore's epidermis.

Why, I kept wondering, was he so absorbed in the riddle of the whore?

*Kiss Me Stupid* expressed and resolved the great dilemma of his imagination. This eluded most of those who hated the film. (Though it is possible that it was this peculiar resolution which may have unwittingly disturbed them.) The film showed us a whore who fantasizes playing a wife for a day and a night—and a wife who fantasizes playing the town whore. There is a good moment when Kim Novak, the town slut, returns to her trailer to find Mrs. Spooner (Felicia Farr), in a nightgown. The women share their experiences with each other. Kim says how good it was to put on an apron and make waffles and coffee for Orville Spooner. And Mrs. Spooner says, a twinkle in the eye, "Well, it was fun being a hooker for one night." She hands over the $500 fee which Dean Martin—who played Dean Martin, a big-time singing star whom two small-town amateur songwriters hope to ensnare into performing their songs—has left in a glass for her services.

Novak looks at the money and says, "I'll swap you for the wedding ring."

Wilder had arrived at a sort of new acceptance in *Kiss Me Stupid* and *The Private Life of Sherlock Holmes.* Did this not reflect the happiness of his life with Audrey? I think so. As one considers the entire body of Wilder's work, as a whole, as an expression of his ruling obsessions, one sees him carefully threading his way through the labyrinthine maze of the Eternal Woman. His films are studies in the varieties of women. A man's yearning for a woman after whom he lusts or whom he loves is counterpointed against his equal and powerful compulsion to do his work, the masculine hunter in the primitive jungles bringing food for the mate. Freud had said, towards the end of his life, that he still did not know what women wanted. And this is one of the riddles of every man's existence, being confounded by a woman's soul and body and mystery from the hour of his birth and his first taste of mother's milk. The Wilder complication was the dilemma of the whore. The presence of woman in one or another variety of independent, self-sufficient role was a dilemma. In *A Foreign Affair,* the "good" woman was posed against the "bad." In *Lost Weekend* the "good" woman was posed against a compulsion. In *Double Indemnity,* the woman is venal, she is evil, she is the corrupter, playing her classical role as the devil's assistant, the temptress, as she does in *Ace in the Hole*—though in both these films the hero is either the willing partner or the leader in the evil. *Sunset Boulevard* was the turning point in Wilder's evolution: the force of the woman, a real woman, is defeated by the "bad" woman, but she is not really "bad"; she symbolizes, as I believe, Wilder's own idea of the movies and how they almost kill him. Audrey Hepburn twice played innocent girls who studied to be sophisticated independent women so they could manifest their true beings to the men they loved. And Shirley MacLaine on two occasions, and Marilyn Monroe on two occasions, also impersonated women who were beyond any simple labels marked "good" and "bad." They were individual persons. Sometimes they were forced to play a charade which a man compelled them to play and sometimes they won their freedom to be who they were. The answer Wilder learned to the riddle of women was that it did not consist in attempting to decipher her inscrutable mysteries, since these varied from one woman to another, *but in looking into oneself.*

In asking himself, "What do *I* want from a woman? What do *I* want from this woman? How can *I* be of service to this woman? What can *I* give to this particular woman whom I love?" When a man once looked into himself and dedicated himself to pleasing a woman he loved, as Billy had come to do with his Audrey, suddenly the old mystery of Woman with the capital W, woman as unscrewable and inscrutable, vanished, and you were face to face with your own mystery as a man, which was even more frustrating because you discovered how little you knew about yourself, and that was the resolution of *The Private Life of Sherlock Holmes.* You were given the choice of being a worse detective—and a better person—or a splendid detective and a crippled human being. In the end, Holmes gets Ilse von Hoffmanstal her freedom. He gets his brother to release her and he receives a final and beautiful letter from her as she is about to be executed as a spy in Japan.

*Avanti,* Wilder's next film, was, like *Sherlock Holmes,* filmed in color, romantic color. Billy was the last of the great American directors to resist color. He had made *Seven Year Itch* in color because Monroe's contract demanded it of Twentieth Century-Fox. Except for *Irma,* he was still working in black and white. *Some Like It Hot, The Apartment, One, Two, Three, Kiss Me Stupid, Fortune Cookie*—all were made in black and white. I think it was while he was filming *Holmes* that Wilder became enamored of color. *Avanti* is bathed in the same romantic pastel shades as *Holmes*—the lemon yellows and aquamarines and turquoises and pinks. Pamela Piggott of *Avanti* is partial to pink negligees and romantic music. On this one, Billy also had collaborator agonies. Iz Diamond was under contract to Columbia. He was writing *40 Carats.* Wilder tried to collaborate with Julie Epstein of the famous Epstein brothers, and Norman Krasna, and finally the Italian writer Luciano Vincenzoni, who had written *Seduced and Abandoned* and *Divorce Italian Style.*

He could not fabricate a screenplay with any of them and ultimately Iz Diamond came back and they wrote the screenplay. The situation was this: a rich old American has been killed in a car accident on Ischia. His son, Jack Lemmon, a stiff, detached, somewhat prissy, gentleman, goes to the Italian island to bring back the body. He learns that for ten years his father has been summering here with a British lady. The lady's daughter, Pamela, played by Juliet Mills, has come to the island to give her mama a proper burial. Jack and Juliet meet and fall in love and play once more the idyll of their parents.

There was one amusing Wilder touch here, almost like a little signature in a corner of a canvas. You remember that in *Bluebeard's Eighth Wife,* Cooper and Colbert meet cute in a haberdashery—he wants pajama tops and she wants pajama bottoms? In *Avanti*, there is a scene in which we see the lovers in bed in the morning: Juliet is wearing the pajama tops—and Jack is wearing the pajama bottoms.

*The Front Page*, a 1975 remake of the old Hecht-MacArthur comedy, was not a story which struck Wilder's ruling obsessions. For this was a love/hate story between two men and the woman is quite peripheral. Wilder knew these aspects of life and he was willing to explore them as he had done in *Double Indemnity* but it would only strike fire in his hands if there was also a powerful woman present. There was no Barbara Stanwyck present in *The Front Page*. Wilder tried to make one out of Molly Molloy, the prostitute who befriends the anarchist. She also was a peripheral character in the original play. Wilder cast Carol Burnett in the role. He was driven by his need to establish an important woman, preferably a hooker, to make her role larger and thus, as several critics noted, an unbalance was created.

I now knew that Wilder was, deep in his subconscious, compelled to play with this theme. I still did not know why. What made him turn the question over and over and over? What drove him to make Molly Molloy an important character in *The Front Page*? Why was he forever seething with these problems of money and love, and money and sex, and money and women? I wanted to know why. Why, for instance, was he intrigued by the woman who disdained prostitution? I saw an example on the set of *The Front Page*. Lemmon had announced to Matthau that he's quitting the paper to get married. "Ah," says Matthau, "another one of your sluts—like that hostess at the Hotsy Totsy Club?"

LEMMON
You're not even close. This is a very classy dame—Philadelphia—studied to be a concert pianist . . . actually she's a widow. Her husband cracked up in a brand-new Packard—only had eighteen miles on it . . . so now to support herself she's playing the organ at the Balaban and Katz Theater . . .

Wilder asked for a second take and a third take. Then he said, "Jack, you are speaking too apologetically. Don't apologize for her. Get it up, *up, up.* You are proud of her. She is supporting herself. Her husband was killed in an accident. You are speaking all in her

favor. She could be a chippie—or a hooker. Instead she gets a job.
She plays the organ in a movie house. 'How about that for guts?' is
what you're telling Walter. She's a real dame. You're proud of her—
proud of her."

*She's a real dame.* What is the nature of a "real" dame? What is
the nature of an "unreal" dame? Can you ever be sure with a woman—with any woman—that, if she isn't a prostitute, she may be one
anyway, or that if she is, there lurks within her the "guts" of an
honest woman? And is any woman ever honest?

And how do you ever know? How the hell do you ever know?
Does she take money? Is that the answer? One might subtitle *Avanti!* the consciousness-raising of Wendell Armbuster IV. It is the
morning after the first night of love. Pamela and Wendell are lying
abed in divided pajamas. There is breakfast on small tables bedside.
Jack Lemmon broods about going home. Pamela has endeared herself to him. He wants to do something for her, give her something.
She won't accept any presents. He nervously paces the room. Now
there ensues the following exchange:

WENDELL

Pamela, tell me—my father and your mother—in all those years—
didn't he ever give her any—uh—I mean, just have helped her out
from time to time—financially—

PAMELA

You want to know whether my mother was a kept woman?

WENDELL

Well, after all—a man likes to show his gratitude—maybe an occasional present—

PAMELA

Oh yes. Every Christmas he would send her a dozen long-stemmed
roses. To the Savoy Hotel.

WENDELL

Oh, then your mother was well-to-do.

PAMELA

No. She was making fifteen pounds a week, and tips.

WENDELL

On fifteen pounds a week, she was living at the Savoy?

PAMELA

She wasn't living there. She was working there. As a manicurist.

WENDELL

Did my father know that?

PAMELA *(shakes her head)*

She didn't want him to know.

WENDELL

Why not?

PAMELA

I told you the first day. She loved him. She didn't want any tips.

*Wendell looks at her, affected by this new bit of information. The phone rings in the living room. He does not react. Another ring.*

# 23

# THE END OF
# THE SEARCH

What you have read up to now I had written by the end of 1975 in a long and formless first draft, almost a thousand pages, and still I was not satisfied that I had grasped the source of Wilder's ruling obsessions. There had to be—there ought to be—some crucial event, some series of occurrences, perhaps, which had been so traumatic in nature that they or it had engendered this powerful thrust of his imagination. I could not find it. Perhaps I was trying to force a man into the shape of a jigsaw puzzle or a Byzantine mosaic and looking for missing pieces—when there were no pieces, missing or otherwise, when there was just the disorganized chaos of life as it is lived. The idea that somewhere, someplace, the biographer will find a sled trademarked Rosebud to explain the psyche of his subjects, haunts every biographer. You may tell yourself that a man is the end result of many, many factors, social and genetic, the accidents of his unique experiences . . .  and yet . . . and yet . . .

I remembered the last conversation with Vicki Wilder Settember as we stood outside her house. She had said, "I hope you will explain him to me in your book. I love him but I don't understand him. Never did. Wonder what made him the way he is?"

There was a note typed on an index card after a meeting with Billy. "I am saddened by the time it took to make it [ *Private Life of*

*Sherlock Holmes* ] And what was left out . . a flashback . . . Oxford . . . Holmes falls in love with a girl who turns out to be a prostitute . . ."

While I was writing the second draft of this book—what you are reading is the fourth, by the way—I finally was able to secure an interview with Shirley MacLaine. She had been traveling a great deal and writing her own books and living her own life in New York. At last, early in 1976, we were able to talk. We had the interview on the phone. MacLaine is an articulate person with strong ideas. Many of them I don't hold with. But it was during, and after, our conversation that my mind knew where to look for the missing piece, the significant stone for the mosaic, my own Rosebud . . .

"I think he is a sensitive person," she said, "one of the most sensitive and vulnerable people I've ever known in my life, and that is why this exterior is necessary to him—protection. And, oh, his brilliance, and he is brilliant on every level. He has as much emotional brilliance as he has intellectual brilliance. He has more talent in his little finger than anybody I've ever worked with [has] in their whole body. I had never studied acting (at a school) and I learned more from Billy Wilder than anybody else in the business."

It was when I asked her whether he had ever influenced her tastes in art, travel, clothes, food, as he had influenced other stars whom he had directed, notably William Holden and Jack Lemmon, she began to talk about her relations with Billy and about what she deduced to be his psychology of women.

"No, he didn't, he really didn't. You see, he didn't get involved personally with me at all, except for reminding me that he was very married. I did want to be his friend and learn from him but you have to have some personal contact with a man in order for your ideas about paintings or food to be affected. So I had very little personal contact when he said that to me, that he was very happily married. I did not understand why, but his relationship with women stars are different from his relationship with men stars."

Was it, I wondered, that he might have felt himself vulnerable to her as a woman, and therefore avoided any intimacies lest they be misconstrued and have an adverse effect on his authority as a director?

"Well, I don't know if it was ever sexual with anybody—woman star, that is. It certainly wasn't with me. I just felt that I was being held at arm's length in the social and personal area. He put me off either by his wit, or by his caustic critical humor, or by this way he has of standing back and cocking his head and looking at you as if you were a specimen of—of human nature.

"Billy, in directing, he doesn't usually give you gestures, line readings, ideas, as much as he tells you what is wrong with the ones that you've got. He operates more like an editor, as a judge. To watch him work with Jack [Lemmon] was an entirely different thing than to watch his work with me. I used to stay afterwards, after a scene, or come in when I wasn't called, just to watch him work with Jack. He has this intellectual and emotional and appreciative love affair going with Jack. I had the feeling—well, to him Jack was the master of communicating comedy. Jack would slowly feel his way the first few takes, and Billy would help him improve on it. He gave him much time. Well, he didn't spend time with me. He was not as much in love with my potential in a scene as he was with Jack's. He would build on Jack's because he adored what he was doing in the first place. With me, it was more realistic. He seemed less involved with me. He would watch what I was doing, inform me what was wrong, and then when I cut out what he didn't like, he would print it. With Jack he loved it all, from the beginning, from take one, and he improved on it.

"That's why you see Jack so busy, in movement, in most of Billy's pictures. He has the scintillating treble clef in them. And ultimately why I am more simple in Billy's pictures than I am in my other films.

"The fact that he is a male chauvinist pig we take for granted."

"Do you mean that seriously?" I asked Ms. MacLaine.

"Oh yes, he is, really he is, oh sure," she replied. "Remember this man, Doane Harrison, that was on the set with him all the time? Doane was there to tell him at the end of every day whether his heart had or had not been flopped over that day—because Billy knew his cynicism would get in the way of his feelings. He is a very feeling person, I believe, under it all, that cynicism—well, he is the most cynical man ever to hit Hollywood, you know; it is unparalleled, his cynicism, especially with women.

"Still you think of it, Billy's finest pictures have a central focal character who is a female, genuine strong sincere, around whom everything else happens. Wasn't that the structural setup of both

*Apartment* and *Irma*? And *Some Like It Hot*, and *Sunset* and *Double Indemnity* and *Major and the Minor* and *Witness for the Prosecution*?

"In my opinion, his pictures that really worked have this central female character and the men around her.

"Now in his recent pictures, *Kiss Me Stupid, Fortune Cookie,* they didn't work in my opinion because they lacked a woman at the center, the core. I believe Doane kept Billy in balance, reminding him that he needed heart. When Doane got sick, he had nobody there to remind him and when Doane died that was the end of it.

"And this is the crux of Billy Wilder's career—his male chauvinism. I think this is a real valid analysis of what is wrong with most of our pictures today. The men don't know where the women belong. They don't understand who women are. The only women they understand in womendom are complaining housewives, helpmate housewives, and prostitutes. All the nuances in between—my God, men are completely confused.

"I am not saying this because it is fashionable and I am a woman. I am saying this because, culturally speaking, this attitude has a large effect on art in our society. You have to be courageous enough to grapple with identities when you're making any picture. And identities are made up of men and women and Billy was infinitely more certain of what the identities of the male characters are than the female, but life is composed of both.

"His tendency to a cynical, intelligent, ironical twist on life is his highest priority, but it is tempered in his films when he had those women characters in the heart of it. If he didn't have them he was in trouble. Jan Sterling was just a peripheral character in *Ace in the Hole*, as Felicia Farr and Kim Novak were in *Kiss Me Stupid,* or like many of his other women, they were not the central point on which the action revolves, as Marilyn was in *Some Like It Hot* or Irma was or like Fran Kubelik was. The women in *Kiss Me Stupid* were not very nice persons either. That horrible scene at the end, you know, in the trailer, where he leaves the money."

As the reader knows I did not agree with MacLaine's evaluation of the later films. I said that Dean Martin, when leaving the $500 tip, did not know that the lady in the trailer was a housewife. He thought she was a hooker.

MacLaine did not think that changed it. "It doesn't matter if it is done sideways. The point is that this was how Billy Wilder viewed the relationship and that is my point. He had MacMurray leave Fran a hundred for Christmas. You know, now that I think of it, sort it all out, somewhere under it all, it seems like he feels the only attractive women are the whores. Like he has to make whores out of us all. Remember he was one himself, Maurice; somewhere under it all he is identifying with such women because he was in the same business himself, giving a little love for a little money."

We talked about the interesting gigolo characters who recurred in the Wilder *oeuvre*—Boyer in *Hold Back the Dawn,* Douglas in *Ninotchka,* Holden in *Sunset Boulevard.*

"Yeah, yeah," she said, "and how about Jack? Isn't that what Jack Lemmon was in *The Apartment,* in a way? Selling out. And isn't that what Jack's doing in *Fortune Cookie*?

"It's fascinating when you start thinking of it but that's a conflict in Billy's values. He has never worked it out, this conflict about love and money. I think others have worked out their problems with money." She thought we all had this problem in an acquisitive society like the American society. She suggested this was why she had begun to explore alternative means of living. She said that a few years ago she said to Billy, "I can get you into Red China if you want to go there. Why don't you do a picture there? Even a comedy about the way they live. I can get you in. You really should go there."

And, she recalled, he shrugged his shoulders and quipped: "When I travel, I like to have hot and cold running carpets."

Perhaps it was again his holding her at arm's length, as if resisting any closeness, not just closeness to her as an intriguingly exciting woman but as his intellectual equal. That was what irked her. He could argue with her. He could scorn the Marxian interpretation of life and that degrading effect of the "cash nexus" between human beings in bourgeois society which Marx and Engels had described, he could do all that, but to be, as it were, patronized and joked at— this was upsetting. She tries to get him into focus and it is troubling to her, because she admires him so much. She wants him to be in her camp. She doesn't understand how he can be so—so smug?

"And so," she went on, "he has this magnificent apartment and his works of art around him and I guess hot and cold running carpets and he has this thing about money which some of us have grown out of, or resolved in ways. Billy is lagging behind. Maybe he correlates money with success—power.

"Imagine having to resort either to a pimp or a whore as representative of men and women. Well, isn't that something he is trying to work out in his art? We all do that in our art, trying to solve what is personally conflicting in us. Maybe you will track it back to his childhood; yes, maybe you will find it there. My God, such a great man Billy Wilder is, such a strange man—and these conflicts—Yeah, maybe you'll find it there—in Berlin, in Vienna—"

And it was, after all, to be found in Vienna. And I had had it under my nose all the time, the clues being scattered through many notes, remarks dropped in conversation with Billy, hints given by his brother W. Lee Wilder, and friends from Berlin and Vienna. Some of the ground I had to reconnoiter once again.

Billy had told me how the Viennese whores had fascinated him and how he watched them, as boys of his age did, from the distance, knowing that to be with them was, finally, to have the great erotic mysteries of life unveiled. But, he said, he did not have the money to go to them. He had to go with girls he knew at school or encountered at the dance halls. He had to go with girls who were as innocent and frightened of sex as he was. He had learned how to survive in the streets. He had endured the deprivations and hunger of the war. He had endured the insecurities of life after the war. He had survived. He had grown a protective skin around his heart. He was a tough guy by the time he was sixteen years old. But the guy who talked tough and strutted, hands in his pockets, was also a sensitive lad who loved poetry and dreamed of a romantic understanding with one whom he would love eternally. It is difficult for persons like Shirley MacLaine—reared in Richmond, Virginia, maturing into a sophisticated, independent woman in a society in which the prostitute has lived a degraded existence—to understand how, aside from any personal traumatic factors in his youth, Billy Wilder could be obsessed by the whore. It is hard for an American to get into the historical frame of mind in which he can imagine the sensations one experienced in the ancient Vienna red-light district. Throughout Europe, especially in the great cities—Amsterdam, Rotterdam, Hamburg, London, Berlin, Paris, and Vienna—the whore was openly and realistically accepted as necessary. Whores were often granted legal recognition and were, in some places, licensed and supervised by the police, and given medical examinations as precautions against venereal diseases. There were quasi-legal "red light" districts in these cities. The "red light" was not a metaphorical phrase.

There were real red lights which were turned on when the whore was free. One saw the lights. One knew what the women were doing in these rooms. And that was what boys did in Vienna often. If they could get the money, they went to a whore. If they were poor, they could stand in the streets leading off from the Kaerntnerstrasse, in Vienna, and the Kaerntnerstrasse itself, and paint glorious erotic pictures in the mind.

It is important, first, in understanding Billy's unriddling of the whore, to know that she was not the immoral specter of disease she has been in American life. She has always been there in her European milieu and in her quarter, flaunting her wares, accepted as part of life. Americans coming to Paris and London the first time are embarrassed by the whores roaming nonchalantly everywhere. The old red-light districts of Billy's youth still exist in Amsterdam's street-of-the-windows near Central Station or in Hamburg's Herbertstrasse, a street of old buildings and old whores. You see and smell the mystery of women's flesh on public display. Billy's senses were highly stimulated. His imagination ran wild. The writings of Arthur Schnitzler, drenched in sex, stirred up libidinal frenzy.

But why a persistent obsession? Something happened to him during his freshman year at the University of Vienna. I have reconstructed the episode, from the clues scattered through the memories of old friends of Billy's and from the internal evidence of his films. W. Lee remembers an early love and gave a few details, as did Walter Reisch. Both of them said that only Billy knew the whole story. He would not remember. He has a fine amnesia. It works on a conscious level. The painful memories, however, insinuate themselves into the dreams he makes when he writes the screenplays and directs films.

The girl's name was Ilse. The same name as the enchanting spy—German, of course!—in *Sherlock Holmes*. She was blonde and blue-eyed and rather tall. She had long golden hair which she wore in plaited tresses bound around her large head. (It may be interesting to note that except for Ilse, all the women, including his wives, who played a significant role in his life, were dark-haired and dark-eyed.) Ilse was a saleslady in a phonograph and record shop in the First District. She was older than Billy. She was nineteen or twenty. Billy went to the shop to listen to the new imports from the United States. He did not have the money to buy all the records he wanted. He went to the shop to listen to the new records demonstrated on a gramophone, as they did in those days. He talked to Ilse about American jazz and popular music. He went walking with Ilse. He drank coffee *mit Schlag* with Ilse at the cafés. He held hands with Ilse in the parks and by the lakes. It was a lovely autumnal season that year in Vienna. He fell in love with Ilse. He wrote poems in which he declared his feelings for her. He went dancing with Ilse. He dreamed of making her his wife. There was no other girl now in his life. He showed her off, with pride, to his friends. Sometimes she would meet him at the college and his friends were quite taken with her.

Two friends, strolling along the Kaentnerstrasse, after midnight, when the whores came out in large numbers, were shocked to see that Billy's Ilse was soliciting. They went up close to make certain it was she. It was she. She had on rouge and lipstick. Decent girls didn't wear makeup, and she was smoking a cigarette and dangling a handbag and looking very desirable but *cheap*. One proposed that they go to her place but they did not do that. They told Billy what they had seen. He did not believe it. He fought with both of them. Then he went to her corner the next night. He did not see her. He saw her the second night. He confronted her. They had an angry exchange. She wept. She wanted to explain. She wanted him to love her. She loved him. He slapped her across the mouth. He called her a whore. He turned on her. He had experienced a betrayal so deep and so wounding that he was never to recover from it. It remained an unhealed wound. He had been shamed before his friends. These incidents had occurred just before the Christmas recess at school. During the holiday season, he remained alone in his room. He did not eat. He did not sleep. And, in January, *he did not return to college.*

It was this experience with Ilse which drove him into making a career as a reporter and confirmed him in his cynical philosophy. He could not trust a woman. He was always to be *en garde*. And, when he became for a long time, an *Eintänzer* at the Hotel Eden, playing the other side of the street as it were, exchanging compliments with women in return for their tips, he was again forced into the dilemma of money/love/lust/money/sex/men/women . . .

The shock effect of this experience reverberates throughout his life. In one sense, most of his films are an attempt to come to terms with this disillusionment. It was hard, because a shock event like this, coming at an age when one is so vulnerable, tends to narrow one's vision of other women. A narrowed vision—like a microscope—has the advantage of magnifying that small segment of the environment on which it is focused. But as with a microscope, all that lies outside the lens is unexamined. And so, throughout his films, from the very first films he wrote with Brackett, the ones in which Claudette Colbert is out to get money and a husband, and both in the same man, and the films he began to direct after Lubitsch and Leisen, the same motifs recur, over and over again.

The whores are not really whores, and that is the point of it, really, they are not really painted Jezebels selling vaginas to passing strangers, the drunken sailors, the fat war profiteers in Vienna and Berlin, they are not the hags and dregs whom Brecht described in *Threepenny Opera*, whom Grosz drew in his caricatures. The girls and the women who stroll through the Wilder films may or may not be technically whores, like Polly the Pistol and Irma La Douce, but whether it be Ginger Rogers putting on a little-girl act to get home to Iowa, or Anne Baxter, the French servant Mouche in that North African hotel, who sleeps with the Nazi officer to get her brother out of a concentration camp, they become whores, so to speak, because they do not meet a seventeen-year-old romantic boy's fantasy of a love which is true and pure and absolutely unfettered by questions of paying the rent, buying a train ticket, helping a relative in trouble, and other unsettling problems of everyday life like one's daily bread. The wound and the romantic fantasy both tormented Billy and lasted in him, in some hidden place in his character, all through his maturing years, in Berlin, in Paris, in Hollywood. They weathered, as such early experiences often do, all the later events of his life.

And yet, it is precisely this romantic fantasy and the unhealed wound of Ilse's seeming betrayal that generates the emotional energy, the violence, the bitterness, the sadness and the pity as well, in Billy Wilder's greatest films, and makes even his lesser pictures, like *The Emperor Waltz* (in which two dogs in love parody the love between Joan Fontaine and Bing Crosby) interesting and sometimes beautiful and sometimes disturbing—vaguely disturbing, anxiety-provoking, as if he were spewing out a black hatred of humanity.

A growth, an evolution in his vision can be seen, I think, from the films of the middle 1950s. It may have been the experience of directing Monroe in *Seven Year Itch*. She was blonde and somewhat similar physically, as well as in her air of remoteness and airiness, to Ilse. With Monroe, Billy became aware of how vulnerable such persons are, how weak and frightened they can be. It was hard to feel pity for Monroe because her self-centeredness and little acts of cruelty were so repelling, but he did feel it, and he continued to feel it, even through the terrible experience of making *Some Like It Hot* with her.

While coming to feel the sadness of the "whore," he also came, more and more, as his relationship with Audrey Wilder ripened into a unity of tastes and mutual affection, to know the felicities of a life together with a woman, his woman as he was her man.

It is evident that from the time he came to cowrite and create *The Apartment* he was working in himself toward what was for him a new reconciliation of these warring elements in his character. It was to be able to see women, more and more, as persons in their own right, as individuals, as human beings, as vulnerable human beings. It was as though he was trying to bring together what had formerly been separated in his mind—the woman of some strength and personality whom you put into the "whore" category, and the other kind, all pliant and sweet and moral and damn near boring you to death, and this was the "good woman" or "wife" or Olivia de Havilland in *Hold Back the Dawn* or Jean Arthur in *A Foreign Affair*.

And then, gradually, the two seem to melt into each other and become one, as they do in the two Shirley MacLaine films, for meeting MacLaine was an educational experience, as meeting Marilyn Monroe had been. In MacLaine were qualities of quickness of mind, sharpness of wit, intellect, strength, which were like Audrey Wilder's.

Billy had to change. He did. In the films he made after *Irma La Douce*, the films which are unappreciated and unhonored but which I am convinced will stand up and be loved years from now, he went on evolving these conceptions, freeing love from all thoughts of money and all stereotyped feminine poses. That is the meaning of *Avanti!* That is the meaning of Ilse von Hoffmanstal in *Sherlock Holmes*.

He had, finally, forgiven Ilse of Vienna, when he made this picture. He had at last exorcised his raging demon. The bat had made friends with the mouse.

Billy Wilder was at peace with himself.

# 24

# AFTERWORD

In September, 1976, I.A.L. Diamond and Billy Wilder began to write a new screenplay. It is about Fedora. Fedora is the central character of this movie.

Fedora is a woman.

# ACKNOWLEDGMENTS

This book is mainly the product of meetings and conversations with many persons. I am, first of all, most grateful to Billy Wilder for all the hours in which he has, with patient truculence, borne the burden of my company. Researching this book has been the most invigorating experience of my career. It stretched over a period of two years and eight months. Three of these months were spent on the set, or on location, while Wilder was directing a film. This daily immersion in the process of making a picture changed some ideas I had about the movies.

There have been two short books previously published about Wilder: *Billy Wilder* by Axel Madsen (Indiana University Press, 1969) and *The Bright Side of Billy Wilder, Primarily* by Tom Wood (Doubleday and Company, Garden City, N.Y. 1970). Three lengthy magazine essays about him have appeared: Lincoln Barnett's "The Happiest Couple in Hollywood" (*Life,* 1944), Richard Lemon's "Well, Nobody's Perfect . . ." (*Saturday Evening Post,* 1966) and Jon Bradshaw's "You Used To Be Very Big" (*New York Magazine,* 1975). Film critic Charles Champlin's essay on Wilder was useful (*Los Angeles Times,* July 14, 1974). The best critique of Wilder's films is Robert Mundy's "Wilder Reappraised" in the British *Cinema* (October 1969). Two French tape-recorded interviews are good and will be found in *Cahiers du Cinema* (October 1962) and *Positif* (January 1974.)

I have also looked into many—too many—books about Vienna and Berlin in the 1920s and reread many books on my shelves about Hollywood actors and directors involved with Wilder. Most of those which have been useful I have cited in the text. I have decided not to weigh down this biography with a filmography or a bibliography. The Wood and Madsen books contain filmographies up to 1969, if you are interested. I suspect the intoxicated movie fan already knows what he wants to know about the Wilder films—and the common reader will be bored by these trivial names and facts, which have in recent years replaced interesting writing about movie people and the world they live in.

I thank these members of Wilder's family circle who spoke at length to me: Mrs. Audrey Wilder; Victoria Wilder Settember; W. Lee Wilder; and Miles Wilder. At times, I had the feeling I was a character in the Pirandello play *Right You Are (If You Think You Are)* as I rebounded from one version of my hero to another. I am grateful to several women, and friends of these women, for confiding a few—all too few—amatory revelations. These sources asked for anonymity.

Felix Jackson, Walter Reisch, and Curt Siodmak shared their memories of Vienna and Berlin as did the incredible Mia May. Joe Pasternak and Paul Kohner shared memories of the Berlin years and Hollywood. Reisch was immensely stimulating in his recollection of Wilder at several phases of his development. Charles Higham, Gail Cottman and Kaytie Sistrom were helpful.

Jennings Lang, executive vice president of MCA-Universal and an old personal friend since our high school days in Brooklyn, gave me valuable information about studio operations. He arranged to screen for me all the American films in which Wilder had a hand, either as writer or as director.

David Bradley, film scholar and UCLA teacher of film history, was of much help.

I am grateful to James T. Powers, director of publications for the American Film Institute, and to the AFI for a grant.

I feel a special closeness to the cast and crew of *The Front Page*, who had to put up with my queries, sometimes at moments of stress—especially Carter de Haven, Jr., Howard Kazanjian, art director Henry Bumstead, set decorator Jim Payne, cameraman Jordan Cronenweth, unit publicist Lou Dyer, sound mixer Bob Martin, and makeup man Harry Ray.

A fervent embrace to Kay Taylor, Wilder's amanuensis, who was helpful above and beyond the call of duty and managed to solve many difficult problems.

My thanks to Helen Hernandez, who was the right arm of Brackett and Wilder during their partnership. Hernandez is one of those persons with seeming total recall of the past. Rozella Stewart, who took dictation between Hernandez and Taylor, was another good source.

Many actors helped me get a focus on Wilder. I know there's a widely held belief, expressed by Truman Capote and David Merrick most loudly, that actors are overemotional children. During these researches, I was impressed by the intelligence and maturity of the actors who talked to me about Wilder: Walter Matthau, Jack Lemmon, Shirley MacLaine, Cliff Osmond, Fred MacMurray, Jimmy Stewart, Gloria Swanson, Olivia de Havilland, Ginger Rogers, Ray Milland, and William Holden.

William Dozier, who headed the Writers Department at Paramount during the 1940s and was later a movie and televison producer, told me many fascinating stories of the good old days.

I talked to all of Wilder's cowriters who are still alive—and had the good fortune to know several, like Harry Kurnitz and Charlie Brackett, who have passed away. John Bright helped put the screenwriter's life at that time in a framework for me.

I.A.L. Diamond was of immense help and spoke to me over several long sessions, for many hours, as did Ernest Lehman and Wendell Mayes, Edwin Blum, Walter Newman, and George Axelrod. Norman Krasna, who almost collaborated with Wilder, held forth for hours telling me his views. And Ketti Frings finally told me the inside story of *Hold Back the Dawn*.

Among Wilder friends and colleagues who were kind enough to speak with me were Jack Benny (with whom I taped a long interview a few weeks before he died), playwright Leonard Gershe, Matty Malneck, Willie Schorr, Harold Hecht, bridge virtuoso Don Krauss, Sid Boehm, Walter Mirisch, Joe La Shelle, and Irving Paul Lazar.

James Mink and Brooke Whiting of the UCLA Special Collections Library made available to me the Raymond Chandler letters in the Chandler Collection at UCLA. And Mrs. Mildred Simpson and her staff at the Library of the Motion Picture Academy of Arts and

Sciences always seemed to have exactly what I was seeking—and knew where to locate it at once.

To my editor, William Targ, I say, "Thanks, and yes thanks." And, finally, I am most grateful to my agent, Scott Meredith, who has been a friend and a comforter many times in the course of these last years.

# INDEX